Quotation Marks

Quotation Marks

Marjorie Garber

Routledge
New York London

Published in 2003 by
Routledge
29 West 35th Street
New York, NY 10001
www.routledge-ny.com

Published in Great Britain by
Routledge
11 New Fetter Lane
London EC4P 4EE
www.routledge.co.uk

Library of Congress Cataloging-in-Publication Data

Garber, Marjorie B.
Quotation marks / Marjorie Garber.
    p. cm.
Includes bibliographical references and index.
ISBN 0-415-93745-0 (hardback : alk. paper) — ISBN 0-415-93746-9 (pbk.: alk. paper)
1. English literature—History and criticism—Theory, etc. 2. American literature—History and criticism—Theory, etc. 3. Literature—History and criticism—Theory, etc. 4. Literary forgeries and mystifications. 5. Influence (Literary, artistic, etc.) 6. Quotation in literature. 7. Sequels (Literature) 8. Allusions. I. Title.

PR21 .G37 2002
820.9—dc21
                                 2002003450

Cover art: Quotation mark from Caslon 224 Black.
Book design: Karen Quigley

For Don,
the best talker I know

The correct words of a few familiar sayings that are more often wrongly than rightly quoted may be useful.

—H.W. Fowler, *Dictionary of Modern Usage* (1926)

Contents

Plates

Figures

Quotation
and Cultural
Authority

Quotation

3. a. The action or practice of quoting.

   1646 SIR T. BROWNE, *pseud. Ep.* 279, This translation . . . if often followed . . . by our Saviour himselfe in the quotations of the Old Testament.
   1765 *Museum Rust.* IV. lxiii. 286 Nothing can be more unfair than false
   quotation. 1781 JOHNSON in *Boswell* 8 May, Classical quotation is the
   parole of literary men all over the world. 1875 EMERSON *Lett. & Soc.*
   Aims, Quot. & Orig., Quotation confesses inferiority.

   b. A passage quoted from a book, speech, etc.

   1690. LOCKE *Hum. Und.* IV. xvi. (1695) 383. He . . . cannot doubt how
   little Credit the Quotations deserve, where the Originals are wanting.
   1711 STEELE *Spec.* No. 11 He . . . enforced his Arguments by Quotations
   out of Plays and Songs. 1771 *Junius Lett.* xlvi. 245 After giving a false
   quotation from the journals . . . he proceeds. 1828 D'ISRAELI *Chas. I,* I.
   viii, 249 That prodigal erudition which delights in inexhaustible quotations from writers whom we now deem obscure. 1887 BOWEN *Virgil*
   Pref. (1889) 7 Hundreds of Virgil's lines are for most of us familiar
   quotations.

   (*Oxford English Dictionary*, second edition)

Whether greeted with Samuel Johnson's tempered approbation or Ralph
Waldo Emerson's tempered scorn, the topic of quotation has long fascinated
those who quote—and those who are quoted. Among the combining-forms
listed by the *Oxford English Dictionary* are several that betray their own

ambivalence, or worse, about this common practice of intellectuals, scholars, divines, poets and politicians: *quotation-capping, quotation-monger, quotationist.* Yet no kind of utterance or reference is more powerful when accurately deployed, for as Emerson also remarks—and as I will have occasion to quote—the quotation creates authority by its very nature and form. It instates an authority eslewhere, and, at the same time, it imparts that authority, temporarily, to the speaker or the writer.

The quotation resides somewhere in the territory between the aphorism and the echo—which is to say, between the essay and the lyric voice. It is sometimes an excuse for not thinking, and at other times a goad to thought: Polonius's anodyne bromides ("This above all: to thine own self be true") and Oscar Wilde's acerbic epigrams.

Quotation, writes Walter Benjamin, is the interruption of context. To quote a text is to break into it, to "tear" something out of it, to become a "thought fragment" and thus a focus for critical attention. In a famous simile he asserted, "Quotations in my works are like robbers by the roadside who make an armed attack and relieve an idler of his convictions." Hannah Arendt put the point succinctly when she wrote, about the brilliant aperçus of Benjamin and his despairing engagement with the present, "he discovered that the transmissibility of the past had been replaced by its citability."[1]

Many of the essays in this book take as their starting points—and frequently as their points of return—a word or phrase that is uttered in quotation marks—or, perhaps one should write, "in quotation marks." The title essay discusses the odd circumstance of *speaking* in quotation marks, from the double-finger-squeeze gesture on the podium to the unexpected voices of John Keats's oracular urn and Edgar Allan Poe's uncannily iterative raven. In other pieces in this volume I ponder the odd careers of words that seem to carry their own invisible quotation marks: "fashionable," a word that has become fashionable to employ as a standard dismissal of critics deemed too clever for their own good, and the title "Ms.," which, while it was coined as a way of eliding certain categorical divisions among women, in fact wound up by creating more, and different, categories among which women could choose.

In other cases I engage words that seem to require a set of qualifying quotation marks, as with the ubiquitous "compassion" or the problematic "human nature," which is now, as I suggest, a term more comfortably employed by sci-

entists than by humanists, with important, and not entirely happy, consequences for the general public's view of the humanities. In a discussion of
"work" I explore the doubled meanings of that term and the related concept of
"invention," both used, over time, for both the most intellectual or cognitive
activities (poetry as invention) and the most physical or practical. In a moment
of high panegyric, Thomas Alva Edison, the "Wizard of Menlo Park," bestows
his highest accolade on Shakespeare: "He would have been an inventor, a wonderful inventor, if he had turned his mind to it."

Some essays address the case of historical personages and authors who frequently appear "in quotation marks" in our culture: William Shakespeare, Jane
Austen, Cleopatra, Monica Lewinsky. "Shakespeare" these days is a metaphor
as well as a man, a belief system and a literary standard as well as a set of
works: the word "Shakespearean" is likely to appear as an adjective describing
cataclysmic political events, or sports contests, or massive outpourings of
grief, without any but the most general reference to the playwright or his plays.
Austen, like Shakespeare, provokes spontaneous expressions of "love," which
should properly be written as love, without the scare quotes, because there is
nothing ironic about the emotion or its expression. Contemplation of these figures has, as the reader will see, often led me to speculate about some larger
questions central to reading and to humanistic thought, questions that have, to
a certain extent, receded from view in recent decades: questions of character,
for one, and (as I have noted) human nature, for another.

In an essay called "Historical Correctness" I investigate the ways in which
an overinvestment by literary scholars in certain notions of history as causality
has narrowed the focus of research, and has obscured, or rendered more difficult, certain overarching inquiries of a more theoretical and speculative nature.
In this essay as elsewhere—despite my own insistence throughout this volume
on philology, on the fascination and importance of historicizing the uses of
words and terms—I offer a defense of, and a plea for, a return to *anachronism* as
a powerful way of reading. To quote the German romantic critic August
Wilhelm Schlegel, whose own remarks of 1808 are shrewdly pertinent today,
Shakespeare "considered himself entitled to the greatest liberties."

> He had not to do with a petty hypercritical age like ours, which is always seeking in
> poetry for something else than poetry; his audience entered the theatre, not to learn
> true chronology, geography, natural history, but to witness a vivid exhibition. I

undertake to prove that Shakespeare's anachronisms are, for the most part, committed purposely, and after great consideration. It was frequently of importance to him
to bring the subject exhibited, from the back ground of time, quite near to us.[2]

The word "us" is what linguists call a *shifter*, a word that refers in different
utterances to different persons: my "us" and your "us" may be identical, but
they are far more likely to be different in some particulars, and may, in fact, be
completely at odds with one another. "Us" is precisely the kind of word that is
written and spoken rhetorically as if it transcended boundaries and encompassed everyone; it is, arguably, the most softly yet strongly polemical of pronouns, at its most coercive when it seems to be at its most generous and inclusive. Yet Schegel's "us," a term enclosed by invisible quotation marks, is the
word that drives home his argument. The fact that audiences, readers, and
speakers change over time means that the authors, figures, terms, and concepts
they discuss, though they bear the same names, also change. Language and
culture are always in quotation marks for us. (It would be tedious and
supererogatory to write this sentence as it might be inflected under the sign of
quotation marks as I describe them in this volume: "Language" and "culture"
are "always" in quotation marks for "us.") But the engagement with a world
that is made up of quotation, a feature of culture and society from the ancient
world to the present, is the definition of modernity—that ultimate shifter—for
any readership that imagines an "us."

At least one other kind of shifter is present as a fulcrum of argument in
these essays, and since it is one that has been the object of complaint over the
centuries, it may be good to acknowledge that here. The shifter I mean is the
pun, or the play on words, what Johnson dismissively calls a "quibble" and, in
a famous passage I discuss in the essay that borrows Johnson's phrase as its
title, a "Fatal Cleopatra." Puns or homonyms are always set out in invisible
quotation marks; they are invitations, sometimes strong-armed, to double
reading and to close reading or (to use Reuben Brower's phrase) "reading in
slow motion." The "Ms" in "A Case of Mstaken Identity"; the "moniker" in
Monica Lewinsky's name; the double-take produced by Janet Rickus's delectable portraits of produce in "Vegetable Love"; and perhaps especially the
deliberate and important root word of the "essay" form, the French *essai* (try
or attempt), first used by Montaigne and reworked by virtually every subsequent essayist of note, which I link in a piece in this collection to the "Try-

Works" or rendering vat of Herman Melville's *Moby-Dick*—all these are examples of the way wordplay can be a very serious business, a way of getting at the radical capacities of words to *mean* their various and often contradictory meanings. Quotation marks are a time-honored mode of typography for marking such multiple meanings for the reader. I do not always employ them, since I think the double meanings in these terms tend to emerge clearly from the context without excessive textual ornamentation. But the mode of argument that takes words seriously—and takes them the most seriously when confronted with their capacity to and for play—is an aspect of rhetorical criticism that has historically frightened some rationalist readers, by confronting them with their poets'—or their own—unexpected inner thoughts.

Other essays in this book offer additional and complementary ways of understanding the "quotation marks" of the title. My essay "Sequels," for example, argues that a sequel or prequel implicitly places quotation marks around the so-called "original," changing it in important and unforeseeable ways. In this way sequels are functionally similar to the editorial emendations I discuss in a piece called "MacGuffin Shakespeare," an exploration of the fascinating world of conjectural Shakespeare editing, where early editors tried to improve upon the playwright by guessing what was really in his mind. I take the term "MacGuffin" from the film director Alfred Hitchcock, for whom it denoted the missing thing that everybody wants, the plot pretext (the secret plans, the photographic negatives, the cipher or code), the "deliberately mysterious plot objective" that made the story go. Both sequels and emendations are additions or corrections in quotation marks, offering the reader's responses to, or fantasies about, the original and its origins.

Earlier I cited Walter Benjamin, who compared quotations in his works to "robbers by the roadside who make an armed attack and relieve an idler of his convictions." It will perhaps be fitting to close these brief introductory remarks by returning to Benjamin, whose monumental *Arcades Project* is his own personal *Bartlett's*, a collection of observations and perceptions, gleaned over a period of thirteen years, and likened by his twentieth-century translators to "the methods of the nineteenth-century collector of antiquities and curiosities, or indeed to the methods of the nineteenth-century ragpicker." The translators, Howard Eiland and Kevin McLaughlin, add that it was "[n]ot conceptual analysis but something like dream interpretation [that] was the model."[3]

Benjamin's *Arcades Project* (in German, *Das Passagen-Werk*) consists of dozens of short pieces and hundreds of brief notes, aphorisms, and aperçus, among which are more than a few that reflect upon the nature of his own task. "This work has to develop to the highest degree the art of citing without quotation marks," he declares at one point.[4]

The art of citing without quotation marks: to cite this from Benjamin while removing the quotation marks is to participate in the critical, historical, and political project he set for himself, in defining modernity as a theory of montage. But without Benjamin's cultural authority his observation floats free, sidles into the realm of philosophy (or "philosophy") rather than critique. The world we inherit and inhabit is just such a montage, a palimpsest of citations and quotations that are half-recognized and, in their flashes of recognition, of literal "reknowing," come back to us as wisdom.

Wisdom itself was once a set of quotations, wise sayings or precepts, as in the "wisdom" books of the Bible, where the term "wisdom literature" denotes the books of Job, Proverbs, Ecclesiastes, the Wisdom of Solomon and Ecclesiasticus, and the Epistle of James. Wisdom was a form and a genre, as well as a mode of judgment or knowledge. "Wisdoms" in the plural was a common term for such precepts. It is symptomatic of our time that the phrase "in his wisdom" (or "her" or "its" wisdom) is now usually ironic, as if wisdom was always, through its own smug certainty, shortly to be proven self-interested and unwise. Yet it is wisdom rather than knowledge that is conventionally regarded as the special province of the humanities, the thing that, above all, the study of arts and letters (as contrasted with science and social science) is thought to provide. The essays that follow will explore the function of quotation marks, visible and invisible, in framing, conveying, resisting, or querying such wisdom or wisdoms. It is the claim of this book that the centrality of the humanities in a world increasingly skeptical of their value depends upon taking language seriously, no matter how unexpected its authorities, how multiple and contradictory its associations, and how circuitous its path to meaning.

(Quotation Marks)

> If, for the sake of a crowded audience you do wish to hold a lecture, your ambition is no laudable one, and at least avoid all citations from the poets, for to quote them argues feeble industry.
>
> —Hippocrates, *Precepts*

When Representative Henry Hyde addressed the U.S. Senate in January 1999 on the solemn occasion of President Bill Clinton's impeachment hearings, he gave his remarks the requisite element of gravity by salting them with familiar quotations—or quotations that seemed as if they ought to be familiar. For example, he cited Sir Thomas More, whose conscience would not permit him to acquiesce in the tricky business of Henry VIII's divorce and remarriage. But Hyde's quotation from this Tudor statesman had an oddly contemporary ring. "As he told his daughter Margaret," the congressman from Illinois informed the Senate, "'when a man takes an oath, Meg, he's holding his own self in his own hands. Like water. And if he opens his fingers *then*, he needn't hope to find himself again.'" Here the voice of Thomas More comes through slightly muffled; it is in fact the character of More from Robert Bolt's 1960 play *A Man for All Seasons* that is talking.[1]

The staffer who found this quotation apposite might have been inspired by Bolt's ardent preface, which explained the playwright's choice of hero: "A man takes an oath only when he wants to commit himself quite exceptionally to the statement, when he wants to make an identity between the truth of it and his own virtue; he offers himself as a guarantee. And it works. There is a special kind of shrug for a perjurer; we feel that the man has no self to commit, no guarantee to offer."[2] But quoting Robert Bolt lacks the force—historical, religious, canonical—of quoting Sir, later Saint, Thomas More. Perhaps mindful of Robert Burton's famous declaration about quoting from the classics, "A dwarf standing on the shoulders of a giant may see farther than a giant himself,"[3] the tall, stooped Hyde craned across the ages, speaking to the future through a voice from the "past."

That I elect to stress the spuriousness of this "past" by enclosing the word in quotation marks will indicate, at the outset, one of the curious properties of these typographical signifiers; for in their present condition of use, they may indicate either authenticity or doubt. (Make that "authenticity" or "doubt.") This is a property to which we shall want to return. But let us continue, for a moment, with the impeachment hearings.

In quest of authority Hyde also, it is almost needless to say, quoted William Shakespeare in his opening remarks. And here the author was so familiar that he did not need to be named. "Our cherished system of justice will never be the same after this," Hyde intoned. "Depending on what you decide, it will either be strengthened in its power to achieve justice, or it will go the way of so much of our moral infrastructure and become a mere convention full of sound and fury, signifying nothing."[4]

It's probably unsportsmanlike to fault Hyde for wrenching this quotation out of context; both "sound and fury" and "signifying nothing" have long ago passed into the general word hoard, having been borrowed by everyone from William Faulkner to Malcolm Evans.[5] But Macbeth's famous cry of despair on the meaninglessness of (his) life, uttered in response to the news of his wife's death, seems in a way singularly inappropriate for a political speech whose entire point is to mark the meaningfulness of the moment. "Life," in Macbeth's formulation, is

> A poor player
> That struts and frets his hour upon the stage
> And then is heard no more: it is a tale

> Told by an idiot, full of sound and fury,
> Signifying nothing.
>
> *Macbeth* 5.5.24–28

The point of Hyde's citation was to rouse the Senate to greatness by urging it to *avoid* reducing justice to "sound and fury, signifying nothing." Nonetheless, the proximity of "poor player" (a bad, unskilled, or hammy actor) and "idiot" seem slightly risky in the context of an address to a group of U.S. senators. The New York *Daily News* found some amusement in the omission: "Hyde said a violated oath was 'full of sound and fury, signifying nothing.' But he left out the preceding line that life 'is a tale told by an idiot.'"[6] Identifying these as "Shakespeare's words from *Macbeth*," the paper implied that this view of "life" was somehow Shakespeare's rather than his character's. But at least the *Daily News* got the play right. An article in *Newsday*, written by "an attorney specializing in intellectual property law," blithely described Hyde as beginning his remarks with "a quote from *Hamlet*—'full of sound and fury, signifying nothing.'"[7]

A scholar once wrote of Shakespeare that "to cite him in a lecture or an essay was to give lustre and prestige to the words and ideas that surrounded his magic name."[8] But does that "lustre" attach itself to the speaker as readily as to the writer? Or does the "poor player" syndrome kick in, reminding the audience all too clearly that the speaker is *not* Shakespeare, or, to cite another once-canonical text, "not Prince Hamlet," but rather

> an attendant lord, one that will do
> To swell a progress, start a scene or two,
> Advise the prince; no doubt, an easy tool,
> Deferential, glad to be of use,
> Politic, cautious, and meticulous;
> Full of high sentence, but a bit obtuse;
> At times, indeed, almost ridiculous—
> Almost, at times, the Fool.[9]

By the end of the impeachment process even the *New York Times* had grown slightly restive. "Mr. Hyde," the *Times* reported, "mustered a veritable *Bartlett's* in offering his last impassioned plea for conviction. 'We happy few,' he said, turning in Shakespearean tribute to his fellow House Republicans." And, "Quoting Gibbon, Mr. Hyde acidly denounced the President by comparing him to a corrupt Roman emperor, Septimius Severus: 'Severus promised, only to

betray; he flattered, only to rule; and however he might occasionally bind himself by oath and treaty, his conscience, obsequious to his interest, always
released him from the inconvenient obligation.'"[10] A journalist writing for
another newspaper had earlier dismissed the impeachment debate in the
House as "blue suits quoting from *Bartlett's*."[11] The implication was that they
were doubly out of fashion; they were not, in any way, saying something new.
Under these circumstances, was the quotation *more* authoritative and convinc-
ing than the speaker's own voice, or *less*?

Who is speaking when we speak in quotation? In the case of Henry Hyde's
address to the Senate, was it Hyde, More, or Robert Bolt? Hyde, Macbeth,
Shakespeare—or J. Alfred Prufrock?

II

"Quotation is a constant reminder that writing is a form of displacement," suggests Edward Said. "As a rhetorical device, quotation can serve to accommo-
date, to incorporate, to falsify (when wrongly or even rightly paraphrased), to
accumulate, to defend, or to conquer—but always, even when in the form of a
passing allusion, it is a reminder that other writing serves to displace present
writing."[12]

Quotation reminds us that *writing* is displacement. What does it tell us
about speech? How does one indicate that one is speaking in quotation? Or,
"in quotation"? At scholarly conferences it has become conventional for a
speaker to raise his or her hands above the shoulders and rapidly flex the first
two fingers of each hand, miming the look of (American-style, double) quotation marks on the page. The effect is rather retro Rogers and Hammerstein; as
one friend commented, this gesture always makes him think the speaker is
auditioning for "Happy Talk." Do speakers from the British Isles, or others
whose primary publication venue is Britain, gesture with single-finger quotation marks? (Nursery habitués might then be reminded not of *South Pacific* but
of "The Itsy-Bitsy Spider.") In fact, the two-finger flex has become conventional rather than strictly mimetic, a sign of quoting rather than a quote-sign.
For some divas of the podium the gesture involves the shoulders as well as the
hands and offers an opportunity to express not only the activity of quotation,

but also a certain attitude—often of wry skepticism—about the authority of both the quotation and the quotee. Some users call these protestation marks, indicating that they are the performed equivalent of what Jacques Derrida, following Martin Heidegger, has termed being "under erasure"—a word with a horizontal line drawn through it to indicate that it demarcates a nodal idea for which the present word is inappropriate or insufficient: *man*; *freedom*; *justice*. Others who employ the finger-waggling gesture refer to these airy points as "scare quotes"—both the word being framed, and the witchy gesture, contributing presumably to the currency of the term.

It was not always thus. Conferencegoers with longer memories or grayer hair may recall the days when a sotto voce "quote . . . unquote" demarcated the boundaries of a cited phrase. (Without these oral punctuation marks the quoted passage often melted into the speaker's own text with no perceptible boundary, especially when the quotation was lengthy and unmemorable.) On the other hand, the necessity could itself invite dramatic improvisation. The rabbi of the temple of my youth, a Russian émigré with a grandiloquent flair for performance, used to wind up to a sonorous "and I am qvoting" before delivering whatever words of wisdom he had quarried for his sermon. Senators and other public figures, as we have seen in the case of Henry Hyde, often footnote their learned quotations in the text, lest the audience fail to register either the quotation or the erudition: "As Abraham Lincoln so wisely said"; "In the immortal words of John F. Kennedy"; "The Book of Isaiah tells us."

This practice works well when the figure being quoted is eminent, recognizable, and honored; in fact, all three attributes then seem to attach themselves, in a rather ghostly fashion, to the present speaker, who appears in the act of quoting to have virtually incorporated the predecessor and to speak from the vantage point of the ages, as if the speaker were a Russian doll who had somehow swallowed up these articulate authorities and was therefore able to ventriloquize them from within. When the figure being quoted is *less* eminent or reputable, however, the old-style "quote-unquote" is deployed, but with a lawyerly edge, casting doubt on the veracity of the person quoted or underscoring the suspicious significance of the utterance. The effect is one of distancing rather than incorporation.

Thus, to return yet again to the House managers' presentation to the Senate, the words of principals in the case against President Clinton were cited in deliberate, and exaggerated, oral quotation marks: "Ms. Lewinsky testified, quote, 'No one ever told me to lie,' unquote. When considered alone, this statement would seem exculpatory. In the context of other evidence, however, we see that this one statement gives a misleading inference. Of course, no one said, 'Now, Monica, you go down there and lie.' They didn't have to. Based on their previous spoken and even unspoken words, Ms. Lewinsky knew what was expected of her."[13] Or, again: "According to Ms. Lewinsky, Mr. Jordan told her that he has spoken with the president, that she came highly recommended, and that, quote, 'We're in business,' unquote. However, the evidence reflects that Mr. Jordan took no steps to help Ms. Lewinsky until early December of that year, after she appeared on the witness list in the Jones case."

"Quote-unquote" often functions in this manner; thus a character in crime fiction can report of another that "he did have quote, a jolly good reason for bumping off one special person, unquote,"[14] while in Peter Ustinov's *Loser* we are told that someone "expressed the personal opinion that the picture was quote great for America unquote."[15]

And "quote-unquote" when spoken as a whole before the word in question indicates the greatest possible degree of skepticism. "The mayor's quote-unquote dedication to duty" means the speaker does not think the mayor is very dedicated.

Monica Lewinsky herself took note of the slippery problem posed by unmarked oral quotation when she was deposed by House managers in the impeachment hearing. "'Sometimes in the, in my grand jury testimony, they've put quotations around things when I'm attributing statements to other people, and I didn't necessarily mean that those were direct quotes,'" she said; and several times in her deposition she cautioned, "'This is not a direct quote.'"[16] This lawyerly caution, however belatedly introduced, throws some doubt on the whole question of transcription and its authority. When "he said—she said" becomes "he said something like this" and "she said something like that," the effect of authenticity and evidence produced by direct quotation becomes blurred and etiolated.

Paradoxically, as I have already noted, quotation marks, when either written or spoken, can convey both absolute authenticity and veracity, on the one hand, and suspected inauthenticity, irony, or doubt, on the other ("this 'leader' we elected"[17]; or, from an article in an 1897 article in *Century* magazine, "I must put 'play' in quotation-marks to express the sarcasm of it"[18]). It is either, "This is exactly what was said," or, "Can you imagine saying or believing this?"

The House managers, of course, did not waggle their fingers at the Senate as they quoted, either from the literary classics or from Monica Lewinsky. (It would have been far more entertaining had they done so.) And sonorous quoters of the classics do not, in general, do the "Happy Talk" finger dance; it's virtually impossible to imagine citers of "Ask not what your country can do for you" or "I have a dream" pausing to clench and unclench their fingertips before launching into the rhetorical stratosphere. In fact, this practice is pretty much limited to professors and graduate students, and even they do not usually perform it when quoting purple passages. "To be or not to be" has seldom, in my experience, been prefaced by a gesture of digital "quotation."

III

Consider for a moment how curious it is that we should pronounce any punctuation marks aloud. "Period!" is sometimes used as an intensifier ("No ice cream before dinner. Period!") that marks the closure of the conversation. No reply is invited or welcomed; the matter is closed. The Danish-born comedian Victor Borge often performed in the 1950s, to the delight of audiences, a routine called "Phonetic Punctuation," in which he gave appropriate popping and whirring noises to commas, question marks, and exclamation points, reading a passage aloud with its full oral complement of punctuation and accompanying these sounds with gestures. Borge's quotation marks were two commas (squeaky pop; squeaky pop) and a mimed scare quote gesture. Apart from the sheer energy and inventiveness of his comic routine, Borge succeeded in defamiliarizing the role of punctuation in imparting meaning. Like Molière's gentleman who was astonished to find himself speaking prose, Borge's audiences often discovered, three centuries after the shift from rhetorical to syntactical punctuation practice, that these little squiggles were part of how they listened, and spoke.

Early printed quotations appeared not in the run-in text but in the margins, as glosses or evidence of what was being claimed; sometimes they looked more like modern footnotes than quotations. As R. B. McKerrow writes, "Inverted commas were, until late in the seventeenth century, frequently used at the beginnings of lines to call attention to sententious remarks.... They were not especially associated with quotations until the eighteenth century."[19] But almost from the beginning, there was a real question about the relationship of quotation marks, and indeed all punctuation, to speech.

In English typography the *comma*, a word originally traceable to Greek rhetoric and prosody and meaning a short phrase or group of words, became a punctuation mark used to separate the smallest members of a sentence. Renaissance grammarians, reasoning from the fact that the comma makes clear the grammatical structure and thus the sense of a written passage, as does a short pause in speech, sometimes tended to describe the comma as the mark of such a spoken pause. Thus George Puttenham's *English Poesie* says, "A little pause or comma is geuen to euery word," and Ben Jonson's *English Grammar* says, "A comma is a mean breathing."[20] But there is a difference between Puttenham's emphasis and Jonson's: Puttenham's notion of the purpose of punctuation is elocutionary, while Jonson's is syntactical. That is, Puttenham follows the largely medieval practice of treating points or stops as indications to the reader, especially one reading aloud to an audience, while Jonson is among the first writers in English to consider punctuation as a necessary guide to the grammatical construction of sentences. In this period quotations in the text were not marked by quotation marks, but by a word like *quoth* followed by a comma in run-in text (in Puttenham, for example, *ye may see, quoth the king, what it is to runne away and looke backwards*[21]). In other words, the mark of quotation was an oral, and aural, cue. It was the ear and not the eye that still predominated.

In the seventeenth century in England this began to change. The comma began to appear above the line as a quotation mark. The mark at the beginning of the quotation or line was inverted, and in later years these began to be called *inverted commas*. The commentary accompanying quotations in learned texts indicates both the use of, and some textual anxiety about, such designations. "To authenticate the date of the author's ideas, the parts of it which are contained in the present letter are marked with double commas," wrote one.[22] "The reader must not take it for granted, even where inverted commas denote a closer attention to the text, that nothing is omitted," cautioned another.[23] A third drew the reader's attention to "turned commas, which designate extracts."[24] One nineteenth-century account of *Modern English Literature: Its*

Blemishes and Defects took a passage to task for appearing "without inverted commas, or any other marks to show that the writer intended it as a quotation."[25]

If such anxieties—was it a quotation? was it authentic? was it complete?—could attend upon the *written* text, what were the implications and ramifications for speech? How was the *hearer* now to be sure when what was spoken was "in quotation"?

A similar history attends the onset of "quotation marks" on the continent of Europe. The French mark of quotation, the *guillemet*, was first used in 1546, according to the *Grande Encyclopédie*.[26] In the earliest printing in France, as in other European countries, the marks of quotation are absent. French typographical style differs from that of other languages in that dialogue is generally set without quotation marks. The words of each successive or alternate speaker are marked, instead, by an em-dash. This is sometimes done in Italian, as well. (In French, passages of quotation can be prefaced or, more frequently, followed by the information that this is the beginning or the end: *fin de citation*.) German language quotations are marked either by pairs of commas or by reversed guillemets. As with the English punctuation, these typographical practices all have consequences, not only for how passages are read with the eye, but also for how they are read aloud. And this in turn will affect their cultural currency, the way in which they are valued. Are these pearls of wisdom, gems of language, or clichés and curiosities? Snobbery, or common talk? Better, or worse, than "plain language"?

IV

Some of the most quoted men and women in history have expressed themselves, quotably, on the question of quotation. Doctor Johnson roundly countered the criticism that quotation was pedantry: "No, sir, it is a good thing; there is a community of mind in it. Classical quotation is the *parole* of literary men all over the world."[27] Johnson's *parole* is a password, an "open sesame," a code of belonging. Literary men recognize one another by the classical tags that ornament their language. This guild-recognition system was still in effect two hundred years later among what naysayers like to describe disparagingly as the "cultural elite" (please note my quotation marks). As Justin Kaplan wrote in his preface to the sixteenth edition of *Bartlett's*, "We use quotations, like the Biblical Shibboleth, as passwords and secret handshakes, social strategic signals that say, 'I understand you. We speak the same language.'"[28] But we could also associate Johnson's term with the modern linguistic sense of *parole*, meaning "(spoken) word" or "utterance," the speech event, as contrasted with the linguistic system, or *langue*.

We might call to mind a well-known instance from the popular film *Ghost*, when Whoopi Goldberg, playing a supposedly spurious medium, is inhabited by the spirit of the murdered Patrick Swayze. Swayze speaks through Goldberg: her voice speaks his words. Commentators have noted the frisson that attaches to this cross-gender and cross-race haunting, as Goldberg (should I call her Goldberg or Swayze here? In any case she is clearly "in quotation," like all ghosts) moves to kiss the bemused widow, Demi Moore. The director and the camera chicken out, it has been said, by dissolving Goldberg into Swayze, so that the kiss is "correctly" sexed and raced: white woman kisses white man, not black woman. But we can read the Goldberg/Swayze pairing here also as an incarnate allegory of quotation: who is speaking when Swayze's words come out of Goldberg's mouth?

Henry James's Verena Tarrant, a "high-class speaker" who is "the daughter of Doctor Tarrant, the mesmeric healer" may offer another (and "higher-class") model of speaking *through*. Verena is a hit on the Boston social circuit, an eloquent orator on behalf of women's rights whose facility for public speaking depends on her father's art. "'I heard her last spring,'" reports a young man. "'They call it inspirational. I don't know what it is—only it's exquisite, so fresh and poetical. She has to have her father to start her up. It seems to pass into her.'" Verena's freshness and poetical speech are hers and not hers. Once "started up" by her father, who strokes and smoothes her head, "she proceeded slowly, cautiously, as if she were listening for the prompter, catching, one by one, certain phrases that were whispered to her a great distance off, behind the scenes of the world. Then memory, or inspiration, returned to her, and presently she was in possession of her part."[29]

In some ways quotation is a kind of cultural ventriloquism, a throwing of the voice that is also an appropriation of authority. "He wrapped himself in quotations—as a beggar would enfold himself in the purple of Emperors," wrote

Rudyard Kipling of an ambitious young writer who "rhymed 'dove' with 'love' and 'moon' with 'June' and devoutly believed that they had never so been rhymed before."[30] The English poet and diplomat Matthew Prior had made the same point, more satirically, almost two hundred years earlier, writing, "He rang'd his tropes, and preach'd up patience; / Back'd his opinion with quotations."[31]

Here, as you can see, we have entered the murky *mise en abîme* world of the quotation about quotations. Books of quotations, whether intended for inspiration, spiritual comfort, instant edification, or self-aggrandizement, have been around at least since John Bartlett's first edition of *Familiar Quotations* in 1855. (Current avatars, all published in the 1990s, include *Bartlett's Book of Business Quotation*, *The Executive's Quotation Book*, *The Golf Quotation Book*, *The Mother's Quotation Book*, *The Military Quotation Book*, *The Eccentric's Quotation Book*, and *The Culture-Vulture's Quotation Book*, to name just a few.) The young Winston Churchill, in later years the source of obsessive quotation by politicians across the spectrum (for one of the slippery qualities of a quotable quote is that it can be used to point almost any moral) delivered himself of an encomium to Bartlett's work that could readily serve as a dust jacket blurb.

> It is a good thing for an uneducated man to read books of quotations. Bartlett's *Familiar Quotations* is an admirable work, and I studied it intently. The quotations when engraved upon the memory give you good thoughts. They also make you anxious to read the authors and look for more.[32]

But clearly there is a difference between quoting an apposite phrase and knowing what you are really saying. So widespread had become the habit of quoting for parole or entry into an exclusive club by the beginning of the twentieth century that Fowler felt impelled to warn against it in *A Dictionary of Modern English Usage* (1926):

> QUOTATION. . . . A writer expresses himself in words that have been used before because they give his meaning better than he can give it himself, or because they are beautiful or witty, or because he expects them to touch a chord of association in his reader, or because he wishes to show that he is learned and well read. Quotations due to the last motive are invariably ill-advised; the discerning reader detects it and is contemptuous, the undiscerning perhaps is impressed, but even then is at the same time repelled, pretentious quotations being the surest road to tedium.[33]

When Henry Hyde quotes Gibbon on Severus, a political cartoonist can lampoon him as beating a literal dead horse. But Hyde, a man in his seventies, reared and educated in the same state that produced the Lincoln-Douglas debates, came of age at a time when rhetoric and oratory were requisite parts of the education of a citizen in the liberal arts. It was only in the 1960s that the Harvard University Department of English discontinued its offerings in public speaking, rhetorical theory, and the oral interpretation of dramatic literature (English N, P, and Q). The advanced course in principles and practice of public speaking promised study of "speech composition and rhetoric; logic; the psychology of audiences; persuasive presentation. A large proportion of the speech practice will consist of public appearances on selected occasions before various audiences."[34] English Q (for Quotation?) and its fellow public speaking courses did not count toward the concentration (Harvard jargon for major) in English. Presumably their ranks were filled, not with the aspiring young John Updikes, but with the aspiring young John Kennedys—or Henry Hydes. With the demise of public speaking as an academic subject at the elite universities came a shift in the value, and valuation, of oral quotation from the classics. It would not be too long before Walter Mondale, in an attempt to connect with the electorate, would find himself quoting instead from a hamburger commercial: "Where's the beef?" Here the exclusive club was the highest office in the land, and the *parole* was, supposedly, in lingua franca.

In his *Essay Concerning Human Understanding* John Locke recorded the pitfalls of quotation "where the originals are wanting":

> Passion, interest, inadvertency, mistake of his meaning, and a thousand odd reasons, or capricios, men's minds are acted by, (impossible to be discovered,) may make one man quote another man's words or meanings wrong. He that has but ever so little examined the citations of writers, cannot doubt how little credit the quotations deserve, where the originals are wanting; and consequently how much less quotations of quotations can be relied on.[35]

Being quoted "out of context" is one of the most frequent complaints of politicians, so it might seem surprising that they give themselves permission to take such liberty with the literary classics. The *Bartlett* version of a famous quote often omits not only the context but also, in the case of fiction, drama, or poetry, the speaker, with the result that such profoundly ambiguous utterances as Shakespeare's Iago on reputation, Polonius's "This above all: to thine own self be true," and Alexander Pope's "Hope springs eternal in the human breast" appear regularly in political speeches without a trace of irony as the ringing "philosophy" of the (often uncited) author—and, by implication, of all good men. I do not mean to attribute this practice only to the collection called *Bartlett's*—as we have seen, there have been hundreds of books of quotations, "beauties," and "household words," and most follow the same schema, excerpting passages with the minimum of context and explanation. The result is, again paradoxically, the elevation of a local observation to the status of oracular truth.

Quotations, especially disembodied quotations, can serve an educative function, providing (or counterfeiting) wisdom. Detached from their contexts, they seem not only "true" but iconic, monumental. But as we noticed in the analogy to *Ghost*'s Whoopi Goldberg, a quotation does not remain disembodied for long. Once it is reincarnated in a new speaker, it takes on a new set of meanings, and often sheds or alters the "original" meaning it may be thought to have possessed.

Ralph Waldo Emerson remarks in his essay "Quotation and Originality" that "a writer appears to more advantage in the pages of another's book than in his own. In his own he waits as a candidate for your approbation; in another's he is a lawgiver."[36] This seems almost depressingly true these days, when the iteration of theoretical catch phrases (for example, Michel Foucault's definition of the homosexual, or Judith Butler on gender as a repetition of stylized acts) seems all too often to replace systemic thought or argumentation. Such quotations are inserted into a borrower text as precisely what its author did not claim: a ground of fact. In her fine study of quotation in Ralph Waldo Emerson and Emily Dickinson, Debra Fried asks, "[T]he equivocal stance of American writers to quotations—are they truly the voice of one's genius, or are they unreliable promptings from tired ghosts?"[37]

When a quotation becomes so familiar that it slides, almost imperceptibly, into aphorism or maxim, the cautionary quotation marks will disappear entirely, leaving the cultural residue: *doxa*, or "wisdom." Locke insists that quotations never become truer over time ("This is certain, that what in one age was affirmed upon slight grounds, can never after come to be more valid in future ages by being oft repeated. But the further still it is from the original, the less valid it is, and has always less force in the mouth or writing of him that last made use of it than in his from whom he received it").[38] Yet the doxa effect of quotation, especially, I would contend, in an oral context and in an increasingly less classically educated society, has today a strong free-floating force. T. S. Eliot's smugly complacent view of the ancients—"they are what we know"—has been replaced by a suspiciousness of too much learning that is oddly gratified by "familiar quotations" that function as sound bites, not "they are what we know," but, "they are what we *quote*." Old authors are regarded as having written not books, but quotes. Classical tags have turned into "tagging," a practice of graffiti artists. "Capping" quotations is an arcane activity largely engaged in by the louche heroes of 1920s drama and detective fiction.

Even more problematic than this practice of misquotation by quoting out of context, however, is what might be described as quotation by free indirect discourse: the invention of phrases that famous speakers *should* have said. These bon mots often show up in books of quotations under the hazy label "attributed," the equivalent in the world of quotation of the phrase "school of" in art history. Thus Voltaire's famous, and frequently cited, "I disapprove of what you say, but I will defend to the death your right to say it" is found nowhere in the works of Voltaire, but is offered instead in a 1906 volume entitled *The Friends of Voltaire* as a paraphrase of something Voltaire wrote in his *Essay on Tolerance*. At issue was a current literary contretemps that ended in a book-burning. What the volume's editor, S. G. Tallentyre (the pen name of Evelyn Beatrice Hall) wrote was this, in double quotation marks: "'I disapprove of what you say, but I will defend to the death your right to say it,' was his attitude now."[39] Asked about the quotation many years after her book was published, Hall explained that she had not intended to imply that Voltaire used those words verbatim, and would be very surprised if they were to be found in any of his works.

To give just one more example from a legion of possibilities: Alice Roosevelt Longworth, credited with wittily remarking, "I do wish [Calvin Coolidge] did not look as if he had been weaned on a pickle," was in fact, as she acknowledged, quoting someone else, a patient of her doctor's. After the doctor had passed on the quip, Longworth gleefully reported, "Of course, I repeated it to everyone I saw." She *became* its speaker, though she was not its originator.[40]

V

A well-known passage from Derrida sets out the stakes of iterability in terms that specifically engage the question of marking a quotation as a quotation, either in writing or in speech:

> Every sign, linguistic or nonlinguistic, spoken or written (in the current sense of this opposition), in a small or large unit, can be *cited*, put between quotation marks; in so doing it can break with every given context, engendering an infinity of new contexts in a manner which is absolutely illimitable. This does not imply that the mark is valid outside of a context, but on the contrary that there are only contexts without any center of absolute anchoring [*ancrage*]. This citation, this duplication or duplicity, this iterability of the mark is neither an accident nor an anomaly, it is that (normal/abnormal) without which a mark could not even have a function called "normal." What would a mark be that could not be cited? Or one whose origins would not get lost along the way?[41]

Signs, linguistic and nonlinguistic, can be put in quotation marks. In order to be recognized *as* signs, they have to be able to be repeated—to be iterable and citational. (In French the word *citation* means "quotation.") And since every repetition is a repetition with a difference, duplication becomes "duplicity." The "same" spoken again will always be "different." Derrida's "quotation marks" are here, so to speak, uttered in quotation marks. (With genial rhetorical ingenuousness he would inquire, fifteen years after the appearance of this influential essay, "Why does deconstruction have the reputation, justified or not, of treating things obliquely, indirectly, with 'quotation marks,' and of always asking whether things arrive at the indicated address?"[42]) To what extent, if at all, can these figurative quotation marks be understood as speaking to the question of quotation?

By extension, we might say that *every* quotation is a quotation out of context, inevitably both a duplication and a duplicity. Emerson, famously ambivalent about quotation as a practice—"I hate quotation," he wrote in his journal. "Tell me what you know"[43]—noted both that "all minds quote . . . the originals are not original." (Even this observation is of course not "original"; compare it to Robert Burton's *Anatomy of Melancholy*: "We can say nothing but what has been said. Our poets steal from Homer. . . . Our story-dressers do as much; he that comes last is commonly best."[44]) And Emerson also saw that citation changes meaning: "We are as much informed of a writer's genius by what he selects as by what he originates. We read the quotation with his eyes, and find a new and fervent sense; as a passage from one of the poets, well recited, borrows new interest from the rendering. As the journals say, 'the italics are ours.'"⁴⁵ In fact Emerson goes so far as to endorse, though again ambivalently, the made-up quotation: "It is a familiar expedient of brilliant writers, and not less of witty talkers, the device of ascribing their own sentence to an imaginary person, in order to give it weight,—as Cicero, Cowley, Swift, Landor and Carlyle have done."⁴⁶

"Ascribing their own sentence to an imaginary person": this gesture of othering or displacement pairs oddly but pertinently with the converse practice of appropriation, described by Kaplan as "converting other people's words to our own use" and thereby giving them "meanings quite different from what their authors may have intended."⁴⁷ Both are authority moves. And both depend upon the floating power of the quotation *as* quotation. "Attributed" is a powerful author, in the sense that the phrase marked by this sign-of-a-missing-signature is manifestly familiar enough to demand recognition.

J. L. Austin's *How to Do Things with Words* offers two ways for the performer of a performative utterance to refer to the fact that he or she is "doing the uttering, and so the acting": "*(a)* in verbal utterances, *by his being the person who does* the uttering—what we may call the utterance-*origin*, and *(b)* in written utterances (or 'inscriptions') *by his appending his signature.*"⁴⁸

Austin, we may note, is very much the kind of educated reader/writer who does communicate in unmarked quotations, tags, and allusions: "To feel the firm ground of prejudice slipping away is exhilarating, but brings in its revenges"; "there are many transitional stages between suiting the action to the word and the pure performative."⁴⁹ Indeed, and perhaps unsurprisingly given his subject, "suiting the action to the word" is for Austin a favorite phrase, one that returns (bringing in its revenges?) when he finally, at the very end of his series of lectures, comes around to discussing the verb "I quote."

"I quote" is for Austin one of a group of words he calls expositives, words "used in acts of exposition involving the expounding of views, the conducting of arguments, and the clarifying of usages and references." We may dispute, he acknowledges, "whether they are not straight descriptions of our feelings, practice, &c., especially sometimes over matters of suiting the action to the word, as when I say 'I turn next to,' 'I quote,' 'I cite,' 'I recapitulate.'"⁵⁰ Those

who have followed the fortunes and felicities of Austin's *Words* over the last
thirty years or so may find themselves wondering whether quotation and allusion might fall under his doctrine of etiolations: performative utterances that
are, as he claims, "*in a peculiar way* hollow and void if said by an actor on a
stage, or if introduced in a poem, or spoken in soliloquy."[51] But a quotation, at
least if marked by quotation marks, seems clearly voiced *as* an act of quotation.
It would seem to be performatively valid, at least in terms of its quoting function, if not in terms of its truth content. What about an allusion? Leonard
Diepeveen, a modern critic, has nicely described the difference between quotation and allusion as "a difference signaled by the formal signs of an alien tex-
ture," locating the two practices at different points along a continuum of textual appropriation. "Most allusions have some textural fringes which lead to
effects which pure quotations more fully exploit."[52]

   Much has been said about the category of etiolated or "hollow" utterances,
and I will not attempt to recapitulate it here. But let me cite one key passage
from Derrida's rather spirited riposte to Austin, a passage, a quotation, that is
itself, of course, also by now familiar:

> given [the]structure of iteration, the intention animating the utterance will never
> be through and through present to itself and to its content. The iteration structur-
> ing it a priori introduces into it a dehiscence and a cleft [*brisure*] which are essen-
> tial . . . this essential absence of intending the actuality of utterance, this structural
> unconscious, if you like, prohibits any saturation of the context.[53]

In the case of a quotation, the absence of the primary intending subject is itself
a normative structuring element (phrases like "as Emerson says," "to quote
Hamlet," "in the words of the immortal Bard" all imply that the first speaker is
not present but is being invoked by the quoter). And, as we have seen, the juxtaposition of contexts between the two utterances (the "original" quotation
and its iteration or reuse) can indeed function much like a structural unconscious. Henry Hyde's invocation of the "sound and fury" line from *Macbeth* was
not "intended" to label his Congressional colleagues as idiots, any more than,
in the Clarence Thomas hearings, Senator Alan Simpson's quotation of Iago's
famous speech on reputation was "meant" to cast doubt on Thomas's veracity.
But the quoted line does work very much like an "unconscious," bringing
unwelcome and unvoiced associations to light.

What Derrida calls "saturation," full presence, is by his argument never possible in any citation. But in the special kind of citation known as quotation, a citation of a citation, the dehiscence and the cleft are particularly manifest. This may be the case of a letter *never* returning to its sender. Both the addressee and the "author" are, in the parlance of the post office stamp, unknown.

VI

I want now to turn to two famous literary quotations in which the intention of the speaker has always seemed enigmatic and where the utterance is apparently a nonce utterance, with no other words from the same speaker against which to test it. The first of these quotations can be found in Keats's "Ode on a Grecian Urn," and the speaker, it would appear, is the urn itself.

Here is Helen Vendler's account of the last lines of the poem:

> The poet himself utters the closing words in which the urn's motto and commentary are encapsulated as a quotation:
>
> > When old age shall this generation waste,
> >   Thou shalt remain, in midst of other woe,
> > Than ours, a friend to man, to whom thou say'st,
> >   "Beauty is Truth, truth beauty"—that is all
> > Ye know on earth, and all ye need to know.
>
> The last two lines are spoken by the urn, which places special emphasis on the mottolike epigram before going on to comment on its unique worth. But the whole last sentence of the poem is the sentence of the speaker who, in his prophecy, recounts what the urn will say to succeeding generations.[54]

Vendler explains, in a footnote after the phrase "spoken by the urn," that "This crux now seems settled," and refers the reader to a discussion in Jack Stillinger's *Twentieth-Century Interpretations of Keats' Odes,* "where the *consensus gentium* seems to be that the last two lines are spoken by the urn to men."[55]

Let us leave aside for a moment the question of whether a crux settled is, in literary studies, a happy or an unhappy development. In the phrase "the *consensus gentium*," the wisdom of wise men seems redoubled by the Latin phrase (he who can understand it is part of the insider group, part, indeed, of the *consensus gentium*). And despite the fact that the poet/speaker says "say'st," one could perhaps argue that he is reading the motto on the urn, or rather (since there is no implication that the urn is in fact inscribed with words, and if it were the words would presumably be in a language that antedates even that of the native speakers of *consensus gentium*) that he reads the motto *into* the urn's "message."

Who is speaking here? What do the quotation marks mean? And where, indeed, do they or should they end? I remember lively classroom discussions about this poem that included the termination of the quote marks as part of the—then not-yet-settled—"crux." Here is Earl Wasserman on the question, writing in 1953:

> If man is to "know" that beauty is truth, he must learn it, not by direct experience, but indirectly; it must be told him by the urn ("to whom thou say'st"), for otherwise he could not know it, since it is not true of the sphere of his direct experience...
>
> [O]n implies a commentary, and it is Keats who must make the commentary on the drama that he has been observing and experiencing within the urn. It is the poet, therefore, who speaks the words, "that is all Ye know on earth, and all ye need to know," and he is addressing himself to man, the reader. Hence the shift of reference from "thou" (urn) to "ye" (man).[56]

And here is Walter Jackson Bate's authoritative account, in his 1964 biography of the poet:

> The perennially disputed close of the poem then follows. The focus of the dispute is the final two lines, discussion of which already fills a small book of critical essays.... [Keats] was probably too ill to oversee the publication of the 1820 volume, where the lines were printed:
>
> > "Beauty is truth, truth beauty"—that is all
> > Ye know on earth, and all ye need to know.
>
> Hence it was long assumed that the final remark is the poet's own personal comment on the aphorism, either as a consoling admonition to his fellow human beings (addressed as "ye" though he has been speaking in terms of "us" and "other woe/than ours") or else as a congratulatory bow to the figures on the urn (though the whole burden of the stanza is what the urn, as a "friend," is offering to man). The texts of the transcripts make it plain that the entire two lines are meant as the message or reassurance to man from the urn, without intrusion by the poet.

Here Bate includes a footnote that directs the reader to fuller discussions of the transcribed text, adding "all four transcripts (those of George Keats, Brown, Woodhouse and Dilke) lack a full stop after 'truth beauty,' lack quotation marks, and by dashes break the final lines not into two parts but into three. That of Dilke is typical: 'Beauty is truth,—truth beauty,—that is all. . . .'"[57]

So the "originals," or rather the period transcriptions of Keats's "original," all lack quotation marks. Bate (at least the Bate of the 1964 biography) insists that these texts "make it plain" that the entire two lines are the message from the urn. Vendler appears to agree ("are spoken by the urn") but goes on to declare that "the whole last sentence of the poem is the sentence of the speaker who, in his prophecy, recounts what the urn will say to succeeding generations." The speaker thus imagines what the urn will say and translates it for posterity. Vendler encloses only the words from "beauty" to "beauty" in quotation marks. Bate, printing the lines as he thinks they should be printed, has

> "Beauty is truth, truth beauty,—that is all
> Ye know on earth, and all ye need to know."

He explains, "the final two lines are in the vein of the inscriptions on Greek monuments addressed to the passing stranger. The elusive message is meant to be that of the urn, not of the poet speaking for himself." And he adds this deduction from the life of the poet: "Keats never comes close to anything as bald as the simple equation of these two abstractions, 'beauty' and 'truth,' that he permits the urn to make here (least of all does he advance anything seriously comparable to the words that follow)."[58]

The sentiment "Beauty is truth, truth beauty—that is all / Ye know on earth, and all ye need to know" is, we are thus told, *out of character* for John Keats. Bate deftly associates this kind of bromide with the "pseudo-statements" criticized by I. A. Richards, and emphasizes the distortion that comes with phrases taken out of context. Let us look once more at Bate's own reading of the problem:

> [P]artly because of the aphoristic nature of the final lines, they are constantly being separated not only from the context of the poem but even from the sentence in which they occur, and the efforts to put them back into the context only increase the concentrated focus on these innocent words. Perhaps the modern critical irritability with the phrasing would be less sharp if the Victorians themselves

had not so frequently isolated the lines from their context and quoted them enthusiastically as what I. A. Richards calls a "pseudo-statement."[59]

In the case of the "Ode on a Grecian Urn," then, the final, aphoristic lines are often quoted out of context, as a pseudo-statement, and placed in quotation marks. The quotation marks, apparently absent in the earliest transcripts of the poem, are inserted as intended clarifications: the encapsulated speaker, the urn, starts speaking *here* and stops *there*. Where *here* and *there* are depends upon whether the critic thinks Keats believes the sentiments of the last two lines of the ode, and also upon whether he or she thinks the diction in which they are expressed is appropriate to the poet's (or the poem's "speaker's") voice. The itinerant and shifting nature of the lines, their "quotability," the very quality that seems to further banalize them (Eliot calls them a "serious blemish," and faults them for being "grammatically meaningless"[60]) is in fact exacerbated by those "Victorian" quotation marks that, perhaps as a mark of emphasis, seem to translate the last two lines from the realm of free indirect discourse to that of direct (if slightly obliquely attributed) speech.

In this most canonical of examples, the presence and absence of quotation marks indicates the presence and absence of an origin, and the presence and absence of a truth. Much earlier we noted the paradox that quotation marks can be signs of both authenticity and suspicion: the real thing and the "pseudo." In the "Ode on a Grecian Urn," one of the most famous sound bites in all of romantic literature is framed by quotation marks and then disavowed. It is the urn that speaks, not the poet. Or if the poet/speaker is speaking, he is paraphrasing "what the urn will say to succeeding generations." The absence of quotation marks in the transcripts of Keats's contemporaries is characteristic of early-nineteenth-century punctuation. Subsequent attempts to fix and clarify meaning, by enclosing either the first half-line or the entire two lines in quotation marks, introduce authenticity, authority, and voice as effects of interpretation masquerading as originary fact: what the poet meant, or meant to do. And because quotation marks are themselves by convention marks of origin—indicating that this is the real thing, not a paraphrase—the "crux" can be finally "settled," if we don't mind mixing our metaphors, by the imposition of anachronistic punctuation that is clearly spurious.

A certain faction of the poetic establishment is so determined to protect Keats from the claim that he speaks (and espouses) this sentiment that even *Bartlett's* goes to the extraordinary length of appending a literary-critical footnote. After the phrase "beauty is truth, truth beauty" (enclosed, as in Vendler's text, by quotation marks) there is a footnote from W. H. Auden that reads,

> If asked who said, "Beauty is truth, truth beauty!" a great many readers would answer, "Keats." But Keats said nothing of the sort. It is what he said the Grecian Urn said, his description and criticism of a certain kind of work of art, the kind from which the evils and problems of this life, the "heart high sorrowful and cloyed," are deliberately excluded. The Urn, for example, depicts, among other beautiful sights, the citadel of a hill town; it does not depict warfare, the evil which makes the citadel necessary.[61]

But time, to paraphrase Austin's felicitous paraphrase, will bring in its revenges. The crux will not stay settled in the popular imagination. Urn, schmurn—the public knows who is speaking, and it is not the pot but the poet. Here are some media allusions to this famous passage:

- *From a scientific report about waist-to-hip ratio (WHR) in the human species*: "Beauty is truth and truth beauty, to quote John Keats. But what is the truth about beauty? A scientific investigation of what men find beautiful in a woman's shape suggests that concepts of beauty are more to do with Western influences than what comes as an inbuilt, or innate desire."[62]

- *From an article about fall foliage in New England*:

  > "'Beauty is truth—truth beauty—that is all Ye know on earth,
  > and all ye need to know.'
  > —John Keats

  By now, anyone who has passed more than a few autumns in New Hampshire knows why the state's fall foliage is colored so flagrantly. . . . 'Beauty (or ugliness) is not out there in a man's environment but here, within a man's brain,' wrote Faber Birren . . . a craftsman, [and] pioneer in the study of the psychology of color."[63]

- *Lead sentence in a newspaper article about the merits of live-performance recording*: "According to John Keats, beauty is truth and vice versa. Some recording artists disagree."[64]

- *Headline in the* New York Times, *drawing attention to "a new Israeli esthetic along the Mediterranean"*: "THE SECULAR JEWS: Beauty Is Truth. That Is All the Stylish Need to Know."[65]

- *Headline of an editorial on the National Endowment for the Arts:* "BEAUTY IS TRUTH: Government has a role in nurturing the arts."[66]

- *Headline for a* Los Angeles Times *column:* "If 'Beauty is Truth, Truth Beauty,' That's Not All We Need to Know Today: What's 'Telegenic'?"[67]

- *And, somewhat ironically in view of subsequent developments, this opening paragraph from a 1983 piece in the* New York Times: "John Keats wrote that 'beauty is truth, truth beauty—that is all ye know on earth, and all ye need to know.' But is that all we need to know about Vanessa Williams, the new Miss America?"[68]

In none of these citations does the "famous crux" figure at all, nor does anyone seem to wish to credit the urn. Exactly what Eliot seems to have feared, that Keats will be blamed (or praised) for the bathetic sentiment behind the aphorism, comes resoundingly true. No one is interested in the views of an Attic shape, however fair or unfair its attitude. The canonical figure of the poet guarantees the "beauty is truth" line as a touchstone, unironized, unqualified— except for the vicissitudes of fallen modern life.

It is tempting to end this discussion of quotation marks and the quotation as floating signifier on this note. But I would like to interject one more famous utterance into the equation—one that has been, in the history of modern literature, as problematic and teasing as that of the urn. The speaker in this case is not a vase but an *avis*: specifically, Edgar Allan Poe's enigmatical raven. And what it speaks, of course, is the single word "nevermore."[69]

What is fascinating about the raven (and "The Raven") is the mixture of pertinence and impertinence generated by its steadfast iteration. Once it arrives and perches on the pallid bust of Pallas (and here I do in fact suspect a little intertextual allusion to Keats's Grecian urn) the raven has only one word for the increasingly importunate narrator. No matter what the query—"tell me what thy lordly name is"; "will you leave me, as have my other friends?"; "is there balm in Gilead?"; "will my soul clasp Lenore's in heaven?"—the all-purpose answer, superbly overdetermined and always infuriatingly apt, is "nevermore." "Much I marvelled this ungainly fowl to hear discourse so plainly," says the narrator, "though its answer little meaning—little relevancy bore." But perhaps the problem was not that the single word "nevermore" had little meaning and relevancy, but rather that it had too much. "Floating (or, to use Poe's own word for the bird, *flitting*) signifier" seems an understatement for this word that, as the narrator is quick to observe, breaks into the silence with a "reply so aptly spoken":

> 'Doubtless,' said I, 'what it utters is its only stock and store
> Caught from some unhappy master whom unmerciful Disaster
> Followed fast and followed faster till his songs one burden bore—

In stanza after stanza the word "nevermore," sometimes in quotation marks and sometimes not, is repeated with a difference, gaining "meaning" both from the act of repetition and from the uncanniness of the too-aptly spoken reply. "Nevermore" is an empty signifier that becomes, precisely, saturated, or even supersaturated. It has no "origin," no intending subject; it is from the beginning a quotation, and a quotation out of context, since no one—not the narrator, not the reader—presumes that the raven is actually hearing and responding to the questions hurled at it by the increasingly agitated narrator, often called a student, and clearly suffering from an etiolating ("weak and weary") excess of learnedness ("many a quaint and curious volume of forgotten lore"). (Perhaps this "quaint and curious volume" is the same "very rare and very remarkable volume" that was the occasion for the first meeting between C. Augustus Dupin and his unnamed colleague and friend.[70] But this may be to consider too curiously.)

Explaining his choice of language and his cast of characters in the fascinating little piece called "Philosophy of Composition," Poe himself insists that the word "nevermore" was the key to the whole: it answered fully the needs for sonority, melancholy, and the *o* and *r* sounds required by the refrain. "In such a search it would have been absolutely impossible to overlook the word 'nevermore.' In fact, it was the very first which presented itself."

> The next *desideratum* was a pretext for the continuous use of the one word "nevermore." In observing the difficulty which I at once found in inventing a sufficiently plausible reason for its continuous repetition, I did not fail to perceive that this difficulty arose solely from the pre-assumption that the word was to be so continuously or monotonously spoken by a *human* being—I did not fail to perceive, in short, that the difficulty lay in the reconciliation of this monotony with the exercise of reason on the part of the creature repeating the word. Here, then, immediately arose the idea of a *non*-reasoning creature capable of speech; and, very naturally, a parrot, in the first instance, suggested itself, but was superseded forthwith by a Raven, as equally capable of speech, and infinitely more in keeping with the intended *tone*.[71]

Now, whatever the "intended tone" of Poe's own enigmatical text here, the phenomenon he produces is instructive: a specifically *non*reasoning creature capable of speech carries the burden of meaning or, more accurately, is the occasion for wild interpretation. (That ravens were imagined to speak may be attested to in literary terms by another famous speaker—one well known to Congressman Henry Hyde :"The raven himself is hoarse, / That croaks the fatal entrance of Duncan / Under our battlements."[72]) "Nevermore" migrates from stanza to stanza, sometimes marked as something the raven "quoth" and some-times appropriated by the narrator. The progression from "nothing more" (the refrain word of the first stanza) to "nevermore" (the refrain word of the last), neither enclosed in quotation marks, is made possible by the intervention of an authoritative speaker whose word is taken *as* authoritative partly because it is repeated with a difference and partly because it is "in quotation." That the ori-gin of the word is *elsewhere*, and is *lost*, does not undercut its authority. The raven, we could say, quotes (or "quoth") "out of context"—and this becomes part of the force of his freestanding, and free-ranging, utterance.

When the Cleveland Browns football team moved from Cleveland to Baltimore in 1996 the new owners had a contest to rename the team. The win-ner, to the amusement of many and the pleasure of some, was the Ravens—a tribute to Poe, who died in and was buried in Baltimore. Sportwriters had pre-dictable fun imagining a "Nevermore Defense" and a team that, if it failed, could be labeled "a pallid bust."[73] One prophesied a change of fortunes for the club: "Why a raven? To make the 'Nevermore!' believable."[74] Headline writers could not resist quoting perhaps the most notorious of all lines about quoting: "Quoth the Ravens, Play Everymore, Kelly"; "Quoth the Ravens fans, Nevermore, after Pizza Hut Promotion"; "Quoth the Former Raven Everitt, Evermore"; "Quoth You on the Ravens; Nevermore!"[75] But perhaps the most striking, if inadvertent, effect was that these Ravens, too, began to be quotable, and enigmatic: "The Ravens are involved in preliminary talks that might lead to acquiring [a new quarterback]" read one account. "Neither Ravens owner Art Modell nor team vice president of player personnel Ozzie Newsome would comment. . . ."[76]

The choice of the name Ravens may have been overdetermined by the existence, in another sport, of a long-standing Baltimore team that bears the name of a bird: the Baltimore Orioles baseball club. *Baltimore Orioles* is felici-tous in at least two senses: (1) there is an American songbird called the

Baltimore oriole, and (2) both the double-dactyl scansion and the repetition of the *o* or *or* sounds (Balti*more* *Or*ioles) seem to make the name sound right. Baltimore Ravens lacks both ornithological and metrical inevitability. But we should not entirely forget the unarticulated but latent mantra of Poe's oft-quoted talking bird: behind the same open *o*s and *or*s of Balti*more*, and concealed by the aural brightness of Raven, may lurk the same ghostly word, in context more a spondee than a dactyl, "Never*more*."

I want to offer this kind of poetic event as a model, sign, or epitome of the fate of spoken quotation. Always "in quotation," whether its quotation marks are showing or not, the quotation often blends, apparently seamlessly but with its seams and its semes showing, into the parent text of the quoter. As in the philosophical brainteaser, "'This statement is false' is true," the location and comprehension of a quotation's limits, and the degree to which *its* voice is marked as different from the speaker's, can radically alter both our sense of its truth value and our interpretation of its meaning.

Fashionable | 2

Taste...is the *only* morality.... Tell me what you like, and I'll tell you what you are.

—John Ruskin, *The Crown of Wild Olive*

What is the relationship between morality and style? Are they opposites or allies? Is the very concept of style inimical to morality, or is it, contrariwise, morality's surest sign? Or, put another way, is morality an artifact of style? Is style an artifact of morality?

In what follows I will begin with the function of the fashionable as an epithet. And I will end with a theory of the fashionable as a genre.

It has become quite fashionable to condemn being fashionable. Indeed, in certain contexts, including some wings of the profession of scholarship, there is nothing so unfashionable as being *fashionable*. The word itself is an insult, usually hurled from the supposed right to the supposed left. One hears of "fashionable theories," "fashionable philosophizing," "fashionable evils." The adjective connotes unseriousness, and, more important, suggestibility, fandom and followerdom (consider terms like "fashion victim" and "slave to fashion," both imported from the newspaper "style" pages, where celebrity gossip is found). To be "fashionable" is to lack that word that so entranced journalists and commentators during the early phases of the presidential political season: *gravitas*, a word that itself became fashionable, the topic of innumerable public parsings.

Like its equally suspect cousins, *fad* and *trendy*, *fashionable* seems to speak of the new and the now, the passing fancy, as in this celebrated passage from William Shakespeare's *Troilus and Cressida*, where the crafty Ulysses tries to warn Achilles that fame is fleeting:

> For Time is like a fashionable host,
> That slightly shakes his parting guest by th' hand,
> And with his arms outstretch'd, as he would fly,
> Grasps in the comer; welcome ever smiles,
> And farewell goes out sighing.
>   (3.3.159–63)[1]

Indeed temporality, or what might be called lack of timelessness, has always been the Achilles heel of the word *fashionable*.

What then is the other, or the opposite, of *fashionable*? Its other might conceivably be *unfashionable*, or indeed *sensible*, but I think the real functional opposite to the word *fashionable* in the world of literature and culture, morality and style, is *classic*. That which exists in the realm of the "timeless" (or, the "timeless classic," to use a phrase that is applied variously to children's literature, on the one hand, and the Talbot's clothing chain, on the other).

An ad for Louis Vuitton's "Monogram Bucket Bag" declares

> Fashion trends come and go.
> Too bad for them.[2]

But this is not the worst that can be said about *fashionable*. Because to be fashionable is not only to be time bound or timely rather than timeless, it is also something else equally unreliable: to be fashionable, it seems, is to be French.

The title of Alan Sokal and Jean Bricmont's diatribe against what they call "postmodern intellectuals' abuse of science" says it all: *Fashionable Nonsense*. The two words offer what is in effect a tautology: to be fashionable is to be nonsensical, to create *non-sense*. It is far from an accident, of course, that

Fashionable Nonsense targets French theorists. American writer Barbara Ehrenreich's cover blurb exults, "Take the most hallowed names in current French theoretical thinking, divide by one of the sharpest and most irreverent minds in America.... render in good clear English—and you have a thoroughly hiliarious romp through the postmodern academy." Sokal's famous hoax article is described in the first page of the book as having appeared in "a fashionable American cultural-studies journal, *Social Text*."[3] To be fashionable *is* to be French, or (worse yet) to *want to be* French—which is to say, frivolous, lacking in moral fiber, fascinated by surfaces.

This may be the time to mention the existence of an upscale clothing line called *Façonnable*, with a cedilla and two *ns*. How fashionable can you get? (Although the ads still read, in French, "Fondé en 1950," the company is now part of Nordstrom.)

Listen to a perhaps unlikely "fashion critic," Belgian Paul de Man, who writes that

> in a long tradition, more familiar even in the world of *haute couture* than of literary theory, what is made in Paris is often thought of as more fashionable than sound. What is in fashion in Paris is tolerable only as window display, not for everyday wear. Yet, as we know from Baudelaire, fashion, *la mode*, is itself a highly significant and, precisely, aesthetic and historical category that historians should not underestimate. When it becomes fashionable to dismiss fashion, clearly something interesting is going on, and what is being discarded as mere fashion must also be more insistent, and more threatening, than its frivolity and transience would seem to indicate.[4]

French fashion: the term sounds almost like a tautology. Ever since the Norman Conquest, the Anglo-Saxons have defined Englishness as in opposition to "Frenchness"—in literary style as well as in sartorial style.

Here is an English account of linguistic changes in the medieval period: at first, says the author, a nineteenth-century scholar,

> few French words crept into English, and for most of those which did we can see a distinct reason. But, as the fusion of races went on, as French became, not so much a foreign tongue as a fashionable tongue, the infusion of French words into English went on much faster. The love of hard words, of words which are thought to sound learned or elegant, that is, for the most part, words which are not thoroughly understood, is, I conceive, not peculiar to any one age. What it leads to in our own day we see in that foul jargon against whose inroads lovers of their native tongue have to strive.[5]

For three centuries after the Norman Conquest many English writers wrote in French. In a way, then, by the logic of the narcissism of minor differences, French, the near other, *had* to be a "foul jargon" in order for English to be English.

The standard alternative to this French fanciness was "plain speaking," often a cover for the most successful and duplicitous (or at least manipulative) speech. Consider this clear opposition between straightforward English conduct and suspect French fashionableness from Shakespeare's *Richard III*:

> Because I cannot flatter and look fair,
> Smile in men's faces, smooth, deceive, and cog,
> Duck with French nods and apish courtesy,
> I must be held a rancorous enemy.
> Cannot a plain man live and think no harm . . . ?
> (1.3.47–51)

This plain speaker, of course, is Richard III himself.

"Plain" would come to have another rhetorical or stylistic sense in the Renaissance, one also pertinent to our inquiry, for its opposite was "pointed"—the plain style or the pointed style. Epigrams, satires, and other modes of wit were "pointed"—stinging, sharp, precise. The notion of a "pointed style" was given legitimacy (and point) by the supposed etymology of the word *style*, thought to derive from *stylus* or pin, a sharp-pointed instrument for writing. Here material culture and figurative language go, as so often, hand in hand, since *style*, in the sense of "pen" or "pen point," became a symbol of literary composition. ("Death, with his keen-pointed style / Hath writ the common doom."[6])

Since "pointed" also meant "punctuated," and was in addition a sartorial term, meaning "fitted or furnished with tagged points or laces," the possibility for confusion or crossover was omnipresent, and overdetermined; overdetermined because of the long history of association between style and dress, or style and fashion, or the "fashionable."

Georges Louis Leclerc de Buffon's famous formulation, "the style is the man" ("*Le style c'est l'homme même*" or, as it might be better translated, "style is man himself"[7]) aligns style in its most general as well as its most particular sense with morality, with the moral. The idea was that the writer's or speaker's style was formed by the way he thought and reasoned—this was not a psycho-logical view about inadvertently disclosing something personal in one's style, but what might perhaps be called an ethical view.[8] Perhaps symptomatically, Buffon wrote his famous phrase for a particular occasion, which itself was a celebration of style, French style—his induction into the French Academy in 1753. And just as symptomatically, we might think, Jacques Lacan held the mirror up to Buffon, in his introduction or "overture" to the French edition of his own *Écrits*, in a passage omitted from the English edition:

> "Style is man himself," people say without seeing any trick at work, or worrying about whether "man" is any longer such a definite reference. . . .
>
> Style is the man, we would agree, simply by lengthening the formula: the man we are addressing.[9]

Style, in other words, comes from outside, from the other, not (as Buffon implied), from within.

In any case, Buffon's dictum—the dictum of a naturalist inducted into a society for the preservation of the purity of the French language—has had a curious itinerary in the twentieth and twenty-first centuries, since it has been, like all really good quotations, repeatedly quoted out of context. Thus we have, on the one hand, the use of the phrase to characterize *writing style*, as in the title of Louis Auchincloss's book of literary essays, *The Style's the Man: Reflections on Proust, Fitzgerald, Wharton, and Others* or John Bayley's praise of William Empson: "what matters is his unformal and colloquial style, and the style is the man: it makes literary criticism seem wholly human."[10]

But "the style is the man" has also been used, increasingly, to describe *clothing style*, and the messages sent through clothing, as in fashion scholar and upscale haberdasher Alan Flusser's book, *Style and the Man: How and Where to Buy Fine Men's Clothes*. In this case Buffon seems to have been crossed with Virgil: not only "style is the man" but "style and the man I sing."

To complicate things further, the same quotation from Buffon appears as an epigraph for an article in *USA Today* (a newspaper I didn't even realize *used* epigraphs) on President Bill Clinton's cross-country bus trip way back in 1993. "Style is this man," said *USA Today*, cheerfully. "Clinton really does like climb-ing on and off buses to meet people. Jogging in baggy short shorts, sagging socks and a baseball cap. Munching or musing at McDonald's. Loafing around the mansion in jeans. But he also cleans up nicely. Looks OK in suit and tie."[11]

As odd an appropriation of Buffon as this might seem, it is not, in a larger sense, really a mistake, since the word *style* has long been taken to refer both to a mode of expression or literary composition and to a mode of deportment, appearance, and behavior. To have style is, precisely, to be fashionable. Thus, *style* is used in an absolute sense to denote a "fashionable air, appearance, deportment."[12]

In the history of the concept of literary style there are two fundamental kinds of theories, the mechanical or ornamental and the organic—the first predominant among Renaissance and neoclassic writers, the second coming to the fore in the romantic period. Both, usefully for our present inquiry, involve some recourse to the question of clothing and style. By ornamental is meant, broadly speaking, something added; by organic, something intrinsic. "Language is but the apparel of Poesy, which may give beauty but not strength," wrote Sir William Alexander, in 1634.

Alexander Pope gave the ornamental view its most celebrated expression in his "Essay on Criticism":

> True wit is *Nature* to advantage drest,
> What oft was *Thought*, but ne'er so well *Exprest*.

And

> Expression is the *Dress of Thought*, and still
> Appears more *decent* as more *suitable*;

And again

> In *Words*, as *Fashions*, the same Rule will hold;
> Alike Fantastick, if *too New*, or *Old*;
>   (296–97; 318–19; 333–34)

John Ward, a professor of rhetoric at Gresham College in London, declared in his *System of Oratory* (1759) that

> polite and elegant speakers distinguish themselves by their discourse, as persons of figure do by their garb; one being the dress of the mind, as the other is of the body. And hence it comes to pass, that both have their different fashions, which are

often changed; and as the vulgar affect to imitate those above them in both, this frequently occasions an alteration, when either becomes too trite and common.[13]

Although the "organic" view is most often associated with Samuel Taylor Coleridge and the romantics, it is found episodically in earlier periods. For example, in the Renaissance George Puttenham wrote of "stile" as the image of man [*mentis character*],[14] and Ben Jonson asserted, "Language most shows a man: 'speak that I may see thee.'"[15] What is more important for my argument, however, is that the image of clothing persisted in overdetermining questions of literary style, no matter what the viewpoint of the critic. Thus Jonson, insisting that style should suit subject matter, produced an image of ludicrous class jumping and cross-dressing from one social rank to another: "Would you not laugh to meet a great-counsellor of state in a flat cap, with his trunkhose and a hobby-horse cloak, his gloves under his girdle, and yond haberdasher in a velvet gown furred with sable?"[16] The appropriate style was determined by the speaker and the topic—it could not be put on, or off, at will.

By the beginning of the twentieth century the figure of speech was alive and well, if somewhat variously deployed. John Middleton Murry could declare, in a series of lectures on *The Problem of Style*, that "style is organic—not the clothes a man wears, but the flesh, bone and blood of his body."[17] Ludwig Wittgenstein wrote in his *Tractatus* that "Language disguises thought. So much so, that from the outward form of the clothing it is impossible to infer the form of the thought beneath it."[18] Meanwhile, Oscar Wilde gleefully proclaimed, "Dandyism is the assertion of the absolute modernity of Beauty," "A really well-made buttonhole is the only link between Art and Nature," and, "One should either be a work of art or wear a work of art."[19]

In France, of course, Charles Baudelaire had already written eloquently of fashion and the dandy, praising cosmetics, makeup and the simplicity of a perfect *toilette*; "Fashion should thus be considered as a symptom of the taste for the ideal which floats on the surface of all the crude, terrestrial and loathsome bric-a-brac that natural life accumulates," he wrote. "Virtue . . . is artificial," he declared. "Nature [is] a bad counsellor in moral matters."[20]

It was partly in the spirit of Baudelaire's essay that Roland Barthes produced his tour de force, *The Fashion System*, reading fashion itself as a mode of discourse, a set of vestimentary codes. Working, as he said, "not on real

Fashion but on written (or more exactly on *described*) Fashion," Barthes explained that his study actually addressed "neither clothing nor language but the 'translation,' so to speak, of one into the other, insofar as the former is already a system of signs."[21] In doing so he pointed, unerringly, to the critical issue: the question of time and the fashionable. For one function of the rhetoric of fashion, he said,

> is to blur the memory of past Fashions, so as to censure the number and the return of forms . . . . it discredits the terms of past Fashion, making those of current Fashion euphoric. It plays on synonyms, pretending to take them for different meanings . . . . In short, the system is drowned under literature, the Fashion consumer is plunged into a disorder which is soon an oblivion, since it causes the present to be perceived in the form of a new absolute.[22]

The "system is drowned under literature." Little did Barthes suspect what might be coming by the turn of the next century, when a journal like *Fashion Theory: The Journal of Dress, Body and Culture* could provoke an outpouring of attention. According to its editor, Valerie Steele,

> *Fashion Theory* has received a lot of press coverage, in newspapers ranging from *The Guardian* and *Die Zeit* to fashion magazines such as *Elle* and *Harper's Bazaar*. The journalists at *Artforum* and *Time Out* were a little sarcastic about the possibility that professors might know anything about fashion. But Robin Givhan at *The Washington Post* thought that a "brainy" approach to fashion was great, and W even suggested that fashionistas who saw themselves as intellectuals might trade in their Comme des Garçons for subscriptions to *Fashion Theory*.
>
> It is true that academic discourse can be at least as opaque as "Voguespeak," and some of the articles in *Fashion Theory* have proved difficult for readers unaccustomed to the vocabulary.[23]

In September 2000 a website called Style.com was launched as a joint venture of *Vogue* and W magazines; it is dedicated to fashion shows, trends, people and parties, shopping, and forums.[24] There is, however, currently no website at morality.com, though I was able to find beliefnet.com, moralityinmedia.org, jewsformorality.org, ourcivilisation.com, and secularhumanism.org, among many others.

Let us come back, then, to the question of morality and style, and the role of the word *fashionable* in connecting them, or in disrupting what we think they might have to do with one another. Barthes analyzed clothing as a mode of speech; the history of style analyzes speech as a mode of clothing. What I propose to do here is to reverse the terms of Barthes's analysis, and to seek the material place of the fashionable in the realm of the literary.

What is the genre, or literary mode, of the fashionable in the realm of morality and style? Despite various claims to the contrary, it is not the novel, nor yet the comedy of manners. It is the aphorism, and its close, sometimes indistinguishable, relatives: the adage, the sentence, and the maxim.

The Renaissance drew distinctions in literary style between the sugared and the salt, between honey and gall, between the pointed and the plain. Eighteenth-century critics were more engaged with the distinction between wit and judgment. Wit was the capacity to find similarities in things apparently unlike. Judgment was discriminating between things apparently alike. A good example comes from Joseph Addison: "I shall endeavor to liven morality with wit, and to temper wit with morality."[25] Another comes from Blaise Pascal: "True eloquence has no time for eloquence, true morality has no time for morality."[26] Not all such distinctions are chiastic, of course. But what I will assert is that the family of aphoristic utterances bring wit face-to-face with judgment, in a formulation, sometimes gnomic, that is the apotheosis and the realization of morality and style.

Theodor Adorno's *Minima Moralia* is a brilliant example of precisely this genre: aphorisms, maxims, adages, and reflections. Adorno is following in the path of La Rochefoucauld, the author of the *Maxims*, titled in full *Reflections or Aphorisms and Moral Maxims*; and of Pascal, the author of the *Pensées*, and of Erasmus, the author of the *Adagia* or *Adages*. He follows Francis Bacon, J. W. von Goethe, Friedrich Nietzsche, and dozens of others, as well.

The maxim is the jumbo shrimp of morality, the little sentence with the name that means big. A maxim is an axiom, a self-evident proposition, assumed as a premise in mathematical or dialectical reasoning. The original term, from Boethius, was *propositio maxima* (greatest proposition)—over time the noun dropped out, leaving only the adjective to stand for the thing. So *maxima moralia* are moral axioms. *Minim* means smallest, extremely small. Like *jot*, it is also a term from writing, a single downstroke of the pen. A minim rest in music is a tiny pause. A minim was thus an insignificant thing, or person; Adorno is being witty and self-deprecating, at least in his title, *Minima Moralia*.

As for the aphorism—which derives from the same word as "horizon" and means to delimit or define—"It is brief, it is isolated, it is witty, and it is 'philosophical.'"[27] John Gross observes that maxim and aphorism were once synonymous (or so thought Samuel Johnson), but goes on to note that "aphorisms tend to be distinctly more subversive; indeed, it is often a maxim that they set out to subvert." Aphorisms, writes Gross, are brief, are generalizations, are forms of literature, and are often retorts or ripostes: "There are times when the very form of the aphorism seems to lend itself to a disenchanted view of human nature."[28] Without begging the question of what "human nature" is (I might want to say that the aphorism is the form in which the very existence of that comfortable construct is challenged), I think I can agree with this general set of formal definitions.

Adage–saying–proverb–maxim–axiom–aphorism: the sequence produces a truth-effect. The *epigram*, or witty saying, is another variant, with the emphasis on the wit rather than judgment. The sound bite is a modern form, as is, curiously enough, the advertising slogan.

"The adage, the *sententia*," says Rosalie Colie, writing of Renaissance small forms, is "a quotation from an authoritative source (biblical, classical, proverbial) which sums up a mass of experience in one charged phrase." Adages become "figures for alluding to a large meaning from an important context. They are keys to culture, or convenient agents of cultural transfer." "An adage," she notes, "bears a coded message, compresses much experience into a very small space, and by that very smallness makes its wisdom so communicable. Trust in adages and axioms can be noted in many different contexts...."[29]

Why do we trust them? Because they always turn against themselves.

Shakespeare puts adages into the mouths of unlikely speakers—it's the drama that makes them turn against themselves. Polonius, the least self-aware of men, turns on "to thine own self be true"; Iago turns on reputation, as he is about to destroy Othello's; Jaques turns on that chestnut of chestnuts, "all the world's a stage" presented not as a startling new idea but as a conventional, even boring, set piece; Ulysses on degree, just as he is about to convince the dull Ajax to take the place of the brilliant Achilles. That very drama, that very irony, drops out in the *Bartlett's Familiar Quotations* version of Shakespeare, leaving the flat, unanswered "wisdom" of doxa, the opposite of the pointed style.

But the maxim form, so elegantly balanced and delicately paradoxical, turns against itself *all by itself*: it is completely self-sufficient, serenely self-contained. It knows its mind, and it knows fashion. It creates the illusion of the timeless with the materials of temporality. In fact, it makes the fashionable into the classic.

Here are some examples from La Rochefoucauld:

- We are never so happy nor so unhappy as we imagine.
- Everyone complains of his memory, and no one complains of his judgment.
- We always like those who admire us; we do not always like those whom we admire.
- We frequently forgive those who bore us, but cannot forgive those whom we bore.
- The greatest fault of a penetrating wit is to go beyond the mark.
- Nothing prevents our being natural so much as the desire to appear so.
- In the misfortunes of our best friends we often find something that is not displeasing.
- Fashions of thought, as well as the fortunes of the world, come round on the whirligig of time.

Notice the recurrence in these maxims of words like *frequently*, *always*, *never*, and *often*. When they do not actually appear, they are implied, as in the maxim on "fashions of thought," which by implication "[always] come round on the whirligig of time." There is no more fashionable art form than the maxim, and it balances, precisely, on the *point* of *style*, as on the heightened temporality of the timely/timeless, and on the tipping point between wit and judgment.

The invention of these maxims was a parlor game in high society, a pleasurable and witty way of passing the time. "The skill," explains Leonard Tancock, "consists in expressing some thought about human motives or behaviour in a form combining the maximum of clarity and truth with the minimum of words arranged in the most striking and memorable order."[30] Though they may have originated with the author, the maxims were communally revised and edited. La Rochefoucauld polished and shaped them over the course of his six or seven years in the Paris salon of Madame de Sablé.

We have already noted some examples from another great master of the maxim, Oscar Wilde, the man who insisted, in "A Few Maxims for the Instruction of the Over-Educated" and "Phrases and Philosophies for the Use of the Young,"

- To be really medieval one should have no body. To be really modern one should have no soul. To be really Greek one should have no clothes.
- The only way to atone for being occasionally a little over-dressed is by being always absolutely over-educated.
- In all unimportant matters, style, not sincerity, is the essential. In all important matters, style, not sincerity, is the essential.
- Only the great masters of style ever succeed in being obscure.[31]

The maxim—the adage, the aphorism—is the apotheosis of the fashionable. It would be easy to spend a pleasurable hour, or an instructive semester, revisiting the authors who write in these small and explosive genres, among the most powerful and eloquent of forms.

More important, perhaps, is our own age's attraction to the form of the aphorism, precisely because of its stylish economy and subversive flair. Stand-up comedians and late-night talk-show hosts, like it or not, are our modern and postmodern aphorists. Their monologues and one-liners intersect, precisely, at the crossroads of morality and style (like the late Victor Borge, who once remarked mordantly, while performing as a Jewish comedian in his native Denmark, that the difference between a Nazi and a dog was that a Nazi raised his *arm*[32]). And if they have speech writers and joke writers to assist them, so—let us not forget—did La Rochefoucauld, surrounded by the witty editorial circle of Madame de Sablé.

The problem of morality and style is the problem of the figure: Is style something that disguises—or discloses—what lies beneath or within? Or is style itself the real thing, from which canons of morality are derived in an act of secondary revision, and then established—via the logic of back-formation—as prior? Which comes first, morality or style? And what do we mean by first? Or rather, *who's* on first? What we have here is not so much a problem of the vehicle and the tenor as of the cart and the horse—or, if you prefer, the chicken and the egg. In the case of the "fashionable," perhaps it is a Fabergé egg, the small, jeweled, perfect thing, described by one curator as "very expensive toys for adults"[33]—like the maxim and the aphorism.

The word *fashionable* ought to be more than a term of scorn or praise, a class putdown or shopper's mantra. It comes by its etymology honorably, being descended, as it is, from both the artist and society. The fashionable is the "fashioned" as well as the stylish, and the suffix, *-able*, tells you everything you need to know. *Fashionable* is an adjective that lives the life of a verb; it is the description of a life act as a speech act. It cuts both ways: it is naive and knowing, it is cynical and hopeful. Its genres are small and perfect, social and sociable, crafted and crafty: the maxim and the aphorism, thinking on paper. We could do worse than to remember with honor and pleasure those societies that played word games so seriously, that tried to capture morality and style in a single, rebarbative, and exquisitely fashioned phrase.

Try-Works

> A novice in the game generally seeks to embarrass his opponents by giving them the most minutely lettered names; but the adept selects such words as stretch, in large characters, from one end of the chart to the other.
> —Edgar Allan Poe, "The Purloined Letter"

Once upon a time "cultural studies" was an exotic and edgy import. Now it is the norm in many—though not all—departments of literature, a marker of "interdisciplinarity" and its discontents. What is the role of literary criticism in an age of cultural studies? A question behind this question would seem to be, "Is literary criticism *over*?" Has literary study changed, changed utterly? Or is literary criticism making a spectacular comeback, perhaps under the auspices of a new aestheticism? Is there a fundamental and irreconcilable difference between literary criticism and cultural studies?

In one sense cultural studies is so ubiquitous that it is virtually invisible as a category (it is a case of Edgar Allan Poe's famous description of the map, naming the continents in letters so large they escape the eye). The listings specified under the rubric Cultural Studies, Folklore, and Popular Culture at a recent Modern Language Association conference were relatively few in num-

ber: on that occasion I counted only fifteen. The listings under Literary
Criticism and Theory (note that prestige-infusing phrase "and Theory") were
almost three times more numerous (my count was forty-three). But these "lit-
erary" sessions included sessions called Postcolonialism and Sexualities,
Moses and Jesus in Hollywood, and Political Constructions in the Future of
Eighteenth-Century Studies, just to name a small, but fairly representative,
sample. Among the theorists cited by name in the Literary Criticism and
Theory session titles are Jacques Lacan, Michel Foucault, Sigmund Freud and
Karl Marx—none of whom are literary critics. I will not take time to cite the
listings under Cultural Studies, but they were really not very different: several
included the terms *popular culture* or *cultural studies*, which may be why they
wound up where they are. Of course, this does not prove much. But it is suggestive. What does it suggest?

If we define literary criticism as something like "literary commentary that
doesn't take its center of gravity to be outside the text," the question of literary
criticism in an age of cultural studies would seem to pose a pair of related
queries:

- Is literature in service of something else, or is it itself the object of contemplation and desire?
- Is literary criticism about the text or about the world?

We may pause to reflect that these are hardly new issues. They are in fact
the oldest issues in the field, and that they go back at least as far as Plato and
Aristotle, ordinarily regarded as the "founders" of literary criticism.

When I refer to the question of literary criticism in an age of cultural studies, I am using *question* here in its time-honored debater's sense, as demarcating
two sides of an argument—the sense in which Hamlet uses it ("To be or not to
be, that is the question"), and the sense in which members of Parliament, and
faculty meetings run according to Roberts' Rules of Order, can "call the question" in order to put an end to debate. I am not ready, yet, to "call the question." But I do want to set up the terms of the debate.

There are two ways of construing the problem posed by our topic: a narrow one that inquires about institutional practice, and a broader one that
inquires about persons and their politics. Thus, we could understand "literary
criticism in an age of Cultural Studies" as asking, "What is the fate, or role, of

close reading and textual analysis—and of works of 'literature,' however defined—in a profession increasingly attentive to matters of historical and sociological concern?"

Or we could understand the same topic as asking, simply, "Can people who teach in departments of literature effect social change through their professional work?" with the follow-up questions: "Should they?"; "Are they professionally competent to do so?"; and, taking this cliché in its literal sense, "Is it any of their business?"

Mediating between these two ways of construing the question has to a certain extent preoccupied both practitioners of our profession and their critics over the past several decades. About ten years ago Ellen Rooney argued, in an essay nicely titled "Discipline and Vanish," that Cultural Studies should avoid going the route of American Studies, losing its political edge and its capacity for critique by seeking and accepting disciplinary status within the American academy. "If cultural studies becomes a new 'period,'" she wrote, "it will inevitably become a natural object for disinterested inquiry, a discipline. The irony is that this process is encouraged by some cultural studies scholars."[1] That was then. This is now.

As John Brenkman maintained in an article in *Critical Inquiry*, "[W]hile cultural studies defines itself as going beyond literature, high culture, and disciplinarity, what defines cultural studies is that it *is* literature, high culture, and a discipline."[2] I hasten to say that this degree of false consciousness, disavowal, and projection is not a particular property of *cultural studies* as an intellectual or institutional movement, but could be said of all "new" critical moments as they define themselves against the recent past and its imagined sway.

For example, Georg Lukács, meditating on the critical infatuation with scientific research, "new methods," and "new facts," wrote, in 1910, that

> every epoch needs its own Greece, its own Middle Ages and its own Renaissance. Every age creates the age it needs, and only the next generation believes that its fathers' dreams were lies which must be fought with its own new "truths."[3]

Every age creates the age it needs. Only the next generation believes that its fathers' dreams were lies that must be fought with its own new "truths." The argument I want to make here will ultimately be presented under the sign of anachronism, but I will begin with the question of chronology, since one of the tacit implications of our question is that there has been a progression, of sorts, or a historical shift, from an Age of Literary Criticism to an Age of Cultural Studies.

I want to suggest that the Age of Cultural Studies, which is now passing and may in one sense itself be "over" (since it is now to such a great extent inside the academy, the very place it needed to resist in order to function, did not "succeed" the Age of Literary Criticism so much as it anticipated it and to a certain extent encompassed and still encompasses) it, like a Venn diagram. Or, to put it another way, and to use a very handy locution I am sorry to see remanded to the ash heap of theoretical cliché, we were *always already* in an Age of Cultural Studies when we embarked upon the great adventure of literary criticism.

To make this case let me turn directly to my title, "Try-Works."

As Americanists and Melvillians will know full well, the phrase comes from Melville's *Moby-Dick*. The "Try-Works" is the place on board ship where they boil down bits of whale. It is often been taken as a thinly veiled allegory for the novel itself, and the process of novel writing.

The word *try* in this case means to refine, or purify by fire. It is related to a whole series of other meanings, from separate to pick, choose, select, ascertain, and test. In the try-works, the whale becomes literally a self-consuming artifact. "In a whaling voyage the first fire has to be fed for a time with wood," writes Melville, but after that the whale provides both fuel and fat, both means and substance: "Like a plethoric burning martyr, or a self-consuming misanthrope, once ignited, the whale supplies his own fuel and burns by his own body."[4] (I think "self-consuming misanthrope" might be a good title for a book.)

"The Try-Works" chapter of *Moby-Dick* (chapter 96), has been singled out by many critics of varying critical persuasions as central to the novel—as indeed what one called "a kind of synecdoche of the symbolic meaning of *Moby-Dick*."[5] But "Try-Works" as a term is also a useful figure for a certain kind of literary argument, a particular kind of reading and writing. I like to think of this term as analogous, in a way, to the rhetorical forms cataloged by George Puttenham in his 1589 *Arte of English Poesie*, each Greek term given as well an Englished name: thus *hyperbole*, the *overreacher* or the *loud lier*. *Metonymia*, or the *mis-namer*. *Ironia*, or the *drie mock*. *Micterismus*, or the *fleering frump*. And so on.

So I want to propose "try-works" as the Englishing of that continental term *essay*, a word that, like *try*, means the action of attempting or testing, the trial of metals, an assay, an attempt, a taste, a first draft, and "a composition of moderate length on [a] particular subject, or branch of a subject; originally implying want of finish ('A loose sally of the mind,' Dr. Johnson defined it, 'an irregular undigested piece; not a regular and orderly composition')" but now said of a composition more or less elaborate in style, though limited in range.[6]

Curiously, describing her own move from the essay form to the novel, Susan Sontag once cited *Moby-Dick*. "The novel form is so free," she noted. "You can put into it anything you want—digressions, reflections. *Moby-Dick* has a whole encyclopedia in it about whaling and whales. The part of me that wrote essays is better employed in the digressive mode in fiction."[7] In one sense Sontag was bidding farewell to the essay; in another she was endorsing its ubiquity, its technique, and its mood.

As Bryan Wolf notes, Melville's Ishmael is himself an essayist, one whose word "essayed" in the "Cetology" chapter of *Moby-Dick* means both "attempted" and "wrote" ("The classification of the constituents of a chaos, nothing less is here essayed.").[8] The double meaning of the word *essay* is characteristic in Melville—Barbara Johnson comments on his use of it in *Billy Budd*.[9] But my interest here is not to offer a reading of Melville's inscribed essayists but to follow the felicitous signifier.

Essay. Assay.

Try-works.

The word *essay* in this sense is taken from Montaigne, whose *Essais* were first published in 1580. Francis Bacon borrowed the term and made it English. In a dedicatory epistle intended for Prince Henry—the son of James I—who died before he could receive these *Essays*—Bacon explained, "The word is late [that is, recent], but the thing is auncient. For *Senecaes* Epistles to Lucilius, yf youe marke them well, are but *Essaies*,—That is dispersed Meditacions."[10] (In the same letter Bacon called his own essays "graynes of salte, that will rather give you an appitite" than fill you up.)

Bacon's "The word is late but the thing is ancient" could be the epigraph of my argument. For the essay, I want to suggest, is "cultural studies" before the letter. (Thus, in my expanded history of literary studies, Montaigne may be thought of as the first Renaissance practitioner of cultural studies before the letter.) By the terms of this argument, it is not cultural studies that has come to displace literary criticism, but rather literary criticism that has interposed itself, as a "late" textual diversion, within a long tradition of cultural studies.

Consider some of Montaigne's essay topics: Of Idleness; Of Liars; Of Sadness; Of Pedantry; Of Cannibals; Of Coaches; Of Smells; Of the Disadvantages of Greatness; Of the Art of Discussion; Let Business Wait till Tomorrow; One Man's Profit Is Another Man's Harm; To Philosophize Is to Begin to Die.

And then consider some of Bacon's: Of Truth, Of Death; Of Anger; Of Parents and Children; Of Marriage and Single Life; Of Seeming Wise; Of Empire; Of Superstition; Of Suspicion; Of Gardens; Of Negotiating; Of Suitors; Of Studies; Of Faction.

And then consider some of William Hazlitt's: On the Conversation of Authors;. On the Old Age of Artists; On the Pleasure of Hating; On Egotism; Hot and Cold (A Comparison of the Relative Cleanliness of Catholics and Protestants).

Now check the MLA program for any recent year. You will find they are there.

The paradigmatic art form of cultural studies is the essay, and the best work of our time can be distinguished as part of an extended "Age of the Essay." Think of the work of Walter Benjamin, or Roland Barthes. Indeed, I would claim for my heretical genealogy of cultural studies not only a brilliant cultural essayist like Virginia Woolf but also a brilliant cultural essayist like Matthew Arnold—often misremembered and misread.

II

One of the markers of the essay since the time of Montaigne has been the preposition: we could say, indeed, the preposition as proposition. In French the word *de*; in English, following Bacon, *of* or *on*. Signifiers of speculation, of thought, of association, of the metonym.

A few years ago I took note in print of a game taught me by a friend, who showed how adding the phrase "in bed" to the fortunes in a fortune cookie could change the meaning for the better: "You will find great happiness—in bed." "Tomorrow is your lucky day—in bed." These were the pleasures of the suffix. I want to suggest a complementary pleasure of the prefix, by suggesting that we might add the word *of* or *on* or *de* to the titles of all critical essays, as a way of indicating their topic, their genre, and their openness: "Of Try-Works." Adding this kind of prefix to some of my own short presentations at previous conferences, just as an exercise, I find that it adds a certain clarity: "Of Fetish Envy." "Of Roman Numerals." "Of Lefthandedness." Try this with your own titles: see how it conveys a sense of genre, and of form.

In her translation of Jacques Derrida's *De la Grammatologie* Gayatri Spivak addresses the power of *of* when she writes of the difficulty of capturing the playfulness and significance of the text:

> Even so simple a word as "de" carries a touch of play—hinting at both 'of' and 'from.'... The translation of the title, suggesting "a piece of" as well as "about," I have retained against expert counsel.[11]

Thus her translated volume is called not *Grammatology* but *Of Grammatology*.

Such prepositions are also propositions, in all senses: statements, invitations, and come-ons. Cheeky, audacious little seductions. It is not an accident that one of the most eloquent essayists of the present day, Adam Phillips, has titled one of his collections *On Kissing, Tickling, and Being Bored: Psychoanalytic Essays on the Unexamined Life* and another *On Flirtation: Psychoanalytic Essays on the Uncommitted Life*.

Some earlier English essayists, like Hazlitt, retain the preposition while Ralph Waldo Emerson, speaking on set general topics, omits it ("Nature"; "History"; "Manners"; "Gifts"), but he is clearly using essay-speak. "He prefigures that peculiarly modern taste for total spontaneity and even disconnectedness in style," writes Alfred Kazin with ambivalent appreciation. We will come back, in a moment, to this question of style.

III

Perhaps the most obvious and obtrusive topic for an "essay" in this sense is the essay itself, and literary history is full of them. (Those who do not essay an essay on the essay directly do so indirectly, by writing essays about Montaigne, as Emerson does. Virginia Woolf does both.) But one of the most compelling essays on the essay is Theodor Adorno's classic piece, "The Essay as Form."[12]

Adorno's friend Walter Benjamin, whom he described as "the unsurpassed master" of the essay form,[13] once wrote a "Program for Literary Criticism" (1929–1930, unpublished in his lifetime) in which he announced,

> Good criticism is composed of at most two elements: the critical gloss and the quotation. Very good criticism can be made from both glosses and quotation. What must be avoided like the plague is rehearsing the summary of the contents. In contrast, a criticism consisting entirely of quotations should be developed.[14]

I am going to follow this excellent, if tendentious, advice and offer a selection of quotations from Adorno's well-known essay.

- "[T]he essay is condemned as a hybrid...the essay arouses resistance because it evokes intellectual freedom."
- "The essay reflects what is loved and hated....Hence it is classified a trivial endeavor."
- "The essay...does not try to seek the eternal in the transient and distill it out; it tries to render the transient eternal."
- "[T]he essay proceeds, so to speak, methodically unmethodically."
- "In opposition to the cliché of 'comprehensibility,'...the essay requires that one's thought about the matter be from the outset as complex as the object itself."
- "[The essay's] self-relativization is inherent in its form; it has to be constructed as though it could always break off at any point. It thinks in fragments, just as reality is fragmentary, and finds its unity in and through the breaks and not by glossing them over....Discontinuity is essential to the essay; its subject matter is always a conflict brought to a standstill."
- "The essay...resists the idea of a masterpiece, an idea which itself reflects the idea of creation and totality."
- "The essay is both more open and more closed than traditional thought would like."
- "The contemporary relevance of the essay is that of anachronism. The time is less favorable to it than ever."

And finally, in the last sentence,

- "[T]he essay's innermost formal law is heresy. Through violations of the orthodoxy of thought, something in the object becomes visible which it is orthodoxy's secret and objective aim to keep invisible."

We might notice the insistent return—it can rightly be called uncanny—of discussions of "form" and "formalism" in accounts of the essay's curious power to enrage, seduce, and persuade. (As Adorno points out, "[H]istorically the essay... is related to rhetoric."[15])

Lukács, in the essay that provoked Adorno's, set out to capture its essence, "on the strength of my feeling that the essay has a form which separates it, with the rigour of a law, from all other art forms. I want to try and define the essay as strictly as possible, precisely by describing it as an art form."[16] Yet everywhere Lukács looked it escaped him: "Fortunately for us, the modern essay does not always have to speak of books or poets; but this freedom makes the essay even more problematic.... The essay has become too rich and independent for dedicated service, yet it is too intellectual and too multiform to acquire form out of its own self."[17] We might think of William Shakespeare's crocodile, teasingly described by Antony to a Roman who will never see one: "It is shap'd sir, like itself, and it is as broad as it hath breadth; it is just so high as it is, and moves with its own organs" (*Antony and Cleopatra* 2.7.1–43).

In her assessment of the particularity of Roland Barthes, one of the most brilliant and accomplished of modern essayists, Susan Sontag cites his "formalist temperament." (And means to praise.) She singles out his gift for aphorism and for making lists, describing these as formal properties of thought:

> His prose constantly reaches for the summative formulations: it is irrepressibly aphoristic.... Being a method of condensed asssertion by means of symmetrically counterposed terms, the maxim or aphorism inevitably displays the symmetries and complexities of situations or ideas—their ideas, their shape.[18]

Barthes, she reminds us, "invokes 'the morality of form.'"[19]

John Brenkman, diagnosing what he sees as a problem in "current criticism, especially... criticism that purports to link literature and politics," calls it a "loss of form." Politics inheres in the specificity of form, otherwise it is merely thematic and dogmatic. Thus, claims Brenkman:

> Literary form is the crux of the question of literature and politics. . . . On the one hand, without grappling with inner form, criticism can't really grasp the work's material or its content. . . . And, on the other hand, the aesthetic experience of form is implicated . . . in the social and political conflicts inherent in the formations of the public sphere.[20]

We have previously seen that literary criticism is enclosed within cultural studies. But now we see that cultural studies, which consciously regards its aims as political, social, and cultural, is also, and perhaps preeminently, enclosed within literary criticism, because it is determined in its effectiveness, however unconsciously, by form: by formal matters, by matters of form and formalism. And of style.

It is time to call the question: Literary criticism in an age of cultural studies.

I quoted above a powerful statement from Lukács: "Every age creates the age it needs." What I failed to mention was that this remark, too, comes from his essay on the essay, to which Adorno's own essay, "Essay as Form," was a reply.

Let me now juxtapose this observation about the "age" with another, Walter Benjamin's remark at the end of "Literary History and the Study of Literature":

> What is at stake is not to portray literary works in the context of their age, but to represent the age that perceives them—our age—in the age during which they arose. It is this that makes literature into an organon of history; and to achieve this, and not to reduce literature to the material of history, is the task of the literary historian.[21]

My observations here have been offered, as I have said, under the sign of anachronism. So let me return, then, finally, to Melville and to "The Try-Works."

The "Try-Works" chapter begins with a highly anatomical vision of the two great try-pots, located within the "flanks" of the structure, braced to the timbers by "knees" of iron, fed by the "mouths" of furnaces, replenished with water from a "tunnel inserted at the rear." When the two try-pots are not in use rendering the blubber into fuel, some cynical old sailors crawl inside and "coil themselves away there for a nap." But let us cut away from this fascinating anatomy of production and rebirth. It is the polishing of the two try-pots ("kept remarkably clean" between uses) to which I want to draw your atten-tion: Ishmael reports that they are almost obsessively cleansed with soapstone and sand. And, "While employed in polishing them—one man in each pot, side by side—many confidential communications are carried on, over the iron lips."[22]

One does not move without the other.

I want to suggest that these two try-pots are literary criticism and cultural studies, both perfectly capable of rendering blubber into fuel, and fed—like the fire that heats the try-pots—with leftovers from a previous rendering, "the crisp, shrivelled blubber, now called scraps or fritters," which "after being tried out... still contains considerable of its unctuous properties. These fritters feed the flames."[23]

So says Ishmael.

We who are polishing the pots, or napping in them, or stoking the fire, might remember this little scene as we move forward into a future (or a pre-sent) that is neither an age of literary criticism nor an age of cultural studies but rather an age of information. The tension now is between *information* and *form*. Literary form, like the whale, has become an endangered species, not because of cultural studies, but because of technology. The freedom inherent in the essay—or in print culture as a whole—seems quaint and slow from the point of view of new information technologies. For that reason polemics between literary criticism and cultural studies may themselves be nostalgic attempts to "save the whale"—that is, to save the form of print culture itself.

Make-Work ⦙ 4

> Who first invented work, and bound the free
> And holiday-rejoicing spirit down?
>
> —Charles Lamb, *Work*

> Milton produced *Paradise Lost* for the same reason that a silk worm produces silk. It was an activity of his nature.
>
> —Karl Marx, *Theories of Surplus Value*

"Inventing Work" is a phrase that has a fascinating plurality of meanings, from economic and social theory to literary studies and popular culture. I want to address here a number of the phrase's possible permutations, with an eye to developing a hypothesis about the way "work" works in culture.

When I was a rebellious suburban adolescent in an era known for its uncritical espousal of the word *conformity* and its unwittingly postcolonial fashion (madras plaid Bermuda shorts, button-down shirts, chino pants with a buckle in the back), my parents tried to sell me on the idea of going to "work camp." "Work camp," I hasten to say, was neither a low-security prison nor a euphemism for forced labor under a murderous and repressive regime, but rather a relatively idyllic, and unquestionably expensive, summer retreat for the hip, progressive, guitar-playing red-diaper-baby set. Teenagers who attended work camps wore denim and flannel shirts and learned about folk songs, barn construction, leftist politics, poetry, and sex—so far as I know. For although all of those topics (except perhaps barn construction) were in fact of consuming interest to me, I refused to attend Shaker Village—a place that would have been far more congenial than Camp Owaissa for Girls, where in fact I did go, and where I learned about makeup, "socials," wearing "flats" (instead of sneakers), and how to pretend to throw like a girl. It wasn't till I went to college—to Swarthmore, then in effect the collegiate version of Shaker Village—that I met all the people I would have encountered at work camp, and who remain my friends today.

The traditional kind of summer camp—the kind that was not a work camp—seemed vaguely militaristic in that unreflective fifties way (there was a flag-raising ceremony every morning and a "color war" to culminate the season; we bought, though we seldom wore, green and white uniforms of shirt and shorts), and it was also infantilizing: we were expected to play games, to flirt with the boys at our "brother" camp, to lie in our bunks and write letters, to expect fancy food packages from home. What distinguished it above all from a work camp was the arcadian, utopian fantasies of urban and suburban parents who wanted their children to be children—to escape the never-mentioned shadows of the Depression and the Holocaust, to inhabit a world in which politics was not an issue, in which all we had to do was "play."

The word *work* in "work camp" signified a solidarity with labor on the part of the affluent, progressive middle class. These progressive work camps of the 1950s and '60s (even the name has disappeared today, a casualty of preprofessionalizing "specialty camps"—theater, tennis, arts, math—on the one hand and perhaps of political sensitivity on the other) were places where work was play.

I want to use this little paradigm—of what we might call "work in quotation marks"—as an example of what I see as a larger phenomenon, and one that is by no means always progressive in its politics: the production of work as make-work, as make-believe work, as a kind of work that resists work while presuming or claiming to support it.

My object is not to expose or condemn this development, but rather to note its dialectical inevitability, and to direct our attention to a critical dyad, and a crucial question: what is the *other* of "work"? The contemporary antonym most in use these days seems to be "leisure," a term that follows Thorstein Veblen and John Maynard Keynes.[1] But I will be making a case here for the more ample, and more productively ambiguous, "play."

Let me start by offering three examples, one from the world of sexual aesthetics, a second from the sphere of women and culture, and the last from the history of literary studies. I will then suggest a brief "coda" that will bring us back, I hope, to the idea of "inventing work."

My first example is a familiar one: the concept of "working out." "Work" in the sense of physical exercise (or exertion in a sport or game) is a common nineteenth-century English usage, surviving in a phrase like "fancy footwork" and in the language of the horse or dog show where the animals are "worked" by their riders or handlers. But to "work out" in a gym is not to do "work" in a cultural or economic sense, even though you may be "working" groups of muscles and "feeling the burn." The sculpted body, the body buffed, is emphatically *not* a worker's body or a working-class body; if you doubt this go down to any construction site and have a look. What is produced at Crunch or Gold's Gym are the abs and pecs of the leisure class. (The famously lower-class lovers of early-twentieth-century novels like *Maurice* and *Lady Chatterley's Lover*—gamekeepers both—are nowhere described as "hunks." The muscle men of Renaissance painting are not laborers but heroes and gods.)

Gym culture is famously autoerotic, as well as good for picking up dates: the key players are the body, the mirror, and you. It has a lot to do with exertion, but very little to do with functional work. In fact, physical labor often builds up the *wrong* muscles from the point of view of contemporary aesthetics. As it was with the cultural prestige of the suntan—once despised because it showed you had to work in the sun, then valued, indeed overvalued, because it demonstrated that you could afford to vacation in the winter, so it is with bodybuilding and "working out": the buffed body is a simulacrum, a powerful fake, an artifact that mimes utility but stays carefully on the right side of leisure. As journalist Gina Kolata wrote in a *New York Times* piece on the relationship between health and beauty, "I lift weights for muscle definition, not explicitly to make myself healthier."[2]

Gender, we should note, is a significant player here. Again, suntanned women were once by definition poor and of the working class; a lady stayed out of the sun. (Today she does again, of course, for other reasons, and the canons of beauty have obediently shifted in response.) The muscular woman was once both low-class and sexually suspect. Now that she pays for the privilege of sweating and lifting weights, her sculpted body is a status symbol.

A hundred years ago Thorstein Veblen had this to say about athletics and exercise:

> The canons of reputable living exclude from the scheme of life of the leisure class all activity that can not be classed as conspicuous leisure.... At the same time purposeless physical exercise is tedious and distasteful beyond tolerance.... [R]ecourse is in such a case had to some form of activity which shall at least afford a colourable pretense of purpose, even if the object assigned be only a make-believe. Sports satisfy these requirements of substantial futility together with a colourable make-believe of purpose.

In addition, he noted, "they afford scope for emulation" (his biceps are bigger than my biceps; keep pumping) and "conform to the leisure-class canon of reputable waste."[3] Indeed, thought Veblen, "success as an athlete presumes, not only a waste of time, but also a waste of money"[4]—making it a perfect icon of American achievement, much more so than classical learning, then still highly prestigious "on the continent of Europe." (This was at a time when the primary meaning of *gymnasium* was "high school." Philologists among you may want to recall that the etymology of the word is "to train naked.")

Gym workouts are make-work, designed to articulate particular groups of muscles, to create (self) "definition," to change the body image, not the culture. We row on rowing machines, not rivers; we lift free weights, not boxes or boulders or booms. What if some enterprising Edison were to harness all that wasted power from stationary bicycles and Stairmasters: how many towns and villages could we illuminate? How many power plants could we run?

And yet, working out is also big business. Arnold Schwarzenegger's *Encyclopedia of Modern Body Building* (itself a workout just to heft, weighing in at over ten pounds) includes key sections on "posing trunks," "tanning parlors," "artificial tans," "posing oil" (Pam spray will work), "hairstyle," "body hair," and "dressing for success" for the competition bodybuilder. So, work that becomes play can again become work.

Women these days "work out" as frequently as men. "Buns of Steel" are not only possessed by male steelworkers (if indeed they are), and abs and pecs are equal-opportunity muscle groups, unlike the gendered bodily regions of breast and hips so dear to cultural institutions like *Cosmopolitan* magazine and Hooters. But "women's work," needless to say, is an entirely different imaginative and social category. "Men may work from sun to sun / But women's work is never done" runs the old saying, and many feminist scholars have studied the paradox whereby such constant and unceasing (and usually uncompensated) work ceases to be thought of or valued as "work" at all. The advent of "labor-saving devices," as other scholars have noted, often increased rather than decreased the amount of work a modern woman did around the house. But the particular kind of "woman's work" to which I want to call your attention is not washing or mending or child care but fine needlework, weaving and embroidery, often merely called "work." Both the activity and the product are designated: a work box holds the work on which a woman (of a certain class) is at work, or pretends to be at work; for this too, however beautiful the result, is make-work.

Medieval and Renaissance historians have traced the gradual *reduction* of women's involvement in the cloth and spinning trades. As Merry Wiesner reported in an important article on women in cloth production, "until the late middle ages, all stages of production, from carding wool or cooking flax to making the final finishing touches on garments, was carried out in the home, usually by female members of the family or servants." From the thirteenth century onward, however, male artisans and guilds of weavers and cloth cutters began to take over the cloth trades, for (political, economic, social, religious, and ideological) reasons explained variously by Marxist and feminist-materialist scholars.

Phrases like "women and other unskilled workers" began to appear in civic trade regulations. Gradually, as the guilds became stronger in the Europe of the early modern period, the concept of the "skilled worker" began to exclude women. Wiesner's reading of this phenomenon is matter-of-fact and powerful: "As more and more women worked at tasks that were unskilled and low paying, any occupation in which a significant number of women were involved became devalued. This vicious circle has been traced in the twentieth century with librarians, secretaries, and telephone operators. . . . 'Women's work' was by definition, low-status, unskilled, and badly paid. . . . Thus women's work came to have an ideological content far beyond its economic significance."[5]

But this is only one side of the story, for by a familiar kind of cultural logic—one I have traced elsewhere, for example, in the changing prestige of Roman numerals[6]—the more "worthless" women's "work" became, the more it became (oddly enough) prized in an elite or genteel sphere. Out with the wife of Bath and her weaving, in with the lady of fashion and her petit point. A grumpily titled tract of 1678 offers *Advice to the women and maidens of London: shewing that instead of their usual pastime, and education in needlework . . . it were far more necessary and profitable to apply themselves to the right understanding and practice of the method of keeping books of account.* The authorship of the book is attributed—in accordance with the custom of anonymity for female writers—only to "one of that sex." But bookkeeping, however necessary and profitable, had little sex appeal.

Fine needlework was the sign of a gentlewoman's gentility, and one of the few such activities to be pursued both before and after marriage. "Your time, my love, passes, I supposed, in devotion, reading, work, and company" wrote Samuel Johnson to a Miss Thrale. "Of work, unless I understood it better, it will be of no great use to say much." Charlotte Palmer in *Sense and Sensibility* hangs in her bedroom "a landscape in colored silks . . . proof of her having spent seven years at a great school in town to some effect." Lady Bertram in *Mansfield Park*, the laziest character in all of literature, "spent her days in sitting nicely dressed on a sofa, doing some long piece of needlework, of little use and no beauty." Indeed, most female characters in Jane Austen's novels do needlework of some kind every day. There is no question but that some of this work was useful—Austen herself wrote of making shirts for her brother Edward and collecting pieces for a patchwork quilt—but it was also display, on a par with watercolor painting and playing the pianoforte.

In a famous scene in *Othello*, Cassio the soldierly lady's man gives a handkerchief to his courtesan "friend" Bianca with the request that she "take the work out" (3.4.279). To "take the work out" is to copy the embroidery, not to remove it—in fact Emilia, Iago's wife, expresses the same intention ("I'll have the work ta'en out / and give't Iago" [3.3.300–301]). Work here means design; combining forms like *drawn work*, *fancy work*, *lacework*, *open work* and *needle work* all describe ornamental work done in textile fabrics. The handkerchief in

Othello is unusual—apparently sewn by a sibyl in a fury using thread dyed from the mummified blood of virgins—but its identification with "women's work" is not. And as time went by, this kind of "work" done by women became the very sign of respectability.

Described as a "distinctively feminine occupation" (*Oxford English Dictionary*, "work," *sb*.16) such "work"—or the thing itself, also called "work"—was a social and sociable, moderately useful and apparently harmless activity for women of a certain class. Heroines in nineteenth-century novels are forever picking up or laying down their "work," or reaching into their work boxes.

Yet it could also be subversive. From the time of Penelope the weaving and unweaving of tapestries has been not only an acceptable activity for well-bred women but a common ruse. When revolution comes in Jean Genet's play *The Balcony* the Queen is said to have retired to her chamber where she is "embroidering a handkerchief." Or is she? According to the character called the Envoy she is "embroidering" and "not embroidering." She is "embroidering an invisible handkerchief." Or so we are told. In fact it is difficult to tell exactly what she's doing, or even if she's alive. Agatha Christie's female sleuth Miss Marple equips herself with balls of wool and knits her way into detective territory through which a man could never pass. Though there are some rather heavy-handed attempts in the later novels to link her with the fates and the figure of Nemesis, the knitting is initially used by Miss Marple herself as a diversion, a blamelessly female "occupation," and a ploy. So in the case of women's needlework, too, "work" goes upmarket when it ceases to be real work, and becomes a mode of diversion, exercise, ploy, or play. Such women's "work" is now often a collector's item, and is to be found in museums and other places of high culture.

It should come as no surprise to find that the same alchemical legerdemain occurs in the case of the "work of art," and more particularly, of the work of literature. Here is Roland Barthes's well-known formulation, from an essay called, quite simply, "From Work to Text":

> It is a fact that over the last few years a certain change has taken place (or is taking place) in our conception of language and consequently, of the literary work which owes at least its phenomenal existence to this same language. The change is clearly connected with the current development of (amongst other disciplines) linguistics, anthropology, Marxism and psychoanalysis.

The "last few years" to which Barthes refers are the late 1960s (his essay was published in 1971) but the change is still taking place, influenced, as he so clearly and presciently saw, by the rise of *interdisciplinarity* and the breakdown of the "solidarity of the old disciplines." Thus, he went on to say, "Over against the traditional notion of the *work*, for long—and still—conceived of in a, so to speak, Newtonian way, there is now the requirement of a new object, obtained by the sliding or overturning of former categories."[7]

This new object was the "text." Here are some of the distinctions Barthes draws between work and text.

- "The work is a fragment of substance, occupying a part of the space of books (in a library, for example), the Text is a methodological field.... "
- "[T]he work can be seen (in bookshops, in catalogues, in exam syllabuses), the text is a process of demonstration.... "
- "[T]he work can be held in the hand, the text is held in language, only exists in the movement of a discourse... the Text is not the decomposition of the work, it is the work that is the imaginary tail of the Text."
- "The work closes on a signified.... the Text, on the contrary, practices the infinite deferment of the signified, is dilatory.... Similarly, the *infinity* of the signifier refers not to some idea of the ineffable (the unnameable signified) but to that of a *playing*.... "
- "The logic regulating the Text is not comprehensive (define 'what the work means') but metonymic; the activity of associations, contiguities, carryings-over coincides with a liberation of symbolic energy.... "
- "The work is caught up in a process of filiation.... The author is reputed the father and the owner of his work: literary science therefore teaches *respect* for the manuscript and the author's declared intentions, while society asserts the legality of the relation of author to work (the '*droit d'auteur*' or copyright)... the metaphor of the Text is that of the *network* [note: this is written long before the Internet became every scholar's and teenager's tool]... no vital 'respect' is due to the Text: it can be *broken* (which is just what the Middle Ages did with two nevertheless authoritative texts—Holy Scripture and Aristotle); it can be read without the guarantee of its father... It is not that the Author may not 'come back' in the Text, in his text, but he then does so as a 'guest.'... He becomes, as it

were, a paper-author; his life is no longer the origin of his fictions but a fiction contributing to his work."

It is easy to see how both gender and parental authority are put in question (or challenged; or undermined) by the shift to text and to play. No wonder this created a stir. Marcel Proust and Jean Genet (not coincidentally both gay authors) are Barthes's illustrative examples here (embroidering and not embroidering), but he claims that the case is general rather than particular, or modern, or French. And finally, he adds,

- "The work is normally the object of a consumption," the text, instead, a place of "play, activity, production, practice."

To Barthes, who urges an abolition of the distance between writing and reading, "*reading*, in the sense of consuming, is far from *playing* with the text," especially if "play" is understood in its rich variety of meanings, from give or shimmy ("play in the machine") to performance.

The distinction between "work" and "text," not to put too fine a (petit) point upon it, is really the distinction between *work* and *play*: a very familiar, and at the same time uncanny, situation. Moreover, once again, as with physical labor and needlework, we encounter the conjunction of belatedness, excess, and nostalgia. For it is just at the time when authorship becomes "work" in the sense of being a paying profession and a respectable one, that a distinction between high and low culture, or elite and popular culture, emerges. We might recall the famous temerity of the Renaissance playwright Ben Jonson who, in publishing his plays in folio format under the audacious heading *Opera* ("Works") in 1616, brought down upon himself both ridicule and scorn. Plays, those raffish, popular things, were not "works." And indeed, in Barthes's terms they are far more like "texts"—open, polysemous, intertextual, atemporal, performed. Plays, in short, are play.

The itinerary of the literary and artistic *work* includes the "masterpiece," initially a rite of passage, the material evidence of the apprentice artist's accession to mastery of a craft.[8] And this piece of "work," too—the union card of early craftsmen—became alchemically transmuted into a transcendent benchmark of quality, a palpable but ineffable monument rather than a kind of "master's thesis," the tangible, earned evidence that the artist had now risen to the rank of "master." The modern sense of masterpiece drops out this sense of earned credit in a guild, letting the "work of art" float free in the etherial realms of greatness. The phrase *work of art* has come to connote "high artistic quality," whether in poetry, painting, sculpture, or music. Thus, Walter Benjamin's celebrated essay "The Work of Art in an Age of Mechanical Reproduction" queried the very possibility of such a "work" if the aura of the unique, unreproduceable object were lost. Karl Marx long ago made this point about the fetishism of objects by the erasure of labor. The dislocation from utility makes the work into art. What is striking is that the word *work* remains, and is inflated and enshrined, by the subtraction.[9]

There is of course another kind of make-work, celebrated by C. Northcote Parkinson in his memorable formulation: "Work expands to fill the time available for its completion." Parkinson's Law wittily recounts the story of the spread of bureaucracy and middle management via his "two almost axiomatic statements, thus: (1) 'An official wants to multiply subordinates, not rivals,' and (2) 'Officials make work for each other.'" The tale of how "a civil servant, called A," feeling himself overworked, generates the hiring of B, C, D, E, F, G, and H, so that "seven officials are now doing what one did before," is, we might say, the bureaucratic version of Falstaff's eleven buckram men grown out of two. For it turns out that "these seven make so much work for each other that all are fully occupied and A is actually working harder than ever":

> An incoming document may well come before each of them in turn. Official E decided that it falls within the province of F, who places a draft reply before C, who amends it drastically before consulting D, who asks G to deal with it. But G goes on leave at this point, handing the file over to H, who drafts a minute that is signed by D and returned to C, who revises his draft accordingly and lays the new version before A.

What does A do? Parkinson's conscientious civil servant does not, as he has "every excuse" for doing, merely sign the thing unread, but

> reads through the draft with care, deletes the fussy paragraphs added by C and H, and restores the thing to the form preferred in the first instance by the able (if quarrelsome) F. He corrects the English—none of these young men can write

grammatically—and finally produces the same reply he would have written if officials C to H had never been born.[10]

This is make-work with a vengeance, and it is too familiar a story (in academia as elsewhere) to be dismissed, even in an electronic age that is supposed to downsize clerks in favor of networks. We might note that author Parkinson went on to contribute to what might be called a Parkinson's law of publication, by producing, in addition to a series of scholarly books on economics, a volume called Mrs. Parkinson's Law, and Other Studies in Domestic Science.

But while this too could be construed as a kind of "play in the system," my interest here is more in the kind of make-work that makes things rather than jobs, whether the things are muscles, samplers, poems, or machines. I want therefore to move on from this account of "make-work" and what might be called, for lack of a more felicitous phrase, the *aesthetic materialization* of the work of art in its contestatory relationship to labor and play, to take note of yet another key term, the word *invention*. Rather than "inventing work," this matter could be called "inventing 'invention'"—or rather, "reinventing invention." And here I will return to a personage whose fleeting and spectral presence I invoked, in passing, a bit earlier.

Invention in nineteenth- and twentieth-century America has tended to refer to the creation of machines for living. Its preeminent cultural icon was Thomas Alva Edison, whose inventions included an improved telegraph, the telephone, an electric pen, the phonograph, and the electric light. Often described as the link between the nineteenth-century "lone inventor" and the twentieth-century industrial researcher, Edison founded, as well, the modern "research park," with its emphasis on collaborative problem solving and commercial productivity. Certainly to Edison himself invention meant objects, machinery, and "work"—sweat equity; he was the very definition of a "workaholic" *avant la lettre*. He spent most of his days and nights in the lab, nicknamed his first daughter and son Dot and Dash, and wrote in his notebook a month after his first marriage that "My wife Dearly Beloved Cannot invent worth a Damn!"[11] (After his wife's death he proposed to the second Mrs. Edison by tapping out the proposal in Morse code as they traveled together on a tour of the White Mountains.) To him the phonograph was essentially a business machine, not an artifact for entertainment. And motion pictures, he thought, might make their best contribution as part of the educational system, not as a new mode of leisure or art.

Yet inevitably it was not the language of science but the language of art that enshrined him. Lauded in his lifetime as the Wizard of Menlo Park, the Inventor of the Age, and the Nation's Inventor-Philosopher, Edison was a media celebrity of almost unimaginable proportions, the object of innumerable newspaper articles, "funny papers," and "school girl . . . compositions"—a veritable "mania," according to an observer in 1878. In 1886 the French symbolist Villiers de l'Isle-Adam published a novel with Edison as its fictional hero, claiming in his preface that "the personage of this legend—even while the man is still alive who inspires it—belong[s] to the world of literature." A journalist, writing his "Talks with Edison" in *Harper's* magazine compared the "imaginative aspect" of Edison's mind with that of "men having creative musical or poetic or artistic genius."[12] (The electric light became the universal sign of inventive genius, the "bright idea,"[13] and would spawn in the late twentieth century a series of dumbed-down jokes about how many *thises* or *thats* it took to change a light bulb.) The editor of a two-volume *Popular History of Invention*, writing in the *New York Times Magazine* after Edison's death, eulogized him as "the last and greatest of experimenters who followed only the dictates of their inner selves and who were as willful and unrestrained as poets. With him the heroic age of invention probably ends."[14] As if to mark this fact, on the date of Edison's funeral in 1931 President Herbert Hoover asked that the nation extinguish its electric lights for a minute, and suspend radio broadcasting, to pay him due tribute.

It is only a very slight irony to recall that the word *invention* from the fifteenth through the early nineteenth centuries meant, precisely, a work of writing produced by the exercise of the mind or imagination, a literary composition, or the devising of a subject, idea, or method of treatment for a work of art. "Laboring in invention" is Shakespearese for "trying to write a poem," and John Dryden, reaching back to the etymology (from Latin for "find") would write, "The first happiness of the poet's imagination is properly invention, or finding of the thought."[15] Indeed, literary *invention* may be the converse of literary *convention*—a flash of originality that alters and disrupts the accepted, and expected course of things. "Invention" was a word used by all the arts—painting, sculpture, and music, as well as poetry.

The cultural "forgetting" of this meaning of the term in the twentieth century is exemplified by a remark made by no less exalted a figure than Edison himself, when, late in life, he recalled an important model for his own creativity: "Ah, Shakespeare!" he exclaimed to an interviewer. "That's where you get the ideas! My but that man did have ideas! He would have been an inventor, a wonderful inventor, if he had turned his mind to it."[16]

That Shakespeare was an "inventor" in his own century's primary sense of the term might have surprised the pragmatic machinist Edison, whose own favorite character was Richard III. But analysts of what one biographer has called Edison's "cognitive style" have emphasized the degree to which his own imagination was what we might—with some license—call literary. One of his chief tools was analogy. Thus, for example, he imagined that the moving picture would be the visual equivalent of the phonograph, "an instrument which does for the Eye what the phonograph does for the Ear, which is the recording and reproduction of things in motion." Historian Thomas Hughes has written that Edison had "an ability to find metaphors that allowed him to draw on what he knew to suggest order in what he did not know."

Yet *metaphor* does not seem quite the right word here. True enough, Edison's analogy (movie camera is to eye as phonograph is to ear) sets up the inventor's quest as a kind of metaphor, yet we could say that his way of getting results is more like metonymy: association or contiguity. If analogy is conventionally aligned with necessity and contiguity with chance, as Paul de Man observed, invention in its modern sense proceeds by the *necessity of contiguity* and the *chance* (or happenstance) *of analogy*. How many stories of scientific invention begin with a "chance" observation? An apple falls on your head; unwanted mold grows in a petri dish. If the experimenter had been a better housekeeper the world would be without penicillin. So for the "inventor," invention is partly a matter of making mistakes. Or, we could say, of play: play in the system, play in the laboratory, plays upon words, the "lively play of fancy."[17]

"Genius," Edison himself once famously declared, "is one percent inspiration and ninety-nine percent perspiration."[18] This puckish and calculated deflation raises again the question of invention as make-work. Which part is work, and which part is play?

For the Edison who preferred lab life to home life the question seems nicely moot. But what is most useful for us is to realize that these are commutable categories. "All work and no play makes Jack a dull boy." "If all the world were playing holidays, / To sport would be as tedious as to work." In a world increasingly concerned with managing leisure time, we cannot get rid of the binary of work and play, for it performs (or "plays") a vital social and psychological role. We need it in order to transgress it.

When an activity coded as *work* becomes *play*, it jumps classes. Thus, for example, where once river rafting and rough-terrain hiking were activities for workers and pioneers, today "extreme sports" are a big-business leisure-time activity. But this class jumping is also true of the "play" that becomes work (professional writers; professional sports). The necessary contamination of these categories does not mean that we should abandon them. Quite the contrary. If "work" did not exist, we would have to invent it. (As Voltaire once famously said of God, who might be called the Original Inventor of work.)

Make-work is excess, or in contemporary philosophical terms a *supplement*—both an addition and a substitution. To quote one of my favorite authorities, Agatha Christie, "I don't think necessity is the mother of invention—invention, in my opinion, arises directly from idleness, possibly also from laziness. To save oneself trouble."[19] "Necessity is the *mother* of invention":—here is that gendered note again, with women as mothers and men as inventors. But in fact it is the invention of necessity that is the invention of work. *Necessity* is what is invented.

Sequels : 5

"She would, if asked, tell us many little particulars about the subsequent career of her people," Jane Austen's nephew wrote in his *Memoir* of his aunt.

In this traditionary way we learned that Miss Steele never succeeded in catching the Doctor; that Kitty Bennet was satisfactorily married to a clergyman near Pemberley, while Mary obtained nothing higher than one of her uncle Philips' clerks, and was content to be considered a star in the society of Meriton; that the "considerable sum" Mrs. Norris gave William Price was one pound; that Mr. Woodhouse survived his daughter's marriage, and kept her and Mr. Knightley from settling at Donwell, about two years; and that the letters placed by Frank Churchill before Jane Fairfax, which she swept away unread, contained the word "pardon." Of the good people in *Northanger Abbey* and *Persuasion* we know nothing more than what is written; for before those works were published their author had been taken away from us, and all such amusing communications had ceased for ever.[1]

In the days before Hollywood sequels Jane Austen enthralled her young relations by telling them what every reader wants to know: What happens after the book's last page, or the play's last scene? It is unusual to have so close a glimpse of the offstage author spinning consequences (and since Austen was only entertaining her family, it is far from sure that she would have written up the story in quite this way; she was far from averse to teasing the earnest young nephew who wrote up this account). But the desire for a sequel is part of the impulse to hear stories and to tell them, the desire that they never come to a definitive end. William Shakespeare gratifies this curiosity to a certain extent in his history plays, both English and Roman, but he, like Austen and any other talented portrayer of character, leaves much unresolved and open to speculation. Do Beatrice and Benedick make a go of it after their marriage, or will their talent for mutual truth-telling do them in? Does Iago hold by his vow of silence, or will the magnificos "induce" him to speak and put him on trial? What's the fate of Caliban?

The eighteenth century went through a phase of "improving" the imperfect Shakespeare, as for example in Nahum Tate's version of *King Lear*, which allowed Cordelia not only to survive but to marry Edgar—a much more "satisfying" result.[2] And the nineteenth century produced one of my favorite "prequels," Mary Cowden Clarke's *The Girlhood of Shakespeare's Heroines*, which offered the Victorian reader a chance to make the acquaintance of the infant Rosalind, Portia the toddler, and the pre-pubescent Lady Macbeth.

But as extensive as the "improvements" and revisions and adaptations of Shakespeare have been, from Tate to Aimé Césaire and Tom Stoppard, they have not been carried out in recent years with the same pointed zeal as have the sequels to Austen. In the twentieth century dozens of sequels, from *Margaret Dashwood, or Interference* (a sequel to *Sense and Sensibility*, 1929) to *Consequence: Or, Whatever Became of Charlotte Lucas* (1997) and *Desire and Duty: A Sequel to Jane Austen's Pride and Prejudice* (1997) have appeared in print. The further adventures of Isabella Thorpe, Mrs. Rushworth, and even the family of Mr. Collins; the events of *Pride and Prejudice* told from Mr. Darcy's point of view, the events of *Mansfield Park* as seen by a maidservant; a play about Anne de Bourgh's wedding—no minor character or plot line is left unturned. Not only do Austenians buy and read these books, but they maintain a lively conversation, in person and online, about sequels, continuations, adaptations, and completions.

"The sequel," wrote Gérard Genette in *Palimpsests,* "differs from a continuation in that it continues a work not in order to bring it to a close but, on the contrary, in order to take it beyond what was initially considered to be its ending. The motive is generally a desire to capitalize on a first or even a second success."[3] Genette distinguishes between the "allographic sequel," written by a "shrewd inheritor," who, driven in part by commercial motives, produces "interminable sequels to adventures that were terminated over and over again," and the "autographic sequel," which is not an imitation but a prolongation—like Sir Walter Scott's or James Fennimore Cooper's novel cycles, or Honoré de Balzac's *Human Comedy*. Both types are tied to market forces.

Collections like *To Be Continued: An Annotated Guide to Sequels* (1995)[4] and *The Whole Story: Three Thousand Years of Sequels and Sequences* (1996)[5] attest to the present-day fascination with the sequel form, and not unexpectedly, the film sequel has generated its own little library, from *Haven't I Seen You Somewhere Before? Remakes, Sequels, and Series in Motion Pictures, Videos, and Television, 1896–1990* (1992) to *Science Fiction, Fantasy, and Horror Film Sequels, Series, and Remakes* (1998). Books like *Dirty Dancing with Wolves: And Other Movie Sequels That Never Made It off the Drawing Board* (1992) take note of the comic nature of sequelmania; the first time as tragedy, the second time as farce.

Functionally, the sequel is a good cultural model of what Freud, describing the activities of the psyche, calls "secondary revision," one of the key elements in the construction of dreams—the rearrangement of the dream-thoughts into an intelligible and apparently consistent scenario that "makes sense." As Havelock Ellis jauntily personifies the process, "Sleeping Consciousness we may even imagine as saying to itself in effect: 'Here comes our master, Waking Consciousness, who attaches such mighty importance to reason and logic and so forth. Quick! Gather things up, put them in order—any order will do—before he enters to take possession'" (quoted in Sigmund Freud, *Interpretation of Dreams*).[6] In essence, secondary revision is a kind of mental censorship—Freud compares it to the way the mind corrects misprints and typographical errors, so that we "have the illusion that what we are reading is correct."[7]

In a very similar way the sequel "corrects" and amplifies, gratifying a desire not only for continuation but also for happy endings. Thus, Alexandra Ripley's *Scarlett: The Sequel to Margaret Mitchell's Gone With the Wind* (1992) sends Scarlett and her children to Ireland, where she meets up with Rhett Butler, whose wife has conveniently died, and falls (back) into his arms.[8]

There is, in fact, a paradox implicit in the very concept of the sequel. In *experiental terms*, a sequel is a highly conservative genre that supplies the comfort of familiarity together with the small frisson of difference. Publishers, film studios, and TV executives love sequels, since they seem to guarantee a ready-made audience. A glance at the *New York Times* best-sellers list at the time of this writing shows one sequel at the top of the list (the further adventures of Hannibal the Cannibal in Thomas Harris's continuation of *The Silence of the Lambs*—"second helping," quipped one reviewer archly) and at least three more sequels and a prequel (predictably, the book version of *Star Wars, Episode 1*) among the contenders.[9] One of the sequels is a children's book, among the genres most prone to the sequel form. Another (*Encore Provence*) takes pains to announce its sequel-status in its title.

In *theoretical terms*, however, the sequel is a more adventurous if not radical departure from the expectation of closure and the boundedness of the text; thus, it can be connected with the other "paratextual" inquiries into borders, frames, glosses, titles, footnotes, prefaces, and dust jackets.[10]

It did not take the advent of postmodernism—or, for that matter, the making of *Star Wars, Episode 1: The Phantom Menace*—to make the point that the "second" could sometimes really be "first." We could put the blame on Horace, who in his *Ars Poetica* enjoined the poet to hasten into the midst of things, and not "begin the Trojan war by telling of the twin eggs," the birth of Helen from the coupling of Leda and Zeus. A modern-day prequel would, precisely, go back to that dramatic moment—as did William Butler Yeats in his retelling and remaking of the myth: "A shudder in the loins engenders there / The broken wall, the burning roof and tower / And Agamemnon dead." Virgil wrote the sequel, Edmund Spenser and John Milton sequels to the sequel, William Wordsworth the sequel to them, James Joyce a new version of the old story... the rest, as they say, is history. In this case, literary history. The sequel and prequel are not anomalies but fundamental elements in the literary canon—as they were, indeed, in classical times.

Yet in a literary-critical era that glories in prefixes like post-, pre-, early, and new (*post*structuralism, the *pre*novel novel, *early modern* culture, *new* historicism) and that has for decades focused on the margins rather than the center, the sequel (and its near relation, the prequel) seems in a way the perfect topic for a rigorous, and pleasurable, unpacking. Recent work on the relationship of copy to original, speech to writing, and manuscript to print has nicely troubled the question of priority, precedence, and origin.

Where critics of a few years ago wrote books that addressed—and compli-
cated—our ideas about *Beginnings* and the *Sense of an Ending*, their successors
have increasingly been fascinated by margins, footnotes, glosses, and the
process of editing as it alters the "original" text.[11] "Originality" in the
Renaissance meant "going back to origins," not warbling your native wood-
notes wild. It was only with Edward Young's eighteenth-century *Conjectures on
Original Composition* that the emphasis on novelty became linked, in a way
many moderns find axiomatic, with a creativity that supposedly owed little to
imitation and the great models of the past. But canon formation as we know it
might well be regarded as the quest for the perfect sequel.

Way back in 1973—it seems eons ago in the chronicles of literary
theory—Harold Bloom argued in *The Anxiety of Influence* that "strong poets"
inevitably resist the priority of their literary predecessors, but (or *and*) that
writing in the wake of others, paradoxically, did wonders for the originality of
their work: "Poetic influence need not make poets less original; as often it
makes them more original, though not therefore necessarily better."[12]
Competition between later poet and "precursor" was inevitable; misinterpreta-
tion ("*in their poems*") was the way strong later poets dealt with the Oedipal
father who both blocked and showed the way (Samuel Taylor Coleridge with
Milton, Milton with Spenser, Alfred, Lord Tennyson with Keats). According to
Bloom "A poet antithetically 'completes' his precursor, by so reading the par-
ent-poem as to retain its terms but to mean them in another sense, as though
the precursor had failed to go far enough." The Bloom of 1973, who blithely
dedicated his most important contribution to literary theory to his own strong
precursor, William Wimsatt, seems curiously at odds with today's Bloom, who
will not go gently into the role of father rather than son. But this is perhaps less
curious than inevitable, according to the logic of his own argument. Bloom has
become, willy-nilly, the precursor of a whole generation of critics whose own
coinages and "swerves" he declines to acknowledge as legitimate progeny, but
rather condemns as "resentment."

More recently, the question of originality and essence has been articulated
by Judith Butler in terms that combine philosophy and the history of sexuality.
Butler's assertion that "gay is to straight *not* as copy is to original, but rather, as
copy is to copy. The parodic repetition of 'the original'. . . reveals the original to

be nothing other than a parody of the *idea* of the original"[13] is a passage very frequently quoted by gender scholars interested in the "constructedness" of heterosexuality, but it is not always fully appreciated for its powerful insight into literary history.

Sometimes the "sequel" radically revises the "original" by the very act of coming second. Thus—to take a deliberately tendentious example—one version of the set of scriptures known to Jews as the Bible is to Christians known as the "Old Testament" (compiled from the thirteenth to the first century B.C.E.). The "New Testament" (probably written in the first century but surviving only in manuscripts from the third and fourth centuries) has been read as the embodiment of God's covenant with man—set forth in the "Old Testament"—in the coming of Jesus Christ. The New Testament thus purports to complete the Old Testament, thus rendering the Hebrew Bible retrospectively "incomplete" from the Christian point of view. Typology—the study of persons, objects, and events in Old Testament history, prefiguring "some person or thing revealed in the new dispensation"—essentially regarded what was past as prologue, a set of signs predicting their own fulfillment. The word Bible has thus come to mean, in countries in which Christians are in the majority, the combination of Old and New Testaments. The "sequel" here performs an act of theological and textual legerdemain, not only "completing" the previous text but in doing so declaring the prior text to be "incomplete," in effect the "prequel" to the revealed word.

The biblical example is particularly striking, but what we might call the sequel-effect always functions in this way, making the reader or audience rethink the various meanings of the work. As Michael Zeitlin notes in an essay on the "postmodern sequel" in an anthology called *Part Two: Reflections on The Sequel*, "a text conventionally defined as a 'sequel' can work a transformative effect upon its precursor, which thereby becomes derivative, secondary, subsequent."[14] *Part Two* is a collection of literary-critical essays on "the phenomenon of secondary narrative," with attention to authors from Homer, Geoffrey Chaucer, and Charlotte Yonge to Donald Barthelme and John Barth. A number of the contributors focus on eighteenth-century fiction, and others on twentieth-century film, two places where one might most readily expect to find evidence of sequelmania. Arnold Schwarzenegger's self-fullfilling prophecy in *The*

Terminator, "I'll be back," used as the title for one of the essays (by Lianne McLarty), hovers over the sequel as something between a promise and a threat.

Yet two problems haunt this collection of essays—one, we might say, related to its own status as a sequel, and the other to its status as an anthology. It is a familiar kind of backhanded compliment for a strong critic to be taken to task for a sentiment that may seem only an incidental remark. In this case the irritant appears to have been a brief passage embedded in the middle of *Masquerade and Civilization*, Terry Castle's groundbreaking book on the carnivalesque in eighteenth-century fiction, published in 1986. No fewer than five times in *Part Two* the contributors lash out at Castle's intelligent observation that "sequels are always disappointing" because they are offshoots of the "bestseller syndrome," attempts within a capitalist economy to "profit further from a previous work that has had exceptional commercial success." Castle calls these generative works "charismatic texts," and gives *Robinson Crusoe* and the first *Pamela* as examples.

"The readers of sequels," she says, "are motivated by a deep unconscious nostalgia for a past reading pleasure," and "the producers of sequels have always recognized and tried to exploit this subliminal desire for repetition." The problem is that "the sequel cannot be the same" as the original text, and that readers cherish two impossible hopes in one: "that the sequel be different, but also exactly the same."[15] This is the best kind of psychoanalytic cultural analysis, taking into consideration, with judicious balance, the economic and psychic motivations for authors, publishers, and readers. Any quick mental checklist of literary and cinematic sequels, from *Henry IV Part 2* to *Terminator 2* (both analyzed in the volume), will suggest that Castle's views are borne out—which does not mean that sequels don't give pleasure; they do. But—or and—the pleasure they give is very much the pleasure of repetition and nostalgia: something familiar, and something lost. For loss—or the memory trace that comes with the sense of something lacking—is itself, in this cultural realm, a kind of pleasure.

Without being over-ingenious, it seems possible to say that what is troubling the authors of some of these solid and thoughtful essays is— paradigmatically—that they are playing "sequel" to Castle's prior—and more "charismatic"—articulation. It is that Castle is, in the main, *right* rather than *wrong* that constitutes the problem. As a result, in order to make space for new arguments on the question, the authors have to prove that she has "oversimplified," "assumed," or "simply overlooked" key issues about the sequel. The introduction to the volume (by Betty Schellenberg, a scholar of the eighteenth century with a special interest in the emerging professionalism of women writers, and Paul Budra, who has published on Renaissance literature and twentieth-century popular culture) thus frames its project as "to problematize, examine, elaborate on and nuance" the assumptions they find in Castle's brief remarks. As if in resistance to the scope of her speculations, the book as a whole downplays strong overarching claims (from psychoanalysis; from economic imperatives) in favor of local particularity (the situation of the woman writer in the eigtheenth century; the relationship of a popular nineteenth-century author to his literary agent). The result is a group of scholarly essays that does not go quite far enough in grappling with the fascinating conceptual and theoretical questions posed by the sequel as a cultural phenomenon as well as an effect of local history.

It is impossible to assess the sequel-effect without taking account of the swift dissemination of information or the increased breaching of the boundaries among categories like "literature," "entertainment," and "news" that have characterized the end of the twentieth century. "Closure," once a formal property of narrative, has become a soundbite nostrum for every televised and media-mediated tragedy from the Oklahoma City bombing to the O. J. Simpson, JonBenét Ramsey, and Louise Woodward cases. Mourners and survivors say they need it, readers and audiences claim they desire it, and yet the files remain open. "Closure" is not news. The mechanism of cultural *Schadenfreude* ensures the endless recycling of the story, with variations that keep it alive. The follow-up, the in-depth revisitation, the videotaped "instant replay" in sporting events, have become part of the news story and the essential fodder of the "news magazine."

And even the most tragic and affecting of news stories seem to be happening again, for the first time. The death of John F. Kennedy Jr. was a signal for the revival of old Camelot tapes, the twinning of father and son, both handsome and charismatic, both early lost. The nickname John-John, never—it appears—actually used by the family, is an icon of the sequel-effect, even more than the very American suffix, "junior." American politics, founded in resis-

tance to monarchy, has always longed for "dynasties," as the Bushes have discovered along with the Kennedys. (This may also account in part for the current American mania for genealogical research, aided and abetted by the
Internet.) George W., or "W," as columnists have come to call him, is a sequel
as well as a scion—and "compassionate conservatism" is a self-declared revision of the "kinder, gentler" mantra of his father. The Janus-like cultural logic
of the sequel has sweetened memories of the Bush administration while also
enhancing the aura of the son: "When you have a son who seems the likely
favorite to be a Republican nominee and possibly the next president, it causes
people to look for good things about his father," a presidential historian told
the *New York Times*. Another observer suggested that the revisionism could cut
both ways: "the romanticism of his being the son of a former President just
makes it that much more sexy."[16]

"There are no second acts in American lives," F. Scott Fitzgerald famously
wrote. Yet Fitzgerald himself, named for his father's ancestor Francis Scott Key,
the author of "The Star-Spangled Banner," acted out his own ambivalence
toward American life in a way that belied the truth of his statement. He could
just as easily have written its contrary, that in twentieth-century America there
are only second acts, and longings for a grand original.

Vegetable Love

> In the nineteenth century the Germans painted their dream and the outcome was invariably vegetable. The French needed only to paint a vegetable and the result was already a dream.
> —Theodor Adorno, "Dwarf Fruit," *Minima Moralia*
>
> The pears are not viols,
> Nudes or bottles.
> They resemble nothing else.
> —Wallace Stevens, "Study of Two Pears"

Here are two questions: How do we represent sexuality in visual terms, and—what is for me a directly related matter—how do such representations relate to the cultural ideology of the couple in the Western Imaginary of the late twentieth and early twenty-first centuries? In order to address questions like these, I will need—even in the course of these relatively brief comments— to touch on the whole matter of authority in allegorical reading, and also upon the tensions, however comic and charming, that exist in different registers of signification. Despite these heavy-duty terms, what I actually want to do is just to look at a few pictures. I will thus be taking what may seem to be a somewhat circuitous and anecdotal route, but my anecdotes will all be pictorial.

Let me propose as an additional epigraph for these observations a famous line by the English poet Andrew Marvell, from a seventeenth-century poem called "To His Coy Mistress":

> My vegetable love should grow
> Vaster than empires, and more slow.[1]

We might also consider what I take to be a not too oblique reply to that famous line from the libretto to the 1881 comic opera *Patience* by Sir William S. Gilbert (and Sir Arthur Sullivan), in a song describing a young aesthete:

> "If he's content with a vegetable love, which would certainly not suit *me*,
> Why what a most particularly pure young man this pure young man must be!"

My topics, then, are what may at first appear to be diverse, but will—I hope—come together: human sexuality and vegetable love.

An artist I know has recently been working on a series of paintings called "Couples." She is not a portraitist—at least of the conventional sort—nor does she do figure studies. What she paints is still lifes: fruits and vegetables in beguiling, often provocative, interrelation. Her "couples" are pears—and peaches, and squash, and Cranshaw melons. She does not restrict herself to high-brow fruits like apples and oranges, the familiar occupants of fruit bowls and cozy domestic interiors. Some of her "models" are butternut squash, and pumpkins, and carrots, and gourds.

The artist's name is Janet Rickus, and she lives in the Berkshire Mountains in western Massachusetts. It may be useful to discuss a few of her paintings.

Rickus's two grapefruit [Plate 1] seem companionable and innocuous enough, sitting on a checked kitchen tablecloth. They are side by side, and touching—if they were people, which they emphatically are not, we might say they were holding hands. Familiar, domestic, anchored, and safe. There are two of them; are they (therefore) differently gendered? The one on the left is a little bigger, more "perfectly" shaped, the one on the right a little dumpier and more misshapen. Also, is it blushing? And if so, is its blush reflected in, or echoed by, the grapefruit on the left? If we *had* to gender them would we say that the one on the left is male, and the one on the right—a little fuller in the "hips," a little more in the shadow—is female? But why would we have to gender them? Just because there are two? It would be vulgar, wouldn't it, to compare them to a pair of breasts—or, for that matter, to a pair of testicles. Instead, let's move on.

The pair of Cranshaw melons [Plate 2] appear in a slightly more formal setting (this highly realized white tablecloth is a frequent feature of Janet Rickus's work). I like particularly the little curly stems at the tops of the melons, almost like topknots of hair. One melon, the one on the left, is more mottled on its surface than the other, a characteristic of this kind of melon. In "human" terms, would we call this "weathered," or "experienced," or even "pock-marked"? It's not a flaw, though, or a blemish, it's what the mature Cranshaw melon strives to look like. Still, a pair of melons, painted as a "couple." Would we gender *this* couple? If we did, how many of us would say the one on the right is male? Probably few of us; it is smoother, just a little smaller, maybe more "made up" (cosmeticized?) for the artist's sitting.

These melons, like the grapefruit, could be a same-sex couple—why not? Cranshaw melons as Gertrude Stein and Alice B. Toklas, for example, with the little stems as locks of very short hair. But this is to resist the overdetermination of binary opposition, the cultural tendency to see a "couple" as male and female, indeed to model other binary oppositions upon the heterosexual couple—if, that is, we are not resistant to allegorizing and anthropomorphizing them—as perhaps we should be, out of a desire to avoid what might be called "fruitism." ("Fruit," after all, is a common, though somewhat dated, slang term for "male homosexual." If someone were to say to you "so-and-so is a fruit" they might be saying he was a peach—but they also might be saying he was a lemon. It depends, once more, upon your point of view. And "fruit fly," I am assured by friends in France, is the equivalent of "fag hag"—a woman who likes to hang out with gay men.)

Are these erotic couples? Are they heterosexual? Are they sexual?

A third couple [Plate 3] may serve as a kind of "control," as social scientists like to put it. These are orange and yellow peppers. One is leaning, the other is—can we say this?—lying down. If the stems are their "heads" then they are in a kind of *a tergo* position, perhaps, though who can tell what is the front of a pepper, and what is the back? Their curves are, however, curvy enough, and their relation more intimate and playful than that of the melons or the grapefruits. And doesn't the tablecloth seem a little rumpled? These peppers are having a good time.

Now obviously, in the history of art, and indeed in the history of visual and literary culture, the identification of fruits, or fruits and vegetables, with human beings or human body parts is hardly unknown. Consider the use of the emblematic fruit in caricature and political satire. The unforgettable figure of Louis Philippe as caricatured by Honoré Daumier [Figure 1] satirized the pear-shaped monarch and his vulgarity for all to see. The famous *poire* was the invention of Charles Philipon, Daumier's editor and collaborator.[2] In this case the human being as pear is hardly a sex object. The pear shape seems to describe both his face and his body—he is like a nineteenth-century Mr. Potato Head, though one inconceivably powerful in political terms.

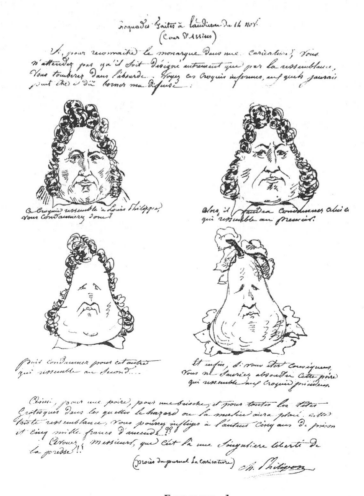

FIGURE 1

But the use of fruits and vegetables to signify and anatomize the human is by no means always satirical or comic. The sixteenth-century Italian painter Giuseppe Arcimboldo produced grotesque combinations of fruits and vegetables arranged to look like human portraits [Plate 4]. This may strike us as a perverse or eccentric vision; it appealed enormously to the twentieth-century surrealists, and especially to Salvador Dalí, in part because of its dislocation of human and vegetable forms. But Arcimboldo was a highly celebrated figure in his own time; though his work seems to us unusual (and it is) it clearly spoke to a sixteenth-century audience attuned to visual puns, jokes, and allegorical meanings. Arcimboldo became one of the favorite court painters to the Hapsburg rulers; one of his commissions was a portrait of Rudolph II [Plate 5].

Arcimboldo's gnomic paintings are in a way peculiarly literal (and *male*) versions of the traditional poetic blazon, comparing the features of the human face to stars, roses, jewels, and fruit (her eyes are like stars, her cheeks are like roses, and so on)—as in English poet Thomas Campion's little song of 1617, "There is a Garden in Her Face":

> "A heavenly paradise is that place,
> Wherein all pleasant fruits do flow,
> There cherries grow, which none may buy
> Till 'Cherry ripe!' themselves do cry."

("Cherry ripe" was the call of the London fruit sellers; despite the romantic and idealizing language, it seems that the lady may be bought and sold.)

This, indeed, is often a subtext lurking in the image of a woman as a paradisal garden. One of the most celebrated poems in English begins, "Of man's first disobedience and the fruit," and Ben Jonson's poetic celebration of the Sidney household, "To Penshurst" (1616), describes the marriageable daughters of local farmers arriving to pay tribute to the lords of the manor:

> their ripe daughters, whom they would commend
> This way to husbands, and whose baskets bear
> An emblem of themselves, in plum or pear.

The ripe, round fruit (plum or pear, already plucked) is carried by the round maidens ripe for the plucking.

I am here reminded of Linda Nochlin's brilliant reworking of a nineteenth-century French erotic photograph, *Achetez des Pommes* ("Buy some Apples")

[Figure 2], a scantily clad girl carrying a tray on which were perched both apples and her breasts. On an unforgettable occasion at a meeting of the College Art Association, Nochlin unveiled her own feminist version, a photograph she herself took [Figure 3] of a naked man, dressed in the parodic equivalent of the woman's sexy stockings and shoes, also carrying a tray, and inviting the viewer via the title to *Achetez des Bananes* ("Buy some Bananas"). Notice the wrinkled backdrop, which could be a coarse piece of fabric or a sheet. Notice also the space left on the tray.

Are the apples (and, indeed, the bananas) "emblems" of their sellers, as the plum and pear were "emblems" of the virgins in Ben Jonson's domestic paradise? Or are they instead *part* of them? Equivalence or detail? Analogy or continuity? Part or whole? Eve turned apple seller, or, "Yes, we have no bananas"?

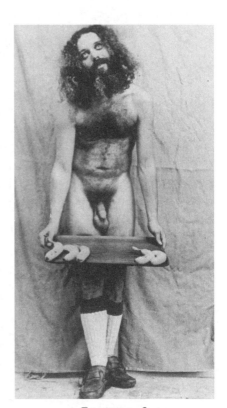

FIGURE 2   FIGURE 3

The commodification of human sexuality and of human bodies ("*buy* some apples") here deliberately undercuts the romance. And by turning the conventional erotic blazon around, Nochlin exposes the commercial transaction, as well as the objectification (and the human comedy). Her bearded model with his eyes made up as if for a Theda Bara movie offers himself, and his wares, in a gesture at once mocking and servile. This is an offer, he seems to say, that *can* be refused. (Or, as Allen Ginsberg put it in a poem called "A Supermarket in California," where he imagines Walt Whitman shopping among the produce and the grocery boys, "what price bananas?")

Yet in each of these instances—Daumier's pear, Arcimboldo's allegorical portraits, the poetic blazon, Jonson's ripe virgins carrying emblems of their own ripeness, Nochlin's fruit sellers—the human element has been directly and insistently present: it is a human being, a human body, a human face that is being described through its likeness to pears, plums, cherries, or grapes. But, for me at least, the magic—and the sexiness—of Janet Rickus's paintings is that the relationships are all, so to speak, purely vegetarian: melon calls to melon, grapefruit flirts with grapefruit, without any necessity for human attributes to mediate their interactions.

Detached from even the trace of a human figure—though not from the trace of human society: who irons those tablecloths?—Rickus's paintings pose the question in stark and loving terms. How do we "see," or "read" sex and gender? How do we "see," or "read" relationship? Are ways of seeing ways of loving?

Let me return, then, to the paintings.

In one of her group portraits of fruit, for example, [Plate 6] all the subjects seem to be showing off their all-purpose sexual organs. Is it a nipple? A navel? A clitoris? An eye? Which side of these fruits is the front, anyway? Is this a chorus line, a curtain call—or a bowl game? Or have the models all, rather rudely, turned their backs on the viewer, and cheekily stuck out their rears?

At this point you may well be thinking that I am just making this up. But here is what the artist herself has to say.

"I become deeply involved, intimate with all the things I depict," said Rickus in an interview. "I'm aware that my fruits and vegetables exhibit personalities, and I have them engage in fitting situations based upon occurrences and observations in my own life."[3]

Rickus says she "auditions" her fruit and vegetable models while she is standing in the aisles of local markets. "I hope I don't make a spectacle of myself," she says, "but I do have to consider the produce very carefully as I seek just the right shapes, textures, colors, sizes and 'identities.'" In addition "The length and posture of stems are also very important story-telling elements," she says.

As for the relative positions of the "models," they are critical. Rickus calls them "touchings," and she emphasizes that "the 'touchings' are always 'nice.' There are no angry or aggressive encounters in my art," she says, "but lots of camaraderie, loving and snuggling sexuality."

Let me say that again: "the 'touchings' are always 'nice'" with "loving and snuggling sexuality." Perhaps sometimes, I would add, both naughty and nice.

Consider Rickus's painting of a couple of gourds, sitting on a white lace tablecloth [Plate 7]. The tablecloth almost says "wedding dress" to me. This could be a marriage portrait of sorts, the participants on their best behavior, serious, rather formally posed, stems pointing resolutely into the air.

Once we have marriage on our minds, we are trapped—let's relax and enjoy it just for a moment—in the heterosexualizing of the couple.

A pair of butternut squash [Plate 8], look almost as if they're posing on the top of a wedding cake: all of that "hair," or "bridal veils," or—what would you say these extravagant stems are suggesting? It's just a little over the top, don't you think? One friend of mine felt it was ridiculous to think of these as formal hats or headdresses—to him this was clearly an image of a couple a little the worse for wear after a busy night. At the least, they were having a bad hair day. But in any case, again there is one relatively upright squash—square-shouldered, we might almost describe it—solid, classic, and classical (except for that Medusa hair), a solid citizen. And on the left, the smaller squash is much more curvaceous, and leaning—I'd like to say even "snuggling" against its—"her"?—partner.

With butternut squash it is especially hard to say, since their "natural" shapes can be both exaggeratedly "femme" or "feminine" and (to use a word that has become almost passé these days) exaggeratedly *phallic*. This playful eroticism can be seen in *Squashed Squash VII* [Plate 9]—actually the seventh in a series. (The word *squash* as a verb means to squeeze, crush, or flatten; the British, I'm told, drink a beverage known as "lemon squash." Interestingly—at least to me—the two kinds of squash, the noun and the verb, vegetable and crush, come from entirely different roots. The vegetable is Native American, from *isquoutersquash*, or Massachuset *askootasquash*; the verb is from Old French and Vulgar Latin, *esquasser*, or *exquassare*, to break to pieces; so the two kinds of squash are, well, squashed together in a single term. A good linguistic equivalent of Rickus's own visual pun.)

We'll consider a few more of these squashed squash in a moment. But this particular squash is a purposive little vegetable, quite determined, assertive, and cheeky, I would say. Some have called it lewd. It's not going to stay in its box for long.

A perhaps more "traditional" pair of squashes [Plate 10] might be read as a squash in the world and a stay-at-home squash. Is the one on the left free, and the one on the right confined? Or is the one on the right cozy, just fitting into its box—*her* box?—while the one on the left wishes it had a place to fit? Notice that this "free" squash is touching the box of the boxed-in squash, nicely, of course. Does it want in? And what are we to make of the all-too-humanoid shapes of these astonishing vegetables? Do they look like human torsos, or like sexual organs? The innate surrealism of fruits and vegetables is here almost casually on display, especially when rendered with such technical fidelity, a realism that is almost hyperreal.

Are these pairs of melons, or grapefruit, or gourds or squashes pairs of same or pairs of different? This is a question to which we shall want to return.

But why—should we restrict ourselves to this binary system, or to the concept of "the couple," much less the banal, domestic, bourgeois couple? Janet Rickus in fact does not.

She offers a promising group of three pomegranates [Plate 11]; a buxom foursome of honeydew melons [Plate 12]; a stand-up bunch of what the artist called *Carrots Casting Shadows* that provoked a few ribald comments when it was exhibited in the window of a Nantucket gallery [Plate 13]; and a sociable group of four rather chunky (or hunky?) pears (two "pairs of pears"? How would you assort them?) flirting with one another on that same, rather femme, lace tablecloth [Plate 14].

Even when the number exceeds two, however, what we might call the "culture of the couple" (or, more harshly, the ideology of the couple) often prevails. As Hélène Cixous observes, "To be aware of the couple, that it's the couple that makes it all work, is also to point to the fact that it's on the couple that we have to work if we are to deconstruct and transform culture."[4]

In one mixed fruit and vegetable arrangement [Plate 15], the two eggplants seem to be calling to one another across the space of the painting. (In fact, the title of the work is *Eggplants Facing*.) The artist likened this scenario to that of a couple (male, female, heterosexual, here it wouldn't matter) meeting on a cinema queue, standing in line among a heterogeneous group of strangers. To me, in a way the eggplants look like parentheses or quotation marks, enclosing the conversation among melons, while the lime at the one end, and the pear at the other, furnish opening and closing punctuation marks. See what the seduction of narrative can be—and the appeal, however retrograde, of formalism?

Janet Rickus's squashes seem more often than not to wind up in "families," whether twentieth-century nuclear families [Plate 16] (mother, father, two offspring), or extended families [Plate 17], each in its own room or apartment. In this second "extended family" [Plate 18], some members seem to be exercising their option to leave the nest (if I may mix my metaphor here), or are, at least, potentially exogamous. Since the small squash on the extreme left of this painting has quite a large box all to itself, it seems not so much a matter of the outsiders not fitting, as of their "not fitting in." Or choosing not to fit in. Here too, though, the couple reigns, after a fashion; in both of these large groupings (and these are quite large paintings) one key box is occupied by a pair. In each case one of the pair is larger than the other, and the smaller of the two seems to lean toward the larger one. Given the cozy suburbanism of their compartmentalized dwelling, it is a little hard *not* to read the "couple" in Plate 17 as male and female, even "mom" and "dad." The tassel of the stem of the one on the right might seem "feminizing," or at least a signifier of long hair. Even if we are determined not to gender this partnership, it seems indisputable that these couples are couples, that they stand—or lean—in *some* relationship to one another, whether that relationship is comic, erotic, complacent, or sexual.

Again, though: why see these as families? After all, these compartmentalized and crowded spaces could be college dormitories. Or perhaps office buildings. Or naked men in a gay bathhouse. I have not been describing what a spectator already resistant to the heterosexual couple would see, but what the dominant culture educates us to see *unconsciously*. Does the number two *automatically* connote heterosexuality and the cultural constructs that go along with it?

One recent Rickus painting of a couple seems to me, when read in the context of her other work, to be clearly readable as a drag painting [Plate 19]. In this painting of watermelons, they are too big for the table they sit on. They seem to be jostling each other for position even as they stand (or lie) still. The artist could, of course, have provided them with a bigger platform, or stage. But these are wannabe Rickus fruits: the watermelon as queen. (I might note that it's unusual not to see the *inside* of a watermelon in a painting; painters, like fabric designers, love the contrast of red, white, black, and green. But Rickus's fruits are models and "persons," never picnic snacks. The dignity of these plus-size big beauties is maintained even, or especially, through the artist's characteristic use of wit.)

Yet one more Rickus "couple" will show how wittily the artist plays with the erotic associations of her work. The painting, of a pumpkin-colored gourd and a large, fleshy gourd-like white pumpkin, both swathed in white drapery [Plate 20], will (perhaps) immediately remind you, as it did me, of René Magritte's *The Lovers* (*Les Amants*) of 1928 [Plate 21]. In Magritte's well-known painting the heads of the two lovers are wrapped in a shroud-like white drapery, giving the encounter an eerie, funereal, and at the same time highly charged erotic atmosphere that is exacerbated by the "anonymity" of the exchange. The architectural molding and detail in the Magritte's upper right-hand corner is echoed in the sculptural detail of the table in the lower left quadrant of Rickus's painting. *Her* "lovers," wrapped in a tablecloth that could be a sheet or a shroud (since after all they are the same) lean toward one another companionably. Are these postcoital gourds? Surely this is to consider too curiously. But can we doubt that they are "lovers"? To gender them seems in a way like an impertinence. But the rounded shape of the white fruit and the more idiosyncratic shape of the orange one do resemble the shapes of the heads of Magritte's shrouded male and female lovers. And the two heads are in the same *spatial* relation as the vegetables, the right one slightly higher than the left. Are they then gendered *by association*? by allusion? These are non-identical "lovers"—that is, one is orange and one is white. Does their twoness, and their apparent difference, make them opposites? Make them a pair? Is this a racially mixed marriage, or just a heterosexual couple? Does this painting make Rickus's other couples seem homosexual, engaging in "same-fruit" relations? You see what problems can arise.

Pairs of same, or pairs of different? As so often when this question is posed, it seems on second thought to be the wrong question, or a question (perhaps the *right* question) to which only wrong answers can be given. Same or different is one binary we are reluctant to let go of: our pundits agonize over same-sex relations and conflicts of different cultures. "In language," says linguist Ferdinand de Saussure, "there are only differences."[5] But would it be completely false to say that, in *visual* representation, there are only similarities, that this curve echoes that; this shape inverts that one? Difference and similarity, different and same, become two sides of a Möbius strip, where the inside is sometimes the outside.

Interestingly, Saussure, who is often thought of as the father of binary oppositions, actually himself posits *three* as the essential number for the possibility of analogy—that is, the creation of new language forms. "Every analogical fact is a play with a cast of three," he writes. "(1) the traditional, legitimate heir . . . ; (2) the rival . . . ; and (3) a collective character made up of the forms that created the rival." His theatrical and sexualized language (play; cast; rival), when talking about *linguistic* formations, should alert us to the stakes here. For what is at stake is nothing less than the very concept of social analogy; relations and functions, not causes. "In semiological systems like language," Saussure tells us, "where elements hold each other in equilibrium in accordance with fixed rules, the notion of identity blends with that of value and *vice versa*."[6]

I want now to turn from Rickus's "Couples" series to a different but related question of representation: the way in which sexuality, or sexualities, can be represented in visual art. These two questions are related, because my own interest in Janet Rickus's work is long standing, and as it happens I used one of her paintings on the cover of my book on bisexuality, a book called *Vice Versa: Bisexuality and the Eroticism of Everyday Life*. The painting, called *Three Pears* [Plate 23], immediately posed for me—and indeed began to dismantle and critique—the important question, "What is a pair?"

What is a pair? This is a question evocatively and teasingly asked by Jacques Derrida in his discussion of Vincent van Gogh's paintings of "pairs" of shoes [Plate 22], a discussion I found very germane to my own understanding of bisexuality. Left and right, inside and outside are for Derrida markers of difference, sameness, and gendering.

Writing against the readings of van Gogh's shoes proposed by the philosopher Martin Heidegger and the art historian Meyer Schapiro, Derrida opened up the question of what a pair is by reading first the morphology, and then the symbolism, of the pair of shoes.[7]

"If one let oneself slip into the facility of the symbolism," he suggested, citing psychoanalysts Sigmund Freud and Wilhelm Stekel, "the obvious bisexuality of this plural thing would stem from the inside-out passivity, open like a glove, more offered, more undressed, of the [one] shoe while the other... is more right/straight, narrow, strict, less open. In short, what one would in the past have called more masculine."[8]

"What proves that we are dealing with a pair?" Derrida asks again and again. "Shall we speak from now on of... an argument of the two-shoes, rather than of the pair, rather than of the couple (homo- or heterosexual). Bisexuality of the double in two shoes."[9]

A pair is a social institution, like marriage. "If there is a pair," notes Derrida, "then a contract is possible, you can look for the subject, hope is still permitted."[10] The concept of the pair works in a social sense, it functions to normalize. "*This*," he writes "is where I would situate the stake of the pair, of the parity or the pairedness of the shoes. A pair of shoes is more easily treated as a *utility* than a single shoe or two shoes which aren't a pair. The pair inhibits at least, if it does not prevent, the 'fetishizing' movement, it rivets things to use, to 'normal' use.... It is perhaps in order to exclude the question of a certain uselessness, or of a so-called perverse usage, that Heidegger and Schapiro denied themselves the slightest doubt as to the parity or pairedness of these two shoes."[11] In other words, the couple, the pair, are not perverse—because they are paired. "You reassure yourself with the pair," Derrida insists; but "what is a pair?" he asks. "What is a pair in this case?"[12]

Here is what I wrote in my book on bisexuality, under the heading, "What Is a Pear?":

Three Pears, a painting by American artist Janet Rickus, presents just that: three pears on a cloth-covered table. One is a comice pear, golden yellow and conical; one an Anjou, stubbier, with a tight green skin; the third is a red pear, deep vermilion in color. There they stand, side by side, in a row, touching. The green one is in the middle, between the other two. The red pear leans jauntily to the right. They have a lot of personality, these pears. Do any of them make a pair?

Look closely at the painting and you will see that you can pair them up, if you want to. The Anjou and the red pear are stubbier in shape; the comice is the odd pear out. But the comice and the red pear, warm-hued, both lean to the right, while the cool green pear in the middle stands upright. In attitude or comportment, then, the two outside pears are paired, the gold and the red. The one in the middle is the one outside. But couldn't we say, on third thought, that the comice and the Anjou are classically "pear-shaped," while the red pear, perhaps because it is posed at an angle (or in profile?) seems less conventionally curved and rounded? So perhaps it is the two on the left, the comice and the Anjou, that are the pair of pears.

Three pears. Or three pairs. If we were looking for an allegory of bisexuality we might take this image into account. The pears, the pairs of pears, will not stay paired. Like the "bisexual" shoes that are or are not a pair, whose story would be so much more explicable, so much more "useful," if they were a pair, a man's pair or a woman's pair, these pairs of pears are perverse. There are, for one thing, three of them, three pairs, a threesome not a pair. But the pear in the middle is only placed there, it would seem, by accident—or by the paradoxical "accident" of a perfect design.

I chose this image because I wanted to avoid the three-body-in-a-bed form of representation. It seems that whenever publishers want to show "bisexuality" at a glance they opt for an image of tangled bodies, as for example in this quite beautiful photograph by Tom Carabasi that was chosen by *Mirabella* magazine to illustrate an article on bisexuality [Figure 4]. Three in a bed is a favorite image, perhaps because it's many people's fantasy, and others' worst nightmare of jealousy or sexual competition [Figure 5]. I wanted something other than nakedness to stand for erotic connection. And it was important to me not to show any particular persons, or any "real" genders. My idea was a cover image that would *signify* bisexuality rather than *picturing* it. So this was the image that my New York publishers, Simon and Schuster, and I agreed upon.

However beautiful this image of Rickus's *Three Pears*, its commercial readability turned out to be too subtle. Certainly the English publishers seem to have thought so. They chose a different image [Figure 6] to use, though they showed the cover design to me early on to get my approval—which I gave.

FIGURE 4

FIGURE 5

F I G U R E 6

Actually, I like this cover very much. It's representational, but the bodies it shows are not clearly gendered, or, rather, don't seem to belong clearly to "males" or "females," at least at first glance. Indeed, at first you might not think these were human bodies at all. In some lights this looks to me like shifting desert sands—if desert sands had navels, nipples, and buttocks.

But a *third* design soon interposed itself for the American paperback edition. And here the language of the "sign" was doubly unmistakable. Instead of representation, symbolic or mimetic, this third cover was itself a sign of a sign [Figure 7]: specifically, a traffic sign, in the traditional diamond shape and yellow color that indicates a road hazard or warning.

The more expensive version was an overlay (of the kind that you often see, incidentally, in pop or trash novels): a cover for the cover, with a hole cut in it. This first image, then, was the road sign, "bisexuality"—with an arrow pointing both ways. "Go either way," it said, in effect, or "go around." If you are looking for a directional signal, this one may offer consternation rather than clarity:

FIGURE 7

Which way should I go? Go both ways. All roads lead there. Both the left and the right. In essence, you can't miss it. But still, this sign may not reassure.

When you lifted up the flap you saw a blurb from Gore Vidal and a number of other subsidiary pieces of information, like the full title of the book and the author's name. In later editions the two separate layers of the cover, the overlay and the underlay, were to be combined into a unified design.

What do these three contrasting images tell us about the difficulty of representing bisexuality?

Transvestism, I had found, was a trope, an image: it could be readily represented in visual terms. I had no difficulty in finding a cover image for my earlier book on cross-dressing. I chose German painter Paul Wunderlich's 1979 *Hermaphrodite Shirt* (*Hermaphroditenhemd*)[Figure 8]. But bisexuality is not a trope, but a narrative, a story. It occurs over time. Indeed, one of the claims of my book is that the word *bisexual* should be used not as a noun but as an adjective, and that many, many people *live bisexual lives*, having intense erotic rela-

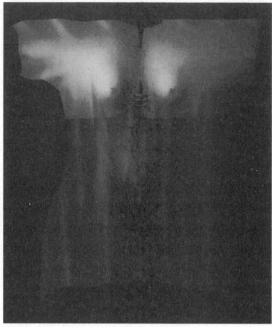

F I G U R E   8

tionships with both men and women over the course of a lifetime. In some cases these relationships are never consummated or even acknowledged—but since when has that undercut erotic intensity? Are such people "bisexuals"? That seems to me the wrong way to look at it. Bisexuality is a story, a plot, not an essence. So it can't be visualized except in narrative terms. Terms like the stories we've been telling, or guessing, or extrapolating, from Janet Rickus's sensationally sensual fruits and vegetables. Call it, perhaps, vegetable magnetism.

The story of the search for an appropriate image for bisexuality illustrates both the problem, and some provisional solutions, for the larger question of erotic representation. The painting of the pears is sensual, though not human. These are fruits. You can eat them. The photograph of the nude bodies is sensuous but abstract, despite the fact that its subject matter is the human figure. There is something paradoxical about the fact that the human bodies are more abstract that the pears—though they are not, at least to some eyes, therefore less erotic. Quite the contrary. The third image, the one that resists mimesis, focuses on the verbal, on the "sign"—and on a rather droll view of what is commonly called sexual "orientation." The arrow points *both* ways. This image, as we have noted, builds in a narrative dimension in time and space, since it requires the reader to turn the cover-page in order to consider both the design and the words of the title.

These three ways of representing bisexuality remind us that sex and sexuality are intimately related to other human qualities like wit, imagination, and storytelling. The "touchings" of Rickus's natural models are "nice" in every sense: exact, calibrated, likeable, tasteful—even tasty. But as "nice" as they are, they are also "touching"—moving, suggestive, and evocative in a way that human images can sometimes fail to be.

This story about imagery and eroticism has a postscript, and a somewhat surprising one, visually speaking. A cover image chosen for a subsequent edition of the same book seemed to solve some of these problems by drawing on a different set of associations, taken this time not from the language of fruits or persons, but from the language of electricity. Electricity, I should note, with just a suggestion of foreignness—just enough to suggest that all everyday currents are not alike [Figure 9]. A three-pronged object, beautifully and precisely rendered in white and copper, seems to jut forward into the pictorial space, ready for action. Since the lexicon of electricity includes words like *male* and *female*, and since in this image three replaces two as the normative number for a successful connection, the use of the converter/adapter/continental plug seemed to me, when I saw it, to be quite an appropriate idea. It sings the body electric. And the fit between topic and image was not only visual but also verbal: one of the most common early euphemisms for bisexual, dating from the 1940s, was drawn from the same language of electricity: AC/DC, alternating current/direct current.

On the back cover [Figure 10] is another version of this same trope. Here is a way of connecting three or more wires and plugs in a socket designed, again, originally for two. The wires seem a little messy, but the connection is made. The clumsiness of this device could be said to match the clumsiness of the term *bisexual*, a verbal placeholder in culture, I believe, until we coin and accept a better word. *Pansexual* seems too random and randy. As I've said, I prefer merely *sexual*, which acknowledges and incorporates the notion that desire and sexual love need not be oriented in a single direction. I hope we'll get to a time when sexualities can be plural without shorting out.

FIGURE 9   FIGURE 10

The difference between the back cover and the front cover can be allego-
rized as anatomical, but I think that's the least important issue. The metaphor-
ical senses of electricity, the "thrilling effect of the electric shock," come
through pretty clearly here. You can get a charge out of it, the design seems to
say. This is a sleek and modern image of "everyday life," both unplugged and
plugged in.

It is an image, we might say, conceived not under the sign of Derrida but
under the sign of Gilles Deleuze and Félix Guattari. "Desire causes the current
to flow, itself flows in turn, and breaks the flow," they write in *Anti-Oedipus*.
The human being "ceaselessly plugs an organ-machine into an energy-
machine," and "[a] connection with another machine is always established,
along a transverse path, so that one machine interrupts the current of the other
or 'sees' its own current interrupted." Deleuze and Guattari speak of "the satis-
faction the handyman experiences when he plugs something into an electric
socket." (The French term for handyman is *bricoleur*, our term for the postmodern maker of culture). And it is of more than secondary interest that this
connection between electrical circuits is called "coupling."[13]

What is at stake here is far more than a few attractive or provocative or witty
images, for image reading, like image production, is a powerful way of thinking, made all the more so in this highly visual and global age where words are
far more partial and limited than pictures. How *do* we represent unrepre-
sentable concepts like bisexuality, concepts that require not a fixed but a

mobile understanding? Concepts that cannot be captured by mimesis, by direct representation? Understanding how we read sex and gender, and how we perform and visualize theoretical concepts, is one of the key steps not only for changing social ideas but also for making what we do as scholars matter in the world.

Any "difference" can be sexualized; "same" can also be understood in a variety of ways. Straight and gay, like masculine and feminine or male and female, are points on a continuum, not rigid and exclusive alternatives. Moreover, many of these "differences" (and "samenesses") can exist *within* a category as well as between categories, whether that category is man or woman, melon or squash, converter, adapter or switch. We are only beginning to deal with the mythologies of erotic representation and the embeddedness of the binary "couple." In the meantime, it is an instructive paradox to find that in leaving the animal kingdom for a while we can learn a great deal about the human animal.

A Case of
Mstaken Identity | 7

"The title of this essay has enacted in brief the story I have to tell, for it has itself been singled out as an impostor. Repeatedly copyeditors and printers have corrected what seemed clearly to be my inadvertent spelling error, in leaving out the letter "i," producing the word *Mstaken*, rather than *Mistaken*, which was taken for a misprint—or, indeed, a *msprint*.

The reinsertion of that "i"—the return from Ms to Miss, is the burden of my tale. For my topic is the abbreviation *Ms.*, used as a mode of address, and what it tells us about the noninclusiveness of so-called "inclusive language."

A poll taken in 1999 revealed that members of the U.S. Presbyterian Church are "far more likely to refer to God as 'Father' than 'Mother.'" Only 13 percent of members were "extremely likely" or even "somewhat likely" to say that they imagined God as "Mother."[1] (Favored titles for the supreme deity were, in order, "Creator," "Redeemer," "Father," "Healer," "Master," "King," "Friend," "Judge," "Liberator," "Lover," "Mother," and "Spouse.") Inclusive-language Bibles ran into resistance from readers who viewed them as "compromis[ing] scripture just to make women feel included,"[2] and as an attempt to "emasculate Christianity,"[3] although in fact the new translations were closer to the original meanings of Greek and Hebrew words that had been (mis)translated into English with masculine gender. To offset criticism, the British publishers of the *Inclusive Language* edition of the New International Version offered customers a money-back guarantee if they failed to find the translation spiritually satisfying.[4] When the Catholic Diocese of Buffalo offered inclusive-language guidelines in 1993 it was attacked for denying the "maleness" of Jesus and "making him genderless." In this case, as in many others, the changes were derided as a "victory for radical feminism," despite the measured response of the director of the diocesan Office of Worship, who mildly observed that "if they are carefully read, it is quite obvious they are not in line with what might be found in the writings of radical feminists."[5] But these arguments, and indeed the fantasy of radical feminism, seem—at the beginning of the twenty-first century—a long time ago.

Even longer ago the French Revolution tried to effect a change in structures of address, substituting for titles of rank and status the common term *citizen*; in French the word had a feminine as well as a masculine form: Madame Defarge was a *citoyenne* (a female citizen), not a *citoyen*. English writers of the period, like Samuel Taylor Coleridge, dutifully coined and wrote *citizeness*, a term that was picked up by Harriet Beecher Stowe, though its vogue was over by the turn of the century. The Communist Revolution tried a similar move, replacing titles and ranks with the one-size-fits-all *comrade* for communists and socialists. Here there is no functional feminine form (no *comradess* in English), but instead a tacit rhetorical presumption of maleness and male bonding. *Comrade* comes from the word for bedchamber, and means originally someone who shares your quarters, a chamber-fellow, a tent-fellow, a fellow soldier. It is "[l]ess commonly said of women," comments the *Oxford English Dictionary*, which gives two examples from the late nineteenth century. It is consistent with the word's history that Edward Carpenter, the author of *The Intermediate Sex* and a socialist influenced by Walt Whitman and Havelock Ellis, could define "comradeship" as "male friendship carried over into the region of love."[6] So *citizen* was not quite gender neutral, since it could have a feminized form, while *comrade*, used to address both men and women, had a history, both social and erotic, that largely tied it to the language of men.

How is our modern and postmodern world coping with this challenge? Here is a symptomatic text, of no intrinsic literary value, that I would like to introduce as evidence: an editorial from the *Boston Globe*, celebrating the turn of the seasons. This kind of fluff piece is a staple of newspaper editorial pages, tacked on as a light "cultural" extra to the more serious political concerns of the day. Thus, quite typically, this piece of journalistic musing came fourth and last in a series of editorials that dealt with (1) the racial politics of the school system, (2) federal drug policy, and (3) "housing cuts in prosperous times." The expectation, quite reasonably, was that the newspaper reader, having cogitated about these vital issues, would be ready for something different. The fourth editorial on this particular day—it happened to be Labor Day—was about taking a day off at the end of summer, and about the way necessary tasks tend to get in the way: "So rather than plopping in a hammock and staying there, a person feels he or she must haul hoses up to filthy gutters, put gardens to bed, and clean out garages."[7] This is impeccable "inclusive language," complete with the clunky awkwardness that has come to accompany some of its uses: "a person feels" (something we'd almost never say); "he or she." "A person feels he or she" is in fact just the kind of phrasing that has brought out the style police, spraying their anti–political correctness mace on offending protesters.

But as the editorial meanders to its speculative close something happens to its gendered language. As it waxes philosophical, its gender inclusiveness almost reflexively wanes. Here are the final two paragraphs of this forgettable—but, as I say, symptomatic—text:

> The September mind-set will take over soon enough, for man is a slave to his calendar and circadian rhythms. He knows that the daylight hours are growing shorter, that the nights are getting cooler, and that leaves are turning early. He knows he is like a migrating bird, returning to the winter nesting places: On Monday he will travel in flocks on the nation's roadways.
>
> He knows all this but doesn't have to go there yet. For now, he can rest on the cusp of change, still enriched by summer's pleasures.

What has happened here? "Man," thought to be retired from active service, here makes a cameo appearance as hero and star. Everyday chores can, and are, performed by "a person"; but the philosophical, existential, cyclical, and eternal being, "slave to his calendar" but knowing and speculative, is still the general, collective, and supposedly nongendered "man."

It seems clear that the writer, gearing up for a kind of transcendental sermon, merely dipped into the usual lexicon of lay pulpit sonority. "Great ideas" are rendered greater (and small ideas can pretend to importance) if they are translated into this universal key. "Man" doesn't clean gutters, but he does look up at the stars. (And, apparently, commutes "in flocks on the nation's roadways.") There is no harm in this, surely. Pretentious diction—especially diction that pretends to a biblical simplicity—is not a crime.

To underscore the point here I want to juxtapose this editorial, very briefly (and at the risk of quite literally comparing small things with great), to a moment in John Locke's *Essay Concerning Human Understanding*, where Locke undertakes to explain why, as they grow up, human beings come to need general terms in language. This is Locke's account of "by what steps we enlarge our ideas from our first infancy":

> There is nothing more evident, than that the ideas of the persons children converse with (to instance in them alone) are, like the persons themselves, only particular. The ideas of the nurse and the mother are well framed in their minds; and, like pictures of them there, represent only those individuals. The names they first gave to them are confined to those individuals; and the names of *nurse* and *mama*, the child uses, determine themselves to those persons. Afterwards, when time and a larger acquaintance have made them observe that there are a great many other things in the world. . . . they frame an idea, which they find those many particulars do partake in, and to that they give, with others, the name *man*, for example. And thus they come to have a general name, and a general idea. Wherein they make nothing new; but only leave out of the complex idea they had of Peter and James, Mary and Jane, that which is peculiar to each, and retain only what is common to them all.[8]

Nurse and *mama* are Locke's examples of particular terms. *Man* is a general name, and a general idea—for Mary and Jane, as well as for Peter and James.

Reading the *Globe* editorial on the cusp of the twenty-first century, I myself was struck, suddenly, by an idea. My idea was that we should give up the struggle for gender-inclusive language. If "man" keeps popping up in public discourse whenever important (or self-important) thoughts are under consideration, then let us just all become men. I mean this grammatically, of course, not medically or surgically. "What, shall we turn to men?" asks Nerissa of Portia in Shakespeare's *Merchant of Venice* when her mistress proposes that they cross-dress and masquerade as a lawyer and his clerk.

My plan is not as radical or culturally discomposing as Portia's. It is, in fact, merely an accession to popular taste and the (apparent) majority will.

Since so many people, from philosophers to lawyers ("the reasonable man" standard) to journalists to conservative pundits seem to think that we cannot do without the generic "man," the hero of humanist discourse for hundreds of years, my suggestion is that we just get rid of female pronouns altogether. If the majority resists inclusiveness that in their view distorts language, let us include ourselves in the majority by using only "he," "him," and "man." Thus, for example, my students would refer to me as "he": "What did Professor Garber assign?" "He assigned us all of *Paradise Lost* by next week." One's parents would still be (in most cases) male and female, addressed or referred to as "Dad" and "Mom," but the pronouns used to describe them would all be male. "Mom asked me to get his purse from upstairs." Why not? If Dad also has a purse, and the objection is that I won't know whether to fetch his or his, the sentiment can always be rephrased for clarity: "Mom's purse is upstairs and he asked me to get it."

I make this suggestion somewhat in the spirit of Jonathan Swift's *Modest Proposal* (1729), the full title of which was *A Modest Proposal for Preventing the Children of the Poor People in Ireland from being a Burthen to their Parents or Country, and for making them beneficial to the Publick.* Swift's ironic proposal, you will recall, was that the poor should devote themselves to rearing children that could be sold and eaten; his pamphlet includes recipes as well as an argument about the advantages of this idea. His objective was not to get his proposal accepted, of course, but to point out the folly (and in his case, the callousness and cruelty) of prevailing Whig economic policy.

But in a way I am attracted to the concept of a single singular pronoun, rather than the he-she-it of English usage.

A number of years ago I had a similar idea, not so radical as this one—an idea that I talked about a good bit with friends but was discouraged from putting in writing, since at the time it was regarded as breaking with feminist solidarity. The idea was encapsulated in the title of the article I never wrote, which I envisaged as an op-ed piece with a headline that read: "Ms-ing the Boat." My argument was that the coinage *Ms.*, produced in optimistic good faith, had in fact divided women from one another rather than making common cause among them, separating adult women into three notional, and instantly ideological, categories: Mrs., Miss, and Ms. (In France all women of a certain age stop being called Mademoiselle and become Madame.)

What I wanted to observe was that, instead of coining a third term, *Ms.*, which immediately came to mean "feminist woman," or "woman in sympathy with feminist goals of equality," we should, strategically, have pressed for a similar, automatic transition from *Miss* (for a young girl) to *Mrs.* (for an adult woman). Since some of the chief objectors to Ms. were those married women who were eager to announce their married state ("earning the M-R-S degree," as people used to say) and were completely out of sympathy with any universalizing terminology that would take that label away from them, *Ms.* was from the outset a contestatory term. It was always extremely unlikely to become the dominant, much less the exclusive, title for adult women. As a term of address it in fact often became italicized and ironized when in the mouths of contemptuous speakers: "Well, *Ms.* Smith, are you satisfied now?"

Here is a brief history of terms: *Mrs.* is an abbreviation of *mistress*, in earlier times prefixed as a courtesy to the first name (Mistress Elizabeth Jones) and more recently to the last name (Mistress Jones) of a married woman. But from at least the sixteenth through the eighteenth centuries "mistress" was also prefixed to the first name or surname of an *unmarried* woman or girl.[9] Mistress Anne Page in Shakespeare is a marriageable young girl, not yet a "merry wife" (*Merry Wives of Windsor*, 1.1.197). *Miss*, or *mis*, was simply a shortening of mistress.[10]

Just for comparison's sake, how about "*Mr.*"? In modern use it is a title of courtesy prefixed to the surname of a man. But originally Mr. was the short form not of *mister* but of *master*. (*Mister* is really a kind of made-up word or back formation, the out-loud-pronunciation of the abbreviation *Mr.*, used in writing only "with more or less of jocular intention." Like *missis* or *missus* or, indeed, the pronounced word *Ms.*) In upper-class households the boys and young men of the family were often designated "the young master" or "the little master"—from which there derived, "after the phonetic separation of *Mr.*," the usual prefix "master" for a young man not old enough to be called *Mr.*[11]

Master had a strong class association. From the seventeenth century it was applied to any man "below the rank of knight and above some humble but undefined level of social status," although "as with other titles of courtesy, the inferior limit for its application has been continually lowered," so that "at the present day any man however low in station would be styled "Mr." on certain occasions." (The *Oxford English Dictionary* cautions that this applies only to a man "not entitled to be addressed as 'Sir' or 'Lord.'") What we have here then is social status, or rank, layered over gender, in a way that is both interesting and suggestive. As *Mr.* descended lower in the social scale by Debrett's version of Gresham's law, *Mrs.* became a title bestowed by a man upon a woman by his invitation to marry, together with his name. "Will you do me the honor of becoming Mrs. Willoughby?" No longer was *Mrs.* (short for *mistress*) a prefix to which a woman automatically acceded as she reached adulthood. It was tied, in English-language usage, to marriage.

As the romantic critic Coleridge pointed out in his ruminations on the way language changes over time, "In all societies there exists an instinct of growth, a certain collective, unconscious good sense working progressively to desynonymize those words originally of the same meaning," either by "giving to the one word a general, and to the other, an exclusive, use," or even by changes in pronunciation that made two words with distinct meanings out of an original one. "Thus 'property' and 'propriety'; the latter of which, even to the time of Charles II was the *written* word for all the senses of both. Thus too 'mister' and 'master,' both hasty pronunciations of the same word 'magister,' 'mistress,' and 'miss.'...For each new application, or excitement of the same sound, will call forth a different sensation, which cannot but affect the pronunciation." Over time the old similarities disappear, "till at length all trace of the original likeness is worn away."[12]

Can we imagine a social system that would distinguish adult *males* by marital status? ("Check your preferred box: Mr., Master, or Mester.") If instead of pushing *Ms.*, and feminist difference, we had followed the models of male English language and female French language usage and all become *Mrs.*, there would have been very little the diehards could have done about it. No anti-*Ms.* *Mrs.* would, I am fairly confident, have doffed her M-R-S in protest. Within a few years all adults would have been *Mr.* or *Mrs.* and *Miss* would have remained for girls, to the extent that it was still used at all.

The original plan for *Ms.*, at least in some quarters, was that it would become the universal designation for adult women. "Use abbreviation Ms. for *all women* addressees. This modern style solves an age-old problem,"[13] suggests a 1952 pamphlet called *The Simplified Letter.* Well, maybe. A revised version of the same pamphlet, published by the Philadelphia-based National Office Management Association in the same year, was already anticipating trouble: "Use abbreviation Ms. if not sure whether to use Mrs. or Miss." And by the

1970s *Ms.* was a choice, not a solution. The British Passport Office "conceded" the right of women to call themselves Ms. rather than Mrs. or Miss on their passports,[14] and an office circular reported that "Female staff in this depart- ment may... use the Ms title (usually pronounced Miz) as an alternative to the Miss or Mrs."[15] In a tellingly awkward sign of the times, *Publishers Weekly* in 1975 reported the republication of *Sanditon* by Jane Austen and Another Lady, identifying it as "Ms. Austen's seventh and unfinished novel."[16]

The advent of *Ms.*, so patently a coinage, produced predictable resistances and anxieties. How should it be pronounced? A series of letters to the *New York Times* worried this question throughout 1971 and 1972. One correspon- dent suggested it be pronounced "Mistress," correctly (as we have seen) citing that term as the etymological root of both *Miss* and *Mrs.* Another proposed the pronunciation "Munus," which happened also to be a Sumerian term that could denote a woman of any age, marital status, or profession, human or divine. The associate editor of the *American Heritage Dictionary* offered a range of pronunciations, from "mis' to "miz" to "em es."[17] Yet another letter writer offered the view that although the title *Ms.* conceals a woman's status, it still identified her as a woman, and proposed instead a unisex title, "Mx," to be used for both males and females; x, of course, stood for "unknown."[18] Columnist Russell Baker suggested jokingly back then, as I have here, that instead of using Ms. as a universal title for women, two new terms for men should be introduced, telling more about them.[19]

Many people had doubts from the beginning. Julie Nixon Eisenhower, meeting with a group of Girl Scouts in the White House, said she did not think Ms. as an alternative form of address for Miss or Mrs. was necessary.[20] President Richard Nixon said he disliked it.[21] The highest-ranking woman in the min- istry of the USSR, appealed to for her judgment, said it was not important how women were addressed. Instead she urged the election of an equal number of woman and men as governors and senators.[22] Meanwhile, in the U.S. Congress, the *Congressional Record* used Ms. for the first time on October 4, 1972, to des- ignate Representative Bella Abzug—but retained "Mrs." as the title for the eleven other women members of Congress.[23] So much for the neutrality of this new term. The fact that it quickly emerged as the title of a frankly feminist magazine may have doomed its universalism from the start.

Miss, Mrs., or Ms.?

Today more and more women are "keeping their names," as the *New York Times* Sunday wedding pages routinely announce. And when they do, how does the "Style" section style them? Why, as "Ms.": "Ms. X, who is keeping her name, is a freelance magazine writer." "Ms. Y, who will keep her name, graduated from the University of New Hampshire...." "Ms. Z, 29, is keeping her name."[24] *Ms.* has become the default term of female adulthood. This is, we might think, a sign of its success and acceptance, but on the same wedding page there are half a dozen brides who have been metamorphosed by the dual agency of clergy and journalism to the status of *Mrs.* The alchemy of this writing formula is completely standard. The first paragraph of the wedding announcement begins with the full name of the bride (Jane Hilda Jones) and names the groom (John Hancock), the location, and the officiating clergyman. By the second paragraph Jane Jones has become Mrs. Hancock. So the wedding page, the society chart of rites of passage, chronicles the change of marital status of two categories of women—or rather, of women who seem to belong to (and to establish) two categories by virtue of their changing, or retaining, the surnames by which they were previously known. Headline writers carefully fine-tune these distinctions; thus the headline for a woman who was taking her husband's name would read "Miss Plunkett, Mr. O'Connor," and the headline for a woman who was retaining her name would read "Ms. Plunkett, Mr. O'Connor." Should these women appear in the pages of the *Times* subsequently, as, let us say, politicians or performers or even participants in a news story, they will all be called "Ms." Thus, for example, Bill Clinton's Secretary of State Madeleine K. Albright, who married a man called Albright, was called Ms. Albright. (In former years the *Times* used only Mrs. or Miss.) Even women in public life who are best known by their married names, and their husbands, are sometimes called Ms.: Before she became Senator Clinton, Hillary was known as Mrs. Clinton, but also Ms. Clinton, in recent published reports; Elizabeth Dole, wife of a senator, but a public figure in her own right, was occasionally called Ms. Dole. Laura Bush, however, is never Ms. Bush, although Ms. Bush is used for her daughters and her nieces.

It is far from my interest here to engage in the old feminist argument about male ownership and female capitulation in marriage, or about the question of whether a woman's father's name is more authentically "hers" than a husband's name. I am interested, for the moment at least, only in the prefixes that mark these women's appearances in print—not in their names, or surnames.

And *mark*, here, is a key term. For in the history of linguistics the question of whether the feminine is always (i.e., in all language systems) the "marked" category has been much discussed. The oppositional relation of markedness emerged in linguistic theory in 1921 with Roman Jakobson's account of *marked/unmarked* as a binary opposition; for Jakobson the unmarked term was not on a par with the marked term—in other words, as with all binary oppositions, the two terms established a hierarchy. What do we mean by "marked" in this case? Consider poet vs. poetess, or waiter vs waitress. The *-ess* suffix means "woman," and the normative term stands as male. "Woman" itself is of course another such word, built on the word "man." The original Old English term was *wyfman*, where *wyf* meant "woman." *Man* meant not "male person" but "human being." A poet writes poems; a poetess is a *woman* who writes poems (and by implication, "womanly," "feminine," or indeed "feminist," poems).

Think for a moment about what would happen (following our earlier hypothesis) if we universalized the *female* form: "Michelangelo was the greatest sculptress of the Renaissance." "T. S. Eliot is a major poetess of modernism." You can see that this will not do, culturally speaking. This is not a kind of inclusiveness we are likely to see hit the mainstream any time soon.

But we do not have to look to the canons of literature and culture to find a crisis of terminological inclusiveness. For it was not *Ms.* that raised the question of redefinition, but, as it turned out, *Miss*. A term that we have already seen to be a back formation from the more "universal," less controllable *mistress*. And in fact it has always been Miss that has been the real problem.

The cultural baggage surrounding the mysterious survival of *Miss* came to a pretty little head during the 1999 Miss America campaign, when pageant officials decided to open the contest to women who had been divorced or who had had abortions. The decision, which produced an instant flurry of protest, was impelled by the fact that the present rules violate New Jersey's antidiscrimination laws. What was a "Miss"?

Since Miss America Jacque Mercer married and divorced during the course of her reign in 1949, causing consternation to pageant organizers, contestants have been required to sign a pledge saying they have never been married or pregnant. The new rules would have asked entrants to swear "I am unmarried" and "I am not the natural or adoptive parent of any child," thus permitting divorced women and women who had had abortions to compete. Notice that adoption was included here; Miss America, whatever else she may be, is not a mother. But is she a virgin? So far as I know, a gynecological exam is not part of the present tests for eligibility: we are talking image here, not fact. But the uproar was amazing (the Associated Press called it a "stunning departure from tradition,"[25] and it turned, not surprisingly, on the all-important (and virtually outdated) prefix *Miss*.

"The word 'Miss' stands for something," said Miss Delaware, Kama Boland. The rule change "would change the image of Miss America, and not necessarily for the better."[26] A 1970 runner-up, Kathrine Baumann, whose niece became a subsequent Miss Ohio, alleged, "There's a purity and an integrity and a morality that would be violated if you let in women who are divorced and had an abortion." She acknowledged that "People get divorced. But if that happens, let them compete in the Mrs. America pageant."[27]

Reaction against the changes was so strong that convention officials ultimately rescinded them. But as the *New York Times* observed in an editorial, the key issue was nostalgia, not behavior. "It is doubtful that the 300,000 citizens who work in state and local pageants really think virginity is as common as it used to be. What animates the local pageants is not analysis of the real world, but nostalgia for a fictionalized American past."[28] And the sign word for that nostalgia was the iconic term *Miss*. The pageant's national board, the *Times* noted, "thought, rightly, that anyone who was a 'miss' at contest time ought to be able to compete." For many, however, *Miss* meant more than current marital status. "We have a certain responsibility as celebrities to live up to a certain standard," said a former Miss Massachusetts (whom the *Boston Globe* described, deadpan, as "a marketing representative who lives in Quincy"; celebrity, like virginity, just ain't what it used to be). "We probably don't want a divorcee as a title next to Miss America. I just think it takes away from what the people in our society expect of Miss America."[29]

"There she is," carols the Miss America theme song, "your ideal." The president of the Massachusetts chapter of the National Organization for Women asked, "Is the ideal woman a woman who has never been pregnant or married?"[30] "There She Is, Miss...Anachronism?" read a headline in the *Christian Science Monitor*, over an article that quoted the director of the Center for the Study of Popular Television (located at Syracuse University) as saying, "Miss America is in many ways a perfect reflection of a slice of American values as they stood a quarter-century ago." He described pageant watching as "almost the experience one gets when one opens a time capsule."[31] Meanwhile, a spokeswoman for the conservative Family Research Council offered a rationale that, if it had come from another source, might have been derided as nihilistic postmodernism: "We know absolutely that women are divorced, we know women have abortions. We may or may not approve of those decisions, but you have to understand that this is a contest...and it is predicated as an ideal."[32]

I agree with both the bifurcated view here and the value of an ideal that may not be embodied in the here and now. In effect, by this reasoning, Miss America offers *Miss* under erasure. "Faux virginity" is what one journalism professor called it, commenting on the flap.[33] In fact the virginity test was itself, like so many other such things, a back formation in the history of the contest.

The first pageants, staged in Atlantic City in the 1920s to attract tourists in the off-season, were condemned by local civic and religious leaders—not to mention women's clubs—for their indecency (women in bathing suits) and their corrupting power (money prizes bred competition and rivalry among women). Contestants, often sponsored by amusement parks, were compared to prostitutes "entertaining in cheap bars," and in some cases they *were* prostitutes, or "professionals."[34] In order to "get the class of girl that we should have," in the words of the reform-minded pageant director who presided over the festivities from the mid-1930s to the '60s, new and stringent rules were invented: each girl had a high-society "hostess" or chaperone, assigned to watch over her day and night, and the pageant was officially limited to young, single women between the ages of eighteen and twenty-eight who had never been married or divorced or had a marriage annulled.[35] Respectability was the initial goal; patriotic sentimentalism soon came to its support, and Miss America, in unofficial use since 1921, became the pageant's official name in 1940. The *Miss* in Miss America, was just what had been missed, and missing: it was the mark of nostalgia personified, the virginity effect. But even lost virginity is reversible these days (a solution foreseen five hundred years ago in the Spanish classic *La Celestina*[36]). A Los Angeles plastic surgeon not only per-

PLATE 1

PLATE 2

PLATE 3

PLATE 4

PLATE 5

PLATE 6

PLATE 7

PLATE 8

PLATE 9

PLATE 10

PLATE 11

PLATE 12

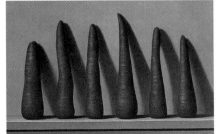

PLATE 13

PLATE 14

PLATE 15

PLATE 16

PLATE 17

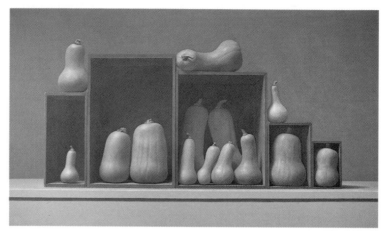

PLATE 18

PLATE 19

P L A T E   2 0

P L A T E   2 1

PLATE 22

PLATE 23

forms breast augmentations and tummy tucks, but will "in some cases" also "restore hymens in brides-to-be."[37] (Come to think of it, what do the Miss America pageant rules say about plastic surgery?) In this case "Miss" is a hard-won affectation, not a guarantee of anything.

"There she *was*, Miss America," quipped the editorial page of the *Boston Globe*, arguing that the pageant marked "the irrelevance of an event rooted in the past." The pageant, thought the *Globe*, should stop pretending to change, by fiddling with the one-piece/two-piece bathing suit rule, or insisting (in its most profoundly disingenuous claim) that this was a "scholastic" competition. "Real change would eliminate inappropriate questions about a woman's private life and would open the Atlantic City stage to single mothers, natural or adoptive. Who is in greater need of a scholarship than a teenage parent?"[38]

On the same page ran a Rob Rogers cartoon in which a transgendered contestant, in pageboy hairdo, tiara, lipstick and stubble, strode victoriously down the runway in two-piece swimsuit, high heels and hairy legs, draped in the distinctive sash that read "Miss America." "I'm all for them changing their definition of the 'ideal' woman," comments a female audience member, "but *that's* my ex-husband up there!" Is this "Miss America" a male cross-dresser, or a transsexual? The revised rules, too radical for many, make no mention of sex changes. But *Miss* is a title that may legally be claimed by those who have undergone sexual reassignment surgery. (It also has, of course, a long history in the gay community.)

FIGURE 11

What if we were to adopt a variant of Baumann's suggestion and take it one step further, by merely changing the name of the Atlantic City contest to Mrs. America and putting into practice the continental usage of *Mrs.* as a term of address for all adult females? But of course there already is a Mrs. America contest—and it has had its troubles, too. The 1991 winner, Jill Scott Chance, was sued by the pageant for $100,000 after it was revealed that she was separated from her husband when she won the crown.[39] The runner-up for Mrs. Illinois in 1999 argued that she should be declared the winner, and thus eligible to compete in the finals for the title of Mrs. America, because the woman crowned Mrs. Illinois had won the contest before, under a different name. ("It says in the rules that you can't have won the pageant before," the runner-up claimed.) Monica Skylling-Kraus—then Monica Skylling-Burke—had won the state contest in 1992, but was forced to give up her title without competing for Mrs. America because she was getting divorced. "We have to have a husband," explained the pageant sponsors.[40]

Other state contests have equally rigid guidelines. The Mrs. Wisconsin pageant says it seeks "married women who believe they exemplify what a modern wife should be. Contestants participate in private interviews and have an opportunity to tell judges what makes their marriage special. There is no talent competition and no experience is required."[41] Incidentally, although the Mrs. America competition is held in September, it is telecast in May, on Mother's Day (or at least it was in 1997–1998).[42]

So far as I know there is no Mrs. Divorced America pageant, though this is a market niche that might well find an audience. There is, however, a *Mr.* America contest. Mr. America—like Mr. Universe—is a bodybuilding competition.

Contemplating the potential entry into millenial politics of numerous contenders from the world of entertainment, like former pro wrestler Jesse Ventura, basketball star Bill Bradley, and actor Warren Beatty, *Boston Globe* columnist Diane White suggested that the entire presidential election be reinvented as a contest, "The Mr. President Pageant." The event would begin with a parade of candidates marching down a runway dressed for a state dinner, and would include a talent session, a "fitness segment" (in which "the candidate would parade in athletic gear while a physician reads selected portions from their medical records"), and a key question designed to bring out presidential character (White suggested: "If you could go out on a date with

Arianna Huffington or Eleanor Roosevelt, who would you choose? And why?"). This cheerful fantasia ended with a national vote conducted by a 900 telephone number and a victory lap down the runway for the winner, smiling, waving, and blowing kisses while the U.S. Marine Band played "Hail to the Chief."[43]

Actually, it is hard to say what part of this fantasy is considered improbable.

The 2001 Pageant had imagined itself as a site of cultural change, yet again. The bathing suit competition was renamed "Lifestyle and Fitness" (though the high-heeled shoes were back; not the standard poolside wear at most health clubs I know). The evening gown event was to be called "Presence and Poise," and the excluded or banished contestants were rewarded, not with the old good-sport/smiling loser title of Miss Congeniality, but with a collective vote ("Survivor-style," noted all the culture columnists) as the "eighth judge" selecting the new Miss America. But then came the tragic events of September 11, and the pageant wrapped itself in the flag—literally—sending out 10,000 photocopies of the Stars and Stripes, one for every member of the audience. On this occasion, the emphasis was on the "America," not the "Miss." And yet in the new quiz show format, in which the contestants were asked to answer multiple-choice questions about current events, these American heroines stumbled, several failing to identify correctly the living U.S. presidents, or the first African-American justice of the Supreme Court. Only some of the five finalists knew that "Give me your tired, your poor, your huddled masses yearning to breathe free" was inscribed on the base of the Statue of Liberty (the Miss America to end all Miss Americas); others thought it came from the Lincoln Memorial or the Washington Monument. In a curious ceremonial innovation, halfway between a debutante ball and a wedding ceremony, the Misses were escorted down the aisle—or at least, across the stage—by their fathers or brothers, who kissed them goodbye and left them, center stage, to face the nation (and Tony Danza). The symbolism was unmistakable. Like Queen Elizabeth I, who famously declared herself England's virgin bride, these women ("the girls," in insistent pageant lingo) were marrying America.

So how should a woman be called? When President Bill Clinton pretended not to remember the name of the intern in his office, he called her "that woman—Ms. Lewinsky." *Ms.* was thus a coded term for youth and estrangement ("I don't remember her") that quickly turned into a sign-word for loose sexuality. It is a category that will not stay put, a category that questions the use of category. In doing that cultural work, far from being unsuccessful, it has been (somewhat ironically) invaluable. But as a vocative—the role such titles play in France or England—Ms. is a dismal failure, as are Miss and Mrs., for that matter. Where the French can say "your table is ready, Madame," and the English say "Madam," your typical U.S. restaurant says "ladies," or, indeed, "you guys." "Guys," I submit, is the low vernacular vocative form of "man" in twenty-first century English. Here "man" again returns, under yet another guise ("the second time as farce"), acting out on the level of usage the very conflation and appropriation from below that I—slightly facetiously—proposed at the outset. ("Shall we turn to men?") Which is the real imposter here: Miss, Mrs., Ms., or man?

Arguably *all* identity is "mistaken identity." And gender inclusiveness, despite its real effects in transforming firemen into firefighters, or policemen into police officers (and thus recruiting more women into the fire and police departments), will ultimately find its limits at the level of rhetoric. Gender is precisely what can never be inclusive. There is always something "missing." Putting "man" under erasure may turn out to have been the wrong strategy, even with the right reasons. The task of literary studies might better be to remind him that he, too, was always a figure of speech.

Moniker | 8

"Why don't we hear very much about Monica Lewinsky being Jewish?" joked comedian Emily Levine at a Los Angeles fund-raiser for the Morning Star Commission, a group of professionals from the media and academia who have organized to combat the stereotype of the "Jewish American Princess." (The group gets its name from the eponymous heroine of Herman Wouk's novel *Marjorie Morningstar*, about an aspiring Hollywood star who changed her name from Morgenstern.) "A Jewish girl with oral sex? I don't believe it," quipped Jackie Mason to a Florida audience. "An oral surgeon, maybe, that's what a Jewish girl wants."[1]

The question of Monica's Jewishness, and her mother's name change from Lewinsky to Lewis was hardly been glanced at in media accounts in this country. In Israel, interestingly, there was more attention, pro and con. When I asked conservative columnist George Will why, he said it was because there were so many other interns who had been involved with Bill Clinton; Monica was only the one who'd gotten caught. The implication was that Clinton was an equal opportunity seducer, fairly "catholic" in his tastes. Monica by this account was just a "Jane Dubinsky," the Jewish Jane Doe. Yet the deep (throat?) structure of the Monica story does have fascinating resonances with Jewishness, and with the historic narratives, fact, fiction, and stereotype, of the seductive "Jewess" and her political role.

Overseas, in Europe and in the Middle East, Monica's Jewish identity was very much part of her story. As we will see shortly, it made her, in some eyes, an obvious Zionist spy, and in others a cultural heroine. In the United States, however, her Jewishness was seldom mentioned, except when she herself brought it up.When it was reported that Monica had given the president a copy of *Oy Vey! The Things They Say! A Minibook of Jewish Wit*, for example, one journalist cited Henry Kissinger's "Power is the great aphrodisiac!" as a particularly apposite selection.[2] But the fact that Monica was Jewish—something she herself was frank and joyous about in many of her comments, both to the president and to her biographer—was largely ignored by the American press and politicians; ignored—or displaced into other frames of reference. Her signifying traits were distributed across a whole spectrum of discussions. She was "pushy"; she was "ambitious"; she was "zaftig"; she was "typical Beverly Hills." She was physically mature for her age. She was sexy and seductive, "the femme fatale in the soap opera of sex and betrayal."[3] She was rich. She had designs on a political or policy role. She lacked moral *gravitas*. She led a weak Christian man astray.

It is not entirely an accident, I believe, that the moral "hero" of the Clinton sex scandal was the Senate's single (and first-ever) Orthodox Jew, Joseph Lieberman of Connecticut, a Democrat and longtime Clinton friend. Lieberman was widely praised for his courage in speaking up about the effect of the scandal "on our children, our culture, and our national character." As the man who persuaded the Senate to discontinue voting on Jewish festivals and holding sessions on Jewish High Holy Days, Lieberman had enormous moral clout. After his speech the national media wrote admiringly about his daily Torah study and prayer and his seven-mile walk from Capitol Hill to his home in Georgetown when the Senate meets on Friday might, since Orthodox Jews may not ride on the Sabbath. So far as I can tell, Lieberman never commented publicly—or for all I know, privately—about Monica Lewinsky's Jewishness. His opprobrium was aimed at the president, who had failed as moral leader. But the fact that this story was anchored at one end of the moral scale by Bill Clinton's relationship with a young Jewish woman ("disgraceful and immoral"⁵) and at the other end by his relationship with a high-ranking and highly respected Jewish man in public life ("a Jewish hero") is evidence of its overdetermination in the public sphere.

Although some of the story's "Jewish" elements went unnamed and unmarked, they powerfully and uncannily reinscribed the story of Jewish-American assimilation and its late-twentieth-century discontents. For just as Senator Lieberman's "heroism" was almost predictable, given the ingredients of this underlying cultural narrative, so was the public fascination with the behavior and desires of a sensual young woman named Lewinsky. When Al Gore chose Lieberman as his running mate, he was widely regarded as trying to distance himself from the perceived moral turpitude of the Clinton scandal. In this case the tacit hope was that the "good" Jewish man could sanitize the stain of the "bad" Jewish girl. The flood of speeches and articles that publicized his Jewishness said nothing, of course, about hers.

Precisely because it went "unmentioned," Monica's Jewishness was, in a sense, everywhere. It became the cause behind the cause, the story behind the story. And it tapped into old stories, and cultural fantasies, and created a logic of its own. Mentions, when they did occur, were oblique and knowing, tapping into the same reservoir of erotic and sentimental stereotype, an ambivalent overestimation of the object that imbued Lewinsky with particular seductive power.

In the midst of the impeachment hearings novelist John Updike, the nation's most famous chronicler of WASP culture (his fictional protagonist Rabbit Angstrom has been described as "a WASP antihero"⁷) published a jaunty little poem in *The New Yorker* called "Country Music." "Oh Monica, you Monica / In your little black beret," it began:

> You vamped him with your lingo,
>   Your notes in purple ink,
> And fed him "Vox" and bagels
>   Until he couldn't think.⁸

Updike, whose novel *Couples* (1968) offered an early depiction of oral sex as an American way of life, stands in what might almost be considered a godfatherly relation to *Vox*, the "phone sex" novel notoriously presented by Lewinsky to the president. One of his greatest admirers and disciples is Nicholson Baker, the author of *Vox*, and Updike is himself somewhat intrigued by the phenomenon of the older man and the sexy Jewish girl.

After the Rabbit books, Updike turned to a series of books about Henry Bech, described as a "moderately well-known Jewish writer," whose lovers became younger as he grew older. "Bech had a new sidekick," begins a chapter in the 1998 *Bech at Bay*. "Her monicker was Robin. Rachel 'Robin' Teagarten. Twenty-six, post-Jewish, frizzy big hair, figure on the short and solid side." And of course, sexy. "The energy of youth plus the wisdom of age," Bech congratulates himself.[9]

"*Vox* and bagels" is a good joke, an apt telescoping of Monica's seductive charms. And while the "lingo," the purple ink, and even the phone sex might conceivably be generic Beverly Hills mall rat, the bagels (and the slightly occluded lox) hint at the specificity of *Lewinsky*—a name that does not appear in Updike's ballad of careless White House love.

Zaftig

> This demure but *zoftick* freshman, with a brain
> rivalling Spinoza's encased in the body of a
> Lollobrigida.
> —S. J. Perelman, *Baby, It's Cold Inside*

"An independent-minded odalisque, unshackled from sexual modesty and constantly celebrating her *zaftig* sensuality,"[10] is how one critic characterized Lewinsky's erotic persona depicted in women's magazines like *Glamour*. (The occasion was an editorial entitled, with deliberate double entendre, "Why We Should All Get Down on Our Knees and Thank Monica Lewinsky.")

However sex-affirmative *Glamour* and its sisters *Cosmopolitan* and *Marie Claire* may be, *zaftig* is not a word one regularly finds in their pages. *Zaftig* (from the German for "juicy") is the closest term we have today to the somewhat outmoded, regionally nonspecific "buxom," denoting someone, or something, plump and well-rounded. ("*Zaftig* describes in one word what it takes two hands, outlining an hourglass figure, to do."[11]) The same word means provocative, seminal, germinal—"*zaftig* ideas." "Hourglass figure" is a term as much associated in this century with Mae West or Dolly Parton as with delectable Jewishness. (Does Elizabeth Taylor count as a Jew in this connection?) But if *zaftig* makes a comeback in the fashion world—and who can doubt that it will, sooner or later?—Monica Lewinsky will have played a role in its revival.

An odalisque is a female slave or concubine in an Eastern harem, so that the orientalism of "Jewish looks" here encompasses both Turkey and Israel, by way of Lord Byron and nineteenth-century French painting. The lush Jewish woman is sexual and sensual, but with a mind of her own. No sex slave ("unshackled"), she is free to enjoy her own pleasures.

On the other hand, the "book" on Jewish girls is that they are neurotic and even phobic about sex, and that—as Jackie Mason so delicately hinted—there are some things a "nice Jewish girl" just does not do. "My friend Riva is very upset," wrote humor columnist Anne Beatts in the *Los Angeles Times*. "'Monica Lewinsky crossed a line,' she says. 'This oral sex thing—everyone knows Jewish girls don't do that. Now she's ruined it for the rest of us.'" Beatts comments, "I happen to be Jewish, and I believe Riva is operating on a false assumption. But then again I'm only a convert, so maybe that rule was something they forgot to let me in on."[12] A *New York Times* article on television stereotypes of Jewish women—published the same week as Lewinsky's ABC interview with Barbara Walters but making no reference to her—was accompanied by a photo display that neatly summarized the issues: it read "Role Models: The Sexless (Bebe Neuwirth, 'Frasier'), the Dependent (Jennifer Aniston, 'Friends'), the Garish (Fran Drescher, 'The Nanny'), and the Intrusive (Cynthia Harris, 'Mad about You.')"[13] The article's headline offered three other categories for Jewish girls: Princesses, Punishers, and Prudes.

The paradox of the Jewish girl as temptress and siren, on the one hand, and marriage-minded upwardly mobile virgin on the other, is far older than the postwar cliché of the "Jewish American Princess," term whose disparaging acronym, JAP or Jap, indicates something of the same mechanism of displacement and abjection. "Jap" is an insult when applied to a person of Japanese origin. Applied to a Jewish American Princess, "a pampered and usually wealthy young woman who feels she deserves special treatment," it is just an affectionate little joke.

The Jewish American Princess Handbook (1982) includes a glossary of "Jewish jargon" that runs the gamut (not, incidentally, a Yiddish word) from "shagits" ("blond haired, blue eyed forbidden fruit who ends up marrying a shiksa") to "guilt" ("Jewish hereditary disease. Symptoms include a churning stomach and feelings of deep-seated anxiety. Highly contagious, especially when the Princess spends too much time in the company of her mother") and "money."[14] As Sander Gilman points out, "Such lists were standard in all of the anti-Semitic literature of the late nineteenth and early twentieth centuries."[15] At the beginning of the twenty-first century these terms mean differently—or do they? How much self-irony is protection enough for the minority group that coined the phrase "self-hatred"?

"The woman, the Jewish woman as JAP, has replaced the male Jew as the scapegoat," observes Evelyn Torton Beck, "and the Jewish male has not only participated, but has, in fact, been instrumental in creating and perpetuating that image." Beck rightly sees this as a mechanism of displacement.[16] "All the [fantasied] characteristics he cannot stand in himself are displaced onto the Jewish woman." The old slurs about Jews—that they are "materialistic, money-grabbing, greedy, and ostentatious," that they are "manipulative, crafty, untrustworthy, unreliable, calculating, controlling"—resurface in postwar fiction and popular culture as typical qualities of the Jewish American Princess.

Princess

> They could see she was a real princess and no question
> about it.
> —Hans Christian Andersen, *The Princess and the Pea*

In October 1997, according to what she told Andrew Morton, Monica Lewinsky and the president had a phone conversation in which "they started swapping dirty jokes—a Lewinsky specialty—mainly on a Jewish theme. One of Monica's ran, 'why do Jewish men like to watch porno films backwards? So that they can see the hooker give back the money.' The President responded in kind: 'What do you get when you cross a Jewish American Princess with an Apple? A computer that won't go down on you.'"[17]

So it seems that Jackie Mason was right in his estimate of the do's and don't's for nice Jewish girls. (Who guessed that Bill Clinton even knew the phrase "Jewish American Princess"?) Monica Lewinsky's story is certainly the tale of a princess. But which princess? There seemed to be several competing for the starring role.

There was, for example, the (non)-coincidence that the task of writing her biography was given to the same man who canonized Princess Diana, the thinnest and blondest of royals. "It is no accident," *New York Times* television critic Caryn James observed, "that Ms. Lewinsky's forthcoming book is called *Monica's Story* or that it is written by Andrew Morton, the author of the best-selling *Diana: Her True Story*, which so effectively spun the sympathetic image of an emotionally wounded Princess. (Not an easy sell when you think about it.)"[18]

Monica Lewinsky's videotaped testimony played before the U.S. Senate and the world elicited, perhaps predictably, its own set of stereotypes. "Wearing a sensible suit, pearls, heavy makeup and a semi-lacquered hairdo, Ms. Lewinsky was well-spoken, used no slang and showed only trace evidence of the Valley Girl of her taped phone conversations with Linda R. Tripp," said the front-page article in the *New York Times*. "Even her voice seemed different now, more modulated, less high-pitched and breathy." The *Times* suggested that Lewinsky, referred to "simply as Monica" by the House prosecutor throughout the deposition, seemed in "appearance, voice and vocabulary" to be "all grown up—and even a little bit hard."[19] Here the division between Valley Girl and JAP, or, we could say, between "Monica" and "Lewinsky," is making itself felt as a cultural divide. The "Jewess" of old, mature beyond her years, "businesslike," ironic, sexy, savvy, and sage (with too much makeup and a throaty voice), versus the young, vulnerable female "victim."

"'They make her seem like she's typical Beverly Hills,'" said a woman who works in a Rodeo Drive clothing store, reflecting on the Monica phenomenon, "'and in a lot of ways I'd have to say that's true. It's the whole rich, snobby thing, which is a stereotype but isn't really. I mean you can just spot them by their attitude.'"[20] *Them?* Californians? Rich people? Or . . . ?

"'You can see some life in her, a little snappy something,'" said a man in a health club watching Monica on CNN as he pedaled on his stationary bike, "'not a ditzy Californian as many people have made her out to be.'"[21] Other articles called attention to her "go-getter's quality" (read: pushy?) and cited her self-description as a "pest" in putting the pressure on Vernon Jordan to help her find a job.[22] (The president's secretary Betty Currie was also quoted as calling her "a little bit pushy" and a "pain in the neck."[23])

Reviewing Andrew Morton's book in the *New York Times*, Michiko Kakutani struck the same familiar chords, noting that "Mr. Morton tries to present Ms. Lewinsky in this book not as a ditsy Valley Girl or pushy tart but as a die-hard romantic who loves roses and shabby chic furniture."[24] So Monica was not California (ditzy) or New York (pushy) but, as Morton tried to tell her, much to the astonishment of many, "classic Boston."[25] The Boston mayor and the Boston media, none of whom had apparently ever heard of "shabby chic" (the title of a book and a design store) took offense at the "shabby," disavowed the "chic," and announced to Monica that she was not really their kind of girl.

But there was a Boston Jewish girl in the Monica story after all, as it turned out. Consider the following characterization, from a prominently placed media account: "Despite a popular stereotype as a spoilt Jewish-American princess, she emerged as a fiercely independent and driven young woman, determined to make her way in television, and attracted to power." She had become "a national celebrity."[26] The subject of this analysis was not Monica Lewinsky, but rather the woman she would choose, with uncanny aptness, as her television interviewer: Barbara Walters. And Walters, who emerged in the course of the interview both as Monica's unwitting double and as her clucking, affectionately reproving "mother," was born in Boston.

Barbara Walters, the daughter of Lou and Dena Selett (née Seletsky), lived as a child in Brookline, Massachusetts, and grew up in circumstances that alternated between wealth and poverty. She attended the Tony Fieldston and Birch Wathen schools, and graduated from Sarah Lawrence. Her father was an entertainment entrepreneur, the man who founded the Latin Quarter nightclub in New York. By the time she was eleven, he had bought her a mink coat. The family moved to a succession of penthouses, then lost all their money.

Like Monica, Barbara Walters says she and her mother were exceptionally close and that she felt more distant from her father. Like Monica, too, she is described as "insecure" and "peculiarly vulnerable" (the words are those of CBS's Mike Wallace).[27] And like Monica she enjoys confiding in her female friends. "She is," announced a celebrity profile interview in the *New York*

Times, "a woman's woman who loves the telephone and having lunch with the girls. Not least, she is an excellent gossip."[28]

In 1977 Walters arranged the first interview between Egypt's President Anwar Sadat and Israel's Prime Minister Menachem Begin. *Saturday Night Live's* Gilda Radner immortalized her as Baba Wawa, impersonating her speech, with its soft l's and r's that sound like w's. "This isn't journalism, this is a minstrel show," complained old-line TV journalist Fred Friendly. "Is Barbara a journalist or is she Cher?"[29] (If Barbara Walters was the media's Cher Sarkisian Bono Allman, was Monica Lewinsky its Cher Horowitz? Clued-in, or totally *clueless*?)

At a New York Friars Club dinner in 1994 Walters was saluted by her supposed archrival, now her *20/20* colleague, Diane Sawyer, who sang, to the tune of Judy Garland's "You Made Me Love You," a parody that contained the following lyrics:

> You made me ruthless.
> I didn't want to do it,
> Ambition drove me to it.
> You made me greedy.
> I couldn't bear that you net
> $3 million more than I get.
> Desperate to beat you,
> I thought I'd do what you do,
> I slept with Roone [ABC news chief
>   Roone Arledge] and Hugh [Downs], too,
> Scheming for interviews.

As the punch line of her song Sawyer wound up with this: "I even married a Jew—hoping to be more like you." The Jew Sawyer married was, as everyone knew, director Mike Nichols. Was the "more like you" line intended to refer to marriage (Walters has been married to three Jewish men, Robert Henry Katz, theatrical producer Lee Guber, and television executive Merv Adelson; in college she dated Roy Cohn) or identity?

Indeed, Walters had been the forerunner of Lewinsky in yet another way. Here is how she reported her encounter with President Lyndon Johnson when they met in the Oval Office. "Our conversation had been so disarmingly friendly that I felt courageous enough when it ended to say, 'Mr. President, do you suppose [I] can ask to kiss a president?...I've had such a splendid time, and I would like to kiss you on the cheek.'"[30] An early apostle of flirtation as a way of getting ahead ("My own opinion is that there is far too little flirtation in our country as it is,"[31] she wrote in a 1970 book), she had tempered her views, at least for public consumption, by the time she got Monica to describe flashing her thong underwear at the president as a "small, subtle, flirtatious gesture."

The Lewinsky-Walters television interview attracted some 48.5 million viewers, and many of those watching were impressed, but not all. "If I want to watch two princesses gossiping, I can stop in at Zabar's," complained Lucianne Goldberg, the literary agent who counseled Linda Tripp.[32] (Goldberg had a lot of attitude about Monica Lewinsky, and some of it was expressed in anti-princess mode. When a news wire service asked for predictions about Lewinsky's future—"What next for Monica?"—Goldberg suggested she should "go back to California and marry a Beverly Hills dentist 'with more gold chains than he can swim in.'"[33] She claims some expertise on the subject, having married a Jew; her husband Sidney runs a news syndication service, United Media. "I raised two Jewish kids—and, boy, do I understand the type."[34])

Bigmouth

> Pisk (Yiddish, from Polish: "mouth")
> 1. The mouth of an animal or human.
> 2. (Colloquialism). An eloquent or garrulous speaker.
> 3. A brusque slang word for "mouth," used in expressions such as "shut your trap."
> The diminutive, piskel or piskeleh, is often applied admiringly to a child who speaks precociously. "Does he have a piskeleh."
> —Leo Rosten, The Joys of Yiddish

"You told 10 other people you had this relationship with the president," Walters chided Lewinsky, almost affectionately, it seemed. "I mean, Bigmouth! Why did you want people to know?"[35] "Bigmouth!" seemed a curiously colloquial interjection from the usually more decorous Walters, but then of course Monica's big mouth was, in every sense, the real topic under discussion and on display.

My haircutter, a woman of excellent judgment and forward-looking politics, said she had watched the interview for only the last fifteen minutes or so, but long enough to see for herself what was hardly news: "She's so *oral*." The camera repeatedly sought out her mouth, and her exceedingly white and gleaming teeth. "What's with the Vaseline on her teeth?" asked Lucianne Goldberg. "Can we get a little closer to her mouth with the camera, please! They're gonna go down her throat any minute. Maybe we'll get to see her uvula!"[36]

The ABC website on the night of the interview logged more inquiries about Monica's shade of lipstick than about any other single matter. (It was Club Monaco's "Glaze," and—once the answer was revealed on ABC's *Good Morning America* by Charles Gibson and Diane Sawyer—the Internet obligingly listed major stores in New York and California where it might be found. "We went out to find a tube of this stuff, and it was sold out," said Gibson. "It was literally sold out everywhere in New York."[37]) What she had done with her mouth, and both with and to whom, was what the whole country wanted to know. Indeed the interest was not confined to the United States; a BBC broadcaster labeled her "Hot Lips," and described her appearance on Channel 4 as "pure televisual Viagra." Almost all women, he contended, "regard Lewinsky with tight-lipped distaste," while men have considerable affection "for louche ladies who hold out the prospect of uncomplicated oral sex."[38] The broadcaster was Charles Spencer, the brother of Princess Diana. "Bigmouth!" If it is not a translation from the Yiddish, perhaps it should be. For Jewish girls with big mouths are some of the ambivalent superstars of our culture.

As always seems to be the case with images of Jewishness, and especially of Jewish women, they cross boundaries: between homeliness and beauty; between Jewish mother and wayward daughter; between fat and thin; between proper and raucously improper.

Sophie Tucker, weighing in at two hundred pounds, became the red-hot *Yiddishe Mamme* with a patter that was both racy and sensual. As Eddie Cantor remarked, "Sophie's style and material are hardly what you'd want at a Holy Name breakfast.... She has no inhibitions.... She sings the words we used to write on the sidewalks of New York."[39] Belle Barth, the "doyenne of the dirty line," was another "pudgy Jewish woman" with an uninhibited approach to sexual comedy. ("Only two words you have to learn in the Yiddish language and that is *Gelt* (money) and *Schmuck* (penis). Because if a man has no..., he is a....."[40]) Comedienne Totie Fields (born Sophie Feldman) poked fun at her own size—she was 4'10" and weighed 190 pounds—and continued to joke

about it even after a long bout of phlebitis forced doctors to amputate her leg
and she dwindled to 120 pounds. Her particular "brand of prosthetic humor"
blended pathos with wisecracking.[41] These Jewish comediennes deliberately
distanced themselves from seductiveness, stressing their weight and their sexual misadventures as a way of seeking stage legitimacy.

Singer and entertainer Fanny Brice, later the subject of the musical *Funny
Girl*, came out of the same Jewish comic tradition (her original surname was
Borach), and her "Yiddish facial grimaces" were pictured in an early newspaper
spread. "Lips seemed to push and pull in different directions," wrote a recent
biographer. "The rubber-faced Brice for whom Protestant prettiness was clearly
unattainable was performing very much in the dialect comedy tradition."[42]
When she had a nose job in 1923 the event was headline news in the *New York
Times*: Fanny Brice "feels she has got all she can out of her nose and mouth and
wants new ones to fit her for the comedy roles to which she aspires."[43] Brice felt
that she was "too Jewish" for Hollywood. Dorothy Parker (born Rothschild,
the daughter of a garment manufacturer, and herself never happy about being
Jewish[44]) quipped acerbically that Brice had "cut off her nose to spite her
race."[45] The new nose—and expensively capped teeth—did not keep *Variety*
from speculating (accurately) that her "distinct Hebrew clowning"[46] made her
"too New York" to succeed in America's heartland.

But a direct descendant of these Jewish "funny women," Joan Rivers (born
Joan Molinsky and raised in Brooklyn) "defied the somatype," as Sarah Blacher
Cohen points out, becoming "not a caricature of a femme fatale, but a femme
fatale herself."[47] Rivers's signature "Can we talk?" defines her principal role as
yente or scandal-monger, dishing the dirt, at the same time that she developed
her antitype as "Heidi Abromowitz," a joyous sexual transgressor whose career
encompassed the stages of "Baby Bimbo," "Toddler Tramp," "Teen Tart," and
"Career Chippy"—all titles of chapters in Rivers's best-seller, *The Life and
Times of Heidi Abromowitz*.[48] Heidi, according to Rivers, "did things with her
pacifier that most women haven't done with their husbands."[49] Readers of the
Starr Report who noted Monica Lewinsky's inventiveness with a cigar might
find Heidi an enlightening guide.

And in the current generation of "big-mouthed" Jewish women entertain-
ers, sexuality is a clear asset, no longer in conflict with assimilation or acceptance. "This 43-year-old Jewish mother with the mouth that other mothers

might wash out with soap," is how the *New York Daily News* described wide-mouthed comedian Sandra Bernhard.[50] The *Los Angeles Times* led with the mouth in its own celebrity interview: "Sandra Bernhard, at 5-foot-10, looks like a slimmed-down Barbie with a mouth like an Edsel grill. It's a mouth that never stops as Bernhard tells erotic and neurotic jokes, discusses sexuality, [and] banters with the crowd.... At some point, she usually ends up standing around in her underwear."[51]

The big-mouthed Jewish diva is a staple of the musical stage, from Ethel Merman to Bette Midler to Barbra Streisand. "Barbra does this thing with her mouth. She pulls the top of her mouth over her teeth when she sings," says celebrity impersonator Eddie Edwards. "It's the smallest detail, but people will come and say, 'You captured that about her,'" he says, noting that he's also figured out how to tighten his throat muscles the way she does.[52] (Streisand is known for her wit as well as her chutzpah, cracking after the London opening of *Funny Girl* that if she'd been nicer to Prince Charles "I might have been the first real Jewish princess."[53])

Even in Lewinsky's own age cohort the Jewish mouth does double duty. "Alicia Silverstone's pouty mouth and slouchy poses make her the girl Hollywood is most eager to corrupt today," announced the *Boston Herald* in a feature piece about the actress who starred as Cher Horowitz, the Jewish American Princess of Beverly Hills, in the hit film *Clueless*. Silverstone (like Monica Lewinsky) "actually attended Beverly Hills High School, but far from being the Coolest Chick on Campus, she recalls: 'I didn't have the right clothes. I was a misfit.'"[54] "Silverstone's mouth is a wavy wet line that wriggled when she talks," declared a feature piece in the *Guardian*. The *Guardian*, in fact, seemed fascinated with her mouth: we read that in her next film, *Excessive Baggage*, male lead Benicio Del Toro "thrust[s] his fingers in Silverstone's mouth to retrieve the car keys she's hiding." (Says Silverstone, "when he's got his hand down her throat, that's a love scene," explaining why she is not interested in doing conventional sex "stuff" on camera. Asked what she means, she "spreads her legs and lets her eyelids flop and her mouth slacken."[56]) In *Clueless* her character offered the following seduction advice: "Anything you can do to call attention to your mouth is good."

Is it necessary here to underscore the connection between sexy, provocative, "smart-talking," Jewish women and "big-mouthed" sex?

Sex and the Jewish Girl

'Is she also a typical Rumanian beauty?'
'I think...she is a typical little Jewess.'
—John Updike, *Bech: A Book*

The story of the dangerously seductive Jewess is, of course, a very old story in Europe, and is often linked with the stage.

The mother of the French actress Sarah Bernhardt was a courtesan, whose Jewishness "did nothing to hinder her career. On the contrary, it was a promise of carnal pleasure in a city where every self-respecting bordello offered at least one Jewish girl and one black girl for connoisseurs of exotica."[56] Bernhardt herself, the model for the actress La Berma in Marcel Proust's *A la recherche du temps perdu*, had numerous affairs with rich and titled men, and was the object of anti-Semitic caricatures and allegations about her "vile Jewish habits" throughout her life.[57] (Unlike the weight-obsessed Monica, Sarah was preternaturally thin—and equally unfashionable in her time for being so.)

Bernhardt's predecessor on the French stage, sometimes credited as the first stage actress to achieve "international stardom," was Rachel (Elisa) Félix, a celebrity so well known that she did not use her last name, but became simply Rachel. (Félix, a translation of the Hebrew *Baruch*, or blessed, was a common Jewish name.) The daughter of poor Jewish peddlers, with an ambitious stage father much ridiculed in the press (Heinrich Heine wrote that "Père Rachel preens himself with the success of his daughter"[58]), Rachel became the "Jewish queen of tragedy," inspiring characters in novels by Benjamin Disraeli and George Eliot; her "reputation for taking and dismissing men at her pleasure made her a formidable image of sexual voracity."[59] Other Jewish actresses at the time—Mlle. Judith, Mlle. Nathalie—likewise doffed their *prénoms*, or (what are sometimes called in English) "Christian names." Rachel became *la grande Rachel*. Rachel's looks were unconventional for beauty; she was small and dark, with a large head and deep-set eyes.

In fact the sultry "Jewess," a first-order cultural fantasy, became, in part through the agency of fiction and the theater, the very type of sexual desire. Significantly, in literature as in life, she is often paired or partnered by her father, who serves as a foil.

The seductive beauty of Jewish daughters in two famous Elizabethan plays, *The Merchant of Venice* and *The Jew of Malta*, is, essentially, taken for granted; it is not a surprise that young gentile men fall in love with them, despite the fact that these same young men detest and revile their fathers, Shylock and Barabas. In Christopher Marlowe's *Jew of Malta*, Mathias, "a young gentleman," and Lodowick, the governor's son, rhapsodize about "fair Abigail, the rich Jew's daughter."[60] Using his daughter as bait, Barabas, the Jew of the title, schemes to entrap them both, and the hapless Abigail, who loves Don Mathias, sees her two suitors slaughter each other for her sake.

In Sir Walter Scott's *Ivanhoe* (1819), Rebecca the Jewess, the daughter of the wealthy Isaac of York, is a woman of far more character and charm than her Saxon counterpart, Rowena. When Ivanhoe chooses Rowena, Isaac and Rebecca leave England for the Continent. Honoré de Balzac's *Le Cousin Pons* (1847) describes yet another father-daughter pair, the daughter "a beautiful girl, like all Jewesses who incarnate the Asian type in all its purity and nobility."[61]

But of course the paradigm case for the Monica story is a much earlier instance, the story of Queen Esther—a story newly made popular in twentieth-century France through Marcel Proust's repeated citation of Jean Racine's *Esther* in *A la recherche du temps perdu*. "Even today," literary critic Eve Kosofsky Sedgwick wrote in 1990, "Jewish little girls are educated in gender roles—fondness for being looked at, fearlessness in defense of 'their people,' nonsolidarity with their sex—through masquerading as Queen Esther at Purim; I have a snapshot of myself at about five, barefoot in the pretty 'Queen Esther' dress my grandmother made [white satin, gold spangles], making a careful eyes-down toe-pointed curtsey at [presumably] my father, who is manifest in the picture only as the flashgun that hurls my shadow, pillaring up tall and black, over the dwarfed sofa onto the wall behind me."[62] Sedgwick and I are roughly of the same (Long Island) generation, and my mother sewed for me a costume that sounds very like hers. Without question Esther was a heroine and role model as well as a leading costume part to the junior Jewish set. And the plot of the book of Esther is a story of palace intrigue.

Esther, the beautiful ward of her uncle Mordecai (the "father figure" of the story), is brought by him to the palace of King Ahasuerus. Ahasuerus, displeased with his wife, Queen Vashti, who had disobeyed his order that she display her beauty before his courtiers, divorces Vashti and chooses Esther as queen in her stead, selecting her from the "many maidens" who are brought to the king's palace at his decree. Esther, on Mordecai's advice, conceals her Jewishness from the king until a crisis arises: Haman, a court favorite and an enemy to the Jews, had conceived a plot to kill them. Esther reveals her true identity to the king, pleads eloquently on behalf of the Jews, and secures not only their rescue but preferment for Mordecai, who had once saved the king from assassins.

It is quite true, as Sedgwick notes, that one of the secondary lessons of this story for Jewish girls in the 1950s was that the "proud" Vashti, who disobeyed her husband, deserved what she got. I do not remember any discussion of what it meant for her to refuse to "shew the people and the princes her beauty, for she was fair to look on" (Esther 1.11). The Book of Esther is quite clear on the political consequences: "For this deed of the queen shall come abroad unto all women, so that they shall despise their husbands in their eyes, when it shall be reported, the King Ahasuerus commanded Vashti the queen to be brought in before him, but she came not" (1.17). So far were we from seeing this as a laudable act of feminist self-assertion, I think we saw it instead as an intergenerational rivalry: the "bad" queen, a mother figure like all queens, was banished and replaced by a "maiden," a "young virgin"—one of us. No wonder Sedgwick is flirting with her father and his camera. This is the story of the young girl who gets the king.

And the king, in this case, is—*o tempora, o mores*—Bill Clinton. The play casts itself: Hillary is Vashti, the headstrong proto-feminist queen, feasting on that occasion with the women in the royal house, unwilling to drop everything to display herself for his friends. And Monica, it is needless to say, is Esther, the beautiful Jewess.

The Israeli right wing saw the connection right away, calling Lewinsky a modern-day Esther. "Like Esther," according to this analogy, "Monica allegedly slept with the head of state at a time when the people of Israel were in grave peril. And like Esther, her intervention has averted a danger—the likelihood of President Clinton embarking on a personal Middle East peace initiative," forcing the man who was then Isreal's prime minister, Benjamin Netanyahu, to give up more West Bank land to the Palestinians.[63]

But the political message might as easily be read the other way. The nineteenth-century Austrian playwright Franz Grillparzer wrote a tragedy, complete but unpublished at his death, called *The Jewess of Toledo* (1855). In it a king falls passionately in love with a young Jewess, and only regains his sense of responsibility to his country after she is killed at the queen's command.

Next Year in Jerusalem?

> And why should you plead for them, Jewess?
> —Eugene O'Neill, *Lazarus Laughed*

"The Palestinian Authority can be forgiven for thinking that Monica Lewinsky was a Mossad plant (though I personally doubt they would have chosen anyone with such an obviously Jewish name),"[64] wrote a reporter for the *Jerusalem Post*.

Was Monica a spy? A number of people seemed to think so. Nation of Islam leader Louis Farrakhan appeared on NBC's *Meet the Press* and declared that Monica Lewinsky might be part of a Zionist plot to undermine the Mideast peace negotiations.[65] A popular Chinese magazine proposed, in a plot not unlike that of *The Manchurian Candidate*, that Lewinsky had been sent to Washington when she was a child as a Cold War agent on a mission to entrap the president and destabilize the government. "Is Lewinsky with the KGB?" inquired the headline. "Information has exposed Monica Lewinsky as a spy assigned to the former Soviet Union. Her mission was to drag a U.S. President through the mud!"[66]

Meantime the Syrian defense minister, too, announced that the affair was a Zionist plot. "Monica Lewinsky is a young Jewish girl that Mossad hired and pushed into working as an intern in the White House." Since it was a "Jewish lawyer who disclosed the scandal to Ken Starr," said General Mustapha Tlass to the United Arab Emirates' *Al-Khaleej* newspaper, "all this definitely proves that worldwide Zionism and particularly American Jews" are working for Israel. "President Clinton has said it is a conspiracy but unfortunately he did not say by whom."[67] A Syrian newspaper declared that "Netanyahu stands behind the Lewinsky affair."[68] Palestinian commentators noted that many of the principals in the scandal were Jewish: not only Monica Lewinsky, but also

lawyer William Ginsburg and literary agent Lucianne Goldberg, who persuaded Linda Tripp to do the taping. The fact that Vice President Al Gore had
been favorably inclined toward Likud, Netanyahu's party, led some to think
that the impeachment of Clinton would benefit the Israeli hardliners—another
clear sign of conspiracy.

Other biblical analogies were also possible, of course: Monica could be
seen as "a careerist Delilah."[69] A Los Angeles rabbi drew an analogy between
the Clinton-Lewinsky liaison and the story of David and Bathsheba, citing a fifteenth-century Spanish philosopher who had said, "David sinned as a man and
not as a king."[70]

An article in the *Jerusalem Post* took what might seem to be an unusual
tack: it lamented the fact that American Jewry had become so assimilated that
the Lewinskys preferred to send their child to Washington rather than to
Israel. "Given the choice, how many Jewish parents in America would opt for
an internship in the White House for their child rather than a scholarship from
the Hebrew University?" The writer, a former director general of the Israeli
prime minister's office, said, "It seems to me that the behavior and norms that
motivated Monica Lewinsky and her family, which emerged from her detailed
testimony before the Starr commission, were entirely, if not typically,
American."[71] "Israel has never really forgiven Monica Lewinsky," observed a
commentator in the *London Guardian*. "The Jewish heroine of the Washington
potboiler had once promised to flee to Israel if the pressures of fame became
too great in Washington."[72] But other Israelis were wary of both ethnic and
national stereotyping. A correspondent to the *Jerusalem Post* was dismayed at a
columnist's description of Lewinsky as "the Jewish American Princess who
allegedly made it with the president," calling this a "denigrating description"
used almost exclusively by "self-hating" Jews.[73]

Meanwhile, at home in the United States, some Jews felt protective, and
others vulnerable. After the scandal hit, Bernard Lewinsky "had to listen in
helpless, silent indignation as local Orthodox Jewish elders discussed the possibility of using religious law to cast Monica out from the faith," reports
Andrew Morton.[74] The Lewinsky family rabbi, David Wolpe of the
Conservative Sinai Temple in Los Angeles, told his congregation a story about
his nine-year-old niece, who had blurted out that she never wanted to be of
President Clinton's religion. Wolpe, the author of *Teaching Your Children about*

God, Why Be Jewish? and *The Healer of Shattered Hearts*, said of the president, "He was a brilliant, talented, extraordinary child, and for the leader of the United States we need an adult."[75] Two former congregants now residing in Israel promptly wrote to reprove the rabbi for meddling in the moral instruction of a Southern Baptist, and urging him to look closer to home. "Monica Lewinsky attended Temple Sinai's religious school. Perhaps Rabbi Wolpe should review the school's curriculum to learn whether it includes lessons on proper behavior, including feminine modesty, by the Temple's boys and girls."[76] Another Israeli reader chimed in to say, "My nine-year-old daughter says she never wants to be the same religion as that of Monica—Conservative Jewish. With a student like Monica coming from his synagogue's religious school, it would be wise for the rabbi to examine exactly what is and is not being taught there."[77]

Although it was never mentioned specifically by the mainstream media in the United States, Lewinsky's religious affiliation had, perhaps inevitably, some effect upon political oratory and public discourse. Gary Ackerman, a Democratic congressman from Queens who is himself Jewish, declared that it was "unsavory" and an "outrage" for the House of Representatives to release a videotape and documents of Bill Clinton's testimony in the Monica Lewinsky scandal on Rosh Hashanah. The item was reported in the *New York Post* and (once again) picked up by the *Jerusalem Post* (no relation to the New York paper). Non-Jewish U.S. congressmen representing largely Jewish districts reported the same concern: "I have heard from scores of constituents who are outraged that the testimony would be released during one of the holiest days in the Jewish calendar," wrote Representative Carolyn McCarthy to the House Judiciary Committee. Neither Ackerman nor McCarthy alluded to Monica's religion, though some implication of a connection seemed possible. Would it have been equally outrageous to Jewish sensibilities if the testimony, with its "sexually graphic details," had been that of Paula Jones or Kathleen Willey? Perhaps; but the unwelcome—and unstated—fact that the woman testifying was Jewish must have added to the cultural embarrassment of the occasion. Six of the fifteen Democrats on the House Judiciary Committee were Jewish. None of the Republicans was. "Jews Rip Rosh Hashanah Tape Release," said the New York *Daily News* breezily. Again there was no mention of Monica, just of the holiness of the holiday and the inappropriateness of releasing sexually explicit materials on a day of prayer and reflection. But Abraham Foxman, director of the Anti-Defamation League, had another view, observing that the material didn't pertain to the Jewish community. Monica's Jewishness was not, for him, part of the scandal or the story. And Rabbi Ismar Schorsch, chancellor of the Jewish Theological Seminary, saw a silver lining, noting that observant Jews would not see the tape until after the holiday: "our level of discourse will remain elevated a bit longer than the rest of America," he said.[78]

Meanwhile, Bill Clinton read a passage on repentance from the Yom Kippur liturgy at a White House prayer breakfast of 150 clergymen. It had, he said, been recommended by a Jewish friend.[79]

Prostheses

> Cleopatra's nose, had it been shorter, the whole
> face of the world had been changed.
> —Blaise Pascal, *Pensées*

The Jewish temptress theme had a number of fascinatingly displaced effects in the playing out of the Clinton sex scandals. I wonder, for example, if it occurred to anyone to note that it was Paula Jones, Clinton's undeniably non-Jewish alleged playmate, who underwent a highly publicized, and publicly ridiculed, nose job. For rhinoplasty is a time-honored puberty ritual of American middle-class Jewish girls.

Jones's plastic surgeon—paid, incidentally, by an anonymous donor, and not by Jones herself—was the same man who had performed surgery on Michael Jackson and Barbra Streisand.[80] And her new nose was unveiled, like Monica Lewinsky, on ABC television, and in the midst of the Lewinsky scandal, as if it were a new bid for the public's attention. Fantastically—and fantasmatically—it was as if Paula Jones had had to reenact one of the secular rites of passage of surburban Jewish culture in order to rival Monica Lewinsky for the fickle attention of press and public.

The history of cosmetic rhinoplasty begins at the turn of the last century, with an operation performed by Jacques Joseph in 1898 on a male patient, thereby inaugurating what Sander Gilman calls "the craze for nose jobs in fin-de-siècle Germany and Austria."[81] "Joseph was very charitable," said a woman who benefited from his work in the early thirties, "and when he felt that someone suffered from 'a Jewish nose' he would operate for nothing."[82] "Suffering" from a Jewish nose was of course a self-fulfilling diagnosis.

Joseph, a German Jew who had changed his first name from Jakob when he undertook his medical training, died in 1934 before the full scenario of Nazi anti-Semitism and genocide had unfolded, but his procedure, an instrument for cultural invisibility and passing, became itself a rite of passage among many postwar American Jews. The objective was not so much the obliteration of a cultural heritage—most of those who changed their noses did not also change their names—but a kind of aesthetics of passing, assimilating Jewish looks into the WASP mainstream. The nose job, or nose bob, became a signifying tradition of a certain subset of suburban Jewishness. Once a sign of (attempted) invisibility, the rhinoplasty had become a triumphantly, if somewhat paradoxically, visible sign: a sign of parental ambition for their children, a sign of the endorsement of "universal" concepts of beauty, a sign of affluence and of materiality. And although the first clients for this treatment in German and Austria were men, the preponderance of mid-twentieth-century new noses went to women. In the 1960s and '70s the nose of choice was the "button," which went out in the early eighties in favor of a more "natural" look.

It is ironic that Paula Jones, an Arkansas native with no links to Jewish culture, felt that her nose job itself was both desirable and forbidden. "I have enough people screaming at me, talking about my new nose," Jones told *Inside Edition's* Deborah Norville. "Everybody else has plastic surgery, and has noses done...but I don't have a right, I'm not pretty enough."[83] *Los Angeles Times* television critic Howard Rosenberg took note of the general risibility in the media (and on late-night talk shows) about Jones's nose, writing,

> Noses having been used historically to demean Arabs and especially Jews with Hitler's Third Reich and the old Soviet Union using such caricatures to dehumanize and isolate an entire people. In the German weekly Der Stuermer from the 1930s, for example, you find ugly cartoon after cartoon of Jews depicted as the enemies of humanity, their most prominent feature being beak-like noses that droop almost to their thick lips.
>
> In my case, I recall vividly how some of the older kids in my elementary school would stroke their noses when the passed me in the halls, just because a guy named Rosenberg was obviously Jewish.
>
> I was Jewish trash; Jones is trailer trash—making us both fair game in our respective generations.

It's a stigma she may never outlive, no matter how many times she tries to rein-vent herself. And this new nose business is just another reminder, just as some of its coverage brings to mind the ever-closer ties between mainstream media and tabloids.[84]

Jones was neither a WASP (like Norville?) nor a JAP (like Monica); in the shifting hierarchy of entitlements, her nose was news.

The uncanny displacement of the "nose job" story from the Jewish Monica Lewinsky to the gentile Paula Jones was, I want to suggest, part of a larger mechanism of displacement in the U.S. media, which regularly shied away from any direct acknowledgment of Lewinsky's Jewishness. Although Britain's Jon Snow could elicit from her a televised declaration that she feels "being Jewish is my culture and my heritage," and that her grandparents' experiences in the Holocaust "have instilled in me a sense of courage,"[85] neither Barbara Walters nor any other U.S. commentator went near the topic. The "Jewish American Princess" label was occasionally trotted out by print journalists, but again it was often displaced onto other—non-American—speakers or thinkers, like biographer Andrew Morton (from a Montreal review: "Very early on, Morton identifies what he calls Lewinsky's 'high sense of entitlement,' a rather elegant euphemism for Beverly Hills brat, or Jewish American princess"[86]) or young Arab onlookers at a London book signing ("To these boys she was a spoiled Jewish American Princess, a hate figure, and they didn't bother to hide their contempt."[87]).

"The nice Jewish girl from Beverly Hills whose lips launched a thousand quips,"[88] said the *Irish Times*. Notice again that the overseas press, favorable or unfavorable, was far less skittish than the American media at mentioning the obvious. Which was *not*, in this case, "as plain as the nose on her face." But which was quite clearly declared—if you knew enough to see it—in her name.

Monikers

Their vicinitie, and mutual entercourses, made
the Jews passe under their neighbors names.
—Theophilus Gale, *The Court of the Gentiles*

Lauren Bacall was born Betty Joan Perske, in Brooklyn.
Paulette Goddard was born Marion Levy.
Judy Holliday was born Judy Tuvim.
Shelley Winters was born Shirley Shrift.
Barbara Hershey was born Barbara Hertzstein.
Barbara Walters was born Barbara Walters.
Whoopi Goldberg was born Caryn Elaine Johnson.

This list of stage names or pseudonyms seems harmless enough in the present day, a mere reminder of another prosthetic performance of assimilated Jewishness, like the nose job. And indeed the name, like the nose, was sometimes merely bobbed, or shortened, or in some cases translated, to make it fit into mainstream American culture. Asa Yoelson became Al Jolson; Issur Danielovitch, the son of a Russian Jewish immigrant ragman, became Kirk Douglas; Eddie Cantor, taken through immigration by his grandmother— whose surname was Kantorowitz—was given, by bureaucratic fiat, an abbreviated version of her name. A typical narrative is that of novelist Irving Wallace: "Born the son of Jewish parents who emigrated from Russia as teen-agers and met and married in the United States, his real name should have been Irving Wallechinsky. But an Ellis Island immigration officer shortened the name. (Years later when Irving's son, David, heard the story, he changed his name to Wallechinsky.)"[89]

To change your name, or to have "had it changed at Ellis Island," as family lore sometimes reported (thus rendering the name change not an act of voluntary cultural disavowal or erasure but a timely accident of fate), was just another step in becoming American. Or so Jews might have thought, until the days of the House Un-American Activities Committee and the Hollywood blacklist. Then, suddenly, a changed name was a deception, a lie, perhaps even a treasonous act. Senator John Rankin of Mississippi, a member of the committee, named Jewish names on November 24, 1947. The performers he singled out were all signers of a petition protesting limits to the right of free association:

One of the names is June Havoc. We found out from the motion-picture almanac that her real name is June Hovick.

Another one was Danny Kaye, and we found out that his real name was David Daniel Kaminsky.

Another one is Eddie Cantor, whose real name is Edward Iskowitz.

There is one who calls himself Edward Robinson. His real name is Emmanuel Goldenberg.

There is another one here who calls himself Melvyn Douglas, whose real name is Melvyn Hesselberg.[90]

The revelation or unmasking of the "real name" made the "stage name" false, an apparently deliberate deception, a potentially criminal attempt to pass. To pass, that is, as *not* a Jew; to pass, instead, as an American. It was unimaginable, in those days, that a non-Jewish performer might someday *choose* a Jewish name, like Whoopi Goldberg—or that a popular blond television character might bear a name that is soul sister to Whoopi's—"Dharma Finkelstein."

"I bet you don't even remember my name," an "insecure" Monica is believed to have said to President Clinton two days after their first sexual encounter, "to which he answered," according to Andrew Morton, "'What kind of a name is Lewinsky, anyway?' 'Jewish' was her immediate riposte."[91] Leaving aside whether this qualifies as a "riposte," it is of some interest to note that to Bill Clinton of Arkansas, Yale and Oxford, "Lewinsky" was not a clear and overt signifier of Jewish identity.

If there was anyone (else) in America who had somehow remained unaware of the fact that Lewinsky was a Jewish name, enlightenment came quickly within the pages of *Monica's Story*. In a chapter called "My Little Farfel" (Bernard Lewinsky's baby name for his daughter, from the German/Yiddish word for "noodle") the reader learns about her father's family's flight from the growing power of the Nazis in the Germany of the 1920s, and her mother's father's flight from Lithuania during the Stalinist purges of the 1930s. Marcia Vilensky married Bernard Lewinsky in 1969, the family moved to Los Angeles in 1976, and the young Monica, "a bright, lively Jewish girl," began attending the academically and socially prominent John Thomas Dye School in Bel Air, characterized by Morton as "a quintessential example of WASP culture."[92] We read of Monica's resistance to the strict Sinai Temple (she "wanted to attend a less orthodox synagogue with her schoolfriends"[93]) and her desire for a fancy Bat Mitzvah party ("it is customary in Beverly Hills for Jewish children to have very elaborate Bar/Bat-Mitzvah parties at the age of thirteen, usually held in a ballroom or the reception room of the temple with friends and parents' friends: 'like a wedding for one,' recalls Monica"[94]).

Morton assures the reader that Marcia Lewis was a "pen name," adopted when Monica's mother began to write a monthly column for the *Hollywood Reporter*. The clear implication is that she had not adopted a new name, or disguised her Jewishness, for anything other than professional reasons. (The implication *behind* the implication was that "passing" for personal reasons—or separating herself from her husband's obviously Jewish name—would have been less admirable or understandable.) In the midst of the impeachment hearings, one Hollywood journalist wondered in print whether Lewis would have thought twice about changing her name if she had known her daughter was going to be so famous.[95]

Yet it is the first name, as well as the last, that has become famous. Note that Morton's book was called, simply, *Monica's Story*. The first name, standing alone, reinforced the analogy with that other princess, Di, but it also signaled fame pure and simple. Her "Lewinsky," we might say, was in rhetorical terms "understood," just as her Jewishness, so readable if you had the clues, was, in the lexicon of poststructuralism, "under erasure." *Monica*, say the baby-name books, is a name of uncertain origin. It has been linked to words meaning "alone" (from Greek *monos*), "adviser," "pure," and "nun"—all, inevitably, telling and even comical associations in the present case. *Monica* is also a variant spelling for *moniker*[96]—which is how Lewinsky's first name would have been pronounced in the Long Island neighborhoods of my youth, or indeed in some districts of present-day Boston. During the course of the scandal, Monica's "monica" became itself a powerful signifier. Like the Valley-speak terms in *Clueless*, a "Betty" and a "Baldwin" (denoting a sexy, attractive woman or man), a "Monica" appeared to the media to be a type as well as a person. Her Jewishness—so readable to the rest of the world, and to American Jews—would, as we have seen, render her (for history does indeed repeat itself as farce) a suspect for both heroism and treason.

But to Bill Clinton she was an exotic. "What kind of a name is Lewinsky?" he wanted to know. The cluelessness of Bill Clinton, surrounded as he was by numerous male Jewish advisers (Sidney Blumenthal, Robert Rubin, Alan

Greenspan, Samuel Berger, James Rubin) may stand as our final, Ahashueran, symptom. Clinton, a relatively sophisticated man who knew not only Jews but Jewish jokes, looked at Monica Lewinsky and both saw and failed to see. His relationship with her, retold by the press and the special prosecutor, re-created the stereotype it did not name ("pushy," "ambitious," "seductive") and dispersed it to the diaspora and to the world.

MacGuffin
Shakespeare

> I had my father's signet in my purse,
> Which was the model of that Danish seal,
> Folded the writ up in the form of th'other,
> Subscrib'd it, gav't th' impression, plac'd it safely,
> The changeling never known.
>
>   —*Hamlet* 5.2.49–53

> "But what purpose had you," I asked, "in replacing the letter by a *fascimile*? Would it not have been better, at the first visit, to have seized it openly, and departed?"
>
>   —Edgar Allan Poe, "The Purloined Letter"

Recent Shakespearean scholarship has been much preoccupied with the fascinating business of editing. Once famously dismissed by Alexander Pope, the "dull duty of an editor" has become among the liveliest scenes in early modern studies, bringing together a social and material interest in what is called "print culture" (from printing houses to title pages to the London book trade) and the history of the book, with a persistent interest in "textuality," the language of the plays. New or renewed emphasis has been placed upon collaboration in writing and staging, and on the role of the theatrical company and the audience in shaping and reshaping play texts.

I am not an editor, nor was meant to be. Although I have learned enormously from these recent explorations, what I want to focus on here is a
slightly different phenomenon: the production, from within Shakespeare studies itself, of textual problems—problems about ambiguities of sense and
meaning—that are generated by the ingenious speculation of editors and critics; the production, in other words, of what might be called ghosts in the
machine. Editors from the eighteenth century on have called this "conjectural
criticism" or "conjectural emendation." I am going to call it—for reasons I will
explain in a moment—"MacGuffin Shakespeare."

I

In his response to Pope's "dull duty" phrase, already notorious in the eighteenth century, Samuel Johnson had offered an amplification and a correction.
Pope, he suggested, "understood but half his undertaking." He wrote,

> The duty of a collator is indeed dull, yet, like other tedious tasks, is very necessary;
> but an emendatory critic would ill discharge his duty, without qualities very differ-
> ent from dullness.... Out of many readings possible, he must be able to select that
> which best suits with the state, opinion, and modes of language prevailing in every
> age, and with his author's particular cast of thought, and turn of expression. Such
> must be his knowledge, and such his taste. Conjectural criticism demands more
> than humanity possesses, and he that exercises it with most praise has very frequent
> need of indulgence. Let us now be told no more of the dull duty of an editor.[1]

Johnson had a good deal to say about "conjectural criticism," which he found
both daunting and unavoidable: "The collator's province is safe and easy, the
conjecturer's perilous and difficult"; "As I practiced conjecture more, I learned
to trust it less"; "Conjecture has all the joy and all the pride of invention, and
he that has once started a happy change, is too much delighted to consider
what objections may rise against it"; "Yet conjectural criticism has been of
great use in the learned world; nor is it my intention to depreciate a study, that
has exercised so many mighty minds."[2]

Many of the mighty minds of recent years have spoken out against conjectural criticism, or at least against the kind of conjectural emendation that alters
and "improves" the language of the plays, urging instead the "unediting" of

William Shakespeare's texts. Nor is this resistance—or rather, this impulse to leave things alone—a concept of modern manufacture. Almost a century and a half ago, C. M. Ingleby warned against "a destruction now in progress . . . latent, insidious, slow, and sure," in the "constant and unstaying process of supplantation and substitution" that had overtaken the editing of the plays, the "innocent-looking little modifications which we now introduce into Shakespeare on the plea of textual misprinting will sooner or later themselves require modernizing." For Ingleby the saving technology was photography, which had enabled the "multiplication of copies" from the folio of 1623, and thus preserved the text against well-meaning learned corruption.[3] Later critics would praise their own technological advances, from collating machines to digitization.

Yet a relatively short time ago a textual scholar like Fredson Bowers could defend, with pleasure and excitement, the uses of conjecture—at least in the past. Bowers and his fellow "new bibliographers" had set as their goal the rediscovery of the original, or rather, the ideal of that original, dedicating their labors "to approach as nearly as may be to the ideal of the authorial fair copy by whatever necessary process of recovery, independent emendation, or conflation of the authorities."[4] This process was especially exciting, it is fair to say, when the author to be approached and summoned from the past was William Shakespeare. "Sometimes an inspired guess gives us with absolute conviction of rightness what Shakespeare must have written, even though we rely on faith and not on concrete evidence," writes Bowers. He points to "the old critic Theobald" and his emendation of the "nonsense" phrase "A Table of green fields," in the story of Falstaff's death in *Henry V*, to "a babbl'd of green fields." Here, says Bowers, Theobald had "what was surely a real meeting of minds with Shakespeare."[5]

"Admittedly, if we follow one editor's version of *Hamlet* rather than another's, we shall not discover Claudius emerging as the hero, nor will Hamlet suddenly be exposed as a woman in disguise." So says Bowers, setting aside what he jovially calls "these scary possibilities" for the relative comfort zone of editorial decision making: "whether Hamlet's father's bones were *interred* or *enurned*; whether the *safety*, *sanity*, or the *sanctity* of the Danish state is involved; or indeed, whether Hamlet's flesh, he regrets, is *too*, *too solid* or *too*, *too sullied*."[6] The folly of such a view must be much on Bowers's mind, since he repeats it later in the same book: "No blinding new revelations about plot or character are to be anticipated [by advances in editing techniques]. Hamlet will not be revealed as a woman in disguise, nor will Lear save Cordelia from hanging."[7] Some of the "scary possibilities" Bowers discounts—Claudius as hero, Hamlet as woman—have in fact been urged by one or another critic over the years, from E. P. Vining's *The Mystery of Hamlet* to John Updike's *Gertrude and Claudius*. But Bowers is concerned to decide "what Shakespeare must have written."

I want to turn our attention, for a moment, away from *what Shakespeare wrote*, and toward the dangerous pleasures of conjecture on the part of editors, readers, and stagers of the Shakespearean text. I am interested, in particular, in textual problems and traces that have been brought to light, and to life, by the exertions of editors and lay scholars, and that remain, like unlaid ghosts, hovering about the page and the stage. This is what I call "MacGuffin Shakespeare."

II

Mac means "son of" in Gaelic, and these spinoff problems—which have engaged some of the finest minds in the field—are in a sense sons of, or offspring of, or artifacts of, the critical and editorial process. Many of them derive from a certain fantasy of what Shakespeare was like, or what he had in mind, or what his characters have in mind. For as will quickly become clear, the quest for what Shakespeare wrote, and even more tellingly, for a real "meeting of minds" with Shakespeare, always returns, even if the editorial permutations have led us, apparently, far afield.

I take the term "MacGuffin," of course, from the film director Alfred Hitchcock. The MacGuffin (also spelled McGuffin and Maguffin) was Alfred Hitchcock's term for the missing thing that everybody wants, the "plot pretext,"[8] the "deliberately mysterious plot objective—the non-point."[9] The secret plans, the radioactive isotope, the photographic negatives, the cipher or code: Uranium 235 in Hitchcock's thriller *Notorious*; the "project" in David Mamet's *Spanish Prisoner*; the "proof" in playwright David Auburn's recent play of that name—a play that the author said could have taken off from "any number of Maguffins."[10]

The founding narrative for the term, its supposed source, is an anecdote told by Hitchcock's old friend the film editor Angus MacPhail. Two men were traveling to Scotland on a train from London, when one of them noticed that the other had an odd looking parcel stowed in the luggage rack.

> "What have you there?" asked one of the men.
> "Oh, that's a MacGuffin," replied his companion.
> "What's a MacGuffin?"
> "It's a device for trapping lions in the Scottish Highlands!"
> "But there aren't any lions in the Scottish Highlands!"
> "Well, then, I guess that's no MacGuffin!"

This is a famous story, frequently retold, and the "moral" seems to vary with the teller. Hitchcock's biographer Donald Spoto writes that "the point is that a McGuffin is neither relevant, important, nor, finally, any of one's business. It simply gets the story going."[11] Thus, for example, in Hitchcock's film *The Thirty-Nine Steps*, the MacGuffin is a set of top-secret plans. But, as Spoto writes, "it is to *prevent* the secret from being known—rather than to reveal it—that the adventure-chase is precipitated; thus the formula, which at first seems crucial, is immediately reduced in significance."[12]

Hitchcock himself was constantly asked—by journalists, film students, colleagues, and biographers—to describe his concept (in one interview he called it simply "my own term for the key element in any suspense story"[13]) and, inevitably, the MacGuffin became itself a MacGuffin, its meaning endlessly pursued, and always just out of reach.

Literary critics will immediately spot the similarity to Edgar Allan Poe's "Purloined Letter." In his essay on Poe's famous story, Jacques Lacan notes that it is a "signifier nothing but whose obverse anyone except the Queen has been able to read." Furthermore, the letter is "destined by nature to signify the annulment of what it signifies."[14] The letter's contents are kept from the reader; we guess at its import and purport by the effects it has on characters in the story.

It is not surprising, then, to find the MacGuffin appropriated by a cultural theorist like Slavoj Žižek and mapped onto the psychoanalytic work of Jacques Lacan. The MacGuffin was, in Žižek's terms,

> "nothing at all," an empty place, a pure pretext whose sole role is to set the story in motion: the formula of the warplane engines in *The Thirty-Nine Steps*, the secret

clause of the naval treaty in *The Foreign Correspondent*, the coded melody in *The Lady Vanishes*, the uranium bottles in *Notorious*, and so on. It is a pure semblance: in itself it is totally indifferent and, by structural necessity, absent; its signification is purely auto-reflexive, it consists in the fact that it has some signification for others, for the principal characters of the story, that it is of vital importance to them.

The MacGuffin thus accorded, said Žižek, with Lacan's *"objet petit a*, a gap in the centre of the symbolic order—the lack, the void of the Real setting in motion the symbolic movement of interpretation, a pure semblance of the Mystery to be explained, interpreted."[15] With or without the analogy to Lacan, this perception is a useful one. Especially when it comes to trying to pluck out the heart of a mystery.

One of the curious attributes of Hitchcock's MacGuffin is what might be called its recursive nature, its tendency to double back upon itself and become true after the fact. Take the notorious case of the bottles of uranium in *Notorious*. Hitchcock often claimed—as he did, for example, to fellow director François Truffaut—that the choice of uranium was an uncanny accident. The plot of the film was to involve a woman working as a government agent who was told "to sleep with a certain spy to get some secret information." What was the information? It didn't much matter. But they needed to make something up.

"Gradually, we develop the story," Hitchcock told Truffaut, "and now I introduce the MacGuffin: four or five samples of uranium concealed in wine bottles." The film's producer wanted to know what uranium was, and what it was for, and Hitchcock told him that it was for the making of an atom bomb. The year was 1944, a year before Hiroshima, and the idea seemed far-fetched. Hitchcock offered to change the MacGuffin to industrial diamonds—the atom bomb "wasn't the basis for our story, but only the MacGuffin and . . . there was no need to attach too much importance to it"—but the studio remained unconvinced. ("We turned it down because it was such a goddamn foolish thing to base a movie on," they recalled.) A few weeks later the whole project was sold to RKO, where it turned a huge profit.

Meanwhile Hitchcock's nosy questions about the atom bomb, which he had first heard about through a friend, landed him on the FBI surveillance list for three months.[16] Or so he said. Spoto, the biographer, contests this account, chalking it up to embellishment and Hitchcock's great "sense of publicity." FBI files reveal no evidence of "surveillance." In fact, claims Spoto, by the time the film was actually in production Japan had been bombed, and Hitchcock had made the acquaintance of several famous German émigré scientists who would finally be cast in the film, and who presumably told him about uranium. But producer David O. Selznick, warned by the FBI that any representation of American intelligence officers would have to get U.S. State Department clearance, advised Hitchcock "that the MacGuffin of spies and intelligence activities should remain just that—a MacGuffin, entirely subordinate to the romance that Hitchcock had always wanted to emphasize in any case."[17]

In this case, again, the MacGuffin was itself a MacGuffin: that is to say, the fiction that Hitchcock was an uncanny prophet—always something easier to accomplish after the fact, as several Shakespearean prophecies make clear—was itself a plot device to forward the Hitchcock myth.

But how does the MacGuffin function in Shakespeare?

III

I want to suggest that "MacGuffin Shakespeare" is an effect that springs to life as the result of an interaction between text and reader, and especially between the text and a certain kind of reader: not the naif, but the learned close reader, the critic and the editor. It is the result, not of careless inattention but of hypervigilant attention. In describing this effect, and its uncanny production of textual ghosts, I will focus my attention on *Hamlet*, which for a variety of reasons has become the MacGuffin of MacGuffins for Shakespeare critics over the years. First, however, let me offer one example of a MacGuffin from another play, just to demonstrate what I mean about the creative energy of editors bent on doing their jobs.

I choose this particular example among a myriad of possibilities because the heated tone of the editorial contestants is so revealing, the textual suggestions so divergent, and the passage itself so pertinent. Again the critic doing the adjudication is the nineteenth-century amateur of Shakespeare, C. M. Ingleby, who was trained as a lawyer and whom we will encounter a number of times, as it happens, in our quest for the Shakespearean MacGuffin. The passage in question is from the opening scene of *Timon of Athens*, where the characters called the Poet and the Painter are discussing their respective arts and the role of the patron. In the First Folio, the only surviving text, the Poet asserts

> Our Poesie is as a Gowne, which uses
> From whence 'tis nourisht. (*Timon of Athens* 1.1.21–22)

The line seemed to make no sense as it stood, and it was conjecturally emended by two eminent eighteenth-century editors, themselves poets not unfamiliar with the vagaries of patronage:

> Our Poesie is as a Gumme [*Pope*] which oozes [*Johnson*].

These emendations, we might note, are still accepted by modern editors; the Norton edition uses them without comment, though the Riverside puts them in square brackets. The Arden editor remarks that "this generally accepted emendation seems probable," and adds his own gloss: "The basic idea is of poetry, like gum, flowing steadily."[18] Here is the Victorian scholar Ingleby's rather overwrought summary of the controversy, which will focus, at least in part, on the view of the German romantic writer and critic (Johann) Ludwig Tieck, himself a translator of Shakespeare:

> Shakespeare undoubtedly wrote,
>
> > Our poesie is as a gumme which oozes,
> > From whence 'tis nourisht.
>
> But in the edition of 1623, the passage was, as we have seen, misprinted
>
> > Our Poesie is as a Gowne which uses
> > From whenc 'tis nourisht.
>
> And Tieck, who set himself up as a critic on Shakespeare and other English Dramatists, defended the nonsense, under the impression, perhaps, that Shakespeare meant to compare poetry to a worn-out robe!
>
> Unhappy passage! In a letter on "The influences of Newspapers on Education," written by Mr. Blanchard Jerrold, in the *Daily News*, he had intended to quote the amended version; but to his horror it appeared in a totally new form,
>
> > Our poesy is as a queen that dozeth;
>
> And it now remains for some conceited foreigner of the future to contend that the bard meant to signalize the drowsiness of our poetry, by comparing it to a queen, who despite the calls of her high station, falls asleep on the throne![19]

The sideswipe against "some conceited foreigner of the future" is of course meant for Tieck and other German critics of Shakespeare, but its interest for us may rest more in the awareness of criticism as a slippery business. Once a textual variant is printed, however unreliable the source, it becomes a possible target for analysis, explanation, and adoption. What "the bard meant" can be extrapolated from almost any piece of "evidence," and then read backward into the text. That poetry should be a sleeping (or dreaming?) queen may not, at least to a modern reader, seem any odder than that it should be an oozing gum, or a worn gown.

IV

Of all of Shakespeare's plays, it is not surprisingly *Hamlet* that seems to have provoked the most eager and earnest MacGuffinism. I say "not surprisingly" because the themes of *Hamlet* are so relevant to this quest for source and certainty. Haunted by ghostly traces, itself a Hitchcockian thriller before the letter, *Hamlet* is also, perhaps most pertinently, a play about homology, about kin and kind, and about communication. The brilliance of the Michael Almereyda film (in which Ophelia wears a wiretap, Rosencrantz and Guildenstern are heard over a speakerphone, Hamlet edits videos, the "sealed commission" commanding his death is found on a laptop and the Player King's lines—"our thoughts are ours"—are read by real-life news anchor Robert McNeill from a scrolling teleprompter) stems in part from his perception that Shakespeare's *Hamlet* reflects a similar concern with technologies of performance and reproduction: the players, their acting styles, the "town crier" who mouths for the general populace, the letter, the signet-ring as stamp or signature, the ghost's injunction to remember, Hamlet's real or mimed note-taking ("my tables, meet it is I set it down"). Himself an inveterate punster, Hamlet stars in a play in which double meanings abound and have made their way into the textual apparatus.

Let us consider a couple of brief examples before coming to the most obvious and fascinating *Hamlet* MacGuffin of them all.

Take the peacock, for instance. You may—or may not—remember him. His cameo appearance takes place in act 3, scene 2, right after the play-within-the-play, when Hamlet is quoting, or rather misquoting, to Horatio a verse about the old king and the new king:

> For thou doest know, O Damon dear,
>   The realm dismantled was
> Of Jove himself, and now reigns here
>   A very, very—pajock. (3.2.275–279)

"This creature, otherwise unknown," writes Arden editor Harold Jenkins dryly, "first appears in this guise in F2 through what is presumably a modernized form of *paiocke* (Q2, F). it is usually taken to be a peacock." Editors have conjectured the omission of the missing letter *c*, and have urged the case of the peacock on substantive grounds: "The peacock's gross and lecherous reputation is held to make it an apt symbol for Claudius; it was said to break its mates eggs and to swallow its own dung," and so forth.[20] Jenkins is dubious ("one may question whether so splendid a creature is altogether suitable for an antithesis to Jove and for the degree of disgust implied here") and notes, following the *Oxford English Dictionary*, that the word "peacock" is spelled correctly (no missing *c*) the five other times it appears in Shakespearean texts.

According to the indefatigable Ingleby, the nineteenth-century writer Eden Warwick (the pseudonym of George Jabet, the editor of *The Poet's Pleasaunce*, 1847, and of a volume called *Nasology, or Hints Toward a Classification of Noses*, 1848), "proposed to substitute for Hamlet's *pajock* or *paiocke* the strange word *patokie*, a word he had coined expressly for the occasion, as a possible derivative of *patocco* or *patokoi*."[21]

It has been claimed that *paiocke* derives from an "alleged northern Scottish" form, *pea-jock*, meaning peacock. But, "There seems no reason," says the *OED*, reasonably enough, "why Hamlet should here use a stray dialect word." Editor Jenkins therefore prefers *patchock*, "a contemptuous diminutive of *patch*," meaning "clown," linking it to similar uses in the work of Edmund Spenser, and also to Hamlet's later comment about "A king of shreds and patches" (3.4.103; it is Shakespeare, not Sir William S. Gilbert, who coins this phrase).

Exit peacock. Except that, having been conjured up, it is hard to banish from our minds completely. Indeed, productions that make Claudius into something of a popinjay may have the strutting peacock somewhere in mind.

As with the reigning "peacock," so with the notorious "sledded Polacks" or "sleaded pollax." Here the phrase is Horatio's, at the very beginning of the play, remembering—apparently from legend—Old Hamlet's warlike air:

> So frowned he once when in an angry parle
> He smote the sledded Polacks on the ice. (1.1.66)

The word is "pollax" in both the quartos and the folio, and is amended to "Poleaxe" in the Fourth Folio, "Pole-axe" by Nicholas Rowe, "Polack" by Pope, and "Polacks" by Edmund Malone.

Does the phrase refer to "inhabitants of Poland riding in sleds," or to a heavy weighted or studded weapon wielded by King Hamlet? Jenkins prefers the Polish invaders to the weapon. Why would old Hamlet smite an axe on the ice if there were no threat—"if no Polanders and no sledges, why ice?" Poland and its king are mentioned elsewhere in the play (2.2.63, 75; 4.4.23) and the name of Polonius is in Jenkins's mind obliquely connected to this theme. But above all he finds the first scenario more stirring than the second: "what, along with the natural sense of *sledded*, gives the preference overwhelmingly to Poles in sleds as the object of [King Hamlet's] smiting is their power to stir the imagination, which a pole-axe so signally lacks."[22]

Leaving aside the comparative capacity of Poles and axes to stir the imagination, this seems reasonable enough. But having misconceived the travelling foes as a mighty weapon and thus conjured up the poleax, it is hard for some critics to give that weapon up completely: After all, axes, also known as "battle-axes" and "polaxes," were used by heroes in what the *OED* calls "olden warfare." The word began as *poleaxe* (one word) and began to be spelled as two (*pole-axe*) in the sixteenth century; by 1625 *pole-ax* was the usual spelling (*OED*, "pole-axe," "poleax"). And while *sleaded* does indeed mean "on sleds," or "sledges," there was also the *sledge*, or sledgehammer, which was wielded by both hands. Those who struck with sledgehammers could be said to be of a different social class from King Hamlet (blacksmiths are often cited), but, for what it's worth, *sledge*, from *slegge*, or *slaegge*, is derived from an old Danish word. Thus some critics have compared King Hamlet's ancient and primordial ax with the more sporting rapier of the civilized courtier sons, Laertes and young Hamlet.

The MacGuffin effect here is a kind of mental fetish ("I know... but still... "). If we believe in the Poles on sleds, do we have to give up the battle-axe or sledgehammer as a regal accessory? Once this crux arises, it may be resolved, but is not forgotten.

The Shakespearean texts are full of such cruxes, some famous, some infamous, and others oddly neglected. Consider for example, as a MacGuffin not taken, the fascinating choice between a "pelican" and a "politician" in act 4, scene 5 of *Hamlet*. Laertes has returned to Denmark, enraged at the murder of Polonius, and Claudius asks artfully whether in seeking vengeance for his father's death Laertes will distinguish between friends and foes. "To his good friends thus wide I'll ope my arms," replies Laertes,

> And, like the kind life-rendering pelican,
> Repast them with my blood. (4.5.145–47)

A modern editor (Jenkins) comments on the "pelican" image, a traditional figure: "the pelican feeds its young from its own breast, in some versions reviving them from seeming death," and notes that "the extravagance of the image here is no doubt meant to characterize Laertes's 'emphasis' and 'rant.'"[23] But in the folio text the lines read

> To his good Friends, thus wide Ile ope my Armes:
> And like the kinde Life-rend'ring Politician,
> Repast them with my blood.

It has been conjectured that the compositor set *Polician*, which was then misidentified as a misprint and "corrected" to *Politician*.[24] The idea of a politician as self-sacrificing and life rendering, then or now, has a certain counterintuitive charm, but there have been few if any champions of the folio reading, although a "politician," or at least the rotted skull of one, does appear in the play in act 5, scene 1.

V

Of all the editorial MacGuffins in Shakespeare's most celebrated play, however, the most ardently sought in the last hundred years of criticism have been the "dozen or sixteen lines" that Hamlet asks the players to insert in *The Murder of Gonzago*—his mousetrap play:

> You could for a need study a speech of some dozen or sixteen lines,
> which I would set down and insert in't, could you not? (2.2.534–36)

The dozen or sixteen lines are a kind of model or template for MacGuffin Shakespeare. Harold Jenkins observes, in the Arden edition, that "The voluminous attempts to locate the speech in the Gonzago play are only a degree less absurd than speculations about how the players came to have this play at all."[25] And it is also worth noting that since the audience is unfamiliar with the text of *Gonzago*, neither they nor we can hear the crucial shift of tone that this supposed insert would supply. But this has not kept scholars and passionately motivated amateurs from trying to find them.

Indeed, needless to say, they have scoured the text of the play-within-the-play for the identity of these lines. The most recent to have "found" them is Harold Bloom, who, perhaps inspired by out his self-identification as Falstaff, discovers that the twelve or sixteen have become twenty six, much as eleven buckram men grew out of two. (Falstaff's buckram men are Shakespearean MacGuffins, in fact.) Here is Bloom's account:

> With a cunning subtler than any other dramatists before or since, Shakespeare does not let us be certain as to just which lines Hamlet himself has inserted in order to revise *The Murder of Gonzago* into *The Mousetrap*. Hamlet speaks of writing some twelve or sixteen lines, but we come to suspect that there are rather more, and that they include the extraordinary speech in which the Player King tells us that ethos is not the daemon, that character is not fate but accident, and that eros is the purest accident.

Bloom goes on to hypothesize that Shakespeare himself might have played not only the part of the Ghost but also that of the Player King: "There would be a marvelous twist to Shakespeare himself intoning lines that his Hamlet can be expected to have written."[26]

This is first-class MacGuffinism: the missing lines are not only found but also connected, by an astounding feat of logic, to the double presence of the playwright as author and actor, as if the conjecture about Shakespeare as Player King were further "proof" of the identification of the dozen or sixteen lines.

The phrase "dozen or sixteen" indicates that Hamlet is making an approximation; the word *dozen* is often used colloquially in the period to mean "a moderately large number." But critics and editors have tended to fixate on the numbers, whether or not they can actually locate them in the text. A. C. Bradley is so sure of the identity of the interpolated lines that he can tell us "only six are delivered." Thus, he writes of "the 'dozen or sixteen lines' with which Hamlet has furnished the player, and of which only six are delivered, because the King...rushes from the room," and, "When only six of the 'dozen or sixteen lines' have been spoken [the King] starts to his feet and rushes from the hall, followed by the whole dismayed Court."[27] The speech to which he points is thus that of Lucianus, the murderer, who utters six portentous lines, in rhyming couplets, before [but in the Folio stage direction only] he *"pours the poison in the sleeper's ears"*:

> Thoughts black, hands apt, drugs fit, and time agreeing,
> Confederate season, else no creature seeing,
> Thou mixture rank, of midnight weeds collected,
> With Hecate's ban thrice blasted, thrice infected,
> Thy natural magic and dire property
> On wholesome life usurps immediately.

John Dover Wilson notes "the vexed problem of the identification of Hamlet's inserted speech, over which much paper and ink have been expended." He too is quite sure he has identified the lines, and they are the same lines to which Bradley points:

> The speech, as we have seen, was one of passion....Moreover, it is the words of the murderer which cause Claudius to blench, and there is therefore a strong presumption that they were Hamlet's contribution....Last, they are the only words in the interlude which point directly at the crime of Claudius.

But in what sense have we "seen" that the speech was one of passion? We have seen it because Dover Wilson insists that Hamlet's advice to the players at the very beginning of this scene ("Speak the speech, I pray you, as I pronounced it to you, trippingly on the tongue..." [3.2.1]) was in fact about *this* speech, the interpolated dozen or sixteen lines added by Hamlet, lines that are given to the First Player, and lines that Hamlet is eager for him not to overdramatize ("if you mouth it as many of your players do, I had as lief the town-crier spoke my lines"). Dover Wilson dismisses Harley Granville-Barker's report that by theatrical tradition the First Player is given the part of the Player King, not that of the murderer Lucianus. "Hamlet expressly asks the First Player...to 'study' his inserted speech, which must, as I show, be the Lucianus speech."[28]

Dover Wilson calls the matter of the dozen or sixteen lines a "vexed problem"; Bradley had addressed himself to the task of identification as an important critical issue. And yet, before the middle of the nineteenth century apparently no one worried much about this question at all.

It was the German critic Eduard Wilhelm Sievers, editing the play in 1851,who identified the lines in question for perhaps the first time, choosing the speech of Lucianus. Among English critics, the first to address the problem in print were the editors of the *Cassell Shakespeare* (1864–1868), Charles and Mary Cowden Clarke, who locate the passage added by Hamlet in the Player King's speech, at the point when the King responds to the Player Queen's vow that she will never remarry:

> I do believe you think what now you speak;
> But what we do determine, oft we break.
> Purpose is but the slave to memory,
> Of violent birth but poor validity,
> Which now, the fruit unripe, sticks on the tree,
> But fall unshaken when they mellow be.
> Most necessary 'tis that we forget
> To pay ourselves what to ourselves is debt.
> What to ourselves in passion we propose,
> The passion ending, doth the purpose lose.
> The violence of either grief or joy
> Their own enactures with themselves destroy.
> Where joy most revels grief doth most lament;
> Grief joys, joy grieves, on slender accident.
> This world is not for aye, nor 'tis not strange
> That even our loves should with our fortunes change,
> For 'tis a question left us yet to prove,
> Whether love lead fortune or else fortune love.
> The great man down, you mark his favorite flies;
> The poor advanc'd makes friends of enemies;
> And hitherto doth love on fortune tend;
> For who not needs shall never lack a friend,
> And who in want a hollow friend doth try
> Directly seasons him his enemy.
> But orderly to end where I begun,
> Our wills and fates do so contrary run
> That our devices still are overthrown:
> Our thoughts are ours, their ends none of our own.

> So think thou wilt no second husband wed,
> But die thy thoughts when thy first lord is dead. (3.2.168–197)

The Clarkes believe that the added lines are those that go from the phrase "Purpose is but the slave to memory" to "Our thoughts are ours, their ends none of our own." This is a passage of some twenty-five lines—plainly they did not feel bound by a strict construction of "a dozen lines, or sixteen lines." And what is their reasoning in singling out this passage? The speech can be readily cut without disturbing the flow of the sense; without it the Player King says merely

> I do believe you think what now you speak;
> But what we do determine, oft we break. . . .
> So think thou wilt no second husband wed,
> But die thy thoughts when thy first lord is dead.
>   (3.2.168–69, 196–97)

This offers a much briefer reply to his Queen, and one far more to the point.

Furthermore, the Clarkes claim that the speech sounds like Hamlet, not like the rest of the play-within-the-play ("it is signally like Hamlet's own argumentative mode"). And why does he want this particular passage inserted—a passage that reflects on the changeableness of the world and of love, on the fickleness of fortune, and on the difficulty of fulfilling one's own purposes? Here is what the Clarkes have to say:

> His motive in writing these additional lines for insertion, and getting the player to deliver them, we take to be *a desire that they shall serve to divert attention from the special passages directed at the king, and to make these latter seem less pointed.*[29]

Thus the "dozen or sixteen lines" are a decoy, not a smoking gun; it is their innocuousness, not their pointedness, that singles them out as the intruders. Without them *The Murder of Gonzago* already points sufficiently at Claudius's guilt. Hamlet did not need to add anything to indicate the identity of the murderer, but rather needed to lull the King into a false sense of confidence and safety. This is subtle indeed. It is based upon a desire to find Hamlet himself—his consciousness, his thinking style, his "self"—even in the place where it might seem to be most unlikely, the voice of a Player King speaking in rhymed couplets in the play-within-the-play.

The Clarkes are not alone in this conjecture. In a lively interchange published by the New Shakespere Society in the year of its founding (1874), two scholars debated the question, which had stirred up considerable interest among the members. History professor J. R. Seeley of Cambridge University, noting that "here is a Shakesperian problem which has been overlooked, that Shakespere evidently meant us to ask which the '12 or 16 lines' were, and that apparently no one (except Mr. and Mrs. C. Clarke) has thought of doing so," directed attention to the one speech in the play longer than twelve lines, the speech of the Player King, the only speech from which lines could be cut (and therefore the only speech into which lines might have been inserted). Like the Clarkes, he maintained that this speech "suits Hamlet's general character," and reflects his preoccupation with his mother ("it is this which really fills his mind"), but Seeley's central argument was that no other speech could satisfy the necessary conditions (be longer than twelve lines; be able to be cut without damage to the action). "No other such passage can be found in the sub-play," Seeley says with serene logic. "Those who reject this passage are driven to the shift of supposing that Shakespere after promising us such a passage and leading us to expect it has not given it."[30]

W. T. Malleson of University College, London, in reply insists that Hamlet's advice to the players—"speak *the speech*, I pray you, *as I pronounced it to you*" leads one to expect that his interpolated lines will exhibit "the torrent, tempest, and whirlwind of passion," and asks, with incredulity, whether the reader can find "anything of passion, with which 'to split the ears of the groundlings,'" in the measured and philosophic lines of the Player King. The answer is no. For Malleson, as for others, the only speech that will do is the speech of the murderer, Lucianus. Indeed, Malleson finds the parallel between the plot of *The Murder of Gonzago* and the death of old Hamlet so uncanny that he suspects "that Hamlet altered the manner of the murder in the old play to make it tally precisely with the awful secret fact. If not, it is strange that so odd, if not impossible a way of committing murder should have occurred in both the plays."[31]

The objection raised by Seeley, that the speech of a dozen or sixteen lines described by Hamlet "must consist of some 12 or 16 lines," and that it must be enclosed in a speech even longer than that in order to be "inserted" as promised, Malleson simply dismisses as "somewhat strained":

> Hamlet never says he *has written* a passage of so many lines and inserted it. If he had said so the matter would be simpler. We only know that he *intended to write* and insert some lines of the number of which he was not himself certain, "12 or 16." When he sat down with the play before him he may have written 20 or 26. . . .

And would they really have to have been plugged into a longer speech? That is, "May not Hamlet have inserted his lines in substitution for others which he struck out?" asks Malleson rhetorically[32]—a conjecture that Seeley, in rebuttal, calls "an unnatural interpretation of the words." Seeley's own interpretation is preoccupied with Hamlet's state of mind. He thinks *The Murder of Gonzago* probably needed no insertion to catch the conscience of the king—"the play did its own work." But as for Hamlet, the composition of additional lines is cathartic: Hamlet "thinks with great delight of the opportunity [the play] affords him of relieving himself of the weight of feeling that has been oppressing him so long by putting it into verse. He will write a poem on his mother, and insert it in the play. It may not have much effect upon her when she hears it; indeed, he probably knows too well already how unimpressionable she is; but his object will be gained if he only writes it, for it will be a relief to his feelings."[33]

I have been describing this debate as if it had only two participants, Mr. Malleson and Dr. Seeley—both, we might say, interested amateurs. But the protocols of the New Shakespere Society meant that the exchange was triangulated, in its published form, via the distinguished English scholar F. J. Furnivall, the society's founder and chair. Malleson read his paper at a meeting of the society; Seeley—whose views had been mentioned and refuted by Malleson—responded in a letter to Furnivall; Malleson offered a "rejoinder"; and the whole discussion was published together with a response by Furnivall that, while printed in smaller type and single spaced as if to underscore its relative unimportance, in fact pulled rank, easily trumping the views of both the lay participants.

Furnivall felt that Seeley's view (the dozen or sixteen lines were part of the Player King's speech) was "technically" strong but weak "on the merits." He inclined to agree with Malleson that the lines Hamlet inserted were the ones he described to Horatio in act 3, scene 2 as the "one speech" that would "unkennel" the King's "occulted guilt." "To me," he writes, "fair criticism requires the identification of the two." Before Malleson can congratulate himself on having won, however, Furnivall immediately proceeds to demolish his claim:

But I hold very strongly that Lucianus's speech, "thoughts black," &c., is not this speech; and that, in fact, the speech is not in the printed play.

Why not? It is simply a matter of the playwright having rewritten as he went along:

The inconsistency of Shakespere's having made Hamlet first talk so much about inserting one speech, and then having afterwards left it out, doesn't trouble me in the least. It's just what one might fairly expect in the recast *Hamlet*.

Perhaps, Furnivall says, Shakespeare found as he wrote the scene that the King's conscience was more quickly stung than Hamlet had anticipated, so that the written scene was never needed, or that Hamlet changed his plan, "and put his 'dozen or sixteen lines' into action instead of words." The fact that the play so exactly resembled the circumstances of the murder, rather than being, as Hamlet had at first said, "*something like* the murder of my father," meant that the lines would be superfluous. This inconsistency seems minor, thinks Furnivall, in comparison with the "really startling" inconsistencies on other matters, like Hamlet's age and Ophelia's suicide. And even about these, Furnivall is serene. On the question of Hamlet's age, the first and second halves of the play "*are* inconsistent," with a youthful Hamlet-as-lover at the beginning and a mature Hamlet-as-philosopher/mourner at the end.

"What matter? Who wants 'em made consistent by the modification of either part?" asked Furnivall briskly. "The 'thirty' is not in the First Quarto; yet no one wants to go back to that." (As I write this, many scholars and actors are in fact "going back" to the First Quarto as a lively, playable text with a legitimate claim to be Shakespeare's.) As for the dozen or sixteen lines, "what can it matter whether an actual speech of a dozen or sixteen lines, though often announct, is really in the play or not? The comparative insignificance of the point is shown by no one having noted it in print before Mr. and Mrs. Cowden Clarke."[34] Other members of the Shakespere Society seemed to agree: "I think that there is no warrant for assuming that the lines announced by Hamlet are to be supposed to exist in the sub-play at all," wrote one, pointing out appositely that in other Elizabethan plays-within-the-plays, like that in *A Midsummer Night's Dream*, there is no connection between the scene rehearsed (act 3, scene 1) and the play as ultimately performed. Likewise, with

Histriomastix, where the play of the *Prodigal Son* is read over to the actors in an early scene, and is acted toward the end. "Not a passage in these two presentations of the same piece agrees." Thus, the writer concluded, "I don't believe that the poet ever meant us to pick out a bit, and say, This is the plum contributed by Hamlet himself."[35] In fact this very modern-sounding solution, the idea that there were no dozen or sixteen lines to find, was one of the earliest conjectures put forward in the nineteenth century. "I do not see symptoms of the lines which Hamlet was to insert," commented Charles Bathurst in 1857.[36]

Indeed, yet another Victorian critic, entering into the debate, vehemently discounted the whole idea that there was any addition to be found. "Hamlet writes no speech at all, whether of six, twelve, or sixteen lines, nor recites such a speech; Shakespeare simply wrote the entire play, *not* writing any additions *in persona Hamleti*, still less writing an addition to a play which he had previously written in the character of the author of an Italian morality," writes H. H. Furness, summarizing the views of "my friend Dr. Ingleby."

This is the same C. M. Ingleby whom we have already encountered as a critic sometimes skeptical of "conjectural emendation" and at other times certain of what "Shakespeare undoubtedly wrote." Ingleby, the author of such works as *Shakespeare the Man and the Book*, *Shakespeare's Bones: The Proposal to Disinter Them*, and *The Shakespeare Fabrications*, was a lawyer who had quit the law to give over his life to Shakespeare and philosophy.

According to Ingleby, Shakespeare had quite a different goal in mind from merely giving Hamlet opportunity to catch the conscience of the King by adding a few lines to *The Murder of Gonzago*. His purpose, in fact, had nothing to do with revenge. It was rather to make the play "a vehicle for the highest possible instruction in the art of elocution." He would "make Hamlet instruct the Player, and through him all players, how to act." But since it would hardly be plausible for Hamlet to tell the Player how to perform roles or scenes that were already part of his professional repertory (roles and scenes the Player would know far better than would Hamlet) Shakespeare invents the idea of the Prince writing "a speech of his own composition," about which he would be entitled to give instructions. The device of the "dozen or sixteen lines" was merely a pretext, in order to enable Shakespeare to achieve "his own object (kept wholly out of view)"—that is, "to prepare the audience for his own lesson (*voce Hamleti*) on elocution." As for the seemingly specific "dozen or six-

teen," Furness insisted, it "does not mean what it says; it is even more indefi-
nite than 'ten or a dozen' or 'a dozen or fourteen,' which Mrs. Quickly uses in
Henry V (II, I); the prefix 'some' adds vagueness to what was vague before.
These lines, by the very nature of the case, can never have been in *Hamlet*."[37]

"'Tis here. 'Tis here. 'Tis gone." From this perspective, the "dozen or sixteen lines" (or, according to the Second Quarto, "*some* dozen lines or sixteen
lines") are very like Poe's purloined letter: we can only see the outside, the fact
of their supposed existence, not the interior, the actual and particular text. And
they are also very like Žižek's understanding of the MacGuffin; it is "'nothing at
all,' an empty place, a pure pretext whose sole role is to set the story in
motion."

VI

One of the most intriguing secondary issues attending upon this editorial scav-
enger hunt for the dozen or sixteen lines is what the quest does to Hamlet's
famous advice to the players. As several scholars point out, the instruction that
begins act 3 scene 1, "Speak the speech, I pray you, as I pronounced it to you,"
draws the actors—and the audience's—attention to *one speech*, as will Hamlet's
later aside to Horatio ("if his occulted guilt / Does not itself unkennel in *one
speech*" [3.1.80–81]). Instructing the players, Hamlet emphasizes his own
authorship: "if you mouth it as many of your players do, I had as lief the town-
crier spoke *my lines*." (3.1.1–3). Thus, this celebrated passage, the locus classicus of a doctrine of "natural" acting and of holding "the mirror up to nature,"
begins not as a piece of transcendent philosophy about theater's relationship to
life, but as a highly particular piece of coached performance: "speak 'my lines,'
the ones that I have written and inserted, the way I pronounced them to you
when I read you the script." As Martin Dodsworth points out, "It is easy to
stretch Hamlet's first-person in 'my lines' to include his author speaking
through him." But this is to miss some of the crucial particularity of the scene.
For Dodsworth, the "immediate business of the episode" is to mark the difference between Hamlet and the actors, a difference of class: the aristocrat
addressing his inferiors.[38] For other readers, especially those concerned or
obsessed with the "dozen or sixteen lines," Hamlet's storied "advice" is actually

pragmatic and instrumental: not pride of authorship or abstract theorizing, but the effectiveness of one key dramatic moment, is what is at stake.

The difference between a philosophical observation on verisimilitude in art and life, on the one hand, and a stratagem for putting across an interpolated set of lines, on the other, makes the "speak the speech" speech a performative crux. Is Hamlet functioning here as Shakespeare or as Hitchcock?

Insertions and enlargements of the text are, of course, the common practice of early modern dramaturgy. "The text in Q1," notes R. A. Foakes, "includes two comic additions, one in Hamlet's advice to the players and a second in mockery of Osric's perfume, that are not in Q2 or F, and presumably these were inserted for or by the players. . . . Playhouse interpolations, in the form of improvised jokes, dying O's, or whatever, deserve more consideration than to be simply dismissed as corruptions." But in the nature of things the acting version is often cut down, rather than enlarged, for reasons of time; it is the Second Quarto, a "text for reading," that announces itself as "Newly imprinted and enlarged to almost as much again as it was, according to the true and perfect Coppie."[39] Recent attention to stage directions, extant or imputed, and speculation about the improvisation of pieces of stage business (from Kemp's jig to Hamlet's leaping in the grave) that subsequently became a conventional part of the play, have likewise emphasized the fact that there is always something "missing" and something "added" in the play texts as we have them, something that escapes being pinned down and enshrined.

VII

Perhaps no version of the "dozen or sixteen lines" story is as uncannily revealing as the story of John Payne Collier, antiquarian, Shakespeare editor and bibliographer, and co-founder of the Shakespeare Society. Collier, who gained early fame with his *History of English Dramatic Poetry to the Time of Shakespeare* (1831), was an acquaintance of John Keats, Samuel Taylor Coleridge, William Hazlitt, and Charles Lamb. He dedicated his *History* to the Duke of Devonshire, and was soon asked to look after the library at Devonshire House. Shortly he was also welcomed by the Earl of Ellesmere to

Bridgewater House, where a rich trove of Elizabethan manuscripts was to be found, many of them previously unexplored.

The diligent Collier explored them, to remarkable effect, and found previously undiscovered letters and other documents with new and sometimes startling information about Shakespeare's life. In his *New Facts Regarding the Life of Shakespeare* (1835), he thanks the noble earl for letting him view the manuscripts: "if the example were followed by others possessed of similar relics, literary and historical information of great novelty and of high value might in many cases be obtained." Although he occasionally detected—and scrupulously corrected—some factual errors in these new documents, Collier's discoveries significantly enlarged, and changed, what was known about Shakespeare's life. In subsequent publications he was able to do the same for the works, discovering key if questionable information about previously unsuspected performances (a performance of *Othello* in 1602, for example, when the play is dated by scholars 1603–1604), and previously unknown sources for the plays.

Collier's reputation blossomed. He became one of the best known and most highly regarded Shakespeare editors of his time. With some scholarly friends he founded the Shakespeare Society in 1840. His biography of Shakespeare, published in 1844, explained the importance of the new factual and textual discoveries he had made. Then, in 1852, he announced an even more breathtaking discovery: a copy of the 1632 Second Folio of Shakespeare, inscribed with the name of one Tho. Perkins, presumably the owner, which was full of marginal and textual annotations—thousands of them, in a handwriting dating to the 1630s.

How had the author of the annotations, who became known as the Old Corrector, come by his corrections? Collier speculated in print about whether it was from better manuscript sources, or from oral evidence—speeches heard in performance. In any case, this was fresh evidence that the Shakespeare text needed careful emendation to restore it to its original state. Moreover, it turned out that many of the suggestions that Collier as editor had proposed in his Shakespeare edition were confirmed and corroborated by the handwritten insertion of the Old Corrector in the Perkins Folio. Collier himself marveled that in the volume he so fortuitously discovered many of "the conjectures of

Pope, Theobald, Warburton and Hanmer are *remarkably confirmed*." (He does not mention his own, which are conveniently proved accurate by the same discovery.) In 1853 he published his *Notes and Emendations to the Text of Shakespeare's Plays, from Early Manuscript Corrections in a Copy of the Folio, 1632.*

The problem was that Collier had apparently himself inserted these corrections, just as he had forged the newly "discovered" documents in Bridgewater House. As one critic later acerbically noted, there was an " extraordinary sympathy" between the "Old Corrector" and Collier.[40] What Collier treats as "*coincident anticipations*," wrote Samuel Weller Singer, were in fact his own belated grafting: "it is not within the doctrine of probabilities that two writers, at distant periods, without any communication or knowledge of each other, should in *hundreds of instances* coincide so exactly as we find the major part of the corrections in Mr. Collier's volume do with the later emendations, slowly elaborated by a succession of commentators, and many of them far from obvious."[41]

Collier fought back. When he was attacked in a pamphlet called *Literary Cookery* in 1855 he sued the author for libel, he swore in an affidavit that "I have not . . . to the best of my knowledge and belief, inserted a single word, stop, sign, note, correction, alteration or emendation of the said original text of Shakespeare, which is not a faithful copy of the said original manuscript, and which I do not believe to have been written, as aforesaid, not long after the publication of the said folio copy of the year 1632."[42]

Meanwhile, the Perkins Folio was itself proving elusive to scholars and literary detectives; Collier put it in the library of the Duke of Devonshire, and for some time it could not be produced to be examined by experts. Among other advantages, this meant that he alone could publish the "emendations," and thus "out-point" his rival editors at a time when there was a fierce contest among scholars to publish new editions of Shakespeare. The arrangement was beneficial to both Collier's bank account and his reputation.

Yet ultimately the Perkins Folio was shown to the Keeper of Manuscripts at the British Museum, Sir Frederick Madden, who, troubled in mind, confided his doubts to his private *Journal*. The ink corrections, it seemed, were retracings of insertions initially made in pencil, and the "ink" was actually a kind of watercolor made to resemble old writing. As Madden wrote in his diary, "These corrections are *most certainly* in a modern hand, and from the extraordinary resemblance of the writing to Mr. Collier's own hand (which I am well acquainted with) I am really fearful that I must come to the astounding conclusion that Mr. C. is himself the fabricator of the notes!"[43]

One of Madden's assistants, N. E. S. A. Hamilton, wrote to the *Times* on July 2, 1859, to declare the Perkins Folio a fraud: "I consider it positively established that the emendations, as they are called, of this folio copy of *Shakespeare* have been made within the present century." Collier's reputation plummeted. Other forgeries and fabrications in his publications were quickly alleged: he had invented "historical" documents and inserted them into the record.

And the chief agent in exposing the Shakespeare forgeries of John Payne Collier—which we have seen to be a much more extended version of the inserted "dozen or sixteen lines"—was none other than C. M. Ingleby, whose 1861 investigation, *A Complete View of the Shakespere Controversy, Concerning the Authenticity and Genuineness of the Manuscript Matter Affecting the Works and Biography of Shakspere, Published by Mr. J. Payne Collier as the Fruits of his Researches*,[44] was published with a facsimile frontispiece from act 1, scene 4 of *Hamlet* taken from the Perkins Folio (Hamlet's apostrophe to the Ghost on rewriting the "Table of [his] Memory," with the interjection "Oh Villaine, Villaine, smiling damned Villaine!") and an epigraph from De Quincey:

> Now, Reader, a falsehood *is* a falsehood, though uttered under circumstances of hurry and sudden trepidation; but certainly it becomes, though not more a falsehood, yet more criminally and hatefully a falsehood, when prepared from afar, and elaborately supported by fraud, and dovetailing into fraud, and having no palliation from pressure and haste.

Ingleby begins his examination of Collier by explaining, for members of the lay public, the state of the Shakespeare text: "Shakspere wrote for the boards, and not for the table. The Globe Theatre was his book; and his admirers used their ears and eyes conjointly in the perusal of his immortal dramas. He died, and made no sign indicative of a care for the preservation of his works as classics for posterity." Thus "we possess no authoritative text at all," and "the door is open to legitimate conjecture as to the readings to be adopted." Because of the corrupt state of the text, editors and conjectural critics "fell into the extreme of loose conjecture; they were more anxious to reform, than to understand."[45]

After some three hundred pages of specific textual and documentary evidence, lawyer Ingleby is ready to sum up his argument for the public, to whom he entrusts "the task of returning a verdict":

> Here then we have a case in which 30,000 manuscript notes, written on the vacant spaces of a copy of the second folio of Shakspere, are simulations of handwritings of the seventeenth century, and written sometimes on the top, sometimes by the side of half obliterated pencil marks and words—such pencillings being in almost every case instructions for the superposed, or at least after-written, ink corrections. (320)

Moreover, the "pencillings" in "Mr. Collier's 'plain round English hand'" were the same as those on a number of supposedly genuine documents also supposedly discovered by Collier, and having a bearing "on the life and character of Shakspere."[46] And this is what concerns Ingleby so deeply. "Shame to the perpetrator of that foul libel on the pure genius of Shakspere!" he writes about the fabrication of the Perkins notes. He deplores the incursions on the native tongue of "Gallicisms" and "(still worse) American slang, and the cant and shibboleth of professions and sects." He continues:

> The texts of Shakespere and of the English Bible have been justly regarded as the two river-heads of our vernacular English. . . . To the texts of Shakspere and of our Bible we must cleave, if we would save our language from deterioration. Yet it is one of these texts that a tasteless and incompetent peddler has attempted to corrupt throughout its wide and fertile extent.[47]

To reinforce his point Ingleby has recourse once again to a literary text, citing, in quotation marks but without attribution, some lines from Samuel Butler's satire *Hudibras*. Collier, he notes, had produced a letter supposedly written by the wife of the Elizabethan actor Edward Alleyn to her husband, in which she reports having seen "Mr. Shakespeare of the Globe"—a reference that Ingleby, among others, insists is a falsification. Collier had defended himself against this charge in his *Reply*, where he mentions "the charge that I interpolated a passage not met with in the original."[48] In forging this anecdotal reference to Shakespeare, says Ingleby, Collier has contrived to

> find void places in the paper
> To steal in something to entrap her—

> or rather to entrap a confiding public in general,
> and the Shakespere Society in particular.[49]

In fact these two lines from *Hudibras*, which appear in the final pages of Ingleby's *Complete View of the Shakspere Controversy* merely as an elegant embellishment to his lawyerly argument, suggest that somewhere in the back of his mind Ingleby may have himself made the connection with Hamlet's dozen or sixteen lines. For Butler's satirical instructions for ensnaring a wife, when viewed in context, allude glancingly both to the insertion of new text and to the *Mousetrap*:

> And if she miss the Mousetrap-Lines,
> They'll serve for other By-Designs:
> And make an Artist understand,
> To Copy out her Seal, or Hand:
> Or find void places in the Paper,
> To steal in something to Intrap her.[50]

VIII

Forgery certainly is on *someone's* mind in *Hamlet*. The elder statesmen of the play are obsessed with it—the word recurs in their speech. Here is the Ghost to Hamlet: "the whole ear of Denmark / Is by a forged process of my death / Rankly abus'd" (1.5.36–38); and Polonius to Reynaldo, about investigating the reputation of his son Laertes in Paris: "put on him / What forgeries you please" (2.1.19–20); and King Claudius on the mysterious and accomplished horseman of Normandy, Lamord: "So far he topp'd my thought / That I in forgery of shapes and tricks / Come short of what he did" (4.7.87–89). As for the forgeries we see, the forgeries of and by Hamlet himself, they become the plot of the *Mousetrap*, the plot of political reversal, and the plot of the play. We may think once again of the key moment of forgery and substitution in *Hamlet*:

> I sat me down,
> Devis'd a new commission, wrote it fair—
> I once did hold it, as our statists do,
> A baseness to write fair, and labour'd much
> How to forget that learning, but, sir, now
> It did me yeoman's service. Wilt thou know
> Th'effect of what I wrote? . . .
>
> I had my father's signet in my purse,
> Which was the model of that Danish seal,
> Folded the writ up in the form of th'other,
> Subscrib'd it, gav't th' impression, plac'd it safely,
> The changeling never known. (5.2.30–36; 49–53)

For thirty years after the publication of Ingleby's *Complete View*, John Collier lived on in disgrace as the most notorious and self-aggrandizing of Shakespeare forgers, although more than a hundred years later at least one recent biographer has sought to absolve Collier of blame.[51] But what is so curious about his saga is that whatever Collier's motives—of fame, fortune, or grandiosity—his story is a progress of sorts, for as he forges and fabricates, erases and invents, he moves from being an editor of Shakespeare to becoming Shakespeare himself. As he wrote late in life, in his unpublished autobiographical memoirs,

> Nobody could deny the excellence of many of [the emendations], they have been gladly adopted since, and they were in fact the foundation of my second edition of 1858. . . . If the proposed emendations are not genuine, then I claim them as mine, and there I intend to leave the question without giving myself further trouble: anybody else is welcome to solve the enigma. —Good or bad, mine or not mine, no edition of Shakespeare, while the world stands, can now be published without them: I brought them into life and light, and I am quite ready to be answerable for them.[52]

A few pages later he repeats this claim, and here, as one modern critic notes, he "brings himself to speak the forbidden word," although in the third person:

> If the emendations be forgeries how the inventor of them, if alive, must laugh at
> the ridiculous result of his unrejectable fabrications: they now form an essential
> part of every new edition of Shakespeare, and never hereafter can be omitted.[53]

The Collier forgeries bespeak a kind of truth. Hamlet is a forger. Collier's forgeries are a textual effect. "If the proposed emendations are not genuine, then I claim them as mine." His additions and emendations change the text to make it into the real thing, into "Shakespeare." Their "authenticity" is the authenticity of MacGuffinism. What has been "lost" has been "found."

The quest for the missing—or masquerading—dozen or sixteen lines in *Hamlet*, a *mise en abyme* of textual studies, is, as we have seen, symptomatic of a pair of linked desires: the desire to "fix" the Shakespearean text, and the desire to experience that "real meeting of minds with Shakespeare" so earnestly sought by readers, actors, and editors. (Recall that the phrase came from editorial scholar Fredson Bowers, and was his highest praise for the eighteenth-century editor Lewis Theobald.) Indeed the ultimate MacGuffin in Shakespeare studies is the Shakespeare authorship controversy, the open-ended quest for the "real" author of the plays, a plot pretext that enables us to fashion a Shakespeare in whatever image we desire. A "meeting of minds with Shakespeare" is the missing thing that everybody wants. As I have argued elsewhere, it is the existence of the authorship controversy that creates Shakespeare's authority.[54] Those who deplore the controversy are those who require it. The act of doubt generates certainty, increases the prestige of the author who needs to be defended against it. And this is also the case with the question of the Shakespeare forgeries. By demonizing the fake, scholars are able to deny, cover up, or repress any doubts about the existence of the real. The forger is in a way necessary in order to enhance the prestige of the authentic.

Historical Correctness

The Use and Abuse
of History for Literature

"

The unhistorical and the historical are necessary in
equal measure for the health of an individual, of a people and of a culture.
>—Friedrich Nietzsche, "On the Uses and
>Disadvantages of History for Life"

—What useful discovery did Socrates learn from
Xanthippe?
—Dialectic, Stephen answered.
>—James Joyce, *Ulysses*

We who profess literary studies have been living through a time of infatuation
with history. This is not the first such crush, to be sure, but it is a heady one.
And like all infatuations, it carries with it a certain overestimation of the
object. History seems to know everything that we want to know, and to offer
"answers" to knotty textual questions: questions of context, interpretation,
and indeed meaning. Earlier in this century articles and footnotes about
Macbeth lay emphasis on the facts of the Gunpowder Plot and the lineage of
James I. An entire mini-industry in what might be called "Essex Studies" grew
up around the Earl of Essex, his marital connection to the circle of Sir Philip
Sidney and his sister the Countess of Pembroke, and his ill-fated rebellion—all

in service of readings, not only of Shakespeare's history plays, but also of his tragedies, comedies, and romances. Readings of *The Merchant of Venice* still routinely incorporate the unhappy story of Queen Elizabeth's Jewish doctor, Roderigo Lopez, and, informed by a growing interest in race, analyses of *Othello* detail the numbers and social occupations of Moors and Africans in sixteenth-century London.

But where these inquiries focused on political history, today's scholars of early modern literature and culture are more likely to turn to conduct books, mothers' manuals, and medical and rhetorical treatises. We have seen in recent years an intense interest in court culture, literacy and reading practices, the printing house, sexuality and the stage, and witchcraft and colonial encounters, all "grounded in material and social determinants."[1] This is the counterpart of the earlier infatuation on the part of historians for literary theory, the so-called "linguistic turn"—a passion now strenuously disavowed, like so many other love affairs gone wrong. Whereas historians were once struck by the nontransparency of their medium and the need to study it rather than simply to look at the past through it, today's literary scholars are fascinated by the task of reconstructing "the real" that must lie behind any of its representations.

My topic is the way that "history" has emerged as a byword for a certain kind of truth-claim in literary studies. New Historicism, nourished and nurtured by interdisciplinary work, by historians and art historians as well as by literary critics, had an enormous impact upon the way emerging younger scholars taught and wrote about literature in the late twentieth century. But the very point that New Historicism tried to stress—that history, or histories, could not be understood as determinative or lineal causes but rather as complex networks of cultural effects—has been eroded by its success. Spawned by postmodernism, New Historicism tried to avoid or complicate causality: it preferred terms like *resonance, circulation, poetics*, and *social energy*. But through its very avoidances this strategy whetted the appetite for causation. To put it another way, New Historicism began by reading history as a text, but it created, despite its best efforts, a desire for history as a ground. In the wake of postmodernism and the general questioning of foundations, a longing to find causality—the priority of history, history as explanation—seems to have come back to literary study even more strongly than before. For many scholars of literature, causality is the unfulfilled desire, the projected or introjected fantasy, the prohibited wish. The question these scholars ask is often a version of *why*—not a version of *how*.

Indeed, recent critiques of New Historicism have taken it to task for not being historical *enough*: too anecdotal, not sufficiently rigorous, "evas[ive] when it comes to causal argument," tending "to adduce a *Zeitgeist* from an accident," in the phrase of one friendly critic.[2] In other words, precisely what distinguishes New Historicism from history, its interest in "the literary," has seemed to some scholars—both historians and literary scholars—to be its weakness rather than its strength.

It occurs to me that some readers might take the title of this essay to refer to the need for "historical correctness," as implied by a headline in the *New York Times*: "We Happy Many, Playing Fast and Loose with History." The point of that article was that although William Shakespeare, like many modern artists and writers, did manipulate history, he had a more nuanced, complex, and learned way of doing so than, for example, director Oliver Stone, or actor-director Tim Robbins. "Shakespeare approached history with depth and integrity," insists the *Times* reviewer. "The contract that he made with his viewers was that they were witnessing an interpretation of history, not an exact reproduction of events. Most historical movies, by contrast, not only reduce history to a simple situation but also strive to give the impression that they are reconstructing what really happened."[3] Whatever the truth value of this distinction—and it does become muddier as time goes on, as Shakespeare's plays are all that many modern nonhistorians know about English or even Roman history—it is not in fact precisely what I mean by "historical correctness." For I intend here to invoke the cognate phrase "political correctness," one of the most denigrated and vilified imperatives in contemporary journalism and academic life.

Political correctness in today's popular parlance is understood to mean an insensitive attack on insensitivity. With its roots in old-style totalitarian discourse (as early as 1947 Vladimir Nabokov could mock it in his novel *Bend Sinister*[4]) the phrase was used in the 1970s with heavy self-irony by the left as a kind of amused reality check on its own excesses, and often abbreviated by its initials as a sign of this ruefully affectionate self-estrangement. Perhaps inevitably, the term was picked up by the right, denuded of any soupçon of irony, and used as a club to beat those very persons who had ironized it to begin with.[5] "Political correctness" is rather old and rather tired news in the United States, where it tends to be employed principally by diehard cultural conservatives and the authors of novels and plays about academic life. A review of *The Winter's Tale* at the American Repertory Theater scolded the director for adding "a politically correct ending," noting that "it is political correctness to disallow Shakespeare's forgiveness."[6]

European commentators often consider political correctness a symptom of both American puritanism and feminist excess. Thus, a French book on the history of flirting deplores the "return to puritanism" and the rise of sexual harassment laws, insisting that "there is nothing politically incorrect in a little ambiguous banter between men and women." In Britain "political correctness" has been decried in the press as having "some of the characteristics of a religious sect." When a popular judge at the Old Bailey stepped down from the bench he did so in a highly publicized speech that inveighed against a new conduct book for judges on how to avoid the perception of racial bias and against "political correctness in all its horrid forms."[7] Horrid or not, political correctness has been regarded as a tendency to turn critique into a new orthodoxy or orthopedic thinking, framing and shaping what can be thought and said.

What, then, is "historical correctness"? We might say that it is the suggestion, either implied or explicit, on the part of literary scholars, that history grounds and tells the truth about literature. The critique of this idea is superbly well made by Walter Benjamin's remark at the end of an essay called "Literary History and the Study of Literature":

> What is at stake is not to portray literary works in the context of their age, but to represent the age that perceives them—our age—in the age during which they arose. It is this that makes literature into an organon of history; and to achieve this, and not to reduce literature to the material of history, is the task of the literary historian.[8]

II

The most specifically *literary* charge offered against those who do not read historically or who deliberately and joyously flout chronology and sequence is the charge of anachronism—in effect, historical *in*correctness. Anachronism, from the Greek for "back" and "time," has itself had a checkered history. As the neglect or falsification of chronological relation, whether intentional or not, it is often regarded merely as a vulgar error. A clock strikes in the Rome of Shakespeare's *Julius Caesar*. An attendant to the Pharaoh in Cecil B. DeMille's *The Ten Commandments* appears in tennis shoes. In the canonical history of art and literature anachronisms are frequent, and some have been naturalized over the years in the service of "timeless" art or the double time of revealed truth. The *sacra conversazione* of Renaissance religious painting brings together Madonna, Christ child, angels, saints, and contemporary donors from the artist's time in a single transhistorical space. In northern European art you may encounter Joseph hard at work in a fifteenth-century shop, or the Virgin Mary as a Netherlandish burgher's daughter. In Florence or in Naples she is an Italian peasant girl. The Belgian painter James Ensor depicts, in 1880, Christ's entry into Brussels.

In literature we find similar "errors," often deliberately contrived for effect. Dido and Aeneas are made contemporaries by Virgil, though they lived three hundred years apart. Shakespeare famously alters history from time to time. He depicts King Duncan of Scotland as an elderly and beloved monarch, rather than the younger and feebler ruler described in Raphael Holinshed's *Chronicles*. He makes his two Harrys, Harry Percy and Harry Monmouth, age-mates rather than a generation apart. He describes the historical Cleopatra, a mere twenty-nine years old when his play opens, as "wrinkled deep in time." In *Titus Andronicus*, a Goth from the time of the Roman Empire pauses "to gaze upon a ruinous monastery" (5.1.121), thus invoking the Reformation context and Henry VIII's dissolution of the monasteries.[9] Mark Twain places a Connecticut Yankee in King Arthur's court. Thornton Wilder moves a single set of characters through a variety of geological and historical periods from paleolithic to modern in his play *The Skin of Our Teeth*. In each of these cases a point is being made about the present day.

Yet often artists and writers are criticized for their anachronisms, like the Gothic novelist Ann Radcliffe or the Roman historian Sallust. In these instances *anachronism* becomes conflated with sloppiness or ignorance rather than aesthetic, political, or satirical effect. The Hollywood speciality known as "continuity" is meant to clean up such inadvertent errors. Forgeries in films are often detected, or detectable, by unwitting anachronisms: too many stars on the U.S. flag, the wrong period fashion in dress or hair, a telephone in the

"Old West" saloon, a piece of advanced technology out of its time and place. The two faces of anachronism (deliberate juxtaposition to make a clever point; awkward and revealing error of fact) are often regarded as different in kind as well as degree. It is the bugbear of "intentionality" again: a knowing error is a cleverness, an unknowing error is a bêtise. But it is sometimes hard to tell the difference. DeMille's *Ten Commandments* stages a Passover celebration that vastly postdates the time of the Biblical event, presenting a modern-looking rabbinic seder rather than a lamb sacrifice. Joseph L. Mankiewicz's version of Shakespeare's *Julius Caesar* (1953) features portrait busts that closely resemble the Emperor Hadrian, who was born about a century and a half later. Josef von Sternberg's 1934 film *The Scarlet Empress* offers Marlene Dietrich in the role of Catherine the Great. The soundtrack of this film about eighteenth-century Russia included the music of Mendelssohn, Tchaikovsky (including the *1812 Overture*), Rimsky-Korsakov, and Wagner's "Ride of the Valkyries."[10] Such anachronisms could be inadvertent or deliberate: whether intended or not, they tell us something about the moment of production and consumption. *Anachronism* in this sense is another term for *bricolage*.

Kathleen Coleman, a professor of Latin and an expert on Roman games, was hired as a consultant to the film *Gladiator* (2000) and found it "an interesting but ultimately disillusioning experience." No sooner did she set the historical record straight, she noted, than "a whole range of fresh inaccuracies and anachronisms" crept in, and were immortalized on film, including fictive inscriptions in bad Latin engraved upon the public buildings. Misunderstanding Juvenal's phrase "bread and circuses," the placating of the hungry and discontented masses with public spectacles like chariot races, the filmmakers invented a slew of imperial caterers tossing bread into the stadium stands.[11] "*Gladiator* ain't history," wrote Philip Howard jauntily in the *London Times*. "Its account of Roman politics is nonsense. Marcus Aurelius never dreamt of restoring power to the people. . . . The heroic general Maximus with republican dreams in the film is a John Wayne fantasy. The Senate gave up any republican inclinations long before." Howard found "the anachronism [he] most enjoyed" was Maximus praying to the shade of his murdered son, and advising him to keep his heels down when riding. "Since the Romans had not yet cribbed the stirrup from the Goths, this was seriously foolish advice." And modern culture, it seems, has the thumbs up/thumbs down gesture backward. "When the crowd in the Colosseum wanted a popular gladiator to be spared they turned their thumbs down into their fists. Thumbs up meant 'Cut his throat,'" Howard explained. (Readers seeking corroboration for this point may consult Montaigne's essay "Of Thumbs."[12]) Nonetheless, Howard liked the film, which he thought embodied modern as well as ancient tastes for blood sport, from boxing to professional football. As he noted, "We continually reinvent the past to match our present concerns, causes and totems."[13]

Nor is the allure of anachronism a new development, a mere artifact of modern or postmodern life. The fashion for dialogues with the dead, modeled after Lucian, provided the opportunity for explicitly anachronistic interchange: Fontanelle's *New Dialogues of the Dead* (*Nouveaux dialogues des morts*, 1683–1684) offered dialogues between Socrates and Montaigne, Seneca and Scarron. Fénelon's *Dialogues des morts* (1700–1718) followed the same pattern, as did English writers like Walter Savage Landor, whose *Imaginary Conversations* (1824) included invented colloquies between Achilles and Helen, Galileo and John Milton, the Earl of Essex and Edmund Spenser, Joan of Arc and Agnes Sorel.

A memorable instance of this once-popular genre was offered by comedian Steve Allen's television show *Meeting of Minds*, which ran for four years on the Public Broadcasting System. On one occasion Aristotle, Sun Yat-Sen, Niccolò Machiavelli, and Elizabeth Barrett Browning debated; on another a lively argument developed among Theodore Roosevelt, Thomas Aquinas, Cleopatra, and Thomas Paine; a third panel featured Florence Nightingale, Plato, Voltaire, and Martin Luther; a fourth, Attila the Hun, Emily Dickinson, Galileo, and Charles Darwin. (Steve Allen to Galileo: "You know, it's most interesting. You sir, Miss Dickinson, and Dr. Darwin all had difficulty with domineering fathers." Attila: "My father, too, was no bargain." Or Karl Marx to Marie Antoinette, from a panel discussion involving Ulysses S. Grant, Marie Antoinette, Thomas More, and Marx: "Did it ever enter your mind, Your Majesty, that . . . empty rituals and customs would in time destroy the people's respect for the monarchy?" Marie: "Nonsense, Dr. Marx, the people adored the rituals and customs!" Thomas More: "Yes, Dr. Marx, . . . rituals and manners aided the people to express their respect for royalty. I understand that in today's Marxist nations there is still room for pomp and circumstance."[14]) These were not séances; actors played the parts. Allen's wife Jayne Meadows performed almost all the female roles.[15]

The pleasure opened up by such deliberate violations of history seems somehow old-fashioned today. But why should that be? What was being disregarded then—or now? Are we simply too conscious of history to be playful in this way? Is there something about the interest in history and politics that gives anachronism a bad name? Or is anachronism simply returning in a new form? A useful analogue to this problem can be found in the current "antichronology" debates among art historians, curators, and art critics—debates inflamed by the thematic, nonchronological installations at such high-profile museums as the Tate Modern, the Tate Britain, the Museum of Modern Art, and the Brooklyn Museum. As art historian Linda Nochlin has noted, "[T]here is a tendency to use chronology as teleology." A "nonchronological hang," she suggested, can "break up the idea of an uninterrupted flow." But other critics have objected, perceiving the loss of chronology as a loss of coherence. Thus, for example, British art critic David Sylvester thought the Tate Modern's decision to follow themes rather than periods was a mistake; chronology, he argued, was "an objective reality, built into the fabric of the work," not "a tool of art-historical interpretation which can be used at one moment and discarded at another."[16]

What was at stake here? Chronology implied evolution and a certain kind of progress narrative, privileging some works and movements above others. History was a history of aesthetic forms: their development and evolution was the ground of meaningful art history. Antichronology (dismissed in some quarters as political correctness because it shifted the focus away from "masterpieces") drew attention to merely looking. It invited pleasure and irresponsibility, not the accuracy of any story. Antichronology, then, is both old and new: both a resistance to an older notion of historical sequence and development and a rediscovery of familiar categories like genre, theme, and structure. These categories were not simply resurrected; they were substantially altered, as, for example, in the notion of many alternative modernisms rather than one.[17] But their chief effect was to open up some kinds of interpretation that might have been closed off by chronology. Placing a Rembrandt painting next to one of Mark Rothko or Norman Rockwell raises issues of similarity and difference, form and mood, that neither chronology nor historical context will address or ground.

This suggests another sense in which the word *anachronism* has been used to criticize and control a development in literary studies: the anachronism not within the text itself but within the framework used to read it. In some ways, of course, the question of history's value for literature is an old and familiar debate. In a 1910 essay called "Anachronism in Shakespeare Criticism," the literary scholar Elmer Edgar Stoll lamented that "Criticism forgets that Shakespeare wrote in the sixteenth century," turning him instead into a "twentieth-century symbolist." (The tension here was partly one between "scholars" and "critics," the latter excoriated as "poets, essayists, gentlemen of taste and leisure, not to mention a horde of the tasteless and leisureless—propagandists and blatherskites.") Stoll's chief culprit was character criticism and psychology, which he thought inappropriate for the discussion of Elizabethan literature. The issue, in short, was one of what I have called respect: respect for sixteenth-century ideas about the preeminence of story and plot, in contrast with "our modern ideas" of character and social problems.

It was anachronistic, Stoll said, to regard Shakespeare as having any interest in "the newer psychology concerning subconscious states, racial distinctions, criminal and morbid types." Ghosts and witches were signs of superstition, not "personifications of conscience." Nor should Shakespeare be read as having any relevance to politics. The English history plays and the Roman plays "are political plays with the politics left out." Here was a gauntlet thrown down on behalf of historical correctness. "Ours is the day of the historical method," Stoll declared. "Fetichism [*sic*; what he called the "cult" of Shakespeare] is all that stands in the way."[18]

More recently, when Terry Eagleton's book on Shakespeare was published in 1986, reviewers zeroed in on what they called its "anachronisms." "Mr. Eagleton does in print what directors regularly do on stage," said the *New York Times*: "change the century, stitch up new costumes, but preserve the story-line and language." Herbert Mitgang found Eagleton "bold" and "courageous" but also sometimes "maddening." "Rather ingeniously, Mr. Eagleton united Freud and Marx in discussing *The Merchant of Venice*," he notes, although by 1986 this had become a fairly common starting point for discussions of the play. "Inevitably, Mr. Eagleton turns to Lady Macbeth to interpret militant feminists," he observes, adding that "it is doubtful if present-day women's organizations... would accept Lady Macbeth as a role model. The parallel is too narrow and strained." (Little did he know what a goldmine Hillary Clinton was going to be for Lady Macbeth hunters in the daily press. The comparison between these two politicians' wives became a standard trope of journalism in the 1990s.) When Eagleton alleges slyly that "Though conclusive evidence is hard to come by, it is difficult to read Shakespeare without feeling that he was almost certainly familiar with the writings of Hegel, Marx, Nietzsche, Freud, Wittgenstein and Derrida," Mitgang regards this as more playful than persuasive. There seems to be something exciting about anachronism, then, and at the same time something illicit. What does this have to do with the relations between history and literature?

III

Let me offer an example of the seductiveness of history for me that also rang some alarm bells, reminding me of where my own resistances and textual predilections lay. A gifted young teacher of colonial American literature and culture recently explained a technique he had developed for teaching the seventeenth-century American poet Anne Bradstreet, whose work, he suspected, might seem temporally distant to his presentist young students. The poem he wanted to discuss was Bradstreet's "The Author to Her Book." Bradstreet wrote it after her brother-in-law, without her knowledge, brought a manuscript of her verses to London and had them published under the title *The Tenth Muse, Lately Sprung Up in America*. Here is the beginning of the poem in which Bradstreet addressed her pirated book, describing it as a victim of kidnapping:

> Thou ill-formed offspring of my feeble brain,
> Who after birth didst by my side remain,
> Till snatched from thence by friends, less wise than true,
> Who thee abroad, exposed to public view,
> Made thee in rags, halting to th' press to trudge,
> Where errors were not lessened (all may judge).
> At thy return my blushing was not small,
> My rambling brat (in print) should mother call,
> I cast thee by as one unfit for light,
> Thy visage was so irksome in my sight:
> Yet being mine own, at length affection would

> Thy blemishes amend, if so I could:
> I washed thy face, but more defects I saw,
> And rubbing off a spot still made a flaw,
> I stretched thy joints to make thee even feet,
> Yet still thou run'st more hobbling than is meet.... [19]

The poem is clearly imagined in the genre of the title, "The Author to Her Book." The phrase "even feet" denotes "regular metrics," the "rags" suggest rag paper, and so forth.

My acquaintance, a scholar of puritan America, knowing the social and medical history of the period, and mindful of another poem by Bradstreet, "Before the Birth of One of Her Children," in which the poet anticipated the possibility of dying in childbirth, handed out to his students, as a way of making Bradstreet's words vivid and her historical predicament clear, photocopies of early-seventeenth-century articles and woodcuts of deformed children and monstrous births, a familiar preoccupation of recent early modern scholarship. When his students had sufficiently put themselves in the place of a mother contemplating anxieties attendant upon childbirth in a medically rudimentary context, he gave them another historical grid to defamiliarize their own sense of corporeal vulnerability. In puritan America, deformed children signified that the mother had consorted with the devil. Thus the fear and fascination was itself a sign of religious, not just medical, history. For this literary scholar—and here is my point—the cause or ground of interpretation was the historical situation—the historical fact and the historical framework through which it was viewed. Bradstreet's references to the "ill-formed offspring" were troped on a mother's hopes and fears. [20]

But Anne Bradstreet, who wrote in the mid–seventeenth century, was well read in sixteenth- and early-seventeenth-century English literature, including the works of Sir Walter Raleigh, William Camden, Sir Philip Sidney, and Joshua Sylvester's Du Bartas's *Divine Weeks*. [21] Imagine if, instead of contemplating the fate of deformed children in the colonies, we were to juxtapose to her poem "The Author to Her Book" with the following passage:

> It had been a thing, we confesse, worthie to haue bene wished, that the Author himselfe had liv'd to haue set forth, and ouerseen his owne writings; But since it hath bin ordain'd otherwise, and he by death departed from that right, we pray you

do not envie his Friends, the office of their care, and paine, to haue collected &
publish'd them; and so to have publish'd them, as where (before) you were abus'd
with diuerse stolne, and surreptitious copies, maimed, and deformed by the frauds
and stealthes of iniurious impostors, that expos'd them: euen those, are now
offer'd to your view cur'd, and perfect of their limbes; and all the rest, absolute in
their numbers, as he conceived them.[22]

This is the letter "To the Great Variety of Readers," by Shakespeare's friends
and fellow players, John Heminge and Henry Condell, affixed to the First Folio
of his plays. The similarities are so striking as to be obvious: the parent who
was unable to oversee the publication of his writings, the (consequent) maim-
ing and deformation of the text, the need in particular to regularize the meter
(Bradstreet's "even feet," Heminge and Condell's "absolute . . . numbers") and
so on. It will not escape your attention that this text, too, is from the
past—that is, embedded in the history of the period. It is not a late-twentieth-
century product, juxtaposed to the seventeenth century. I would be quite willing to defend and indeed promote the use of anachronism for reading, but for
now I want only to point out a difference between what might be called the
vehicle and the tenor of historical literary scholarship. To illuminate Anne
Bradstreet's poem "To Her Book" by framing it with images of "real" deformed
children and information about death in childbirth is one kind of reading. To
examine the same poem by considering it to be, itself, a legitimate or illegiti-
mate offspring of a famous textual passage and a familiar figure of speech is
another. The "Author" referred to in the First Folio's prefatory letter is also
(like the speaker in Bradstreet's poem) said to have "conceived" his writings,
which were "expos'd" by thieves just as Bradstreet's works were "snatched" and
"exposed to public view."

Which is the "ground" here? Literary trope or social condition? Text or
life? Figure of speech or historical fact? Every piece of writing inhabits these
various worlds, and every text offers a dilemma, or an opportunity, in terms of
its frames of reference. We have perhaps overcorrected earlier literary histories
that confined texts within a world of other texts. But might not the intertextual
references have shaped this poem as much as the medical realities? It seems
that this question is all the more urgent in the case of a woman poet. Why are
anxieties about reproduction seen as more real or more literal here than anxi-

eties about authorship? Are women more naturally literal—less involved with literary history—than men? And could it be that in this case the desire to have a more complete picture of history impedes, rather than brings out, the female poet in whose name it is often undertaken? It is not necessary to my argument for Bradstreet actually to be referring to, or remembering, or even half-remembering, the Folio letter. If she were, we could perhaps allege that her modest demurral was in fact a bold claim in disguise: Bradstreet as successor to Shakespeare. But I do not care, at least right now, whether this is the (historical) case. And I do not want, either, to dismiss or impugn the usefulness of historical context and the power of contemporary images of childhood and deformity. This is not an either/or issue. It is, instead, a question of the goals sought by a discipline, or the practitioners of that discipline. Why do we read literature? Why do we teach it? What do we teach?

IV

The defense of Shakespearean anachronism has a long and distinguished history. The German romantic critic August Wilhelm Schlegel observes that Shakespeare "considered himself entitled to the greatest liberties. He had not to do with a petty hypercritical age like ours, which is always seeking in poetry for something else than poetry; his audience entered the theatre, not to learn true chronology, geography, natural history, but to witness a vivid exhibition. I undertake to prove that Shakespeare's anachronisms are, for the most part, committed purposely, and after great consideration. It was frequently of importance to him to bring the subject exhibited, from the back ground of time, quite near to us."[23] For Schlegel, Shakespeare's anachronistic mention of Hamlet's education at a university, "though in the age of the historical Hamlet there was not yet any university," was a sign of the playwright's wisdom rather than of his ignorance: "He makes him study at Wittenberg, and no selection could be more suitable. The name was very popular from the story of Dr. Faustus . . . it was of particular celebrity in protestant England, as Luther had taught and written there shortly before, and the very name must immediately have suggested the idea of freedom in thinking." Concerned with Richard III's mention of Machiavelli,

Schlegel "cannot even consider it an anachronism," since the word is used "altogether proverbially." Anachronism, he insists, is an intelligent mode of generalization, as when early Christian painters dressed "the Saviour, the Virgin Mary, the Patriarchs and Apostles in an ideal dress," but the subordinate actors or spectators of the action in "the dresses of their own nation and age," or when an old manuscript shows the funeral procession of Hector, the coffin carried into a Gothic church. As with Shakespeare, so also with these artists: "a powerful consciousness of the universal prevalency and the solid consistency of their manner of being, an undoubted conviction that it has always so been and will continue so to be in the world" were crucial to the power of their work.

Perhaps anachronism—playing fast and loose with history—is not just something that sometimes happens to literature, but is connected to it in a more profound way. Suppose we return for a moment to Shakespeare's *Julius Caesar*, not by accident the locus classicus of some favorite literary anachronisms. That striking clock, for instance. Arden Shakespeare editor David Daniell reminds us, citing Sigurd Buckhardt's important essay on the topic, that the warring systems of the calendars were very much an issue of contention in late-sixteenth-century Europe, and that Julius Caesar had himself sorted out an earlier set of calendrical discrepancies. The Julian calendar, named in his honor, was the official calendar of Protestant England, while the "New Style" Gregorian calendar, named after the Pope, reigned throughout Catholic Europe. The striking clock, which, as Daniell notes, "amused and irritated eighteenth- and nineteenth-century commentators for its anachronistic ignorance,"[24] was in fact a powerful sign. Caesar had not only set the date with his reforms of the calendar, but also "set the clocks of Rome," and his commentaries are full of his concern for timekeeping. The clock and its striking are thus reminders within the play text of Caesar's power over and against Brutus's.

Julius Caesar contains a number of other celebrated anachronistic references, some of them sartorial: a reference to "hats," for example, describing the conspirators before the murder: "Their hats are pluck'd about their ears / And half their faces buried in their cloaks" (2.1.73). Alexander Pope found this so unhistorical that he printed the line "their—are pluckt about their ears"—"as if the word [hat] were some obscenity," observes Daniell, who adds, "Quite apart from the fine dramatic furtiveness of Shakespeare's image, the Romans did wear headgear," and sends the reader to the previous Arden edition, where we are told the particulars of that headgear: "the petasus, a broad-brimmed traveling hat or cap, the pilleus, a close-fitting, brimless hat or cap, worn at entertainments and festivals, and the cucullus, a cap or hood fastened to a garment." We also learn that Pope was "similarly unwilling to accept *hat*" in *Coriolanus*, where he emends the word to *cap* (*Cor.* 2.3.95;164).[25]

The same criticism might be made of the reference to the turned-down "leaf" in Brutus's book (4.1.271–72: "is not the leaf turned down / Where I left reading?"). Living in ancient Rome, Brutus would properly be reading from a scroll, not a codex, a book with leaves. The sleeping Imogen in another of Shakespeare's Roman plays, *Cymbeline*, also folds down the leaf of a book as she falls asleep (*Cymb.* 2.2.4). But of course by the time we get to *Cymbeline*, ancient Britain, Rome, modern Italy, and rural Wales are all nicely mingled in a transhistorical stew. This is not a mistake; it is a point.

Whether such temporal dissonances are admired or scorned, anachronisms in literature have their purposes and their effects. We see this very clearly and obviously as well in the history of performance, where the tension between so-called modernization and equally so-called period costume (also known as "museum Shakespeare") is the frequent target of theatrical reviews. Thus the director JoAnne Akalaitis, often criticized (or lauded) for the chances she takes with Shakespeare, is described in a review of her production of *Henry IV* (parts 1 and 2) as surprisingly conventional: "performed in predominantly period costumes ... the production has only occasional anachronisms—a TV or telephone thrown in to drive home a motivation."[26] Peter Sellars has staged *Antony and Cleopatra* in a swimming pool and put King Lear in a "kingmobile" (aka a Lincoln Continental). The scheming villain Aaron in Julie Taymor's *Titus* (a film version of *Titus Andronicus*, set in ancient Rome) seals Titus's hand in a ziplock plastic bag.

Charles Spencer, assessing Michael Boyd's Royal Shakespeare Company production of *Troilus and Cressida* in 1998, began by declaring that he was "not one of those arch conservatives who believes that Shakespeare should always be staged in period costume," but went on to speculate about the setting: the scene opened with sepia photographs that seemed to evoke the western front during the First World War, but many characters had Irish accents, and it eventually became clear that while the Trojans were Irish, the Greeks were British. "Why then," he wondered, "does Achilles look like a present-day

Serbian war-crimes thug, and Ajax resemble a particularly dim heavy metal rock star?" Spencer admired the production, with reservations, and offered his own interpretation: "What Boyd is presumably trying to suggest is any modern, war-torn territory in which fine words cover vile actions."[27]

Some people love this kind of thing, and others hate it. Opinion was divided on the Baz Lurhmann film *Romeo + Juliet*, with its black drag queen Mercutio and its CNN talking-head prologues. In Michael Almereyda's film *Hamlet* (2000), starring Ethan Hawke, letters are delivered by fax machine; Ophelia wears a wiretap to entrap Hamlet in the lobby scene; Rosencrantz and Guildenstern are heard on the speakerphone in Gertrude's bedroom; the prayer scene happens in a limousine, and Hamlet makes an indie video film of *The Mousetrap* to catch the conscience of the king. (Elsinore is a hotel. Denmark is a corporation. Claudius is a CEO. So runs the world away.) But these uses of anachronism, however startling, function by destabilizing juxtaposition: bringing a metaphor to devastatingly literal life, or striving, like the Boyd *Troilus*, for the postmodern version of timelessness—that is, multitimeliness. Some productions do this via costume, mingling classical dress, Nazi uniforms, 1970s punk, and 1930s gangster wear. Others do it through cross-casting, mixing nations, races, genders, and accents.

Whether or not we like it, we have become accustomed to this mode of theatrical anachronism, as we have to its more moderate and "straight" avatars, modern dress and rehearsal clothes. Indeed, even if we cherish the old ways, and hang an engraving of Mrs. Siddons as Lady Macbeth on the wall, we will have to acknowledge that she too is in "modern dress," and not in authentic "period costume"—whatever that would be. Authentic Jacobean costume—or authentic medieval Scottish garb? As Eric Hobsbawm and others have argued about "the invention of tradition," authenticity is itself a cultural effect.

Using historical data anachronistically is different, of course, from the anachronistic use of theoretical ideas. But the reviewer who accused Terry Eagleton of anachronism seems himself to have conflicting notions of history and chronology as they affect literary interpretation. He subscribes to two inconsistent but widely held fantasies: the fantasy of historical determination, and the fantasy of universality. Thus he can say both that Eagleton's "strongest arguments are backed by history"—for example, the information "that inflation in the 1590's led to debased coinage and speculation" and also that politi-

cal analysis of the plays is misguided: "Is not the range of [Shakespeare's] characters neither conservative nor even neoconservative but universal?"[28] I want
here to contest both of these views—that history is data and that "universality"
is something different from the theories it opposes, rather than being yet
another theory.

There is a great deal that history can do for literary study, and for the study
of Shakespeare and his contemporaries. I am not urging a return to the old
days of timeless transcendence. The criterion for "timelessness" is the most
historically time-bound thing of all, since there is no real evidence for it other
than consensus. The timeless is what has stopped being considered a theory
and has passed into stereotype. But there are some things history cannot do,
and those things are, I want to insist, at the core of the literary enterprise.

V

I will illustrate this claim in my own anachronistic and unhistorical fashion by
citing a well-known passage of literary criticism that addresses not a
Renaissance text but a nineteenth-century one. The writer is discussing a particular kind of "research," the kind called a "search." (The two words search
and research are versions of the same.) Here he discusses a search of the
premises undertaken by detectives:

> We are spared nothing concerning the procedures used in searching the area sub-
> mitted to their investigation: from the division of that space into compartments
> from which the slightest bulk could not escape detection, to needles probing
> upholstery, and, in the impossibility of sounding wood with a tap, to a microscope
> exposing the waste of any drilling at the surface of its hollow, indeed the infinites-
> imal gaping of the slightest abyss. As the network tightens to the point that, not
> satisfied with shaking the pages of books, the police take to counting them, do we
> not see space itself shed its leaves like a letter?
>
> But the detectives have so immutable a notion of the real that they fail to notice
> that their search tends to transform it into its object. A trait by which they would
> be able to distinguish that object from all others.
>
> This would no doubt be too much to ask them, not because of their lack of
> insight but rather because of ours. For their imbecility is neither of the individual
> nor of the corporative variety; its source is subjective. It is the realist's imbecility,
> which does not pause to observe that . . . what is hidden is never but what is miss-

ing from its place, as the call slip puts it when speaking of a volume lost in a library. And even if the book be on an adjacent shelf or in the next slot, it would be hidden there, however visibly it may appear. For it can literally be said that something is missing from its place only of what can change it: the symbolic. For the real, whatever upheaval we subject it to, is always in its place; it carries it glued to its heel, ignorant of what might exile it from it.[29]

The real is what the realist does not find. The belief that the real can be exhaustively measured and mapped is a form of blindness. The real is what escapes that mapping. The real is what literature, not "the world," is hiding.

The passage I have just quoted is taken from Jacques Lacan's reading of Edgar Allan Poe's "The Purloined Letter," and it is conceivable that Lacan's view of Poe may seem far removed from the study of either Shakespeare or history. So let me place next to this an uncannily similar passage from Ralph Waldo Emerson's essay, "Shakspeare; Or, the Poet." In the essay, published in the 1850 volume *Representative Men*, Emerson has this to say about "the researches of antiquaries, and the Shakspeare Society":

> [T]hey have left no book-stall unsearched, no chest in a garret unopened, no file of old yellow accounts to decompose in damp and worms, so keen was the hope to discover whether the boy Shakspeare poached or not, whether he held horses at the theatre door, whether he kept school, and why he left in his will only his second-best bed to Ann Hathaway, his wife....
>
> The Shakspeare Society have inquired in all directions, advertised the missing facts, offered money for any information that will lead to proof; and with what result?... they have gleaned a few facts touching the property, and dealings in regard to property, of the poet. It appears that, from year to year, he owned a larger share in the Blackfriars' Theatre...that he bought an estate in his native village...that he lived in the best house in Stratford; was intrusted by his neighbors with their commissions in London, as of borrowing money, and the like.... About the time when he was writing Macbeth, he sues Philip Rogers, in the borough-court of Stratford, for thirty-five shillings, ten pence, for corn delivered to him.... I admit the importance of this information. It was well worth the pains that have been taken to procure it.

For Emerson, "we are very clumsy writers of history." The questions we ask are the wrong questions, our real is the wrong real. Emerson feels so strongly about this that he prefers to know nothing of the specifically histori-

cal as it affects the case of Shakespeare, lest that knowledge impinge upon
imagination and poetic genius:

> Can any biography shed light on the localities into which the *Midsummer Night's
> Dream* admits me? Did Shakspeare confide to any notary or parish recorder, sac-
> ristan, or surrogate, in Stratford, the genesis of that delicate creation? The forest of
> Arden, the noble air of Scone Castle, the moonlight of Portia's villa, "the antres vast
> and desarts idle" of Othello's captivity—where is the third cousin, or grand-
> nephew, the chancellor's file of accounts, or private letter, that has kept one word
> of those transcendent secrets?

Thus Emerson offers his famous and paradoxical assertions: that "Shakspeare
is the only biographer of Shakspeare," and, "So far from Shakspeare's being the
least known to us, he is the one person, in all modern history, known to us."[30]
Not knowing Shakespeare's history is what gives Emerson his Shakespeare.

This rhetorically framed either/or choice, between the historical-archival
and the imaginative-poetic ("Can any biography shed light on the localities
into which the *Midsummer Night's Dream* admits me?...where is the third
cousin...or private letter, that has kept one word of those transcendent
secrets?") is just what has been debunked and analyzed in late-twentieth-century literary scholarship. To contemporary scholars there is no methodological
contradiction, no doubt that historical research can and does illuminate imaginative writing, enriching rather than impoverishing aesthetic response.

Far from supplying a text's ground, historical study can unground it in a
new way. Productions of *The Merchant of Venice* have been used both to inflame
feelings of anti-Semitism and to critique them, depending upon the director's
and actor's interpretation, and ("always historicize") the culture and circumstances of production. Notice that the word *production* here has two equal and
adjacent meanings. But as the example of *Merchant* suggests, once they are
written, plays and poems and novels take on a life of their own, and even an
"intention" or intentionality of their own—what is sometimes called the
"unconscious" of the text. Their history starts with their writing and reading,
and is never completed, and can never be completely known.

It is worth remembering that the history of literary analysis has itself been
dialectical. Thus, in the course of the past century of literary study, philology

and editing have given way to literary history; then to "character criticism" and psychology; then to close reading and the pursuit of images and themes; then to archetypal criticism; then to philosophical and psychoanalytic theory; then to historicism and an emphasis on socially and culturally produced categories like race, class, gender, and sexuality; and now once again to philology and editing (and "the history of the book") as well as to appreciation (also known as "aesthetics") and value (also known as "ethics"). The return of these last two categories, aesthetics and ethics, was in retrospect virtually guaranteed by their previous abjection, just as that abjection was virtually guaranteed by their enormous earlier success and prestige.

The critique of what is often called "presentism" by scholars of early modern literature and culture has been a necessary corrective for a failure of historical specificity that can obscure what is most striking and powerful about a literary text.[31] The days of Jan Kott's frisky *Shakespeare Our Contemporary* have, to a certain extent, given way to the rigors, and longeurs, of Shakespeare Not Our Contemporary. But it seems equally crucial to acknowledge that some kinds of literary questions—questions about "what repeats"—cannot be posed through a predominantly historical approach.

Furthermore, there is yet another pertinent paradox for us to note: What the best literary historicists look for are not the moments when the author is consciously historical but when he is unconsciously historical. Anachronism or fantasy, which seems to escape historical determination, is intimately connected to it in ways that escape the author's conscious perception. Thus, in neglecting the ahistorical, literal-minded literary historicists are in reality neglecting the historical. And it is the analysis of the historicity of the present that prevents "presentism."

VI

"The injunction to practise intellectual honesty usually amounts to sabotage of thought," writes Theodor Adorno with characteristic acerbity. He continues:

> The writer is urged to show explicitly all the steps that have led him to his conclusion, so enabling every reader to follow the process through and, where possible—in the academic industry—to duplicate it. This demand not only invokes the

> liberal fiction of the universal communicability of each and every thought . . . but is
> also wrong in itself as a principle of representation. For the value of a thought is
> measured by its distance from the continuity of the familiar. . . . Texts which anx-
> iously undertake to record every step without omission inevitably succumb to
> banality, and to a monotony related not only to the tension induced in the reader,
> but to their own substance.[32]

In Adorno's critique of demands for intellectual honesty, we can dimly make
out what we are asking literature to do. Literature, in fact, is the discourse in
which the knowledge of the discontinuity of thought is made fleetingly available. "The demand for intellectual honesty is itself dishonest," he writes, since
it ignores or rejects the messier ways in which knowledge is actually acquired
"through a network of prejudices, opinions, innervations, self-corrections, pre-
suppositions and exaggerations." If "honest ideas" always manifest themselves
as "mere repetition, whether of what was there before or of categorical forms,"
something crucial is missing in intellectual life. To illustrate this naivete, he
adduces an image of a man dying satisfied that his life has all added up. It is, as
it happens, an image that carries a strong, though indirect, whiff of
Shakespeare:

> Anyone who dies old and in the consciousness of seemingly blameless success,
> would secretly be the model schoolboy who reels off all life's stages without gaps or
> omissions, an invisible satchel on his back.

At first recollection, of course, Shakespeare's schoolboy in *As You Like It* is
scarcely a model, that "whining schoolboy with his satchel / And shining
morning face, creeping like snail / Unwillingly to school."[33] Why then associate
this passage with Shakespeare at all? Why not think instead only of the modern German gymnasium student seemingly directly evoked by Adorno? There
are two reasons: first, the indirect line of associative thinking is the one
Adorno himself recommends in this passage ("a wavering, deviating line"; a
kind of thought "which, for the sake of its relation to its object, forgoes the full
transparency of its logical genesis"); second, the "mere repetition" of "categorical forms" is in fact present, in extreme form, in the passage where
Shakespeare's schoolboy makes his appearance—Jaques's famous, or infamous,
"Seven Ages of Man." It is Jaques who, to cite Adorno's phrase again, "reels off
all life's stages without gaps or omissions, an invisible satchel on his back." It is

Jaques, the "melancholy Jaques," who is the model schoolboy, showing off—here in parodic fashion—the well-worn "knowledge" which had by Shakespeare's time become a cliché:

> All the world's a stage,
> And all the men and women merely players.
> They have their exits and their entrances,
> And one man in his time plays many parts,
> His acts being seven ages. (2.7.138–42)

Instead of the diligent schoolboy, Adorno recommends the model of the slug-abed and the truant:

> Every thought which is not idle . . . bears branded on it the impossibility of its full legitimation, as we know in dreams that there are mathematics lessons, missed for the sake of a blissful morning in bed, which can never be made up. Thought waits to be woken one day by the memory of what has been missed, and to be transformed into teaching.

Teaching—like thought—depends upon what has been missed. Upon the gaps in knowledge, the resistance to the idea of a citation of facts, a "discursive progression from stage to stage," the recording of every step without omission. It is in order to resist the inevitability of such a progression that I want to point toward the usefulness of anachronism, play, and all the other ways in which literature shocks us into awareness, and preserves something that cannot be reduced to a ground. Whatever modes of reading are on the way, I hope that they and their practitioners will dare—at least from time to time—to be historically incorrect.

The Jane Austen Syndrome

"Let me say at the outset that I come to this topic as an amateur, rather than a professional. I am not an expert on Jane Austin novels. I am a Shakespearean by training and a critic of contemporary culture by predilection. For that very reason, perhaps, I am in a good position to testify to the existence of something I will call the Jane Austen syndrome.

Like many passionate literary pilgrims these days I have visited Austen's cottage at Chawton and the Austen museum house in Bath; I have walked the Austen trail throughout that beautiful city, and even climbed a nearby hill to Priory Gardens on a rainy day to get a distant prospect over the surrounding hills, thinking as I did so about Catherine Morland. I have walked the length of the Cobb at Lyme Regis, wondering exactly where Louisa Musgrove fell. I have swooned with the best, or the worst, of them, in watching reruns of the BBC *Pride and Prejudice* ("Oh, God, that shirt, those trousers!" as one Colin Firth fan unguardedly confessed in print to an English reporter[1]), and I have doted on elements of décor and landscape in all the delicious recent films, from *Sense and Sensibility* to *Persuasion*.

While working on a book on the unexpected passions generated by home ownership, I found myself repeatedly returning to Austen: to the vacation cottages in *Sanditon* as well as to the greatest erotic scene in all of real estate literature, when Elizabeth Bennet falls in love with Pemberley. "At that moment she felt, that to be mistress of Pemberley might be something!"

Recall Elizabeth's answer to her sister Jane, when Jane asks when she first thought she could be falling in love with Mr. Darcy: "Will you tell me how long you have loved him?" asks Jane, and Elizabeth answers, "It has been coming on so gradually, that I hardly knew when it began. But I believe I must date it from my first seeing his beautiful grounds at Pemberley."[2] Jane takes this as a joke, but the reader, who has had the advantage of a firsthand perusal of volume 3, chapter 1, knows there is more truth in this than Jane—or perhaps even Elizabeth—would like to acknowledge. The handsome grounds, the handsome portrait, and the handsome master of the house present themselves, one by one, to her intelligent attention, and by the end of the chapter she is in love. The perceptive Mrs. Gardiner unconsciously perceives the identification between house and man, calling Mr. Darcy "stately," rather than proud. (He *is* the stately home.) The man and the house combine to produce that remarkable erotic effect that I term "sex and real estate." (Or "real estate and sex." It was never completely clear to me which of the two was the more erotic term.)

My most intimate Austen connection, however, is with my golden retriever, who rejoices in the name of Willoughby. (He was born at a western Massachusetts establishment called Dashwood Kennels, so there was really never any doubt about his name.) Like his namesake, Willoughby is handsome, flirtatious, irresistible, and unreliable. Such are my meager credentials: amateur enthusiasm, Austen tourism and movie-watching, and pet naming. I am, for better or for worse, enunciating some of the chief symptoms of what I have dubbed the Jane Austen syndrome—my way of understanding how "Jane Austen" (the sum total of her language, plots, biography, and landscape) is marketed, consumed, and disseminated today.

A few years ago I found myself trying to distinguish between a cultural symptom and a cultural syndrome. A symptom, I came to believe, was a sign, an indicator. It was not, despite its modern usage, a *pathological* sign or a sign of *illness* or *disease*, but rather a kind of language, something that acts, or acts out, asking to be interpreted. And my chief expert on this kind of nonpathological *symptom* was Jane Austen.

The word appears over and over again in *Pride and Prejudice*. "I can remember *no symptom of affection* on either side," says Elizabeth Bennet about the elopement of her sister Lydia with Wickham.[3] Darcy initially believes that Jane Bennet isn't in love with Bingley, as he later explains to Elizabeth: "Her look and manner were open, cheerful and engaging as ever, but *without any symptom of peculiar regard*."[4] Meantime, when she visits Rosings, the home of Lady Catherine De Bourgh, Elizabeth keeps a close eye on Darcy and Miss De Bourgh, to whom he is said to be engaged, but "Neither at that moment nor at any other could she discern *any symptom of love*."[5] We might notice that all these are *negative* results: detectives of emotion in Austen's novels often seek such "symptoms" and fail to find them.[6] This is, I think, characteristic of how Austen manages the public/private divide, the space of investigation on the one hand, and reticence on the other.

But if a symptom is a sign, what is a syndrome? The word *syndrome*, I said then, and I still believe, "describes a problem, a set of symptoms. It is a word of context and interrelationship....A syndrome is a symptom in the public sphere."[7] Unlike *symptom*, *syndrome* began as a medical term, and crossed over sometime in the middle of the twentieth century to a more general meaning: a characteristic combination of opinions and behavior.

Thus, in addition to such medical and social categories as Dry Eye Syndrome, Failure to Thrive Syndrome, False Memory Syndrome, Peter Pan Syndrome, and Munchausen-by-Proxy Syndrome, we find the description of new cultural syndromes like "road rage" and "air rage" (described as a "national personality disorder") as well as something called "gourmand syndrome," an injury to the brain that results in a craving for fine food and thus led at least one sufferer to change careers and become a food writer.

Literary people have used the term, too. Aldous Huxley wrote of the "gloom-tomb syndrome": and Oxford scholar and mystery writer J. I. M. Stewart of "the withdrawn scholar syndrome." Recent newspaper citations have included such coinages as "Famous Father Syndrome" and the embarrassing "First Brother Syndrome"—the latter a malady that seems to afflict American presidents, and, indeed, actors like Martin Sheen, who merely play presidents on television.[8]

But how can *Jane Austen* be a syndrome? We have only to look at the recent
record. Book sequels to Austin's works continue to proliferate, as do films, literary house tours of what *Fodor's* guide book calls "Jane Austen Country," websites, souvenirs, and Jane Austen theme parks or "living museums." "By visiting
one or two main locales—such as Chawton or Winchester," *Fodor's* suggests,
"—it is possible to imagine hearing the tinkle of teacups raised by the likes of
Elinor Dashwood, Emma Woodhouse, and the bold and dashing Mr. Darcy."[9]
Although I have never personally fantasized about Mr. Darcy's tinkling teacups
(my Darcy fantasies are a tad more robust) I completely see the attraction.
When I visited Chawton cottage there was a strapping young man in servant's
livery at the gate who bade all the "ladies" and the "gentry" good day. If "living
history" thrives at Williamsburg or Sturbridge Village, why not at Chawton?
Another modern guidebook, *Frommer's England*, ups the ante, if possible, by
listing "Jane Austen Country" as among its winners for "The Best of Literary
England,"[10] and cites at least one old Southampton coaching house as "Jane
Austen's choice,"[11] as if she herself was recommending it.

Even the relatively staid and uncommercial *National Trust Handbook* takes
pains to point out that Lyme Park in Cheshire "appeared as Pemberley in the
BBC's recent adaptation of the Jane Austen novel *Pride and Prejudice*," and that
two National Trust sites in Salisbury were "featured in the award-winning film
Sense and Sensibility." Bear in mind that these are not the places *actually
described* in Austen's novels, but rather the period houses chosen to "play"
those locales in recent films. Meanwhile in Houston, Texas, a spokeswoman at
the national headquarters of the Romance Writers of America declared that
"We consider Jane Austen the first romance novelist," and an article in the
Sunday magazine of the *Houston Chronicle* made the point in irresistibly vivid
terms: "Had *Pride and Prejudice* been a Harlequin romance, Mr. Darcy would
have looked like Fabio and heroine Elizabeth Bennet would have been
writhing in her corset long before casting eyes on his Pemberley estate."[12]

I might note that this boom in Austen awareness is in fact very comparable
to what has happened to William Shakespeare, from the dawn of Bardolatry in
the eighteenth century to the present day. The Shakespeare Jubilee of 1759, the
founding moment of Shakespeare worship, was the brainstorm of actor David
Garrick, who had already erected a "Temple of Shakespeare" on his estate, and
placed inside it a life-sized marble statue of the poet, for which, allegedly,

Garrick himself was the model. The jubilee itself has been described as a "mar-
keting masterpiece" that "spawned Stratford's literary tourism industry."[13]
Certainly neither the town nor the industry has ever looked back. Today
Shakespeare is a commodity as well as an author, so much so that books on
Big-Time Shakespeare and *The Shakespeare Myth* have tried to account for his
commodification.

If Shakespeare is a beer mug, a brand of cigars, and a £20 note, is Austen
(allowing for differences of gender?) a tote bag? a style of home decoration? a
television production company? The Jane Austen Centre gift shop in Bath sells
cards, stationery, lace, and needlepoint. You can also have yourself "professionally photographed in period costume, against a choice of backdrops."[14] There is
something slightly disorienting about watching "a specially commissioned
video of Jane Austen's Bath" in the basement of a Gay Street townhouse in that
city, surrounded by two-dimensional painted dioramas of the city
streets—although the center's publicity brochure does note that "if you are
feeling energetic you can take a walking tour of Jane Austen's Bath." I do not
scoff at such historical connectedness; in fact, I am a passionate taker of tours,
the more "guided" the better. In the teashop across from Chawton Cottage I
bought a cream pitcher made of Steventon pottery. It doesn't say "Jane Austen"
anywhere on its modest brown surface, but whenever I use it I somehow wind
up explaining its pedigree. I am, you see, myself in the grip of the Jane Austen
syndrome.

There is one more enormous and striking similarity between Austen and
Shakespeare, beyond the fact that they have so often been compared as master-
ful creators of character and dialogue. More than any other authors I know,
Austen and Shakespeare provoke outpourings of *love*—a word that is used
repeatedly, by students and others, to describe their sense of connection with
these writers. "I love Shakespeare"; "I love Jane Austen." When I have asked
students of all ages to tell me why they want to take a course, they all write,
unabashedly, about "love."

It might be useful, in diagnosing, if not treating, the Jane Austen syndrome, to see what inroads Austen's *Pride and Prejudice*—so "light and bright
and sparkling," and still among the top favorites in a national poll—had made
upon our messier age. To what degree has this most famous of all Austen novels become cultural second nature, in the way, for example, that *Hamlet* has

become cultural second nature? No one, it is said, ever reads *Hamlet* for the first time. (In one of Dorothy Sayers's detective novels Lord Peter Wimsey jokes that something reminds him of "what the good lady said about *Hamlet*—that it was all quotations."[15]) If I were going to try to gauge the cultural capital of *Hamlet* quotations, I would start with "To be or not to be," which has been translated as everything from a cell phone commercial ("to beep or not to beep") to an airline seating-selection system ("2B, or not 2B?"). Was there, I wondered, a comparable quotation litmus test for *Pride and Prejudice*? The place to start seemed obvious: The famous first sentence of the novel. As I had found with other cultural bromides, like Keat's "beauty is truth, truth beauty," so I also discovered that Austen's famous first sentence—"It is a truth universally aknowledged, that a single man in possession of a good fortune, must in be want of a wife" appeared in print, website, and advertisement in a wide and comic variety of guises.

Here are some pieces of evidence about Jane Austen's cultural capital:

- *From an article on personal adornment:* "It is … a truth universally acknowledged that a woman of a certain age in possession of a reasonable body must be in want of a tattoo."[16]
- *From an article on the talents of opera stars:* "It is a truth universally acknowledged that a singer in possession of a good voice must be in want of acting lessons."[17]
- *From an article on low self-esteem among vicars' wives:* "It is a truth universally acknowledged that a quiet woman may be in need of 'assertiveness training.'"[18]
- *From an article on complaints about the high price of modern technological gadgets:* "It is a truth universally acknowledged that a person with a mobile phone is often in need of a thick wallet."[19]
- *From an article about women as investors:* "It is a truth universally acknowledged … that a single woman in possession of a modest nest egg must be in want of a low-risk investment vehicle."[20]
- *From an article on grape allergies:* "It's a truth universally acknowledged that if a group of friends spend an evening together drinking wine, some will feel fine the next day, while others will feel like death."[21]

- *From an article on restaurant service:* "It is a truth, universally acknowledged . . . that no one can make a waiter approach a table before he (or she) is ready to do so."[22]

Some of these citations actually credit the source and cite the original phrase:

- *From an article on the ill-fated TV show* Who Wants to Marry a Multi-Millionaire? *whose supposed hero, Rick Rockwell, turned out to have falsified both his income and his past:* "What a sad denouement for a program that seemed to take its inspiration, incredibly enough, from *Pride and Prejudice.* According to Jane Austen's famous first sentence, "It is a truth universally acknowledged, that a single man in possession of a good fortune, must be in want of a wife."[23]
- *From an article on financier Michael Bloomberg:* "Jane Austen said it well: 'It is a truth universally acknowledged, that a single man in possession of a good fortune, must be in want of a wife.' But not Mike Bloomberg. The gazillionaire media mogul is single again."[24]

Then there are the Austen literary spinoffs and tie-ins:

- *From a review of a new book completing Austen's* Sanditon: "It is a truth universally acknowledged that a manuscript in possession of a good beginning must be in want of an end"[25]
- *From a review of Helen Fielding's book* Bridget Jones: The Edge of Reason, *described as* "borrowing more ideas unashamedly from Jane Austen": "It is a truth universally acknowledged that a novelist having written a worldwide bestseller, is often tempted to produce a sequel."[26] (Fielding's first book, *Bridget Jones's Diary,* was a modernization of *Pride and Prejudice*; its hero, named Mark Darcy, is played in the film version by none other than Colin Firth. The sequel is a rewriting of *Persuasion.*)

And finally:

- *From a review of a stage play based on* Pride and Prejudice: "It is a truth universally acknowledged that a novelist in possession of wit and a gift for storytelling must be in want of a director. Poor Jane Austen. How rotten to turn out so many wonderful novels and then not be alive in the right century to cash in on the endless transpositions of them to stage and screen."[27]

This last example brings us directly to the question of *Pride and Prejudice* in the future. And here we might want to note that the always prescient Austen, who began as an epistolary novelist and many of whose most telling moments in *Pride and Prejudice* come in the form of encapsulated letters (Darcy's to Elizabeth, containing the truth about Wickham; Lydia's to her family, announcing her elopement; Jane's many letters to Elizabeth; and so on) has lapped the technological revolution, so to speak. Having sparked innumerable stage and screen versions, the art forms of the twentieth century, Austen is now featured on twenty-first-century e-mail, the Internet, and chat rooms.

But if "the truth universally acknowledged" is universally acknowledged as a characteristic Austen tour de force, its deft irony and free, indirect style rendering it from the first a proverbial piece of wit (at the expense, to be sure, of the witless Mrs. Bennet), it is not the only element of the novel that has traveled so far, and assumed so many strange guises, at the hands of contemporary media.

Consider the novel's title. Austen's original title for this work was *First Impressions*. What are the "first impressions" that a reader receives from this belatedly chosen phrase, *Pride and Prejudice*? I have to confess that as a school-child the title put me off. I felt about it much as Lydia Bennet felt about Mr. Collins's choice of *Fordyce's Sermons* as evening reading matter. Like Lydia and Kitty, I would have preferred something that sounded more like a novel.[28] From the title, those two forbidding words, *pride* and *prejudice*, I expected something preachy, not—as TV producer Sue Birtwhistle described the novel to the head of drama at London Weekend Television—"the sexiest book ever written." (Cleverly, Birtwhistle and her colleague Susie Conklin refused to name the novel before they pitched it to the studio, instead "[telling] him the story as if it had just been written: 'Well, there's five girls aged 15 to 22 years old and their mother is desperate to get them married to rich men because, though some are very beautiful, they are poor." The studio executive, she says, "became rather excited and asked if the rights were free.")[29]

That was in the 1990s. In the 1950s and '60s, when I was first introduced to Austen's novel, the words *pride* and *prejudice* were in the process of assuming important new meanings. All Austen aficionados know, of course, that the phrase *pride and prejudice* is found in the closing pages of Fanny Burney's novel *Cecelia* (1782), but the phrase had been proverbial—sometimes in the form "prejudice and pride"—for almost two hundred years.[30] In most of these proverbial usages the two terms represent aspects of the same moral or ethical failing, parallel with "envy and sorrow," or "fear and scorn."

By the mid-to-late twentieth century—and the beginning of the twenty-first—*pride*, a term that in Austen designates an attribute of high birth, wealth, or privilege, had become a term especially associated with the underclass, with racial, ethnic, or religious minorities, and with sexuality. *Pride* increasingly meant ethnic pride, racial pride ("black pride"), and gay pride. And *prejudice* meant the entrenched social and societal attitudes that made such declarations of pride necessary. Typical mid-twentieth-century references include "color prejudice," "class prejudice," "personal prejudice," "religious rules and prejudices," "racial prejudice," and "herd prejudice." Gordon Allport's pathbreaking sociological study, *The Nature of Prejudice*, was published in 1954. A book written after that date, and entitled *Pride and Prejudice*, might be imagined as addressing "first impressions," but in a quite different way.

Indeed, today's newspapers and magazines tend to use the phrase "pride and prejudice" in their headlines and articles to describe things like Australian track star Cathy Freeman's victory in the Olympic Games ("Pride and Prejudice: Aboriginal Runner Freeman's Triumph Stirs a Nation and a People"[31]); the sexual preoccupation of Hollywood gossip columnists, ("Pride and Prejudice: Anne Heche and Ellen DeGeneres, Hollywood's Only Publicly Acknowledged Lesbian Couple, Have Split Up. The Truth Is That It's Tough Being Gay in Hollywood"[32]); continuing racial tensions in post-apartheid South Africa; the dispute over U.S. high schools using team nicknames like "Chiefs," "Red Raiders," and "Warriors" ("Pride or Prejudice? Schools Feeling Heat over Indian Nicknames"[33]); and the battle to remove the Confederate flag from the South Carolina statehouse ("the old South battle banner that currently wildly flaps as symbol of either pride or prejudice, depending on who's asked"[34]). *Pride and prejudice*: the phrase has escaped from the boundaries of the text, its author, and its historical moment, to embark upon an unstoppable career of its own. It now means more or less the opposite of what it once did.

Just as is the case with Shakespeare, who is quoted, misquoted, appropriated, and parodied in every medium from advertising to *New Yorker* cartoons, so it is with Austen: at this point in the twenty-first century Jane Austen's characters have exceeded the boundaries of her novels and have become modern types or ideals, and her titles, phrases, and haunts have become part of the public sphere. It's an odd fate for so relatively private a person. This is what it means to be a classic.

But while I rejoice in some ways in the Austenizing of modern culture, I have to say I worry, sometimes, about the increasingly minor place the novels and letters seem to play in the scheme of things, just as I worry, periodically, about the habit of reading in general. When in a cruelly telling scene in the drawing room at Netherfield we are shown Caroline Bingley using a book as a prop, selecting the second volume of a work solely because Mr. Darcy has picked up the first, we may be getting an uncanny glimpse into the future:

> Miss Bingley's attention was quite as much engaged in watching Mr. Darcy's progress through his book, as in reading her own; and she was perpetually either making some inquiry, or looking at his page.... At length, quite exhausted by the attempt to be amused with her own book, which she had only chosen because it was the second volume to his, she gave a great yawn and said, "How pleasant it is to spend an evening in this way! I declare after all there is no enjoyment like reading! How much sooner one tires of any thing than of a book—When I have a house of my own, I shall be miserable if I have not an excellent library."[35]

Miss Bingley is hoping, of course, that the "house of [her] own" will be Pemberley.

If we were to transpose this disingenuous little fantasy into the future we might guess that Jane Austen's delicious, meretricious, and wickedly wise and funny novels are unlikely to turn up on the shelves of a postmodern Miss Bingley's imaginary library. Miss Bingley is instead likely to own the coffee table Austen books, with their delectable glossy photos of architecture, landscape, interiors, and costume—books about Austen's style, Austen's world, and

Austen's Christmas. For Caroline Bingley the book is a tool of seduction, not because she is reading it, but because she is *pretending* to read it. The book has become an accessory, like a hat or a pair of gloves. It would, I think, be an unhappy development for the future if Austen's books were themselves to become accessories, accompanying the more than 32,000 websites and the dozens of coffee table books and spinoffs and house tours and product tie-ins. It would be unhappy not in a moral sense—all these things are not only fun in themselves but good for Austen and for Austen studies—but quite simply because something would be lost, and that something is Jane Austen's incomparable style of writing.

It is a truth *not* universally acknowledged that what the world needs now more desperately than ever is *writing*: writing that exhibits irony, elegance, wit, shrewd observation, economy, and grace. How we handle issues of (lowercase) pride and (lowercase) prejudice in the future may depend upon remembering that good writing makes good thinking; it makes good sense, and also good sensibility. There is a crucial difference between the *plots* and *styles* of these novels (so available for adaptation and appropriation into a variety of media and cultural forms, from television to movies to wallpaper) and the *actual written texts*, the power of wit and language and the authorial persona at work.

Jane Austen knew this, of course, and put her own praise of the novel form right into the text of *Northanger Abbey*: "'Only a novel'... in short, only some work in which the greatest powers of the mind are displayed, in which the most thorough knowledge of human nature, the happiest delineation of its varieties, the liveliest effusions of wit and humor are conveyed to the world in the best chosen language." In this passage Austen is defending the novel against more supposedly serious literary forms: the sermon, the long poem, the moral essay. In the future—indeed, in the present—we may need to sing the praises of her fiction writing against those proliferating *non*literary forms, from films to walking tours, that are among the most pervasive symptoms of the Jane Austen syndrome.

Few pleasures can compare to the sheer joy of curling up with one of Austen's novels, turning the pages, occasionally laughing out loud. It is the experience of reading and rereading her, the perfect phrases, the laser-sharp observations, the balanced repetitions and inversions of her brilliant plot devices, that keeps us always coming back for more. In this sense it can never be said of Austen, in the present or the imaginable future, what Mr. Bennet so dryly says to his earnest daughter Mary at the Netherfield ball when she embarks upon the singing of yet one more song; it can never be said of Jane Austen, "You have delighted us long enough."[36]

Fatal Cleopatra

Most women have no characters at all.
—Alexander Pope, "Epistle to a Lady"

A person whose desires and impulses are his own—are the expression of his own nature, as it has been developed and modified by his own culture—is said to have a character. One whose desires and impulses are not his own, has no character, no more than a steam-engine has a character.
—John Stuart Mill, "On Liberty"

"Much has been written about the characterization of Cleopatra," writes Frank Kermode. "On the ethical level she is irresponsible in every way—lubricious, cruel, self-regarding; but to ignore the divine attributes of this 'triple-turn'd whore' is to ignore the text." Cleopatra, concludes Kermode, "deserves to be called the greatest of Shakespeare's female characterizations."[1]

What is "character"? And can the study of Shakespeare help us to read it? The word *character*, like all the other treacherous touchstones in that quagmire we call "human nature," has two equal and opposite connotations. We say that a person *has* "character" when we find him morally admirable; we also say that someone *is* "a character" when she is odd, eccentric, or extraordinary.

As literary critics from the Renaissance to the twentieth century have delighted in pointing out, the etymology of the word *character* in English comes from engraving and handwriting. By the time of Shakespeare the word could mean a brand, a stamp, a graphic sign or symbol, writing and printing in general, the alphabet; or, by an extension in the direction of the figurative, a trait, a distinguishing feature, an essential peculiarity or nature, the face as an index of moral qualities within, and those moral qualities themselves. The use of the term *character* to describe the persons of a play, which we find completely commonplace today (as in "Hamlet is the main character in the play that bears his name") is in fact a mode that comes into practice *after* Shakespeare, and is itself apparently an extension of the idea of moral essence.

In Shakespeare's own time, the "speech prefixes" designating a particular actor's "part" were just that: indications of who was to speak the lines. In a number of cases the printed text gives the name of the *actor* rather than the fictional speaker—what we would call the *character*. The line between so-called fiction and so-called reality was blurred, as it was, of course, in the material fact that boys played the parts of women on the English public stage. So the part or character of Cleopatra—to look ahead for a moment—would have been played by a boy: a fact that is famously acknowledged by Cleopatra herself late in the play, in a moment of high metadramatic risk, when she imagines herself brought back to Rome in triumph, where

> I shall see
> Some squeaking Cleopatra boy my greatness
> I' th' posture of a whore. (5.2-218–20)

What the original Shakespearean audience would have seen was some version of this very scenario: a boy actor speaking these lines, the extraordinary and "essential" femininity of Cleopatra, so remarked on by later critics, bodied forth by a young man whose voice had not yet changed, and who performed, onstage, the role of an Egyptian queen, wrinkled deep in time, whom age could not wither or custom stale.

In any case, Shakespeare and his contemporaries would not have called such figures *characters* in the plays, but rather *persons*, a word that derives, conveniently, from the mask worn by a player (*persona* = mask). The surviving Latin phrase, *dramatis personae*, persons of the drama, is less pleonastic now than it was then, since the word "person" has drifted in the intervening years from meaning "a character or personage acted" to an agent or a social actor, a human being acting in some capacity, and, in juridical terms, "a being having legal rights." But in Shakespeare we find, for example, an actor in the play-within-the-play in *A Midsummer Night's Dream* being introduced as one who "comes . . . to present the person of Moon-shine" (3.1.62). "Moon-shine" is the name of the character (as we would say). But the word *character* itself, just to repeat, is never used by Shakespeare in this sense: *character* in his plays almost always means letters, handwriting, or sign, though the sign could sometimes be an indication of what later ages would come to call character ("his nose stands high, a character of honor," we hear of one of the knights in *The Two Noble Kinsmen* [4.2.110]).

When character does begin to emerge as a term for a fictive personage in a play, its connotations tend to be linked with distinct personal attributes and qualities. Thus John Dryden, for example, repeatedly couples the word *character* with the word *humour* ("He may be allow'd sometimes to Err, who undertakes to move so many Characters and Humours as are requisite in a Play";[2] "Besides Morose, there are at least 9 or 10 different Characters and humours in the *Silent Woman*"[3]). A "humor" in this sense was a mental disposition, the term itself traced to the theory of humors from medieval physiology. A character, then, was a type, not an ethical ideal.

The literary genre of the "character," which came into vogue in the years following Shakespeare, was that of the set piece. Thus for example a series of eighty-two witty, satirical prose portraits of Jacobean types were published as *Characters* in a volume attributed to Sir Thomas Overbury, an English poet and essayist. Many of Overbury's "characters" were in fact written by playwrights, like John Webster and Thomas Dekker, and poets like John Donne. These "characters" were forerunners to the essay, and give a vivid sense of the persons and mores of Jacobean society. Here are some examples of Overburian characters: An Ignorant Glory-Hunter; A Fine Gentleman; A Braggadochio Welshman; A Roaring Boy; A Virtuous Widow; An Ordinary Widow. Overbury concludes his collection of characters with a short account of "What a Character Is," tracing the word to its Greek origin: "to ingrave, or make a deepe impression." Thus, he says, it was related both to letters of the alphabet and to "an Aegyptian hieroglyphic."[4] To this Aegyptian hieroglyphic, as might be expected, we shall want to return.

In France in the latter part of the seventeenth century, Jean de La Bruyère wrote a set of characters modeled after the fourth-century-B.C.E. character writer Theophrastus. La Bruyère selected a group of qualities, like dissimulation and flattery, and created a set of character portraits that illustrated those qualities, depicting social types from the Parisian court. The "characters," or "characteristics," of the age were held up for inspection, in portraits that could be aphoristically brief or deftly sketched. Of the first kind, we have, for example, these two aphorisms from his chapter "Of Women": "A handsome woman, who possesses also the qualities of a man of culture, is the most agreeable acquaintance a man can have, for she unites the merits of both sexes"; and "We should judge of a woman without taking into account her shoes and head-dress, and, almost as we measure a fish, from head to tail." Of the second kind of portrait, the brief narrative sketch, consider these from the chapter called "Of Fashion":

> Iphis attends church, and sees there a new-fashioned shoe; he looks upon his own with a blush, and no longer believes he is well-dressed. He only comes to mass to show himself, but now he refuses to go out, and keeps his room all day on account of his foot . . . he sometimes rouges his face, but not very often, and does not do so habitually. In truth, he always wears breeches and a hat, but neither earrings nor a pearl necklace; therefore I have not given him a place in my chapter "Of Women."[5]

Although La Bruyère steadfastly denied that any of his composites was an image of a real person, the game of guessing the identities behind the portrait sketches became popular. So popular, and so risky, that it was many years before his friends succeeded in electing La Bruyère to the prestigious French Academy.

More recent examples of this kind of "character sketch" in words would be Charles Baudelaire's dandy, flâneur, military man, and prostitute, from "The Painter of Modern Life,"[6] or even—in a variation that again will demonstrate the dangers and slipppages of the word *character*—the "psychological types" of C. G. Jung, including the shadow, anima and animus, child, trickster, and self.[7]

In the modern theater a "character part" is not a redundancy, but a type of role; the ambivalence in which these roles are regarded may be seen in the way "character acting" is compared to "real" or "legitimate" acting. "What is known as character acting has definitely established its supremacy in England upon the ruins of tragic art," wrote a contributor to the *Atheneum* in 1878, and a few years later *Stage* defined the terms: "By a 'character actor' is understood one who pourtrays individualities and eccentricities, as opposed to the legitimate actor who . . . endeavours to create the role as limned by the author."[8] Again the distinction is between the idiosyncratic and the ideal.

At about the same time Sigmund Freud developed a theory of "character-traits" and "character-types," for which he actually used some of Shakespeare's dramatic characters *as* models. This has had a curious effect upon our notion of universal types, since Freud, reading Shakespeare, promulgated some general theories of human character that post-Freudian readers have then identified as timeless and universal because they can be found in Shakespeare. The normative, typical, and universal instincts on which Freud bases his theories of psychoanalysis are in fact taken from two kinds of case studies: his patients, many of them women, most drawn from the middle- and upper-middle classes in his native Vienna; and the fictional characters he singles out from his reading of literature. Thus, Freud's essay "Some Character-Types Met With in Psychoanalytic Work" (1916) featured character analyses of Richard III (to illustrate "The Exceptions") and the Macbeths (to illustrate "Those Wrecked by Success"). Other essays discussed figures from King Lear to Shylock to Hamlet, each considered as a human type. Theatrical metaphors would continue to be vital to Freud's readings of human character throughout his career. Thus, to give just one example among many, he describes the possible symptoms of neurosis as like the "members of a theatrical company. Each of them is regularly cast for his own stock role—hero, confidant, villain, and so on; but each of them will choose a different piece for his benefit performance."[9]

"Freud has been judged a fatalist about character, and with reason," writes Philip Rieff.[10]

His conception of human sickness *is* dramatic, for Freud sought to understand character precisely by the reversals embedded in it. As the greatest dramatists—

Sophocles, Shakespeare, Ibsen—had pursued "the problems of psychological responsibility with unrelenting rigor," so the great psychologist will pursue unrelentingly a dramatic understanding of character. Freud's dramaturgy is more technical than tragic. By showing that all character develops not in a straight line but through a series of crises by which certain attitudes or roles are exchanged, Freud exhibits at once the commonplace element in tragic character and the tragic element in everyday character.[11]

In order to have a stable notion of "character" in this older sense one needed to believe in essence, in depth, and in the unity or coherence of the person, or subject. Hamlet would behave in a certain way; Othello in a certain way. Each would express his character in his language as well as his actions. Thus, early editors occasionally reassigned certain lines in the Shakespearean texts from the speaker indicated by the Folio or the Quarto to a more appropriate speaker, given their estimation of what would be "in character" or "out of character," for a given person in the drama. For example, Samuel Johnson suggests, following what he calls the "ingenious" suggestion of a "learned lady," that the line "Oh, horrible! Oh, horrible! Most horrible!" in the middle of the Ghost's speech in *Hamlet* "seems to belong" not to the Ghost but to Hamlet himself, "in whose mouth it is a proper and natural exclamation."[12] Even more indicatively, many editors have refused to believe that the sweet Miranda of *The Tempest* could be either cruel or vindictive toward Caliban. Not wanting to hear this innocent heroine address the island's native inhabitant in terms like "Abhorred slave / Which any print of goodness will not take," a "savage," "a thing most brutish," or a member of a "vile race," (1.2.354–365) they have reassigned this speech—clearly given to Miranda in the Folio text—to her father, Prospero.[13]

More recently, critics and theorists have wondered whether, if the person, the subject, was "split," divided, internally *in*coherent or at war within himself or herself—if *this* was what could be called an aspect of "human nature"—was the concept of "character" even thinkable?[14] And if one also bore in mind that literary characters, and particularly dramatic characters, were only marks on paper, traces and clues, indications for the actor to perform (or indeed records of a particular actor's performance in the past) then what happened to the notion of "character"? Did it not become more like the cloud formation so mock-didactically expounded by Hamlet to Polonius ("Do you see yonder cloud that's almost in shape of a camel? . . . Methinks it is like a weasel. . . . Or like a whale." "Very like a whale."[15])? Or, even more germanely, like the cloud formation to which Antony compares himself in *Antony and Cleopatra*:

> Sometimes we see a cloud that's dragonish,
> A vapour sometime, like a bear, or lion,
> A tower'd citadel, a pendent rock,
> A forked mountain, or blue promontory
> With trees upon't, that nod unto the world,
> And mock ourselves with air. . . .
> That which is now a horse, even with a thought
> The rack dislimns, and makes it indistinct
> As water is in water. . . .
>   now thy captain is
> Even such a body; here I am Antony,
> Yet cannot hold this visible shape[16]

In a briefer phrase but one equally compelling, Antony also challenges the identity of Cleopatra when he finds himself betrayed by her in war: "What's her name since she was Cleopatra?" he asks bitterly. (She is and is not Cleopatra, just as, for Troilus, his unfaithful lover "is, and is not, Cressid.") She is not, we might say, "herself"—at least in Antony's eyes—although to us this changeable creature might be said to be exactly who she "is."

To illustrate the problem further, let me quote an inadvertent gloss on Cleopatra's character, in the form of a malapropism or confusion of words. The mis-speaker in this case is another dramatic character, in fact the very one who bears the name of misspeaker, Mrs. Malaprop in Sheridan's play *The Rivals* (1775). Here is Mrs. Malaprop's famous phrase, which in the context of the play she uses to describe her rebellious niece:

As headstrong as an allegory on the banks of the Nile.[17]

You can probably see why one might associate this phrase with Cleopatra. She is headstrong, she is on the banks of the Nile, and the malapropism in question—Mrs. Malaprop's substitution of *allegory* for *alligator*—makes it all too clear that Cleopatra herself is the stuff of legend, the repository of what Lucy Hughes-Hallett, in a fine book on the cultural trajectory of Cleopatra through the ages, called "histories, dreams, distortions."[18] In short, Cleopatra herself is an allegory; she is not merely, and perhaps not ultimately, a historical personage, or even a dramatic character.

Yet Mrs. Malaprop makes, not one but two mistakes, since if we replace her erroneous term *allegory* with its near-homonym *alligator* we are still in trouble, geographically speaking. Alligators are found in the southern United States and also in China; a stuffed alligator skin hangs in the apothecary's shop in Shakespeare's *Romeo and Juliet*, where it may be used as a remedy in folk medicine. But the reptile of *Antony* and *Cleopatra*, the reptile associated with the river Nile and with the goddess Isis, is the crocodile (*crocodilus niloticus*), famous, among other things, for its artful weeping.

The fascinating phenomenon of "crocodile tears" had been described in Richard Hakluyt's *Voyages* of 1565: "[The crocodile's] nature is ever when he would have his prey, to cry and sob like a christian body, to provoke them to come to him, and then he snatcheth at them." In *The Faerie Queene* Edmund Spenser picked up this image and gave the crocodile's tears to the false Duessa:

> As when a wearie traueller that strayes
> By muddy shore of broad seuen-mouthed *Nile*,
> Vnweeting of the perillous wandring wayes,
> Doth meet a cruell craftie Crocodile,
> Which in false griefe hyding his harmfull guile,
> Doth weepe full sore, and sheddeth tender teares;...
>
> So wept *Duessa* vntill euentide[19]

Shakespeare endowed the Duke of Gloucester in *2 Henry VI* with the twin aspects of crocodile and serpent that would surface again in the seductive Cleopatra:

> Gloucester's show
> Beguiles him as the mournful crocodile
> With sorrow snares relenting passengers;
> Or as the snake, roll'd in a flow'ring bank,
> With shining checker'd slough, doth sting a child
> That for the beauty thinks it excellent.[20]

In Nahum Tate's libretto for Henry Purcell's *Dido and Aeneas* (1689) an angry Dido accuses her lover of perfidy:

> Thus on the fable banks of Nile
> Weeps the deceitful crocodile.

Since Purcell's opera was written to be performed by a girls' school, Aeneas would have been performed *en travestie*. Male and female, deceitful and crafty, the crocodile—rumored to be hermaphroditic and self-generating—was the perfect emblematic (and allegorical) figure for Cleopatra.

"What manner o' thing is your crocodile?" the drunken Lepidus asks Antony at an Egyptian banquet, and Antony's answer is something between a joke and a riddle:

> It is shaped, sir, like itself, and it is as broad as it hath breadth. It is just so high as it is, and moves with it own organs. It lives by that which nourisheth it, and the elements once out of it, it transmigrates. (2.7.41–47)

We could translate this as tautology or evasion: a crocodile is a crocodile, that is all you need to know. The same is true for Cleopatra, who "beggars all description," as Enobarbus feelingly announces, and who seems herself to be at once hyperbole and metaphor: "We cannot call her winds and waters sighs and tears; they are greater storms and tempests than almanacs can report."[21] Cleopatra is virtually impossible to describe from the very beginning of the play. These lines are from Enobarbus's great speech in the second scene. The design of *Antony and Cleopatra* is to offer the audience, repeatedly, a series of set pieces describing the incomparable and indescribable lovers, against which their human (and actorly) avatars must strive to compete, and fail. Octavius testifies to the heroism of the absent Antony, Enobarbus to the inexpressible eroticism of Cleopatra at Cydnus. By the end of the play, of course, Cleopatra herself pronounces her own impossibility:

> I have nothing
> Of woman in me. Now from head to foot
> I am marble-constant. Now the fleeting moon
> No planet is of mine. (5.2.237–40)

Nothing and *no* are the key words here, the negation, against all odds, becoming a superlative. The crocodile, "the elements once out of it," transmigrates into allegory, or into an allegory of allegory.

"As headstrong as an allegory on the banks of the Nile": Mrs. Malaprop's famous, or infamous, line was remembered with fondness by, of all people, Louisa May Alcott, who put it into the mind of her alter ego Jo March in *Little Women*. Near the end of the novel Jo is on her own in New York City teaching children for a living and beginning her independent career as a writer. At a New Year's Eve masquerade she "rig[s] up as Mrs. Malaprop, and sail[s] in with a mask on," surprising the other residents, who cannot dream that "the silent, haughty Miss March... could dance, and dress, and burst out into a "nice derangement of epitaphs, like an allegory on the banks of the Nile."[22]

In the *Poetics* Aristotle claims that "characterisation" is the second-most-important element in drama, after plot. "Character," he says, "is the element which reveals the nature of a moral choice."[23] As the translator and commentator Stephen Halliwell explains, "the main challenge for the modern reader is to grasp the great divide between what the *Poetics* understands by the concept [of character] and what we now commonly mean by it," for Aristotle associates character with "ethical purposes and dispositions," and not with "anything like the intricacies of personality or consciousness which more recent traditions of individualism and psychology have associated with the term." Yet, as Halliwell notes, and as we have seen, character in English once meant something closer to Aristotle's sense of the term than it does now: "It is interesting, for example, to learn how eighteenth-century Shakespeare criticism moves from a concern with consistency and morality in characterisation (two of Aristotle's own four requirements) to a more psychological approach to character."[24]

The dictum attributed to Heraclitus, "character for man is fate" or "a man's character is his fate" (*ethos anthropo daimon*) is often understood as the central tenet of Aristotelian tragedy. A classic example of this view can be found in Samuel Johnson's celebrated "Preface to Shakespeare," in which Shakespeare's genius is said to lie in his delineation of character:

> Shakespeare is above all writers, at least above all modern writers, the poet of nature; the poet that holds up to his readers a faithful mirrour of manners and of life. His characters are not modified by the customs of particular places, unpractised by the rest of the world; by the peculiarities of studies or professions, which can operate but upon small numbers; or by the accidents of transient fashions or temporary opinions: they are the genuine progeny of common humanity, such as the world will always supply, and observation will always find. His persons act and

> speak by the influence of those general passions and principles by which all minds are agitated, and the whole system of life is continued in motion. In the writings of other poets a character is too often an individual; in those of Shakespeare it is commonly a species.[25]

It is worth emphasizing this resounding final sentence: "In the writings of other poets a character is too often an individual; in those of Shakespeare it is commonly a species." This was the sentiment to which William Hazlitt took such exception, labeling Johnson's mode of understanding *didactic* rather than *dramatic*: he "found the general species or *didactic* form in Shakespeare's characters, which was all he sought or cared for; he did not find the individual traits, or the *dramatic* distinctions, which Shakespeare has engrafted on the general nature, because he felt no interest in them."

For Johnson, Shakespearean characters transcend the time-bound and the temporary. They are "the genuine progeny of common humanity, such as the world will always supply, and observation will always find." Thus they are exemplary, and, in the profoundest sense, ethical.

What did Johnson think of Shakespeare's Cleopatra, and the play in which she appears? "The play keeps curiosity always busy," he wrote, "and the passions always interested." But the best part of the play was the action, he thought: "the power of delighting is derived principally from the frequent changes of the scene: for, except the feminine arts, some of which are too low, which distinguish Cleopatra, no character is very strongly discriminated."[26] So none of the characters of the play is especially striking except for Cleopatra, and she is distinguished particularly for her "low" feminine arts.

As Lucy Hughes-Hallett points out in her cultural history of Cleopatra, Shakespeare's own audience would have regarded the overmastering passion of the two lovers in this play as highly dangerous to political stability and order.[27] The romantic and post-romantic idealization of love and eroticism as the fullest expression of passionate selfhood is highly anachronistic when it comes to early modern England.

Over the years many of the play's detractors, and even many of its admirers, have found Shakespeare's Antony and Cleopatra—the characters, if not the play—immoral. In the preface to his revision, *All for Love, or the World Well Lost* (1678), John Dryden commented on the necessity of bringing the play to a tragic conclusion, citing "the excellency of the moral: for the chief persons represented were famous patterns of unlawful love; and their end accordingly, was unfortunate. . . . The crimes of love, which they both committed, were not occasioned by any necessity, or fatal ignorance, but were wholly voluntary; since our passions are, or ought to be, within our power."[28]

Three hundred years later the critic T. R. Henn noted that the play "raises certain moral issues which I was forced to consider, in a peculiar manner, early in my teaching career." It seems that a certain pupil ("admittedly from overseas") had threatened a lawsuit against those who had put the play on the required reading list, since it "was calculated to corrupt the mind and morals of any student who was forced, under duress of examinations, to read it."[29]

More typically, readers concerned with character have given the Egyptian queen her due as the embodiment of contradiction. Thus William Hazlitt, whose brief essay in *Characters of Shakespeare's Plays* focuses almost entirely on Cleopatra, remarks that

> The character of Cleopatra is a masterpiece. . . . She is voluptuous, ostentatious, conscious, boastful of her charms, haughty, tyrannical, fickle. The luxurious pomp and gorgeous extravagance of the Egyptian queen are displayed in all their force and luster. . . . She had great and unpardonable faults, but the grandeur of her death almost redeems them. She learns from the depth of despair the strength of her affections. She keeps her queen-like state in the last disgrace, and her sense of the pleasurable in the last moments of her life. She tastes a luxury in death.[30]

This romantic view of Cleopatra is still very much in force; it is not by accident that Hazlitt's sense of her paradoxical power and of the brilliance of her characterization is shared, as we have noted, by Frank Kermode.

"Many unpleasant things can be said of Cleopatra; and the more that are said, the more wonderful she appears," declares A. C. Bradley, the great exponent of character criticism writing in the same years as Sigmund Freud. Bradley goes on to particularize Cleopatra's charms and flaws in a spirit very like that of the reluctantly admiring Enobarbus:

> The exercise of sexual attraction is the element of her life; and she has developed nature into a consummate art. . . . She lives for feeling. . . . Her body is exquisitely sensitive. . . . Some of her feelings are violent, and, unless for a purpose, she does not dream of restraining them. . . . It seems to us perfectly natural, nay, in a sense perfectly right, that her lover should be her slave, that her women should adore her and die with her; that Enobarbus . . . who opposes her wishes and braves her

anger, should talk of her with rapture and feel no bitterness toward her.... That which makes her wonderful and sovereign laughs at definition.[31]

In a footnote that is significant both as a marker of the taste of his time and as an index of its difference from ours, Bradley compares the superlatively bad Cleopatra to the Shakespearean female character he regards as the best of the "'good' heroines," Imogen in *Cymbeline*, quoting with approval A. C. Swinburne's verdict that Imogen is "the woman above all Shakespeare's women," a view that, as Bradley says, is shared by "so many readers" in his day.

Who in our day, less than a hundred years after this confident assertion, would say that Imogen is the apogee of Shakespearean womanhood? How many of today's readers and theatergoers will even recognize her name? Let this stand for us as a humbling reminder that aesthetic and cultural values are of an age and not for all time. But Cleopatra, the serpent of old Nile, wrinkled deep in time, seems to give this temporal relativism the lie. Swinburne himself had called her "the perfect and everlasting woman," and had described *Antony and Cleopatra* as "the greatest love-poem of all time."[32]

It is highly symptomatic of the problem of Cleopatra's character that, faced with the necessity of describing it, many twentieth-century commentators have wound up taking evasive action. Whenever they think they are talking about character, they are really talking about style.

The Problem of Style is the title that John Middleton Murry chose for his lecture series, delivered at Oxford University in 1921. "The highest style," he insists, "is that wherein the two current meanings of the word blend: it is a combination of the maximum of personality with the maximum of impersonality; on the one hand it is a concentration of peculiar and personal emotion, on the other it is a complete projection of this personal emotion into the created thing." And what does Murry offer as an example of "the style that is the very pinnacle of the pyramid of art"? The scene of the death of Cleopatra:

> Give me my robe, put on my crown; I have
> Immortal longings in me. (5.2.279–80)

In four dense pages Murry analyzes this scene between the queen and her attendant Charmian, its management of grand style and simple style, simile and metaphor. As he points out, "Cleopatra's [words] are not those of a queen, nor are they, in reality, those of a lover. A dying woman does not use such figures of speech; and at the pinnacle of her complex emotion, a Cleopatra would have no language to express it." And yet, "in the death scene of Cleopatra [Shakespeare] achieves the miracle: he makes the language completely adequate to the emotion and yet keeps it simple. The emotion is, to the last drop, *expressed*." The achievement is that of "the highest genius and the finest style."[33]

Murry, the great rival of T. S. Eliot as the premier reviewer and essayist of his day, is pretty clearly thinking of Eliot, both in his remarks on "the maximum of personality" and the "maximum of impersonality," and in his description of the death scene's language as "completely adequate to the emotion," an emotion that is "to the last drop, *expressed*." In contradistinction to Eliot's Hamlet, who "is dominated by an emotion which is inexpressible, because it is in *excess* of the facts as they appear," Murry's Cleopatra finds what Eliot famously called in his *Hamlet* essay an "objective correlative": "a set of objects, a situation, a chain of events which shall be the formula of that *particular* emotion; such that when the external facts, which must terminate in sensory experience, are given, the emotion is immediately evoked."

Murry's word "adequate" (in the death of Cleopatra Shakespeare "makes the language completely *adequate* to the emotion") is likewise borrowed from Eliot's essay of two years before, in which Eliot boldly declared *Hamlet* (the play) to be an "artistic failure." "The artistic 'inevitability,'" Eliot had written, "lies in this complete adequacy of the external to the emotion." This was, he thought, "what is deficient in *Hamlet*."[34] By claiming to find this "complete adequacy" (the word *complete*, as well as *adequate*, taken from Eliot's celebrated formulation) in Cleopatra, where Eliot had found it lacking in Hamlet, Murry trumps his rival while paying him homage. In fact Murry's Cleopatra not only *finds* what Eliot famously called in the "*Hamlet*" essay an "objective correlative," she *is* for him that objective correlative, emotion perfectly embodied, perfectly simulated, through language.

For the late-twentieth-century critic Rosalie Colie, Cleopatra was an aspect of *rhetorical* style. Colie observes that both of the major characters in the play are constantly linked with hyperbole—in fact, with a *hyper*-hyperbole. They "demand a language for their love which rejects conventional hyperbole

and invents and creates new overstatements, new forms of overstate-
ment. . . . Nothing is enough for these two, not even the most extravagant figures of speech." ("Eternity was in our lips, and eyes"; "His legs bestrid the
ocean, his rear'd arm / Crested the world"; "Age cannot wither her, nor custom
stale / Her infinite variety.") Their style, says Colie, "*must* in honesty be bom-
bastic," testing the boundaries between sublimity and bombast. In the end
Shakespeare "manages to show us," through what Colie calls "the *ping* and
pong of plain and grandiloquent styles," the "problem and the problematics, in
moral as in literary terms, at the heart of style."[35]

Part of my objective and pleasure in working on this topic has been to
bring back into prominence some of these once-central voices in Shakespeare
studies, especially those who have fallen out of favor in the past few decades.
No critic has been more devalued than A. C. Bradley, whose first lecture on
Shakespearean tragedy set the tone for preeminent critics through the middle
of the twentieth century. In the following passage Bradley is talking about
Shakespeare's creation of character, and especially about his finest achievements in that mode:

> His tragic characters are made of the stuff we find within ourselves and within the
> persons who surround them. But, by an intensification of the life which they share
> with others, they are raised above them; and the greatest are raised so far that, if we
> fully realize all that is implied in their works and actions, we become conscious
> that in real life we have known scarcely anyone resembling them. Some, like
> Hamlet and Cleopatra, have genius. . . . In almost all we observe a marked one-sid-
> edness, pre-disposition in some particular direction; a total incapacity, in certain
> circumstances, of resisting the force which draws in this direction; a fatal tendency
> to identify the whole being with one interest, object, passion, or habit of mind.
> This, it would seem, is, for Shakespeare, the fundamental tragic trait. . . . It is a fatal
> gift, but it carries with it a touch of greatness; and when there is joined to it nobil-
> ity of mind, or genius, or immense force, we realise the full power and reach of the
> soul, and the conflict which it engages acquires that magnitude which stirs not
> only sympathy and pity, but admiration, terror, and awe.[36]

Notice that Bradley singles out Cleopatra, alone with Hamlet, as a
Shakespearean character who in his view has "genius." Implicitly, Murry did
the same, in juxtaposing the "competely adequate" Cleopatra to Eliot's emotionally inadequate Hamlet. G. Wilson Knight would make a similar comparison between these two figures a few years later, calling Cleopatra "Shakespeare's

most amazing and dazzling single personification," and claiming that she has "far more than Hamlet, all qualities potential in her." She is not one character but many: "She is at once Rosalind, Beatrice, Ophelia, Gertrude, Cressida, Desdemona, Cordelia, and Lady Macbeth."[37]

Twice within the passage Bradley has recourse to the word *fatal*: "a *fatal* tendency to identify the whole being with one interest, object, passion, or habit of mind"... "a *fatal* gift," which yet "carries with it a touch of greatness." *Fatal* here is of course related to the problematic word *fate*, to which Bradley will shortly turn, and about which he expresses some fine interpretative doubt that is often ignored by his less careful readers.[38] We have already heard Freud described as a "fatalist" when it comes to character. But this notion of the fatal tendency and the fatal gift, especially in a passage that begins with such high praise of the character of Cleopatra, may lead us back usefully and provocatively to the opinions of Samuel Johnson.

Here then is another, equally famous passage from Samuel Johnson's "Preface to Shakespeare," in which Johnson discusses not Shakespearean character delineation, of which he so profoundly approves, but Shakespearean wordplay, which he deplores:

> A quibble was to Shakespeare, what luminous vapours are to the traveler; he follows it at all adventures, it is sure to lead him out of his way, and sure to engulf him in the mire. It has some malignant power over his mind, and its fascinations are irresistible. Whatever be the dignity or profundity of his disquisition, whether he be enlarging knowledge or exalting affection, whether he be amusing attention with incidents, or enchaining it in suspense, let but a quibble spring up before him, and he leaves his work unfinished. A quibble is the golden apple for which he will always turn aside from his career, or stoop from his elevation. A quibble, poor and barren as it is, gave him such delight, that he was content to purchase it, by the sacrifice of reason, propriety, and truth. A quibble was to him the fatal Cleopatra for which he lost the world, and was content to lose it.[39]

In this celebrated complaint Johnson, the Shakespeare editor, lexicographer, and moralist, performs a striking pair of critical moves. First he evokes a vivid portrait of Shakespeare as thinker and writer, distracted from the proper pursuit of his craft by language, and specifically by what he calls a "quibble," and what we would today call a pun, a piece of wordplay, or a double meaning. The quibble is described in turn as a "luminous vapour," "a golden apple" like the ones that distracted Atalanta from her "career," and a "fatal Cleopatra for which he lost the world, and was content to lose it." This last is surely a reference to Antony (both the Antony of Shakespeare's *Antony and Cleopatra*, and the Antony of Dryden's 1678 adaptation, *All For Love, or The World Well Lost*). This is the first move, culminating in the tacit syllogism "a quibble was to Shakespeare as Cleopatra was to Antony." What do these have in common? Both are "fatal"—distracting, delighting, enchanting. They seduce a man away from the proper pursuit of "reason, propriety, and truth."

So what, then, is the second move? It might be described as recursive, turning back upon itself. For Johnson is himself, as I have already noted, a celebrated editor of Shakespeare. The passage appears in his preface, where he undertakes to explain and justify his editorial principles and practice. The fatal Cleopatra for Johnson is the duplicity of language: figure itself, the doubleness of meaning. Let us return for a moment to the mention of the "luminous vapour" that lures the traveler astray. There is a Latin name for this vapor: *ignis fatuus*, a phosphorescent light that is seen to hover or flit over marshy ground, and that often seems to recede as the traveler approaches, or to vanish and reappear in another direction. It was once believed to be the work of a mischievous sprite. Over time *ignis fatuus* came to mean, more generally, a thing—or in rare cases a person—that deludes or misleads, or a false or foolish hope or goal. But it began as something literal, something empirical or "real."

In earlier days the *ignis fatuus*, literally "foolish fire" rising from the marshes, was apparently a fairly common phenomenon, which is one reason that it was given folk names as well as its Latin name. Among those names were *Jack-o'-lantern* and *Will-o'-the-wisp*.

Will-o'-the-wisp is a name also associated with Robin Goodfellow, the other name for Shakespeare's Puck. The *Will* in *Will-o'-the-wisp* is the abbreviation for William, and means "anyone," "someone," or "some fellow." But in the context of Samuel Johnson's metaphor, his figure of speech, this Will-o'-the-wisp, described merely as "luminous vapours" but clearly identical to the *ignis fatuus*, is an alter ego for the playwright Will, who often quibbles on his own name in his sonnets. "A quibble was to Shakespeare, what luminous vapours are to the traveler; he follows it at all adventures, it is sure to lead him out of his way, and sure to engulf him in the mire." In other words, at the core of this figure for Johnson is a buried pun, the pun on Will as in William Shakespeare, and Will as in Will-o'-the-wisp.

Johnson in fact, is performing the very act he deplores in Shakespeare. He is making a pun, or a quibble, although I think it is almost surely an unconscious one—which does not make it less a quibble. The hidden Will (the Will-o'-the-wisp) in the "luminous vapours" is what is leading *Johnson* astray, down the path of the quibble: *his* Will-o'-the-wisp, we could say, is Shakespeare.

Furthermore, this doubleness of meaning is also intrinsic to Cleopatra. It is her figural function, her function as a figure of speech, that most accurately describes her "character." Antony calls her a "wrangling Queen / Whom everything becomes..." (1.1.49–50). Enobarbus reports, "For her own person, / It beggared all description" (2.2.207–8), that "she did make defect perfection" (2.2.241), and that "She makes hungry / Where most she satisfies; for vilest things / Become themselves in her" (2.2.247–49). Cleopatra, in short, is a walking textbook of rhetorical figures, from *occupatio* to *paradox*, from *hyperbole* to *enigma*. Above all, she and Antony constitute a "mutual pair" which, like a similar pair in Shakespeare's lyric poem "The Phoenix and Turtle" ("co-supremes and stars of love") seem to be emblems of metaphor itself:

> So they loved as love in twain
> Had the essence but in one,
> Two distincts, division none;
> Number there in love was slain.
>
> Single nature's double name,
> Neither two nor one was called.[40]

George Puttenham, the great Renaissance compiler and theorist of rhetorical terms, had observed in *The Arte of English Poesie* (1589) that "figures" are "transgressions of our dayly speech," and that "writing is no more than the image or character of speech."[41] *Character* here is used in the sense of transcription, the written version of the spoken word. But of course it is impossible, either in a written text or in a dramatic text intended to be performed, to separate the question of rhetoric or style from the question of character.

Fatality is in part an artifact of language if "character for mankind is fate." The central pun of *Antony and Cleopatra*, the familiar Renaissance pun on death and dying, which meant both to experience sexual climax and to reach the end of life, establishes the notion of the fatal at the heart of the play. Should Cleopatra learn of Antony's plan to leave Egypt, quips Enobarbus to his master in an early scene, she "dies instantly. I have seen her die twenty times upon far poorer moment. I do think there is mettle in death which commits some loving act upon her, she has such a celerity in dying" (1.2.147–51). Later we will hear Antony call out to her (in her allegorical person as queen), "I am dying, Egypt, dying," as she pulls him up to her monument. "Die when thou has lived; / Quicken with kissing" she implores him (4.15.40–43). By embodying the paradoxes, slippages, and transgressions of wordplay, the character of Cleopatra, whom everything becomes, becomes precisely the "fatal Cleopatra" of Johnson's edgy warning. She is a living pun. Her decorum lies in her indecorousness, or what Puttenham called "indecency"—not in moral terms, but in the terms of style.

At once a goddess and a "triple-turn'd whore," constantly turning and troping herself into new figures, new characterizations, new "characters," Cleopatra is a paradox who makes hungry where most she satisfies. She is a figure of speech, a figure *for* speech, a living emblem of the relation between language and character, character and style. Or, to recall that phrase from Thomas Overbury's definition of character, "an Aegyptian hieroglyphic."

If a quibble was to Shakespeare the fatal Cleopatra for which he lost the world, we may think that it was a world well lost. But since the plays are not only sublime pieces of poetry but brilliantly imagined theatrical vehicles, constantly aware of their own mediation between page and stage, perhaps we should remind ourselves of that other piece of wordplay that marked the sign of Shakespeare's own theater, the Globe, which for him meant both stage and world. In this case the world is not only lost, but also found: made possible by the enchanting infidelity of language, the inevitability of encountering, whether or not you are hunting for one, an allegory on the banks of the Nile.

Compassion

"Either out of humility or out of self-respect (one or the other) the Court should decline to answer this incredibly difficult and incredibly silly question," Justice Antonin Scalia responded to the issues posed by *PGA Tour Inc. v. Martin*, a case of a professional golfer's fight for permission to ride in a golf cart while competing on the tour. Comparing the majority's decision to grant Martin's request to "misty-eyed judicial supervision," Justice Scalia's acerbic dissent began: "In my view today's opinion exercises a benevolent compassion that the law does not place it within our power to impose."[1]

Since justices (and their clerks) are conscious stylists, often especially attentive to the opening and closing phrases of their opinions, the phrase "benevolent compassion" caught the eye of some experienced readers. The executive editor of Inside.com, Noam Cohen, a former copy editor at the *New York Times*, wrote to his friend and former colleague at the *Times*, William Safire, to inquire whether Safire did not find "benevolent compassion" redundant. Could there, he asked, be such a thing as "malevolent compassion"? Safire's subsequent correspondence on the question with Justice Scalia formed the basis of a Sunday column.

Scribal joustings between such elevated wordsmiths cannot always avoid a certain archness of tone. Here is Justice Scalia's response to the question, posed to him by his friend Safire, about whether he was being redundant or "differentiating from some other kind of compassion":

> I shall assume that such differentiation is impossible—that compassion is always benevolent—though that may not be true. (People sometimes identify with others' suffering, "suffer with" them—to track the Latin root of compassion—not because they particularly love the others or "wish them well"—to track the Latin root of benevolence—but because they shudder at the prospect of the same thing's happening to themselves. "There, but for the grace of God, go I." This is arguably not benevolence, but self-love.)
>
> But assuming the premise, is it redundancy to attribute to a noun a quality that it always possesses? Surely not. We speak of "admirable courage" (is courage ever not admirable?) [and] "a cold New England winter" (is a New England winter ever not cold?)....It seems to me perfectly acceptable to use an adjective to emphasize one of the qualities that a noun possesses, even if it always possesses it. The writer wants to stress the coldness of the New England winter, rather than its interminable length, its gloominess, its snowiness and many other qualities that it always possesses. And that is what I was doing with "benevolent compassion"— stressing the social-outreach, maternalistic, goo-goo character of the court's compassion.[2]

Safire, transcribing this document with manifest readerly pleasure, here interrupts to footnote "goo-goo," which, he says, "some may mistakenly take as akin to 'gooey.'" Instead, he explains, it is short for "Good Government," since "goo-goo" was "the derisive appellation given by the *New York Sun* in the 1890's to local action groups calling themselves 'Good Government Clubs.'" The phrase, says Safire, is Theodore Roosevelt's, from the latter's time as New York City Police Commissioner, when he railed at fellow reformers who voted independent as "those prize idiots, the Goo-Goos."

I am willing to believe that this is the meaning of "goo-goo," since it comes from a virtually unimpeachable source in the language business. But perhaps Safire will not mind if I also have recourse to one of his favorite tools—the *Oxford English Dictionary*, where a researcher in diligent quest of "goo-goo" finds "goo-goo, *a.*" goo-goo eyes, "an amorous glance, a 'glad eye' (from *goggle*)," and "goo-goo, *int.*" (echoic), "to talk in the manner of a baby," but no "goo-goo, *a.*" from Good Government Clubs. I do not doubt that the robust Roosevelt, the legendary personification of everything that was not "social-outreach" and "maternalistic," might have thought his contemporary Goo-Goos were guilty of excessively benevolent idealism. Yet Justice Scalia's list of condemnatory terms for "the court's compassion" fits just as well with spoony glances and baby talk as with the politics of reform. Indeed, the contiguity of "maternalistic" and "goo-goo" in his playful sentence suggests that he was thinking of the high chair as much as the high court. And this association of "compassion" with the ironically inflected "maternalistic" (the opposite of "paternalistic," plainly regarded as a buzz word of liberal-speak) suggests where some of the judicial animus may lie; for "compassion," these days, is a "liberal" word, damned with faint praise from both the right and the left. To see how this has come about, despite the high regard with which the concept of compassion is nominally held, is my objective here.

The suit was brought by the Americans With Disabilities Act of 1990 on behalf of Casey Martin. Martin suffers from a rare circulatory condition in his right leg, and sought to pursue his career as a professional golfer on the PGA Tour with the assistance of a cart. Justice Scalia, whose scathing dissent was joined by Justice Clarence Thomas, derided the court's "solemn duty" to "decide What Is Golf." The majority opinion was written by Justice Paul Stevens, who is one of the Court's two members to have shot a hole-in-one; the other is Justice Sandra Day O'Connor.

The word *compassion* was, perhaps inevitably, picked up and bandied about in the wake of the Court's 7–2 decision. Conservative columnist George Will wrote dismissively of what he called "a moral theory in vogue" in prestigious law schools, "that one virtue trumps all competing considerations. That virtue, compassion, is a feeling that confers upon the person feeling it a duty to do whatever is necessary to ameliorate distress." Will imagined a flood of other disability suits arising from this one, like the suit against the San Francisco Ballet by a mother who charged that the ballet company's height and weight standards discriminated against her daughter. "The work of compassionate courts never ends," he concluded with heavy irony.[4] Others had contrary views, like the veteran golfer Chi Chi Rodriguez, a star of the Senior PGA Tour. Rodriguez thought Martin was right to sue."The tour is played for charity," he noted. "It's supposed to be a compassionate tour, but when it came to compassion everyone went against him."[5] A letter to the editor of the *Chicago Sun-Times* shared Justice Scalia's view that it was unnecessary to spend the court's time on this

question, but the writer saw the matter from a different perspective: If Martin
needed a cart he should have the use of one. In that event, to even up the odds,
all the other players should have the option of using carts, too: "Instead of tying
up our judicial system and wasting mega-money on lawyers' fees, this could all
have been settled in 30 seconds with common sense and compassion."[6]

Who would have thought that compassion could become a two-edged
sword in national debate? When George Will and Antonin Scalia both come
close to ridiculing it, at the very time that the President of the United States
(and the leader of the Republican Party) describes himself as a "compassionate
conservative," something interesting is happening at the level of political—
and religious—rhetoric.

Indeed, both of our two most recent presidents have sought to associate
themselves, at least rhetorically, with the concept of compassion. When George
W. Bush campaigned as a "compassionate conservative," the phrase seemed to
convey, in its insistent and alliterating adjective, traces of an intrinsic uneasi-
ness. What would the alternative be, one was left to wonder: A *dis*passionate
conservative? An *unfeeling* conservative? A *cruel* conservative? Where "compassionate liberal" seemed virtually pleonastic, the term "compassionate conservative" appeared to fend off, or hold at bay, intimations of oxymoron. As for
Bill Clinton, his compassionate catchphrase—so successful that it has entered
the world as a seriocomic cliché—was the affective, even bathetic, but consis-
tently successful "I feel your pain," an expression unsurprisingly labeled "feminine" by early media critics:

> If other presidents tended to speak by lecturing the American public ("We have
> nothing to fear but fear itself" or "Ask not what your country can do for you"),
> Clinton often communicates by listening ("I feel your pain").... Call it New Age if
> you wish. But the Clinton style is really a textbook example of a leader who com-
> municates in ways often more characteristic of women than men....A woman
> tends to say, "I feel your pain." A man might say, "Let me tell you why you feel pain
> and what you should do about it." And then he might look at his watch.
>   This is not to say that displaying a "feminine" style is bad....[7]

This debased version of Carol Gilligan or Deborah Tannen, circa 1993, is one
of the first analyses of what would become a famous Clinton watchword.

A few years earlier media analysts had begun tracking what they labeled
"compassion fatigue," a term coined, presumably, on the model of "metal

fatigue" or, more likely, "combat fatigue." The combat in this case was the war against poverty and the cause of human rights. By the mid-1980s the term was in regular use among disaster relief agencies and United Nations officials, though the U.S. media kept "rediscovering" it through the early 1990s, as donations to famine relief in Ethiopia, cyclone relief in Bangladesh, and homeless shelters in New York City began to wane. In this context "compassion" clearly meant donations as well as volunteer aid; "compassion fatigue" was well glossed by one editorial, headed "Compassion Overload," as "the weariness with which Americans are reacting to suffering abroad and the unwillingness to respond to yet another disaster."[8] "Compassion fatigue" entered modern dictionaries, like *Chambers'*, and became an example of late-twentieth-century language innovation, with its typical compression of noun + noun, the noun-as-adjective so familiar from headline practice. Susan Moeller's 1999 book *Compassion Fatigue: How the Media Sell Disease, Famine, War, and Death* described what was, in effect, the commodification of compassion, its use and misuse by a journalism more concerned with celebrity culture—including its own—than by committed in-depth coverage of "unsexy news."[9] But in fact, the *fatigue* had affected the word *compassion* itself.

Once in regular use to describe human kindness, the very "virtues" celebrated in William Bennett's *Book of Virtues*—which contains, indeed, a section on *compassion*, wherein Bennett offers the unexceptional view that we should treat no one with "callous disregard"—*compassion* has increasingly become associated with issues like human rights, children's rights, animal rights, and multiculturalism. Thus, for example Herbert Kohl, an educator and writer, responds to Bennett in *A Call to Character: A Family Treasury* (co-edited with Colin Green), suggesting that Bennett's "family values" are too rigid and underemphasize compassion and social responsibility. Bennett's book includes the text of the Boy Scout Oath; Kohl's reprints, instead, the International Declaration of the Rights of Children.[10]

The problem with *compassion* begins with its etymology and history. From the fourteenth century to the beginning of the seventeenth, the word (deriving from Latin *com*, together, and *pati*, to suffer) was used to describe both *suffering together with one another*, or "fellow-feeling," and an emotion felt *on behalf of another who suffers*. In the second sense the compassion was felt not between equals, but from a distance—in effect, from high to low: "shown towards a per-

son in distress by one who is free from it, who is, in this respect, his superior."
When the first sense fell out of use, which it did fairly quickly, the remaining
sense hovered between charity and condescension.

Later usages, especially in a religious context, stress the emotional benefits
to the nonsufferer. Here is a symptomatic example, from a university sermon of
1876: "Compassion . . . gives the person who feels it pleasure even in the very
act of ministering to and succouring pain."[11] One does not have to be a card-
carrying Freudian to see that pleasure and pain are here intermingled in a way
that is satisfactorily both simple and complex: the pain of someone else provides an access of pleasure for the compassionate one.

The phrase "the Compassionate One," indeed, invokes one of the most
familiar uses of this notion, the idea that compassion is one of the attributes of
God (e.g., from the apocryphal book *Ecclesiasticus*: "For the Lord is full of
compassion and mercy, long-suffering, and very pitiful" 30:33). By extension,
compassion could be regarded as a normative and desirable perquisite of mon-
archs who ruled by "divine right"—as God's deputies—at least in theory ("By
the compassioned mercy of Queene Elizabeth"—John Speed's *History of Great
Britain*, 1611). The aspect of fellow-suffering led to some specific religious
uses, notably in a term like *compassivity*, which described the feelings of a saint
on beholding in a vision the sufferings of Christ, "whereby his soul is tran-
spierced with the sword of a compassive pain."[12] As was the case with *compassion* as a kind of emotionally gratifying condescension, this sense of the word
carries with it a certain occluded erotics.

Although Samuel Johnson called the transitive verb *(to) compassion* "a
word scarcely used," it does appear in references from the sixteenth century to
the nineteenth. The use of the verb in Shakespeare's *Titus Andronicus* gives a
clear sense of its function: "Can you heare a good man grone / And not relent,
or not compassion him?" (4.1.24). To compassion is to have compassion about
something, or someone, to pity him (or them). In a letter written in 1838, John
Quincy Adams expressed himself, "In charity to all mankind, bearing no mal-
ice or ill will to any human being, and even compassionating those who hold
in bondage their fellow men, not knowing what they do."[13] These words, later
adapted by Abraham Lincoln, suggest the crucial role of "compassionating" as
both activity and belief.

The best-known biblical example here is that of the "good Samaritan," who offered succor to a stranger:

> A certain man went down from Jerusalem to Jericho and fell among thieves, which stripped him of his raiment, and wounded him, and departed, leaving him half dead. And by chance there came down a certain priest that way: and when he saw him, he passed him by on the other side. And likewise a Levite, when he was at the place, came and looked on him, and passed by on the other side. But a certain Samaritan, as he journeyed, came where he was: and when he saw him, he had compassion on him. And went to him, and bound up his wounds, pouring in oil and wine, and set him on his own beast, and brought him to an inn, and took care of him. And on the morrow when he departed, he took out two pence, and gave them to the host, and said unto him, Take care of him; and whatsoever thou spendest more, when I come again, I will repay thee. (Luke 10:25–37)

This parable is told by Jesus to a lawyer who asks him, skeptically, how he can attain eternal life. He is told to love God with all his heart, with all his soul, and with all his might (a literal invocation of the language of Deuteronomy 4, the prayer known to Jews as the "Shema," the standard Jewish declaration of faith) and to love his neighbor as himself. The lawyer in true form then demands, "Who is my neighbor?" and the story of the Samaritan is his answer. Which of the three was the neighbor to him who fell among thieves? asks Jesus, and the lawyer responds, the one who showed mercy. "Go thou and do likewise," is the reply.

There is much to detain us in this parable, which seems to depict the high-ranking Jews as more indifferent to the lot of the unfortunate man than the Samaritan, who is a despised member of another sect. (Hence the paradox in the identification of the "neighbor.") The Samaritan's compassion is generosity, but also, by implication, fellow-feeling. The definition of a true neighbor derives from the behavior of the helpful passerby, who does not cross the road to avoid involvement.

We can know little about this particular Samaritan and his motivations: for one thing, he is in all probability a fictional character, summoned to life to play a part in the parable of instruction, rather than a "real" individual with knowable motives. Structurally speaking, what we are given is the story of two "high-status" insiders versus one "low-status" outsider, with the actions of the third acting as a rebuke to the selfishness of the first two. The Samaritan is the third in a series of three; the priest and the Levite, like Cinderella's two wicked stepsisters, are examples of privileged persons who behave selfishly or ignobly, in contrast to the humbler and more virtuous third. A similar sentiment can be deduced from this symptomatic phrase from the Epistle of John: "Whoso hath this world's good, and seeth his brother have need, and shutteth up his bowels of compassion from him, how dwelleth the love of God in him?" (3:17). Again "brotherhood" (like "neighbor-hood") is a matter of feeling, not blood.

It is worth noting that the phrase "good Samaritan" is itself not biblical, but rather developed over time as a way of interpreting the parable. Most English translations call him "a certain Samaritan"; the *New Living Translation* reads "a despised Samaritan." The implication of the adjective *good* when attached to "Samaritan" is oxymoronic (like "compassionate conservative"), and must once have been stressed ("the *good* Samaritan") to emphasize the surprising fact that generosity in this case came from an outsider, from whom little was to be expected. (Matthew Henry's *Commentary on the Bible* calls the Samaritans "That nation which of all others the Jews most despised and detested and would have no dealings with."[14]) The usual modern emphasis on the second term, rather than the first ("good *Samaritan*") forgets this history of anomaly, and turns an oxymoron into something like a redundancy.

The terms *Samaritan* and *good Samaritan* have had their own history, becoming not only proverbial shorthand for a disinterested do-gooder but the honored name of hospitals, organizations, help lines, and missions dedicated to the care of the sick, the suicidal, the homeless, and the despairing. The organization called The Samaritans, founded in 1953 to offer telephone counseling to those in distress, drops the word "good," as presumably implied in the term; by this point the sense of redundancy was so fully established that all sense of surprise at the "goodness" of a Samaritan had been definitively lost. In any case, those who took the name of Samaritan in this sense, like those compassionate passersby so labeled in newspaper accounts, intervened with acts of compassion like their biblical namesake: compassion extended from the better-off to the worse-off, as the Samaritan of the parable gave his own beast, his own money, and his own kindness to the man who fell among thieves. The sense that the Samaritan himself might have deserved "compassion" because he was a member of a disliked outsider sect has completely dropped away.

Where *compassion* quickly tipped in the direction of inequality, charity, or patronage (the nonsufferer showing compassion to the sufferer), *sympathy* remained, historically, a condition of equality or affinity, whether between the body and the soul, between two bodily organs, or, increasingly, between persons with similar feelings, inclinations, and temperaments. *Sympathy's* roots are Greek and Latin: it literally translated as "having a fellow-feeling," from *sym* + *pathos*, "suffering together." (The word *pathos*, of course, survives in English, where it has become a word more often encountered in aesthetic criticism than in ordinary life.)

To be sure, there was a sense of *sympathy* that was analogous or even identical to *compassion* ("the quality or state of being... affected by the suffering or sorrow of another; a feeling of compassion or commiseration"), a sense that became especially prominent in the late eighteenth and nineteenth centuries, and which survives in the material form of the "sympathy card" or "sympathy note" expressing condolence on a bereavement. An example from Edmund Burke's speech on Charles James Fox's East India bill—"To awaken something of sympathy for the unfortunate natives"—makes clear how close this kind of sympathy came to compassion. One could also sympathize with a political party, ideological stance, or philosophical position: again the angle of incidence, so to speak, might be one of *equality* ("he had no sympathy with the anti-opium party") or of *inequality*, again in the sense we have already noted from *compassion*—that is, that the sympathizers were not themselves suffering the same ills as those with whom they sympathized. Here the clearest example is that of the "sympathy strike," engaged in by workers, or students, on behalf of an embattled group elsewhere.

Empathy, we might note, is a modern word, although it has a Greek analogue. Coined in the early years of the twentieth century as a translation of German *Einfühlung*, it has come to denote the power of projecting one's personality into the object of contemplation, and has been a useful technical term in both psychology and aesthetics. It seems possible that the need for this word arose as the strongest sense of *sympathy* began to decline or become merged with *compassion*. But *empathy* also seems to stress the matter of personal agency and individual emotion. A person who displays empathy is, it appears, to be congratulated for having fine feelings; a person who shows or expresses sympathy has good cultural instincts and training; a person who shows compassion seems motivated, at least in part, by values and precepts, often those learned from religion, philosophy, or politics.

It is arguably this question of the abject other in need of assistance that has been the undoing of *compassion* as well as its proudest boast. "Rallying the armies of compassion" is what George W. Bush called it on the campaign stump. "Compassion is a miserable basis for American politics," declared Mickey Kaus in the *New York Times*. "It was a bad idea when liberals were selling it, and it's no less bad now that conservatives are embracing it." Kaus, the author of *The End of Equality*, found three fundamental flaws in compassion: it was "inegalitarian, carrying the condescending implication of charity, inferiority, and helplessness"; it was sentimental, tending "to override traditional, and sensible, moral distinctions," as between, for example, a young working father and a drug addict or a prisoner; and it was fragile, since it "appeals to essentially charitable impulses" and thus can fall victim to market forces. Citizens will give generously when times are good, but not when they themselves feel the necessity to economize. Kaus applauded Al Gore's description of Bush's noblesse oblige as "the crumbs of compassion," and declared "So the Republicans now have compassion? They can keep it."[15]

In fact, no party seems to want to keep it. Justice Scalia's confident scorn about "benevolent compassion" and governmental overregulation is right in the spirit of George Will's allergic reaction to unlimited government. Compassion has become the default currency of nongovernmental organizations and other "goo-goo" agencies, especially those concerned with social services and children's and animal rights. Indeed, despite its high-sounding name, compassion is fast becoming an *alternative* virtue, associated with persons and practices outside the mainstream. Californians for Compassionate Use works to reform laws concerning cannabis. The Compassion Club provides marijuana to chronically ill patients in Vancouver. *Compassionate Souls* is a book about raising your children as vegetarians. *Love! Valour! Compassion!* is the title of a hit play about eight gay men.

Although numerous religious groups—Catholic, Jewish, Unitarian-Universalist, and Christian nondenominational—also continue to reiterate their commitment to compassion, it may be symptomatic that most current books in print on the topic are voiced from the perspective of Tibetan Buddhism,[16] for this connection between an Eastern religion and a disempowered religious and cultural leader of great moral power offers a useful example of the pitfalls of "compassion." George W. Bush, we are told by the Associated Press, "extended a carefully measured welcome to the Dalai Lama" when the exiled Buddhist leader visited the White House.[17] The Chinese government objected to the visit, and the United States did what it could to minimize its "official" nature: Bush greeted the Dalai Lama, not in the Oval Office, but in the White House residence. This spatial decision in itself (taken together, perhaps, with the choice of a woman, National Security Adviser Condoleezza Rice, rather than Secretary of State Colin Powell to join the welcoming delegation) seemed to place the concerns of the Dalai Lama all-too-clearly on the side of what Justice Scalia called the "maternalistic," the admirable but perhaps ultimately inadvisable claims of that worrisome neo-pleonasm, "benevolent compassion," rather than on the side of expedient political action.

Compassion seems to waver politically between two forms of inequality: the benevolence of those who have (the power of the rich) and the entitlement of those who need (the power of the poor). The insoluble problem for society, and for government and law, is to behave as if there were no competition between the two. And in some quarters, at least, "compassionate government" is regarded as either a contradiction in terms or a category mistake. Compassion, it appears, is a good campaign slogan, but not necessarily a winning political strategy. It seems clear that for Bush, as for Scalia, implementing it in any kind of international policy would represent putting the (golf) cart before the horse.

Who Owns "Human Nature"? 14

"

The proper study of mankind is man.
                    —Alexander Pope, "Essay on Man"

In the wake of the events of September 11, 2001, people around the world struggled to understand what the terrorist attacks on the World Trade Center and the Pentagon could possibly tell us about "human nature." The *London Guardian* suggested that "we are struggling to adapt our perception of the world, our safety in it, and our understanding of human nature—to incorporate a new dimension of evil."[1] A letter to *Newsday* remarked that the actions taken by rescue workers at the World Trade Center showed that "when it is required of people to disregard basic human nature, which is greed and selfishness, and put the needs of a civilization first, it can be done."[2] (The author of this sober assessment was a high school senior.) The *Los Angeles Times* observed that the job of a firefighter seemed "almost antithetical to human nature: When everyone else flees from danger, they run toward it."[3] And an obituary notice for one of the thousands of victims lost in the World Trade Center attack began with a poignant observation: "It is a quirk of human nature that the person who does an act of kindness may forget it, but the recipient does not."[4] What is "human nature"? And what kind of measure can define and assess it?

"It's just human nature," people often say with a shrug about cultural, social, political, and moral actions from greed to optimism to studied indifference. It is human nature to think we can win the lottery; it is human nature not to want to "get involved" in reporting a crime; it is human nature to believe that our current affair of the heart is true love. (Thus Samuel Johnson defined a second marriage as "the triumph of hope over experience.") The shameful silence of the thirty-eight witnesses to the rape and murder of Kitty Genovese on a quiet street in Kew Gardens, New York, in 1964 (none of whom called police until after she was dead) was attributed to human nature, but so is kindness to animals, and a passion for team sports. The "dark side of human nature" turns up in many journalistic accounts of mayhem, trickery, and violence. And it is not just "life," but art, that is periodically called to witness. A production of *The Nutcracker* ballet is said by a critic to plumb the "tragic side of human nature." Reality television is said to cast a "bleakly pessimistic light . . . on human nature."[5]

"Human nature" is praised, or blamed, for the good behavior of Samaritans and the bad behavior of politicians. Journalists use it all the time. A reporter writing during the Monica Lewinsky scandal announced that "human nature being what it is" in the case of male politicians and female interns, we have a long way to go before attaining equality between the sexes.[6] The idea that Americans could quickly forget the irregularities of the presidential election "contradicts whatever we might have observed about human nature,"[7] wrote Francine Prose. It was simply "a matter of human nature" that political contributors wanted to go to Senator Hillary Clinton's new house for a fundraiser, observed Democratic strategist James Carville.[8] The national debate about stem cell research suggested to conservative columnist George Will that "the parties represent different sensibilities—different stances toward nature, including human nature."[9]

What in the world *is* "human nature"? Few phrases are used so confidently and promiscuously, by parents and children, religious figures and laity, optimists and pessimists, humanists and scientists. And few phrases have been responsible for so much disinformation, or so much attitudinizing. John Keats thought it finer than scenery. William Wordsworth exulted that it had been born again in the early years of the French Revolution. Karl Marx called it an "aesthetic delusion."[10] Journalist turned fiction writer Anna Quindlen, disclaiming any right to be considered an ethicist or a philosopher, announced, with mock modesty, "I'm a novelist. My work is human nature. Real life is really all I know."[11]

But where writers from the sixteenth to the mid-twentieth centuries—from William Shakespeare to David Hume to Virginia Woolf—felt both the necessity and the right to offer opinions on this key phrase and its ramifications, studies of human nature in the latter years have focused, symptomatically, on science: evolutionary biology and psychology, gene theory, behaviorism, and cultural evolution. It is a suggestive fact about human nature that it was once the intellectual property of poets, philosophers, and political theorists and is now largely the domain of scientists.

"Genome Project Can't Explain Human Nature," declared the caption of a *Boston Globe* letter to the editor responding to the mapping of the human genome by two scientific teams. The letter writer, voicing an opinion shared by many commentators after the reports disclosed that humans had fewer genes than formerly believed, observes that it is absurd to expect "that the answers science provides can explain the unique nature of humanity."[12] The news that human beings had only 30,000 genes, not many more than go into the making of a roundworm, a fruit fly, or a plant, and that only about 300 of those genes are different from the genome of a mouse, raised what the media persistently called "humbling" questions about how to explain "human complexity" and what it means to be human.[13] And yet this is just what is so ardently desired, at least in some quarters—an answer to the question, an answer that science alone is thought, these days, to provide.

In a book entitled *Our Posthuman Future* (2002), political scientist Francis Fukuyama warns against recent developments in biotechnology—from cloning to Prozac, from plastic surgery to genetic engineering—that threaten to modify human nature. At stake was the view, strongly championed by Fukuyama, that an essential and unchanging theory of human nature is "fundamental to our notions of justice, morality, and the good life," and that tampering with the genome may cause us "to lose our humanity."[14]

Is human nature fixed or mutable? Something that science helps us to understand, or something that science itself has the capacity to change? Something that was once powerfully described by literature and philosophy, but that has now become the realm of science? How did "human nature," once deemed the proper study of mankind, get to be the privileged territory of geneticists and biologists?

II

The term "human nature" can be inflected on the first word (*human* nature, as contrasted with that of animals, angels, or God) or the second (human *nature*, what is intrinsic rather than eccentric or acculturated for human beings). The first of these modes suggests a difference *between* humankind and other beings, and thus implicitly asserts the commonality of *human* experience in contrast with that of others. (The paradoxical phrase "the human nature of Christ," common in many works of Christian theology, points up the issue, as does the section of Jared Diamond's evolutionary study *The Third Chimpanzee*, which focuses on a quartet of activities he calls "uniquely human": language, art, agriculture, and substance addiction.) That which is particular to humans in this concept of human nature is, ordinarily, what differentiates them from beasts or gods. In Western thought this has been associated with the so-called Great Chain of Being, derived from Hellenic philosophy and adapted for Christian and neo-Platonic use in the medieval and early modern periods. The *ur*-text here may be the eighth Psalm: "What is man, that thou art mindful of him? And the son of man, that thou visitest him? For thou hast made him a little lower than the angels" (8:4–5), or its passionate adaptation in Hamlet's famous speech of existential despair:

> What a piece of work is a man! How noble in reason! How infinite in faculty! In form and moving how express and admirable, in action, how like an angel, in apprehension, how like a god; . . . And yet, to me, what is this quintessence of dust? (*Hamlet* 2.2.303–08)

If we change the inflection to stress the second term rather than the first ("human *nature*"), we alter the field of interpretation considerably, since what is now emphasized is what could be called a difference *within*. What is "natural" to humans and what is "learned," "cultural," "adapted," or even "unnatural"? Both of these senses are operative in the history of the phrase, and both have had telling effects on how the various disciplines of the humanities have understood their relation to the age-old question, "What is man?" Yet in fact it is a question not frequently posed, these days, within the humanities. This is the conundrum that has provoked my inquiry.

Humanists have, by and large, abandoned their claims to an interest in this most interesting of problems, tending in recent years to regard the phrase *human nature* as a reductive mode of fuzzy thinking. This skepticism is frequently justified, for all too often human nature turns up (on student papers, for example, or in journalistic opinion pieces) as an *answer*, a solution or explanation for a quirk or a kink of character. If the explanation for human action, or human behavior, whether in literature or in life, is simply "human nature," then analysis and interpretation have been replaced by tautology. In addition, for twentieth- and twenty-first-century humanists, the word *human* itself often seems like a version of what has been called "essentializing"—that is, a refusal to acknowledge both cultural difference and the formative influence of history, economics, regionalism, personal biography, and other social and political elements that go into the "construction" of a person in the world. Feminists and other cultural theorists have also called into question the troublesome word *man*, which seemed to some to erase *woman* in a gesture toward the universal subject. Before we conclude that this gesture is a peculiarity of ideologues and latter-day separatists, we might recall that Hamlet himself parses the word in a similar fashion at the end of that same famous speech—a speech that, though it often misremembered as a soliloquy, is in fact addressed to his mischievous schoolfellows, Rosencrantz and Guildenstern. "Man delights not me—nor woman neither, though by your smiling you seem to say so," he tells them, making the artful shift (no one does this better than Shakespeare) from the general to the particular, and thus exposing the intrinsic ambiguities and doubleness implicit in the grandest of ideas (*Hamlet* 2.2.309–10). Is *man* a term that transcends mere gender, or is it a name that produces gender trouble? In any case, *man* has fallen out of favor in literary and cultural studies, together with universal pronouns like *we* and *us*, leaving the field of "human nature" open to other disciplines. Thus anthropologist Clifford Geertz could refer parenthetically, in his groundbreaking 1973 book *The Interpretation of Cultures*, to "(what used, in a simpler day, to be called 'human nature')."

But this shift in the disciplinary custody of "human nature" has serious consequences for the value of that amorphous enterprise called "the humanities." For if the place to investigate "human nature" is not "the humanities," what is the use of the humanistic disciplines? What else gives them cultural authority? And, equally to the point, what is the use of funding, supporting, studying, and teaching them?

"Human nature" is an artifact of culture and language, of fantasy and projection. In other words, the very idea of human nature as a normative, identifiable essence is both a political and a psychological wish, with important side effects. What is most fascinating to me about the concept of human nature is the way the quest for it has become a self-fulfilling dream, a lure of full self-knowledge, a ruse of research paradigms and protocols from the theological to the anthropological, from behaviorism to genomics. In the Enlightenment it was political philosophers; in the nineteenth century it was religious believers, psychologists, and anthropologists; today it is scientists working at the level of the gene.

III

The migration of "human nature" across disciplines in the last several hundred years, from moral philosophy to religion, psychology, Freud and Freudianism, and the new Darwinists, is a fascinating history, represented in literally hundreds of works like *Human Nature and Railroads* (1915); *Human Nature in Business* (1920); *Human Nature and Management* (1929); *Human Nature and Christian Marriage* (1958); *Human Nature in Politics* (1977); *Human Nature and Predictability* (1981); *The Human Nature of Birds* (1993); *Human Nature at the Millennium* (1997), and so on. Starting as early as Thomas Boston's resoundingly titled *Human Nature in Its Four Fold State of Primitive Integrity, Entire Depravity, Begun Recovery and Consummate Happiness or Misery* (1744), phrases like "human nature and . . . " or "human nature in . . . " or "the human nature of . . . " became the watchwords of a certain kind of cultural advice, analysis, and wisdom. "Suffering," "the gospel," "the nature of evil," "the peace problem," "world disorder," and "selling goods"—all have been linked with "human nature" in the titles of books in the last century. The books on business and management, and indeed some of the books on Christianity, are boosterist in spirit: "America" as well as "Christianity" seems to be a consequence of, or a fulfillment of, the best in "human nature."

Eighteenth-century political theorists like David Hume had speculated on the nature of "human nature" in quest of a theory of the individual, of reason, and of human agency. But later accounts by thinkers from Sigmund Freud to Charles Darwin, radically altered the question of control and mastery. Who or what controlled human nature? Was man indeed a rational animal, or rather a creature dominated by the unconscious or by heredity and evolution? Karl Marx's skepticism about the development of human nature as an ideology by political theorists is still a cogent argument today: "The prophets of the eighteenth century," Marx contended, "saw this individual not as an historical result, but as the starting-point of history; not as something evolving in the course of history, but posited by nature, because for them this individual was in conformity with nature, in keeping with their idea of human nature. This delusion has been characteristic of every new epoch hitherto."[16] Whether delusory or not, the relationship of the individual to human nature came to dominate a whole range of social, cultural, political, and religious writings concerned with human betterment.[17]

In some cases medical science seemed to offer specific answers, as if human nature were a pathological symptom. It was the nerves, or the glands, that held the key, in scientific studies like *The Mysteries of Human Nature Explained by a New System of Nervous Physiology* (1857), by J. Stanley Grimes, a professor of medical jurisprudence, or *The Glands Regulating Personality: A Study of the Glands of Internal Secretion in Relation to the Types of Human Nature* (1921) by Louis Berman, a doctor of medicine.[18] "The future," thought Berman, "belongs to the biochemist" since the glands are really in charge: "In short, they control human nature, and whoever controls them, controls human nature." Thus "the answer to the question: 'What is Man?' is 'Man is regulated by his Glands of Internal Secretion.'" The upshot was a theory of glandular social betterment: "The raising of the general level of intelligence by the judicious use of endocrine extracts will mean a good deal to the sincere statesmen" and may thus help to prevent war.[19]

This focus on the operation of a particular internal body part, the glands, to explain everything about human nature, runs counter to the lofty and seemingly timeless generalizations of philosophy. But the borderline between the timeless and the local or situational is constantly being crossed. A good example is offered by the surprising itinerary of John Dewey's *Human Nature and*

Conduct, an influential work of social psychology written in 1918, at the end of World War I, and published in 1922. Addressing issues like "habit" and the "alterability of human nature," Dewey, a philosopher and educational reformer, pointed out that modern warfare operates on quite a different basis from that of the *Iliad*, the "classic expression of war's traditional psychology as well as the source of the literary tradition regarding its motives and glories." Idealized figures like Helen, Hector, and Achilles were long gone, he noted. "The activities that evoke and incorporate a war are no longer personal love, love of glory, or the soldier's love of his own privately amassed booty, but are of a collective, prosaic political and economic nature." This, indeed, was the very reason why literature is invoked to glorify the "mass movements of soldiery" deployed by "a depersonalized general staff":

> The more horrible a depersonalized scientific mass war becomes, the more necessary it is to find universal ideal motives to justify it. Love of Helen of Troy has become a burning love for all humanity, and hatred of the foe symbolizes a hatred of all the unrighteousness and injustice and oppression which he embodies. The more prosaic the actual causes, the more necessary it is to find glowingly sublime motives.

"Such considerations," Dewey continues, "destroy that argument for [war's] necessary continuance which is based on the immutability of specified forces in original human nature."[20] He wrote this dark account of the "alterability of human nature," at the end of World War I. But his sentiments would be invoked by the U.S. government in 1944, when *Human Nature and Conduct* was reprinted by the War Department as *War Department Education Manual EM 618*, "an aid in instruction in certain educational activities of the armed forces." Thus, by the end of the Second World War, John Dewey's ironic and trenchant account of human nature in ancient and modern warfare had become part of the standard curriculum of the United States Armed Forces Institute setting out a program for the manipulation of public perception. Seldom has the timeless been more directly placed in the service of the times. To a twenty-first-century reader, Dewey's resounding phrases about "depersonalized scientific mass war" and the instrumental rhetoric of "unrighteousness," "injustice," and "oppression" will carry yet another set of local meanings.

As Dewey's instrumental reading of Homer will suggest, poetry and litera-ture have not been completely shut out in the gradual move of human nature toward the social and the scientific. Following the emergence of the phrase in eighteenth-century philosophy, the romantic poets adopted the term with enthusiasm, and by the beginning of the twentieth century "human nature" had become both ubiquitous and commonplace in literary language, appearing regularly in the writings of belletrists of all kinds. Virginia Woolf—a writer with a distinctly unromantic sensibility—seems to have employed it as a matter of course. Reviewing an edition of Montaigne's *Essays*, Woolf observes that he "never ceases to pour scorn upon the misery, the weakness, the vanity of human nature." She congratulates Defoe for dealing with it ("He belongs...to the school of the great plain writers, whose work is founded upon what is most persistent, though not most seductive, in human nature") and suggests that Jane Austen was the doyenne of the field: "Her gaze passes straight to the mark, and we know precisely where, upon the map of human nature, that mark is." As for George Eliot, "she gathers in her large grasp a great bunch of the main elements of human nature and groups them together with a tolerant and wholesome understanding."[21] To illuminate human nature is, in all of these cases, something to be sought, and praised.

Woolf is a novelist as well as an essayist, and it may be imagined that she found some authorial utility in the concept of human nature as it plays into the business of creating characters and social dramas. But in the works of her contemporary and fellow essayist T. S. Eliot—a very different kind of writer—the term also surfaces with surprising regularity. Likewise, Eliot speaks easily of "that dolorous aspect of human nature which in comedy is best portrayed by Molière" and of William Blake's "capacity for considerable understanding of human nature." By building "an attitude of self-dramatization" into some of his heroes, Eliot thought, Shakespeare was "illustrating, consciously or unconsciously, human nature."[22] Plainly in the 1920s and 1930s, when these pieces were written, "human nature" as a general category was itself alive and well in the minds of major writers of fiction, essays, poetry, and drama. Yet the appearance of the concept today in literary discourse is something of an anomaly and a throwback.[23] The term itself is suspect. In a multicultural world, how could there be *one* "human nature"?

Literary critic Harold Bloom's insistence on Shakespeare as the inventor of "the human," while hardly a new claim for Shakespeare studies, was startling in its assumption of a single "human" point of view, as embodied in Bloom's freewheeling use of the word *we* to mean *I*: "Can we conceive of ourselves without Shakespeare?" he asked rhetorically. And, "Our ideas as to what makes the self authentically human owe more to Shakespeare than ought to be possible."[24] It is this magisterial and unquestioning *we* that marks the problem for some modern theorists—and made Bloom's approach so comforting for some readers. This *we* is as important to the book's success as its effusive lionization of Shakespeare—a return to an older fashion of speaking.

What do we mean when we say *we* or *I*? or, for that matter, *you* or *they*? Who is speaking when I say *I*? What is "the human" in this sense? And how is it counterpoised to more theoretical notions of the "inhuman" and the "posthuman" with technology, as well as with what philosophers in the last century called "the human condition"? Hannah Arendt contrasts "the problem of human nature" with the "conditions of human existence—life itself, natality and mortality, worldliness, plurality, and the earth," which "can never 'explain' what we are or answer the question of who we are for the simple reason that they never condition us absolutely."[25] Jean-François Lyotard asks, "[W]hat if human beings, in humanism's sense, were in the process of, constrained into, becoming inhuman," and "what if what is 'proper' to humankind were to be inhabited by the inhuman?"—a question increasingly asked, as well, by cyber-theorists and students of modern technology and communication.[26] Are we "electrical," as has been claimed in a book called *The Post-Human Condition*?[27] Or are we in fact relentlessly and deterministically "biological," as has been asserted, with authority, by sociobiologist E. O. Wilson?

IV

I want now to turn directly to an examination of the term "human nature" as it has appeared in the writings of late-twentieth- and twenty-first-century scientists, and principally in the work of E. O. Wilson and his followers. The influence of these books and their claims has been very great, and the implications for the (apparently diminished) role of the humanities in a modern world are far reaching. It is now commonplace for human nature—the term, the concept, and the book title—to appear in conjunction with arguments concerning genetics, evolutionary psychology, the biological mating strategies of the human animal. Yet, as will become clear, the articulation of these arguments depends, both explicitly and implicitly, upon a use of categories, texts, and questions that have been inherited from the long history of the humanities.

E. O. Wilson begins his Pulitzer Prize–winning book *On Human Nature* (1978) with an epigraph from Hume's *Inquiry Concerning Human Understanding* (1748), one of the grandest achievements of eighteenth-century philosophy:

> What though these reasonings concerning human nature seem abstract and of difficult comprehension, this affords no presumption of their falsehood. On the contrary, it seems impossible that what has hitherto escaped so many wise and profound philosophers can be very obvious and easy. And whatever pains these researches may cost us, we may think ourselves sufficiently rewarded, not only in point of profit but of pleasure, if, by that means, we can make any addition to our stock of knowledge in subjects of such unspeakable importance.

Wilson's own ruminations begin by taking up this quotation, and paraphrasing the questions that, he tells us, "the great philosopher David Hume said are of unspeakable importance: How does the mind work, and beyond that why does it work in such a way and not another, and from these two considerations together, what is man's ultimate nature?" For Wilson the last century of scientific inquiry, since Darwin, has altered expectations for any answers to these questions: "We are biological," he asserts. An acknowledgment of natural selection is "the essential first hypothesis for any serious consideration of the human condition":

> Without it the humanities and social sciences are the limited descriptors of surface phenomena, like astronomy without physics, biology without chemistry, and mathematics without algebra. With it, human nature can be laid open as an object of fully empirical research, biology can be put to the service of liberal education, and our self-conception can be enormously and truthfully enriched.[28]

The chapters of Wilson's book address in turn a series of topics that for him make up a map of human nature: Heredity, Development, Emergence, Aggression, Sex, Altruism, Religion, and Hope. Here is a characteristically brilliant crescendo of generalization that displays Wilson comfortably astride his sociobiological hobbyhorse in a chapter on "Altruism":

Can the cultural evolution of higher ethical values gain a direction and momentum of its own and completely replace genetic evolution? I think not. The genes hold culture on a leash. The leash is very long, but inevitably values will be constrained in accordance with their effects on the human gene pool. The brain is a product of evolution. Human behavior—like the deepest capacities for emotional response which drive and guide it—is the circuitous technique by which human genetic material has been and will be kept intact. Morality has no other demonstrable ultimate function.[29]

Ethics and morality are by-products of biological development, essentially defense mechanisms for keeping "human genetic material" intact. "Morality has no other demonstrable ultimate function." Philosophy is thus something like an optical illusion, as are poetry, fable, and aphorism. What we think are our "highest" functions are fully indebted to our "lowest"—to the body, to its self-preservation and circulation.

The glossary of terms appended to Wilson's book, which runs from A for *adaptation* to Z for *zoology*, pauses at the letter H (between *homozygous*, "when the genes located at a given site on [a] chromosome pair are identical to each other," and *hymenoptera*, "the insect order that contains all bees, wasps, and ants") to define *human nature* in a single pithy sentence:

Human nature. In the broader sense, the full set of innate behavioral predispositions that characterize the human species; and in the narrower sense, those predispositions that affect social behavior.[30]

The key words here are *innate*, *behavioral*, *social*, and *predisposition*. A human being can act against his predisposition—biology is not destiny in a completely deterministic sense—but social, moral, and ethical practices have their underlying basis in the "nature" side of human nature. In a section called "Hope," Wilson calls for the development of what he terms a "biology of ethics," which will enable "the selection of a more deeply understood and enduring code of moral values." If dinosaurs had grasped the concept of "nobility," he suggests, "they might have survived. They might have been us."[31]

This is eloquent, and it is also troubling. What is the place of things like art, music, and poetry in Wilson's concept of human nature? Simply put, they are ornamental figures, illustrative metaphors deployed by a writer who has had a broad liberal education. "The processes of sexual pairbonding vary greatly among cultures, but they are everywhere steeped in emotional feeling," he writes. "In cultures with a romantic tradition, the attachment can be rapid and profound, creating love beyond sex which, once experienced, permanently alters the adolescent mind. Description of this part of human ethology is the refined specialty of poets, as we see in the remarkable expression by James Joyce." At this point in his text Wilson quotes a long passage from Joyce's *Portrait of the Artist As a Young Man*, in which Stephen Daedalus sees a girl standing in the water who looks like a "strange and beautiful seabird." It is not surprising that the naturalist's eye is caught by a figure of speech that invokes, and uses as its point of reference, an image from the natural world. The purely decorative role Wilson assigns to literature is clear in the fact that he does not footnote this passage, although he is careful to provide notes to all his scientific references, however glancing. (The notes are genteelly banished to the back of the book, signifying that *On Human Nature* is a piece of "philosophical" writing for the mainstream reader, not an insider text for scientists.)

Sometimes quoting literature out of context has inadvertent effects. Here is a telling example, from a discussion of "Group Selection and Altruism" in Wilson's 1980 classic, *Sociobiology:*

> Selection will discriminate against the individual if cheating has later adverse effects on his life and reproduction that outweigh the momentary advantage gained. Iago stated the essence in *Othello*: "Good name in man and woman, dear my lord, is the immediate jewel of their souls."[32]

There is no mention here of Iago's position as the most arrant hypocrite in all of Shakespeare, nor of his own contempt for "good name" as compared to more material and vengeful rewards. Arguably "cheating" by Iago himself has later adverse effects on his life, since once his machinations are discovered he is led off in chains to be tortured at the play's close, but this does not seem to be the intent of the citation, which rather appears to aim at an endorsement of the sentiment expressed, despite the bad faith with which it is offered, in context, to the credulous Othello.

The literary references in *On Human Nature* tend to be less startling, but also more frequent. William Butler Yeats is invoked to support the belief, ascribed to "the reflective person," that "his life is in some incomprehensible manner guided through a biological ontogeny....He senses that with all the drive, wit, love, pride, anger, hope, and anxiety that characterize the species he will in the end be sure only of helping to perpetuate the same cycle. Poets have defined this truth as tragedy. Yeats called it the coming of wisdom. Here Wilson inserts a four-line poem from Yeats, "The Coming of Wisdom with Time," in this case footnoted, but not commented upon within the text. The poetry is there to reinforce the cultural generalization. Again, and not surprisingly, the metaphors are drawn from the physical world, as if "truth" were a botanical effect:

> Though leaves are many, the root is one;
> Through all the lying days of my youth
> I swayed my leaves and flowers in the sun;
> Now I may wither into the truth.

Yeats makes another brief appearance in Wilson's text ("what Yeats called the artifice of eternity"), as does *Pilgrim's Progress* and a poem by Sappho, the latter again introduced with a now-familiar formula: "Poets have noted it well, as in the calm phrasing of Mary Barnard's [translation of] Sappho." The poem is then quoted.[33] I want here to call attention to the repetition of this move

- "Description of this part of human ethology is the refined specialty of poets..."
- "Poets have defined this truth as tragedy."
- "Poets have noted it well..."

not only because of the supporting or cameo role in which it casts imaginative literature in its relationship to the quest for "human nature," but also because of the gauntlet that Wilson throws down toward the end of *On Human Nature*, in a passage in which he decries the *absence* of modern science and modern scientists from distinguished cultural conversations. Of all the assertions in his book, published in 1978, this peroration is perhaps the most surprising to modern-day readers, since—in large part due to Wilson's own successes, and those of his students and disciplines—it is precisely science and scientists that now, a quarter-century later, dominate the public conversation about human nature. Here is Wilson's long, passionate, and beautifully written conclusion:

In the United States intellectuals are virtually defined as those who work in the prevailing mode of the social sciences and humanities. Their reflections are devoid of the idioms of chemistry and biology, as though humankind were still in some sense a numinous spectator of physical reality. In the pages of *The New York Review of Books, Commentary, The New Republic, Daedalus, National Review, Saturday Review,* and other literary journals articles dominate that read as if most of basic science had halted during the nineteenth century. Their content consists largely of historical anecdotes, diachronic collating of outdated, verbalized theories of human behavior, and judgments of current events according to personal ideology—all enlivened by the pleasant but frustrating techniques of effervescence. Modern science is still regarded as a problem-solving activity and a set of technical marvels, the importance of which is to be evaluated in an ethos extraneous to science. It is true that many "humanistic" scientists step outside scientific materialism to participate in the culture, sometimes as expert witnesses and sometimes as aspiring authors, but they almost never close the gap between the two worlds of discourse. With rare exceptions they are the tame scientists, the token emissaries of what must be viewed by their hosts as a barbaric culture still ungraced by a written language. They are degraded by the label they accept too readily: popularizers. Very few of the great writers, the ones who can trouble and move the deeper reaches of the mind, ever address real science on its own terms. Do they know the nature of the challenge?[34]

This is appropriately fierce, even though Wilson himself may at the end be looking sideways in the mirror; he, after all, is both a "great writer" and a "popularizer," as the success and esteem of this book and its author attest. In a later and equally ambitious attempt at synthesis, a book entitled *Consilience* (literally, "jumping together," or "concurrence," a term from the history of science[35]), he will say explicitly, "The search for human nature can be viewed as the archaeology of the epigenetic rules." In other words, fields that appear to be distinct from one another, like economics and aesthetics, will be unified under this umbrella of genetic understanding. Science will explain the humanities.

Many subsequent accounts of "human nature" have followed Wilson's lead, filling the gap he lamented. In the years since Wilson's announcement of "sociobiology" in the 1970s dozens of books and hundreds of articles have tried to account for, or to rebut, the claim that human nature can be described, if not explained, by science. Consider the title *Man, Beast and Zombie: What Science Can and Cannot Tell Us about Human Nature,* by Kenan Malik.[36] One of the most successful new books on this topic, Paul Ehrlich's *Human Natures: Genes, Cultures, and the Human Prospect,* stresses what Ehrlich, an evolutionary biologist, calls "cultural evolution." His book begins by asking "What is human nature?" and he then goes on to explain why the term needs to be put in the plural. "'Human nature' as a singular concept embodies the erroneous notion that people possess a common set of rigid, genetically specified behavioral predilections that are unlikely to be altered by circumstances." But the study of human evolution in recent decades has taken account of behavioral flexibility and diversity in areas "as different as sexual preferences and political systems." Thus he resolves, "in light of this scientific progress," to "highlight human *natures*: the diverse and evolving behaviors, beliefs, and attitudes of *Homo sapiens*."[37]

Ehrlich writes as a scientist, but he writes against "the extreme hereditary determinism that infests much of the current discussion of human behavior," and in favor of the idea that biology has to be considered in the context of culture, and that "our culture is changing through an evolutionary process that is generally thought of as history."[38] Yet his book's references to philosophers (Immanuel Kant, Jürgen Habermas, Martin Heidegger, Charles Sanders Peirce, Richard Rorty) and poets (Samuel Taylor Coleridge, Percy Bysshe Shelley, J. W. von Goethe) appear almost exclusively in the footnotes, not in the text: humanities, literature, and the arts may underpin scientific observations but they are clearly secondary to his argument.[39] Erhlich's notion of "cultural evolution," however politically progressive, still strongly emphasizes a theory of natural selection. (Characteristically, this softening of a brilliant and powerful paradigm, the shift from Wilson's uncompromising singular *nature* to Ehrlich's more affable plural, *natures*, robs the original insight of some of its force, even as it renders the evolutionary claims of sociobiology more acceptable to critical audiences.)

Of the host of other recent books by biologists on some aspect of human nature, most address questions of genetics, heredity, and evolution—and many bear enthusiastic blurbs by E. O. Wilson. Designed to cross over into the mainstream, these books have deliberately catchy titles. "*Mean Genes* is brilliant," Wilson writes of a book by Terry Burnham and Jay Phelan subtitled *From Sex to Money to Food: Taming Our Primal Instincts*. Burnham and Phelan, who have become talk-show favorites, take on such eye-catching topics as Debt, Fat, Drugs, Risk, Greed, Gender, Beauty, Infidelity, Family, and Friends and Foes. "*Mean Genes* seeks to foster a deep understanding of human existence," they announce in the introduction. "The foundation of the book is evolutionary biology."[40] In *Are We Hardwired?* authors William R. Clark and Michael Grunstein address "the role of genes in human behavior," following in the controversial path of Richard Dawkins's *The Selfish Gene.*[41] Jared Diamond's *The Third Chimpanzee: The Evolution and Future of the Human Animal*, another Pulitzer Prize–winning study, asks, "What were those few key ingredients that made us human?" "*The Third Chimpanzee* will endure," the voice of Wilson asserts on the jacket flap, adding an evolutionary happy ending to the literary enterprise. In fact, though, Diamond's book is both a history and a warning, as is clear from the concluding section, entitled "Reversing Our Progress Overnight."

I might note that Diamond, like Wilson, occasionally uses a literary text to point a moral. Thus Shelley's "Ozymandias," a poem about a once-omnipotent king whose statue lies dismantled—a "colossal wreck"—in a desert wasteland, is quoted at the end of a chapter on golden ages. The inscription on the ruin's pedestal offers an inadvertently ironic commentary, since it too promises to "endure": "My name is Ozymandias, king of kings: Look on my works, ye mighty, and despair!"

These are the books that E. O. Wilson wants to promote in the place of those by "tame scientists." All are clearly aimed at a general readership, and many have become best-sellers. What is most striking to me, as I have already noted, is how completely the dominance in this discussion of human nature has swung around from the humanities to the sciences.

V

"Books," Jean-Paul Sartre wrote, "do serve some purpose. Culture doesn't save anything or anyone, it doesn't justify. But it's a product of man: he projects himself into it, he recognizes himself in it; that critical image alone offers him his image."[42] It seems to be human nature to *believe* in human nature, whatever those terms are taken to mean.

In point of fact, it is literature and the history of the imaginative arts that have *produced* "human nature." In the intellectual parlor game of "Man is the animal that . . . " (e.g., Carlyle's "man is a tool-using animal"; Spinoza's "man is a social animal"; Thomas Jefferson's "man is the only animal which devours his own kind") it is arguable that "man is the animal that speculates endlessly upon human nature," and that the history of that speculation, as much as any forensic tracing of cause and effect, is what constitutes the nature of human nature for our time.

Let me, then, return to my fundamental question: Why is "human nature" now, as it seems, firmly in the custody of biologists and evolutionary psychologists, on the one hand, and journalists, on the other? Why do so many of these books on "human nature" take as their subject politics, or social theory, or psychology, whether of the hard, soft, or pop variety? How can we account for the strong drift away from such questions by literary scholars and theorists, and by humanistic cultural critics?

The answers are not too far to seek, and they are reasonable enough: multi-culturalism, diversity, a respect for cultural difference, a suspicion of the politics of homogenization, a worry about coercive universalism. All of these critiques and displacements are worth taking very seriously, as any history of race relations, gender politics, religious intolerance, and patterns of immigration will make clear. But the reluctance of humanists to generalize on this topic, whether their reluctance is motivated by sophistication (there is no we), politics (the world is global and multicultural), or sheer weariness with what had become an inert and flabby cliché, has produced some unwelcome effects. In fact this may be a classic baby-and-bathwater scenario, in which humanists write themselves out of the story of who gets to describe, and analyze, "human nature."

There are—I want to suggest—three important reasons for the current estrangement between the humanities and human nature that deserve to be addressed. These reasons derive directly from the appropriation of the term by science and scientists, and before that by behaviorists and social scientists, and they can be summed up in three clunky words: *pluralization*, *verbalization*, and *interdisciplinarity*. Let me address them one by one.

- *Pluralization*, or the fear of the universal

The defensive pluralization of analytic concepts has become a hallmark of modern-day work, and speaks in part to commendable political concerns. The title of Paul Ehrlich's book is *Human Natures*, in the plural, and scholars of literature, anthropology, and cultural studies will all recall the move from "culture" to "cultures," as well as that from "history" to "histories," or indeed from

"feminism" to "feminisms." But such welcome reminders about cultural difference are not without their inhibiting effects. One does not need to hanker after
Bloom's magisterial we in order to recognize the value of structural analysis,
generalization, and transhistorical analogy in the production of intellectually
challenging theory—or theories. Humanists who find human nature either
banal or imperialist should take another look, and see if there is a way of moving beyond the impasse of pluralization that has effectively blocked the way for
a whole formal mode of literary and imagistic analysis.

Some insights in fact require one to be a dupe of universalism, because
that is the only way fully to inhabit a culture. There are some things one cannot see from the outside, but only from within, even if that "within-ness"
comes at the cost of a certain global overview. To speak plainly: pluralization
may be good politics, but it produces undue deference to other disciplines, tacitly acknowledging that certain kinds of humanistic inquiry are elite, overspe-
cialized, or without redeeming social value. It emphasizes historical context at
the expense of synchronic relations within the work. It renders the specificity
of language and the formal properties of art secondary, or ancillary, to local
meaning. The opportunity for the humanities to lead rather than to remain
secondary to the worlds of databases, experiments, and statistics is tied to the
power to generalize and to speak and write cross-culturally. It necessarily
involves combining the perspectives of inside and outside. The experience of
the blindness produced by fully inhabiting a partial perspective is still the
experience of "human life." This act of intellectual projection is too important
a task to be left to the scientists, much less the social scientists, although
humanists should welcome their collaboration.

- *Verbalization*, or the fear of taking language seriously

If we return for a moment to E. O. Wilson's final remarks in *On Human
Nature*—remarks as powerful as they are provocative—we can take another
look at his perfectly justifiable putdown of journalistic attempts to talk science: "their content consists largely of historical anecdotes, diachronic collating of outdated, *verbalized* theories of human behavior, and judgments of current events according to personal ideology." Here I want to single out the word
verbalized, which seems to bear a lot of negative weight: to *verbalize* in this

context is to translate, and translate badly, from one language, the language of science, into another language, the language of journalism and popular discourse. *Verbalize* here is cognate to terms like *intellectualize* and *rationalize*— words that suggest that the activity in question is a second-order phenomenon, a stage removed from the thing itself. What Wilson admires in language is its beauty, its decorative capacity. In another telling phrase, he insists that without taking biology into account, "the humanities and social sciences are the limited descriptors of surface phenomena," like astronomy without physics, biology without chemistry, and mathematics without algebra.

Limited descriptors of surface phenomena—it is hard to think of a more genteelly damning phrase. But the phrase itself is a "limited descriptor," which betrays its own bias.

For humanists, verbalization cannot be so simple a process: language is itself the object of our analysis, the thing itself, and it is the inherent (neither "natural" nor "unnatural") tensions within language, the powerful instabilities of meaning, that make up for many humanistic scholars and writers the core material out of which any interesting theory of "human nature" might derive. A similar fate, incidentally, has befallen the word *literacy*, which—transformed into social-betterment formulas like "cultural literacy" and "moral literacy"— has lost its direct connection with the difficult and dangerous act of reading.

"What shall we call human in humans," asks Lyotard, "the initial misery of their childhood, or their capacity to acquire a 'second' nature which, thanks to language, makes them fit to share in communal life, adult consciousness and reason? That the second depends on and presupposes the first is agreed by everyone. The question is only that of knowing whether this dialectic, whatever name we grace it with, leaves no remainder."[43]

• *Interdisciplinarity*, or the return of human nature

Over the last several years a number of new interdisciplinary fields have grown up, and others previously in existence have expanded and prospered. Areas like the history of science and technology, cognitive science (or, as a version of it is called at Harvard University, Mind, Brain, and Behavior), visual anthropology, and "Law and Psychiatry in Society" are interdisciplinary both in method and in scope, crossing boundaries between and among the humanities, the social sciences, and the sciences. Visual anthropology, to use one example, takes as material for analysis elements like ethnographic film, photography, mass media, and other anthropological "ways of seeing."

Fields like this attract younger scholars in great numbers: majors in these areas are increasing. So many interdisciplinary dissertations are being written—and interdisciplinary courses being taught—that it is sometimes difficult to guess which department is the host of a course in, for example, Fraud and Intellectual Property (History of Science); Eighteenth-Century Ethical Dilemmas (Romance Languages and Literatures); Culture, Politics, and Media (Anthropology); or Literature, Science, and Technology in the Nineteenth Century (English). These are all courses taught at Harvard College today. Fraud, ethics, media, science, and technology: this is a pretty fair glossary of terms for "human nature." And these are just courses randomly picked from one college course catalog, where dozens of other course catalogs might tell the same story.

Of course, by this time "interdisciplinarity" is not news. It has its proponents and its skeptics, and the latter include many people who believe that a professional training, or even a degree, is a necessary passport for anyone seeking to embark upon research in a field. We may note that the absence of such a degree in, say, literature, philosophy, or the history of art has not deterred physicists and biologists from saying wise things about poetry en passant. This lack of equity between the sciences and the humanities—the idea that we can all speak about literature, and that, in fact, a professional discourse about literary studies renders the work in that field arcane and obstructive—is part of the problem about the current custody of "human nature"; for the very existence and prominence of interdisciplinary studies in the narrative fields suggests that an interest in human nature has survived, and returned, in those fields. It has, of course, staged its comeback stealthily, as was necessary, lest it be laughed off the platform. But this is human nature with a difference—human nature approached, as it were, from within and from below, rather than magisterially from above.

Interdisciplinarity, we could say—borrowing one term from E. O. Wilson and another from contemporary political philosophy—is *consilience* without *hegemony*. Or, to speak more plainly, it is mutually respectful collaborative work among the disciplines (largely but not exclusively the discursive and narrative disciplines, the humanities and the less-quantitative branches of science and social science). Interdisciplinarity, in short, is the space, or the mode of collective inquiry, in which questions about "human nature" are *now*, at present, being investigated. And this makes perfect sense. It explains, in part, the dissatisfaction with the boundaries of the present-day disciplines, for breaching boundaries—itself arguably a natural human desire—is not in itself sufficient to explain this explosion of integrated interests. The old-fashioned questions about human nature, about ethics and morality, idealization and expression, humankind reaching close to the angels and the beasts, are accommodated in new places and new guises by interdisciplinary inquiry. Often the impetus moves from the apparently popular to the apparently learned or specialized. Thus, for example, the release of a new film version of *Planet of the Apes* (2001) provoked a discussion of the relationship of humans and chimpanzees, orangutans, gorillas, and bonobos, and led to an interesting exchange of views among animal behaviorists, theoretical biologists, anthropologists, and lawyers on the question of rights for apes.[44]

But the humanities have a single, easy-to-forget point to repeat over and over in these intellectual investigations. Language is not a secondary but a primary constituent of human nature, whatever may turn out to be the case in other spheres. Language is not transparent, though fantasies of its transparency, its merely denotative role, have always attracted and misled some of its users, both writers and readers. Language is not only a window but also a door, a barrier as well as a portal, requiring a handle, some unlocking, and a key.

It is precisely because no one kind of inquiry holds the key to "human nature" that interdisciplinary groupings form and re-form. The humanities sometimes play an ironic role in this by appearing to pose a set of framing illusions that science can demystify. But this is true only from the perspective of the humanities themselves. Scientists often take pleasure in demonstrating that William Shakespeare was right about human nature, even though he had no access to modern scientific information. They are frequently impatient, or uncomprehending, about the work of humanists who question the sources, the sincerity, and the consistency of a "Shakespeare" who is to a certain extent the creation of editors, poets, and critics who lived long after his time. Far from demystifying categories like truth and beauty, scientists often write as if the humanities could still be relied upon to be the quaint but lovable guardians of such notions. In this sense many scientists retain a nineteenth-century notion of the humanities, even as they suggest that humanists cling to a nineteenth-century notion of science.

When a leading scientist like E. O. Wilson could aver some years ago that "[m]odern science is still regarded as a problem-solving activity and a set of technical marvels, the importance of which is to be valuated in an ethos extraneous to science," it is well worth asking him to consider the obverse of this proposition: that modern humanistic study is all too often regarded as a style-enhancing activity and a set of linguistic tricks, the importance of which is to be evaluated in an ethos extraneous to the humanities.

As the popularity of programs in the history of science and technology suggests, science itself has a history, and, in the very nature of such things, it is a history of falsehoods in pursuit of truth. The philosopher Miguel de Unamuno put it clearly when he wrote, "Science is a cemetery of dead ideas, even though life may issue from them," and, "True science teaches, above all, to doubt and to be ignorant."[45] From the Ptolemaic universe (the sun rotates around the earth) to phlogiston (the hypothetical substance supposed to be the "matter of fire," whose existence was affirmed through much of the eighteenth century, only to be rejected and abandoned by 1800) science has proceeded by hypothesis, by theory, and by inspired accident and guess. The "beautiful theories" of the past have become either facts or follies. Will today's answers be any more ahistorical, transcendent, and permanent than all those that have gone before?

It is striking that the term "science wars" has been coined to describe the efforts on the part of some nonscience scholars to understand how scientists construct their notions of truth. The term itself has been highly contestatory, producing heated exchanges and a good deal of willful misunderstanding on all sides. What I have been describing here might perhaps have been called "humanities wars," save for the fact that the humanities are regarded not as specialized knowledge or even as a research field, but rather as the ground of our common knowledge and common inheritance, accessible to scientists, social scientists, and humanists alike. Instead of "humanities wars," then, we have the far more aversive "culture wars," as if the progress of scholarship in the humanities was itself a "war" against, as well as for custody of, certain cultural values and touchstones that are thought to be enshrined in literature and art. I share with Ian Hacking a dislike of the facile use of "war" to describe these intellectual debates. As he says, terms like "culture wars," "science wars," and "Freud wars" suggest gladiatorial contests, in which the plea-sure—and the "war" terminology—belongs to "the bemused spectators."[46] But somewhat obscured by the inflammatory rhetoric, fanned by the flames of cul-tural journalists, is a fundamental dissymmetry in the way "scientific knowl-edge" and "humanistic knowledge" are weighed, valued, and assessed.

Is it really necessary to ban all scientific experimentation in order to pre-serve human nature as a constant and unchanging essence? Francis Fukuyama's concern that contemporary biotechnology will "alter human nature and thereby move us into a 'posthuman' stage of history," with "possibly malign consequences for liberal democracy and the nature of politics,"[47] is one that has in fact been contemplated, sans alarm, by many thoughtful scholars in various branches of the humanities, where "posthuman" is not a scare word but an interesting field for philosophical, ethical, and aesthetic speculation. Perhaps we need the humanities more than ever precisely because it is so obvi-ous that scientific progress cannot be stopped. Here is where humanists can do themselves, and the world, a favor by stressing the ways in which all knowl-edge is an aspect of rhetoric as well as an aspect of logic. Increasingly, scientists speak in metaphors and in linguistic coinages in order to explain their work. *Relativity*; *quark*; *revolution*; *game theory*; *prisoner's dilemma*: these appropria-tions of language, analogy, and neologism enrich understanding by becoming figural, by pointing out that the reality of the world itself is a voiced reality, a reality of figure. Humanists might reasonably point out the rhetorical and "poetic" nature of these terms, the impossibility of science without image and figure. But at the same time these humanists also might return the serve, and the favor, by laying claim once again to the most underrated and overliteral-ized of these figures: the metaphor of human nature.

So, to restate the question with which we have been wrestling: Why is it that today's scientists write about human nature, while today's humanists do not? My answer, at least in part, is that humanists *do* write about this question, constantly, but that neither they nor many of their readers—not to mention their critics—have been willing to acknowledge that that is what they are doing. Somewhere along the way, the concept of human nature became both stale and saccharine: a set of bromides or truisms, often inflected with religion, and frequently invoked as a "so there" pseudo-explanation ("it's just human nature . . . ") rather than explored as a conundrum or a puzzlement.

I am eager, here—or, to be franker about it, I am anxious—not to be heard as deploring the present moment in humanistic writing and research, and harking back, wistfully, to a time when men were men, women were women, and humanists cared about human nature. My point is really close to the opposite of this nostalgic, and retrogressive, thought: what I have been contending is that today's humanists are asking "human nature" questions all the time, when they talk about psychic violence, or material culture, or epistemic breaks, or the history of the book, or the counterintuitive. Many of the theoretical explorations and innovations of the last fifty years of humanistic scholarship have been aimed at demystifying a unitary and positivistic sense of "human nature." But to aim to demystify something is tacitly to acknowledge its mystified status, and not only for others; also for oneself. Avoiding the topic of "human nature" is a mistake, one that has political as well as intellectual ramifications—a mistake based on underestimating what and how we read and write today. "Human nature," as a term and as a field of inquiry, need not be solely the concern of social conservatives or of scientists, however well-meaning and however well-placed. In debunking all the illusions fostered under this ubiquitous term, contemporary humanistic scholars have sometimes failed to see in what ways we are working within it.

When I suggest that to discard a big and baggy idea like human nature is a political mistake, what I mean is that it has given aid and comfort to unthinking critics of the humanities. If we are willing to reflect seriously and critically, we will readily be able to demonstrate that fields like cultural anthropology, structural linguistics, women's studies, cybertheory, and posthumanism are indeed addressing the Big Questions: the Who Am I questions, the What Am I Doing Here questions, the What Lies in the Future questions that all attach themselves to the heritage of "human nature." These questions have never been more pressing—nor more "human"—than they are today. And you can quote me on that.

Acknowledgments

Many friends and colleagues have contributed generously of their time and thought in helping me to work through the essays in this volume. My thanks and gratitude to Mary Halpenny-Killip, the Administrator of the Humanities Center in the Faculty of Arts and Sciences at Harvard University, to Mary-Clarie Barton of the Hoorn-Ashby Gallery in Nantucket and New York, to Janet Rickus, and to Bill Germano. I want especially to thank two people who have been most instrumental in helping me to assemble, frame, and present these pieces in their present form: Marcie Bianco, whose assistance, acuity, indefatigable energy, and perceptiveness have been invaluable; and—as always—Barbara Johnson, who read many drafts, offered much wisdom, and forgave many preoccupations, along the way.

Permissions

"Quotation Marks" was originally published in *Critical Inquiry* 25 (Summer 1999) by the University of Chicago Press. "Sequels" first appeared in the *London Review of Books* 21, 16 (August 19, 1999). "Moniker" first appeared in *Our Monica, Ourselves*, edited by Lauren Berlant and Lisa Duggan, published by New York University Press, 2001. "Historical Correctness" was delivered by Marjorie Garber as the Hilda Hulme Memorial Lecture on May 11, 2000 and published by Institute of English Studies, University of London, 2002. The essays appear here in slightly revised form.

Sommer, by Giuseppe Arcimboldo, 1563, courtesy of Kunsthistorisches Museum, Vienna; *Vertumnus*, by Giuseppe Arcimboldo, 1590–1591, permission by Skoklosters Slott Hallwyl Museet, Stockholm, Sweden; *Les Amants*, by René Magritte, 1928, the fractional and promised gift of Richard S. Zeisler to the Museum of Modern Art, New York; *A Pair of Shoes*, by Vincent van Gogh, 1886, permission by Amsterdam, Van Gogh Museum (Vincent van Gogh Foundation); *Achetez des Bananes*, photograph by Linda Nochlin, permission by Linda Nochlin; "Figures, 1987," by Thomas Carabasi, permission by Thomas Carabasi; Cover, *Genre*, October/November 1992, courtesy of Genre Publishing; "Three Women in Italy," by Lucien Clergue © 1993; Cover, *Vice Versa*, Touchstone/Simon and Schuster, 1995, design by Michael Ian Kay; *Hermaphroditenhemd*, by Paul Wunderlich, 1979, courtesy of Paul Wunderlich; Three-Pronged Plug from cover of *Bisexuality & the Eroticism of Everyday Life*, Routledge, 2000, design by Jonathan Herder; Plug Multiplier from back cover of *Bisexuality & the Eroticism of Everyday Life*, Routledge, 2000, design by Jonathan Herder.

The author is especially grateful to Janet Rickus for permission to reproduce her work.

::::::::
: Notes
::::::::

Preface

1. Walter Benjamin, *Schriften* 1: 571; in Walter Benjamin, *Illuminations*, ed. Hannah Arendt, trans. Harry Zohn (New York: Schocken Books, 1968), 38.
2. August Wilhelm Schlegel, "The Art of Shakespeare's Romantic Drama," from *Lectures on Dramatic Art and Literature* (1808), trans. John Black (London: George Bell and Sons, 1909), 356.
3. Howard Eiland and Kevin McLaughlin, "Translators' Foreword" to Walter Benjamin, *The Arcades Project* (Cambridge, Mass.: Harvard University Press, 1999), ix.
4. Benjamin, *The Arcades Project*, 458.

Chapter 1

1. "Front and Center, Five Accusers," *Boston Globe*, January 15, 1999, A26. Robert Bolt, *A Man for All Seasons* (New York: Random House, 1962), 140. Here is how the event was recorded by More's son-in-law and biographer, William Roper:

    [W]hereas the oath confirming the Supremacy and matrimony was by the first statute in few words comprised, the Lord Chancellor and Master Secretary did of their own heads add more words to it, to make it appear unto the King's ears more pleasant and plausible. And that oath, so amplified, caused they to be ministered to Sir Thomas More and to all other throughout the realm. Which Sir Thomas More perceiving, said unto my wife: "I may tell thee, Meg, they that have committed me hither for refusing of this oath not agreeable with the stature, are not by their own law able to justify my imprisonment. And surely, daughter, it is great pity that any Christian prince shold by a flexible council ready to follow his affections, and by a weak clergy lacking grace constantly to stand to their learning, with flattery be so shamefully abused."

    (William Roper, *The Life of Sir Thomas More*, in *Two Early Tudor Lives*, ed. Richard S. Sylvester and Davis P. Harding [New Haven, Conn.: Yale University Press, 1962], 240.)
2. Bolt, *A Man for All Seasons*, xiii–xiv.
3. Didacus Stell, quoting Robert Burton, "Democritus to the Reader," *The Anatomy of Melancholy* (1621; reprint, New York, 1862), 39.
4. "Front and Center, Five Accusers: The Excerpts; Henry J. Hyde," *Boston Globe*, January 25, 1999, A26.
5. Malcolm Evans, *Signifying Nothing* (Athens: University of Georgia Press, 1986).

6. Thomas M. DeFrank, with Richard Sisk, Kenneth R. Bazinet, and Timothy J. Burger, "A Legacy from Era of Nixon," *New York Daily News*, January 15, 1999, 38.

7. Jonathan Kirsch, "Droning Does Not a Good Case Make," *Newsday* (Long Island, N.Y.), January 18, 1999, A31.

8. Esther Cloudman Dunn, *Shakespeare in America* (New York: Macmillan, 1939), 250.

9. T. S. Eliot, "The Love Song of J. Alfred Prufrock," in *Complete Poems and Plays 1909–1950* (New York: Harcourt, Brace and World, 1952), 7.

10. Francis X. Clines, "Slouching toward Deliverance," *New York Times*, February 9, 1999, A16.

11. Richard Roeper, "In Senate, We Haven't Witnessed Nothing Yet," *Chicago Sun-Times*, January 20, 1999, 11l.

12. Edward Said, *Beginnings: Intention and Method* (New York: Columbia University Press, 1985), 22.

13. Rep. Ed Bryant, Tennessee, in "Front and Center...," *Boston Globe*, January 25, 1999, A26.

14. Bruce Hamilton, *Too Much of Water* (1958; reprint, New York: Garland, 1983), 245.

15. Peter Ustinov, *Loser* (London: Michael O'Mara, 1989), 140.

16. Monica S. Lewinsky, excerpts from her deposition in the impeachment trial of President Clinton, in "From Monica Lewinsky: 'I Feel Very Uncomfortable Making Judgments'," *New York Times*, February 6, 1999, A11.

17. Example given by the *American Heritage Dictionary* (Boston: Houghton Mifflin, 1973), 1073, "quotation mark."

18. *Oxford English Dictionary*, 2d ed., s.v. "quotation."

19. R. B. McKerrow, *An Introduction to Bibliography for Literary Students* (Oxford: Clarendon Press, and London: Oxford University Press, 1927), 316.

20. George Puttenham, *The Arte of English Poesie* (1589), ed. Edward Arber (London: A. Constable, 1906; reprint, Kent, Ohio: Kent State University Press, 1970), 3:29, 222. Ben Jonson, English Grammar (n.p., 1637).

21. Puttenham, *Arte of English Poesie*, 3:18, 199.

22. Watt, *Philosophical Transactions of the Royal Society* (1784), 74:330, note.

23. Henry Hallam, *Introduction to the Literature of the Fifteenth, Sixteenth, and Seventeeth Centuries* (London: J. Murray, 1837), 3:3, 99.

24. Andrew Ure, *Dictionary of Arts, Manufactures, and Mines* (New York: Appleton, 1858), 3:647.

25. Henry Breen, *Modern English Literature: Its Blemishes and Defects* (London: Longman, Brown, Green and Longmans, 1857), 272.

26. *La Grande Encylopédie* (Paris, 1885–1903), cited in Douglas C. McMurtrie, *Typographical Style Governing the Use of the Guillemet—The French Mark of Quotation.* (Greenwich, Conn.: Condé Nast Press, 1922), 3.

27. James Boswell, *Life of Johnson* (London: Oxford University Press, 1965), 1143.

28. Justin Kaplan, preface to the 16th edition of *Bartlett's Familiar Quotations* (Boston: Little, Brown, 1992), ix.

29. Henry James, *The Bostonians* (1886; reprint, London: Penguin Books, 1986), 78, 84.

30. Rudyard Kipling, "'The Finest Story in the World,'" in *Many Inventions* (New York: D. Appleton, 1899), 114.

31. Matthew Prior, *Paulo Purganti and His Wife*, n.p., 1708.

32. Winston Churchill, *A Roving Commission: My Early Life* (1930).

33. Henry Watson Fowler and Francis George Fowler, *A Dictionary of Modern English Usage* (Oxford: Clarendon Press, 1926), s.v. "quotation."

34. *Courses of Instruction, Harvard University, 1958–59*, 162.

35. John Locke, *An Essay Concerning Human Understanding*, collated and annotated by Alexander Campbell Fraser (New York: Dover, 1959), 2:379.

36. Ralph Waldo Emerson, "Quotation and Originality," in *The Portable Emerson*, ed. Mark Van Doren (New York: Viking Press, 1946), 296.
37. Debra Fried, "Valves of Attention: Quotation and Context in the Age of Emerson" (Ph.D. diss., Yale University, 1983; Ann Arbor, Mich.: University Microfilms International, 1990), 5.
38. Ibid.
39. Another scholar claims that a closer source—still far from the famous quote—is a letter Voltaire wrote to M. le Riche, February 6, 1770. See Norman Guterman, *A Book of French Quotations* (New York: Doubleday, 1963). ("Monsieur l'abbé, I detest what you write, but I would give my life to make it possible for you to continue to write.")
40. Quoted in Paul F. Boller, Jr., *Quotesmanship: The Use and Abuse of Quotations for Polemical and Other Purposes* (Dallas, 1967), 325.
41. Jacques Derrida, "Signature Event Context," trans. Samuel Weber and Jeffrey Mehlman in *Limited Inc* (Evanston, Ill.: Northwestern University Press, 1988), 12.
42. Jacques Derrida, "Force of Law: The Mystical Foundation of Authority," in *Deconstruction and the Possibility of Justice*, ed. Drucilla Cornell, Michael Rosenfeld, and David Gray Carlson (New York: Routledge, 1992), 15–16.
43. Ralph Waldo Emerson, journal entry for May 1849. In *Emerson in His Journals* ed. Joel Porte (Cambridge, Mass: Harvard University Press, 1982), 401.
44. Robert Burton, "Democritus to the Reader," 38.
45. Ralph Waldo Emerson, "Quotation and Originality," in *Letters and Social Aims* (Boston and New York: Houghton Mifflin, 1875), 194.
46. Ibid., 196.
47. Kaplan, preface to *Bartlett's Familiar Quotations*, ix.
48. J. L. Austin, *How to Do Things with Words* (1962; reprint Cambridge, Mass.: Harvard University Press, 1975), 60–61.
49. Ibid., 61, 81.
50. Ibid., 161.
51. Ibid., 22.
52. Leonard Diepeveen, *Changing Voices: The Modern Quoting Poem* (Ann Arbor: University of Michigan Press, 1993), 4, 7.
53. Derrida, "Signature Event Context," 18.
54. Helen Vendler, *The Odes of John Keats* (Cambridge, Mass.: Harvard University Press, 1983), 134.
55. Ibid., 312.
56. Earl Wasserman, "The *Ode on a Grecian Urn*," in *Keats: A Collection of Critical Essays*, ed. Walter Jackson Bate (Englewood Cliffs, N.J.: Prentice-Hall, 1964), 138–39. Reprinted from Wasserman, *The Finer Tone: Keats' Major Poems* (Baltimore: Johns Hopkins University Press, 1953).
57. Walter Jackson Bate, *John Keats* (Cambridge, Mass.: Harvard University Press, 1964), 516.
58. Ibid., 517.
59. Ibid., 516.
60. T. S. Eliot, "Dante," in *Selected Essays* 1952; cited in Bate, *John Keats*, 517.
61. W. H. Auden, cited in Kaplan, ed., *Bartlett's Familiar Quotations*, 416.
62. Steve Connor, "Science: The Truth about . . . Beauty," *Independent* (London) November 27, 1998, 9.
63. Ralph Jimenez, "Variety Is as Important as Color to Make Landscape Intriguing," *Boston Globe*, October 4, 1998, 10.
64. Hans Fantel, "Is Truth Also Beauty?" *New York Times*, November 26, 1989, sec. 2, 8.
65. Joel Greenberg, "The Secular Jews: Beauty is Truth: That Is All the Stylish Need to Know," *New York Times* April 6, 1998, A12.

66. "Beauty Is Truth: Government Has a Role in Nurturing the Arts," *Houston Chronicle*, July 5, 1997, 34.

67. Jack Smith, "If Beauty Is Truth, Truth Beauty," *Los Angeles Times*, May 18, 1987, 5.

68. "Larger Triumph, Larger Loss: American Beauty," *New York Times*, September 20, 1983, A28.

69. Edgar Allan Poe, "The Raven," *Great Short Works of Edgar Allan Poe*, ed. G. R. Thompson, (New York: Harper and Row, 1970), 75.

70. Edgar Allan Poe, "The Murder in the Rue Morgue," in Thompson, ed. *Great Short Works of Edgar Allan Poe*, 276.

71. Edgar Allan Poe, "Philosophy of Composition," in Thompson, ed., *Great Short Works of Edgar Allan Poe*, 534.

72. Shakespeare, *Macbeth*, 1. 5. 38–40, 1316.

73. Michael Dresser, "Tintinnabulation," *Baltimore Sun*, March 29, 1996, 19A.

74. Gwinn Owens, "Why a Raven?" *Baltimore Sun*, May 1, 1996, 13A.

75. *Houston Chronicle*, January 11, 1998, sec. 2, 21; *San Diego Union-Tribune*, November 18, 1997, D2; *Los Angeles Times*, July 5, 1997, 2; St. *Louis Post-Dispatch* September 17, 1997, 25.

76. "Ravens Aim for Mitchell or Johnson," *Baltimore Sun*, February 5, 1999, 1D.

Chapter 2

1. The passage continues:

> O let not virtue seek
> Remuneration for the thing it was,
> For beauty wit,
> High birth, vigour of bone, desert in service,
> Love, friendship, charity, are subjects all
> To envious and calumniating time.
> One touch of nature makes the whole world kin—
> That all with one consent praise new-born gauds
> Though they are made and moulded of things past,
> And give to the dust that is a little gilt
> More laud than gilt o'erdusted.
> The present eye praises the present object.

2. Louis Vuitton ad, *New York Times*, November 16, 2000, C29.

3. Alan Sokal and Jean Bricmont, *Fashionable Nonsense: Postmodern Intellectuals' Abuse of Science* (New York: Picador, 1998), 1.

4. Paul de Man, introduction to Hans Robert Jauss, *Toward an Aesthetic of Reception*, trans. Timothy Bahti (Minneapolis: University of Minnesota Press, 1982), xx. In context, de Man is explaining the resistance, on the part of Jauss, to the "play" of the signifier, which he describes, with unerring clarity, as "semantic effects produced on the level of the letter rather than of the word or the sentence, and which therefore escape from the network of hermeneutic questions and answers," (xix).

5. Edward A. Freeman, *The History of the Norman Conquest of England* (Oxford: Clarendon Press, 1886), 5: 545.

6. *OED*, style (2b). (Oxford: Clarendon Press, 1989), 1008.

7. Georges Louis Leclerc de Buffon, *Discours Sur Le Style*. Prononce A L'Academie Francaise Par M. Buffon. Le jour de sa reception le 25 Aout 1753.

8. *The Princeton Encyclopedia of Poetry and Poetics* observes, "The traditional view of style as "l'homme même" was a moral view (as in Longinus and Cicero); the modern version, if not actually psychoanalytic, will certainly emphasize the individual creative act."

Princeton Encyclopedia of Poetry and Poetics, ed. Alex Preminger (Princeton, N. J.: Princeton University Press, 1974), 815.

9. Jacques Lacan, *Écrits* (Paris: Éditions du Seuil, 1966), 9. Translation by Barbara Johnson.

10. John Bayley, "Books: The Style Is the Man" *Times* (London), November 8, 1987, n.p.

11. Al Neuharth, ""Bill's Buscapade." *USA Today*, January 15, 1993, 13 A.

12. *OED*, style (24b), 2d ed. (Oxford: Clarendon Press, 1989), 1010.

13. John Ward, *A System of Oratory* (London, 1759) 1:309–10. Delivered in a course of lectures publicly read at Gresham College, London. Printed for John Ward, in Cornhill opposite to the Royal Exchange, 1759.

14. George Puttenham, *The Arte of English Poesie* (1589), ed. Edward Arber (London: A. Constable, 1906; reprint, Kent, Ohio: Kent State University Press, 1970), 160–161.

15. Ben Jonson, *Timber, or Discoveries*, ed. Ralph S. Walker (Syracuse, N.Y.: Syracuse University Press, 1953), 45.

16. Ibid., 46.

17. John Middleton Murry, *The Problem of Style* (1922; reprint, London: Oxford University Press, 1967), 122.

18. Ludwig Wittgenstein, *Tractatus Logico-Philosophicus*, trans. D. F. Pears and B. F. McGuinness (London: Routledge, 1974), 4:002 (19).

19. Oscar Wilde, "A Few Maxims for the Instruction of the Over-Educated," and "Phrases and Philosophies for the Use of the Young," in *The Complete Works of Oscar Wilde* (New York: Harper and Row, 1989), 1203–6. Could it be for this buttonhole that Lacan's evocation of "upholsterers' buttons" (*points de capiton*) or "button, button, who's got the button" (*le jeu du furet*) are designed? None of them are really, of course, buttons, except in language.

20. Charles Baudelaire, "The Painter of Modern Life," in *The Painter of Modern Life and Other Essays*, trans. Jonathan Mayne (London: Phaidon, 1995), 32, 33.

21. Roland Barthes, *The Fashion System*, trans. Matthew Ward and Richard Howard (New York: Hill and Wang, 1983), x.

22. Ibid., 300.

23. Valerie Steele, "Letter from the Editor," *Fashion Theory* 1, no. (1997): 245.

24. Alex Kuczynski, "Media: Fashion Site Finds Gossip Is a Big Draw," *New York Times*, September 25, 2000, C1.

25. Joseph Addison, March 11–12, 1711, *The Spectator*, Vol. I. (Philadelphia: J. J. Woodward, 1829), 14.

26. Blaise Pascal, *Pensèes*, trans by A. J. Krailsheimer. (Baltimore: Penguin Books, 1966; reprint, 1968), 212.

27. The phrase is that of R. J. Hollingdale, quoted by Peter Hutchinson in his edition of Goethe's *Maxims and Reflections* (London: Penguin, 1998), xiv.

28. John Gross, *The Oxford Book of Aphorisms* (Oxford: Oxford University Press, 1987), vii–viii.

29. Rosalie L. Colie, *The Resources of Kind: Genre-Theory in the Renaissance* (Berkeley and Los Angeles: University of California Press, 1973), 32–33.

30. La Rochfoucauld, *Maxims*, ed. and trans. Leonard Tancock (London: Penguin, 1959), 14, 49, 89, 294, 304, 377, 431, 583, 625.

31. Oscar Wilde, In *Oscar Wilde*, ed. Isobel Murray. (New York: Oxford University Press, 1989), 570–573.

32. Stephen Holden, "Victor Borge, 91, Comic Piano Virtuoso, Dies," *New York Times*, December 24, 2000, 26.

33. Henry Hawley, chief curator of late Western art at the Cleveland Museum of Art. Quoted in Gordon Smith, "Fabulous Fabergé," *San Diego Union-Tribune*, September 5, 1989, C1.

Chapter 3

1. Ellen Rooney, "Discipline and Vanish: Feminism, the Resistance to Theory, and the Politics of Cultural Studies," *differences* 2, no. 5 (1990): 24.

2. John Brenkman, "Extreme Criticism," *Critical Inquiry* 26, no. 1 (1999), 110.

3. Georg Lukacs. "On the Nature and Form of the Essay," in *Soul and Form*, trans. Anna Bostock (Cambridge: MIT Press, 1974), 13.

4. Herman Melville, *Moby-Dick* (New York: W. W. Norton, 1967), 353.

5. William V. Spanos, *The Errant Art of* Moby-Dick (Durham, N.C.: Duke University Press, 1995), 218. Thus, for example, R. W. B. Lewis reads its last three paragraphs as a poem, "three stanzas" that accomplish the "transfiguration of figures" in describing the "moral illumination" of the perceiver. R. W. B. Lewis, *The American Adam* (Chicago: University of Chicago Press, 1955), 132–34. Contesting this "Adamic" reading, Spanos draws attention to the technical description of the "final phase of the mass production process" as a critique, seeing Ishmael as a Gramscian figure, an engaged intellectual who perceives the complicity between truth and power. "If . . . we attend to the fact that 'The Try-Works' begins, like so many other chapters devoted to the whaling industry, with a technical description of its composition and function in the mass production process that gradually modulates into a terrific language of hallucination that estranges the sedimented original terms of rational efficiency, everything that follows, including the final passage that Lewis invokes, comes to be understood as a powerful critical/genealogical commentary on this culminating phase of the productive process aboard the *Pequod*." Spanos, *The Errant Art of* Moby-Dick, 219. Jonathan Arac, noting that "Ishmael is repeatedly healed or purged" throughout the novel, suggests that "the 'Try-Works' teaches him the danger of gloomy obsession." Jonathan Arac, "Narrative Forms," in Sacvan Bercovitch, gen. ed. *The Cambridge History of American Literature* Vol. 2: *Prose Writings 1820–1865* (Cambridge: Cambridge University Press, 1995), 728.

6. "Essay," *Oxford English Dictionary*, definition 8.

7. Susan Sontag, quoted in Judy Stoffman, "Sontag About to Hit her Stride as a Fiction Writer," *Toronto Star*, October 12, 1992, C14.

8. "The classification of the constituents of a chaos, nothing less is here essayed." Melville, Moby-Dick, p. 89. Bryan Wolf, "When is a Painting Most Like a Whale? Ishmael, *Moby Dick*, and the Sublime," in *Herman Melville: A Collection of Critical Essays*, ed. Myra Jehlen (Englewood Cliffs, N. J.: Prentice Hall, 1994), 89.

9. Barbara Johnson, "Melville's Fist: The Execution of *Billy Budd*," in *The Critical Difference* (Baltimore: Johns Hopkins University Press, 1980), 92.

10. Sir Francis Bacon, *The Essayes or Counsels, Civill and Morall*, ed. Michael Kiernan (Cambridge, Mass.: Harvard University Press, 1985), 327.

11. Gayatri Chakravorty Spivak, "Translator's Preface" to Jacques Derrida, *Of Grammatology* (Baltimore: Johns Hopkins University Press, 1976), lxxxvi.

12. Theodor W. Adorno, "The Essay as Form," in *Notes to Literature*, vol. 1, trans. Shierry Weber Nicholsen (New York: Columbia University Press, 1991), 3–23.

13. Ibid., 13.

14. Walter Benjamin, *Selected Writings*, vol. 2 (1927–1934), trans. Rodney Livingstone and others; ed. Michael W. Jennings, Howard Eiland, and Gary Smith (Cambridge, Mass.: Harvard University Press, 290, 292.

15. Adorno, "The Essay as Form," 20.

16. Georg Lukács, "On the Nature and Form of the Essay" (1910) in *Soul and Form*, trans. Anna Bostock (Cambridge, Mass.: MIT Press, 1974), 2.

17. Ibid., 15.

18. Susan Sontag, introduction to *A Barthes Reader* (New York: Hill and Wang, 1982), ix.

19. Ibid.
20. Brenkman, "Extreme Criticism," 114–15.
21. Walter Benjamin, "Literary History and the Study of Literature," in *Selected Writings*, vol. 2 (1927–1934) (Cambridge, Mass.: Harvard University Press, 1999), 464.
22. Melville, *Moby-Dick*, 352.
23. Ibid., 352–53.

Chapter 4

1. Thorstein Veblen, *The Theory of the Leisure Class* (1899; reprint, New York: Modern Library, 1934). John Maynard Keynes, "Economic Possibilities for Our Grandchilden" (1930), in *The Collected Writings of John Maynard Keynes*, vol. 9 (New York: Macmillan, 1972); quoted in Keith Thomas, ed., *The Oxford Book of Work* (Oxford: Oxford University Press, 1999), 583: "To those who sweat for their daily bread leisure is a longed-for sweet—until they get it.... [T]here is no country and no people, I think, who can look forward to the age of leisure and abundance without a dread. For we have been trained too long to strive and not to enjoy."
2. Gina Kolata, "A Question of Beauty: Is It Good for You?" *New York Times*, June 13, 1999, section 15, 1.
3. Veblen, *The Theory of the Leisure Class*, 258–59.
4. Ibid., 397.
5. Merry E. Wiesner, "Spinsters and Seamstresses: Women in Cloth and Clothing Production," In *Rewriting the Renaissance: The Discourses of Sexual Difference in Early Modern Europe*, ed. Margaret W. Ferguson, Maureen Quilligan, and Nancy J. Vickers (Chicago: University of Chicago Press, 1986), 191, 204–5.
6. Marjorie Garber, "Roman Numerals." In *Symptoms of Culture* (New York: Routledge, 1998).
7. Roland Barthes "From Work to Text" *Image-Music-Text*, trans. Stephen Heath. (New York: Hill and Wang, 1977). 155–164.
8. See *Oxford English Dictionary*, citations under "masterpiece," 1.a.
9. In a way the source text here is the Book of Genesis, where the doubled sense of work as achievement or art and as labor is concisely framed: "And on the seventh day God ended his work which he hath made; and he rested on the seventh day from all his work which he had made" (Genesis 2:2). With the expulsion of Adam and Eve from the garden, we might say, the two senses of work split apart from one another: the word itself became "fallen." (This is one reason it is fascinating to find Karl Marx, in his *Theory of Surplus Value*, writing, "Milton produced *Paradise Lost* for the same reason that a silk worm produces silk. It was an activity of his nature." Karl Marx, *Theories of Surplus Value* (1905--10), trans. G. A. Bonner and Emile Burns (New York: International Publishers, 1951), 186.
10. C. Northcote Parkinson, *Parkinson's Law, or the Pursuit of Progress* (1958); quoted in Thomas, ed., *The Oxford Book of Work*, 67–69.
11. Thomas Alva Edison, quoted in Paul Israel, *Edison: A Life of Invention* (New York: John Wiley and Sons, 1998), 75.
12. George Parsons Lathrop, "Talks with Edison," *Harper's* 80 (February 1890), 435; quoted in Israel, *Edison*, 366.
13. Israel, *Edison*, 167.
14. Waldemar Kaempffert, "Titan of the Heroic Age of Invention," *New York Times Magazine*, October 25, 1931, 22; quoted in Israel, *Edison*, 463.
15. John Dryden, letter to Sir Robert Howard, in *Annus Mirabilis*, 1667 (rpt. Oxford University Press, 1927), n.p.

16. Waldo P. Warren, "Edison on Invention and Inventors," *Century* 82 (1911), 418; quoted in Israel, Edison, 29.
17. Benjamin, Jowett. *Dialogues of Plato*, trans. B. Jowett. 2d ed., vol. 1 (Oxford: Clarendon Press, 1875), xviii.
18. Wyn Wachhorst. *Thomas Alva Edision, an American Myth*. (Cambridge, Mass.: MIT Press, 1981), 151.
19. Agatha Christie, *An Autobiography*. Part 3, "Growing Up." (London: Collins, 1977), 131.

Chapter 5

1. E. Austen-Leigh, *Memior of Jane Austin* (Oxford: Clarendon Press, 1926, reprint 1967), 157–58.
2. Nahum Tate, *The History of King Lear,* ed. James Black (Lincoln: University of Nebraska Press, 1975).
3. Gerard Genette. *Palimpsests.* trans. Channa Newman and Claude Doubinsky. (Lincoln: University of Nebraska Press, 1982; trans. 1997), 207.
4. Merle Jacob, *To Be Continued: An Annotated Guide to Sequels* (Phoenix: Oryx Press, 1995).
5. *The Whole Story: 3000 Years of Sequels and Sequences*, ed. John Simkin, 2d ed. (New York: Bowker, 1998).
6. Sigmund Freud. "Interpretation of Dreams," In *The Standard Edition of the Complete Psychological Works of Sigmund Freud.* trans. James Strachey (London: Hogarth Press, 1953), 501.
7. Ibid., 499.
8. Alexandra Ripley, *Scarlett: The Sequel to Margaret Michell's Gone With the Wind:* (New York: Warner Books, 1991).
9. "Best Seller" July 18, 1999 *New York Times* 26.
10. Gérard Genette suggested the term *paratext* for the class of items that includes "a title, a subtitle, intertitles; prefaces, postfaces, notices, forewords, etc.; marginal, infrapaginal, terminal notes; epigraphs; illustrations; blurbs, book covers, dust jackets, and many other kinds of secondary signals." Genette, *Palimpsests* (1982), trans. Channa Newman and Claude Doubinsky (Lincoln: University of Nebraska Press, 1997), 3.
11. See, for example, Jacques Derrida, *Margins of Philosophy,* trans. Alan Bass (Chicago: University of Chicago Press, 1982); Anthony Grafton, *The Footnote* (Cambridge, Mass.: Harvard University Press, 1997); Leah S. Marcus, *Unediting the Renaissance* (New York: Routledge, 1996).
12. Harold Bloom, *The Anxiety of Influence* (New York: Oxford University Press, 1973), 7, 12, 14.
13. Judith Butler, *Gender Trouble* (New York: Routledge, 1990; reprint 1999), 31.
14. Michael Zeitlin, "Postmodern Sequel." In *Part Two: Reflections on the Sequel*, ed. Paul Budra and Betty A. Schellenberg. (Toronto: University of Toronto Press, 1998), 162.
15. Terry Castle, *The Carnivalesque in Eighteenth-Century English Culture and Fiction*, (Stanford, Calif.: Stanford University Press), 1986, 133–34.
16. Michael R. Beschloss, Georgette Mosbacher, quoted in Richard L. Berke, "Two-Way Presidential Coattails," *New York Times* July 25, 1999 13.

Chapter 6

1. Andrew Marvell, "To His Coy Mistress," in *Complete Poetry*. ed. George DeF. Lord (New York: Random House, 1968), 23.

2. See Richard Terdiman, *Discourse/Counter-Discourse* (Ithaca, N.Y.: Cornell University Press, 1985), 152–59; 188–89.
3. David and Mary Verzi, "Still-Life Artist Is Choosy about Models," *Berkshire Eagle*, July 16, 1995, E1, E11.
4. Hélène Cixous, "Castration or Decapitation?" in *Authorship: From Plato to the Postmodern*, ed. Sean Burke (Edinburgh: Edinburgh University Press, 1995), 165–66.
5. "A linguistic system is a series of differences of sound combined with a series of differences of ideas; but the pairing of a certain number of acoustical signs with as many cuts made from the mass of thought engenders a system of values." Ferdinand de Saussure, *Course in General Linguistics*, trans. Wade Baskin (New York: McGraw-Hill, 1966), 120.
6. Ibid., 163
7. Jacques Derrida, *The Truth in Painting*, trans. Geoff Bennington and Ian MacLeod (Chicago: University of Chicago Press, 1987).
8. Ibid., 278–79.
9. Ibid., 334.
10. Ibid., 282.
11. Ibid., 333.
12. Ibid., 265, 259, 261.
13. Gilles Deleuze and Félix Guattari, *Anti-Oedipus: Capitalism and Schizophrenia* (Minneapolis: University of Minnesota Press, 1983), 4, 5, 6, 7. See *Oxford English Dictionary*, "coupling," 6f.

Chapter 7

1. Religion News Service, "Most View God As 'Father,' Poll Finds," *Los Angeles Times*, August 21, 1999, B3.
2. Andreas Kostenberger, a professor at Southeastern Baptist Theological Seminary in Wake Forest, N.C., quoted in Bill Tammeus, "Stopping a Bible Translation," *Kansas City Star*, May 30, 1997, C8.
3. Rt. Rev. John Taylor, Bishop of St. Albans, quoted in Victoria Coombe, "Money-Back Offer for Readers Who Dislike New Bible," *Daily Telegraph* (London), November 22, 1996, 11.
4. Victoria Coombe, "Money-Back Offer," 11.
5. Rev. Dennis W. Mende quoted in Dave Condren, "Guidelines on Inclusive Language Irk Some Catholics," *Buffalo News*, January 10, 1993, 1.
6. Edward Carpenter, "Defence of Criminals," in *Civilisation: Its Cause and Cure* (New York: Charles Scribner's Sons, 1921), 131.
7. "A Day to Savor" (editorial), *Boston Globe*, September 4, 1999, A14.
8. John Locke, *An Essay Concerning Human Understanding*, vol. 2 (New York: Dover, 1959), 2:17–18.
9. *Oxford English Dictionary*, "mistress," 14b: 1818 Todd, s.v., *Miss*, "*Mistress* was then the style of grown up unmarried ladies, though the mother was living; and for a considerable part of the [eighteenth] century, maintained its ground against the infantine term of *miss*."
10. In seventeenth-, eighteenth-, and nineteenth-century use—as, for example, in the novels of Jane Austen—the eldest unmarried daughter would be addressed as Miss plus the surname ("Miss Steele"); other daughters would be called by their first as well as second names ("Miss Lucy Steele"). But in dialect use, and especially, we are told, in the United States, *Miss* has also been used as the equivalent of *Mrs.*—as it has, conventionally, in public life (a newspaper will refer, for example, to Miss Kidman rather than to Mrs. Cruise). Noah Webster complained way back in 1790 that "The use of Miss for

Mistress in this country is a great impropriety," and H. L. Mencken noted a century and a half later that "it survives unscathed in the speech of the common people." Interestingly, as Mencken made clear, this was a pronunciation error: "the vulgar American misuse of . . . Mis" (pro[nounced] *miz*)." In a sense, *Ms.*, or *miz*, has a long American history. If we think of it as southern dialect today we are not mistaken, though many of those verbally addressed as Miz might not be so pleased to be orthographically addressed as Ms.

11. *Oxford English Dictionary,* "master," 23a.
12. Samuel Taylor Coleridge, *Biographia Literaria*, IV, in *The Portable Coleridge*, ed. I. A. Richards (New York: Viking Press, 1950), 476–77, n.
13. Pamphlet quoted in Wendy Lesser, *The Amateur: An Independent Life of Letters* (New York: Pantheon, 1999), 32. *Oxford English Dictionary* (hereafter *OED*), "Ms.," 2.
14. *OED*, "Ms.," 2. p. 43.
15. Ibid.
16. Ibid.
17. Richard A. Fireman, "Ms: Pronounce It." *New York Times*, December 9, 1971, 46; Alma Graham, "To the Editor," *New York Times*, December 20, 1971, 34; P. David Kovacs, "Say 'Mistress,'" *New York Times*, May 2, 1972, 42.
18. N. Robinson Sorkin, "A Giant Step for Unisex," *New York Times*, May 24, 1972, 46.
19. Russell Baker, "'Murm' and 'Smur,' Please," *New York Times*, November 24, 1971, 15.
20. "Notes on People," *New York Times*, July 1, 1972, 13.
21. Robert B. Semple, Jr., "Nixon Indicates He'll Run Again," *New York Times*, January 1, 1972, 20.
22. Enid Nemy, "In the Soviet Union, She's the Highes Ranking Woman," *New York Times*, January 19, 1972, 42.
23. "Notes on People," *New York Times*, October 17, 1972, 47.
24. "Weddings," *New York Times*, September 12, 1999, section 9, 10.
25. The Associated Press, quoted in Richard Roeper, "Behind the Smiles Lives a Two-Faced Pageant," *Chicago Sun-Times*, September 15, 1999, 11.
26. Kama Boland, quoted in Benita M. Dodd, "Conversation Starter: Time to Alter Pageant?" *Atlanta Journal and Constitution*, September 18, 1999, 14A.
27. Katherine Baumann, quoted in Maria Newman, "Updating the Permissible for the Feminine Ideal," *New York Times*, September 15, 1999, A27.
28. "Ghost Dance" (editorial), *New York Times*, September 17, 1999, A26.
29. Samira Zebian, quoted in Carol Beggy, "Miss America Pageant May Widen Criteria," *Boston Globe*, September 14, 1999, A1.
30. Cheryl Garrity, quoted in Carol Beggy, "Miss America Pageant May Widen Criteria," A1.
31. Robert Thompson, quoted in Yvonne Zipp and Stacy A. Teicher, "There She Is, Miss . . . Anachronism?" *Christian Science Monitor*, September 17, 1999, 1.
32. Janet Parshall, quoted in Zipp and Teicher, "There She Is," 1.
33. "You know times have changed when the nation's premiere beauty pageant admits that faux virginity is not what counts when it comes to being a role model." Caryl Rivers, "Miss America Joins the Real World," *Boston Globe,* September 18, 1999, A19.
34. Adrian Philips, quoted in Susan Dworkin, *Miss America 1945: Bess Myerson's Own Story* (New York: Newmarket Press, 1987), 90.
35. A. R. Riverol, *Live from Atlantic City: The History of the Miss America Pageant before, after, and in Spite of Television* (Bowling Green, Ohio: Bowling Green University Press, 1992), 33.
36. See Mary S. Gossy *The Untold Story* (Ann Arbor: University of Michigan Press, 1989), a discussion of Fernando de Rojas, *La Celestina* (1499) "'Hacer virgos' means to mend the hymen of a woman who has had sexual intercourse so that it appears to her next sexual partner that she has not—that is, to make it seem that she is a virgin, *virgo intacta*" (43).

37. Lynda Gorov, "The Latest Fad from La-La Land: A 'Designer' Vagina," *Boston Globe,* August 23, 1999, C1.
38. "The Missed America Pageant" (editorial), *Boston Globe,* September 18, 1999, A18.
39. Don Bauder, "Arizona Grand Jury Indicts Ex-Mrs. America," *San Diego Union-Tribune,* December 15, 1998, C1.
40. Tim Novak, "Runner-Up Sues for Crown," *Chicago Sun-Times* June 4, 1999, 24.
41. Mrs. Wisconsin website (http://www.mrswisconsin.com).
42. Louise Continelli, "Meet the Mrs.," *Buffalo News,* September 23, 1997, 1D.
43. Diane White, "Primping for the Presidency," *Boston Globe,* October 4, 1999, C7.

Chapter 8

1. John Fleming, "All's Well with the Shakespeare of Standup," *St. Petersburg Times,* August 31, 1998, 1D.
2. Barbara Hoover, "What's New," *Detroit News,* October 10, 1998, C1.
3. Mary Leonard, "An Uncertain Second Act for a Scandal Figure," *Boston Globe,* September 19, 1998, A9.
4. Joseph Lieberman, "Character and Values and Consequences," excerpt from Senate Speech, September 3, 1998. *San Diego Union-Tribune* September 13, 1998, 65.
5. Lieberman, quoted in Andrew Norton, *Monica's Story* (New York: St. Martin's Press, 1999), 260.
6. Jonathan Rosenbloom, "Joseph Lieberman, a Jewish Hero." *Jerusalem Post,* September 18, 1998. 9.
7. David Streitfeld, "Updike at Bay,." *Washington Post,* December 16, 1998, D1.
8. John Updike, "Country Music," *The New Yorker,* March 8, 1999, 25.
9. John Updike, *Bech at Bay* (New York: Knopf, 1998), 152.
10. Alex Kuczynski, "Enough about Feminism. Should I Wear Lipstick?" *New York Times,* March 25, 1999, sect. 4, 4.
11. Leo Rosten, *The Joys of Yiddish* (New York: Pocket Books, 1968), 452.
12. Anne Beatts, "What Jews Don't Do Besides, Well, That." *Los Angeles Times,* February 8, 1998, E8. "Part of the mythology is that the Jewish woman will suck, but she won't swallow," observes Evelyn Torton Beck in her account of the JAP stereotype. Evelyn Torton Beck, "From 'Kike' to 'JAP': How Misogyny, anti-Semitism, and Racism Construct the 'Jewish American Princess,'" in *Race and Ethnic Conflict,* ed. Fred L. Pincus and Howard J. Ehrlich, (Boulder: Westview Press, 1994), 166.
13. Joseph Hanania, "Playing Princesses, Punishers and Prudes," *New York Times,* March 7, 1999, 35.
14. Debbie Lukatsky and Sandy Barnett Toback, *Jewish American Princess Handbook* (Arlington Heights, Ill.: Turnbull and Willoughby, 1982), 142–43; quoted in Sander Gilman, *The Jew's Body* (New York: Routledge, 1991), 32.
15. Gilman, *The Jew's Body,* 32.
16. Evelyn Torton Beck, "From 'Kike' to 'JAP'": 163, 167.
17. Andrew Morton, *Monica's Story* (New York: St. Martin's Press, 1999), 139–40.
18. Caryn James, "Video Shows an Image Sympathetic and Human," *New York Times,* February 7, 1999, 26.
19. Melinda Henneberger, "Public Hears Lewinsky's Story As Videos Are Played in Senate," *New York Times,* February 7, 1999, 1.
20. Lynda Gorov, "On Rodeo Drive, Something Familiar about Lewinsky," *Boston Globe,* February 7, 1999, A27.
21. Michael Prince, quoted in Susan Sachs, "Some Compassion for Lewinsky, but Fleeting Interest by Viewers," *New York Times,* February 7. 1999, 26.

22. "Lewinsky Confident and Cool in Her Deposition," *New York Times*, February 6, 1999, A8.
23. Mary Leonard, "What's to Become of Monica?" *Boston Globe*, September 19, 1998, A9.
24. Michiko Kakutani, "Books of the Times," *New York Times*, March 5, 1999, B54.
25. Fred Kaplan, "'She's Classic Boston,'" *Boston Globe*, March 5, 1999. "She's classic Boston," Andrew Morton told the interviewer, "that sort of shabby chic, roses, a mix of urban and country—she loves that" (A3).
26. Susan Ellicott, "The Lady's Not for Spurning." *Times* (London), March 8, 1999, "Features" section, n.p.
27. Quoted in Elisabeth Bumiller, "So Famous, Such Clout, She Could Interview Herself," *New York Times*, April 21, 1996, sec. 2, 1.
28. Quoted in Elisabeth Bumiller, "So Famous, Such Clout, She Could Interview Herself," *New York Times*, April 21, 1996, sec. 2, 1.
29. David Lugowski, "Barbara Walters," in *Celebrity Biographies*, Baseline II 1999. See also the *Complete Directory to Primetime TV Stars and Contemporary Theatre, Film and Television*, vol. 6.
30. Barbara Walters, *How to Talk with Practically Anybody about Practically Anything* (1970), quoted in Rebecca Mead, "Thoroughly Modern Monica," *The New Yorker,* March 15, 1999, 29.
31. Walters, quoted in Mead, "Thoroughly Modern Monica," 30.
32. Maer Roshan, "'Oh, Barbara! Your Dignity!' Lucianne on the Monica Show," *New York,* March 15, 1999, 16.
33. Muriel Dobbin, "What Next for Monica?" *Pittsburgh Post-Gazette*, February 14, 1999, A25.
34. Charles Laurence, "'I'll Eat Hillary Alive,'" *Daily Telegraph* (London), March 25, 1999, 25.
35. March 3, 1999, ABC *20/20* interview. Cited in Linda Matchan, "Can We Talk? Lewinsky Not Alone in Confiding Intimacies," *Boston Globe*, March 5, 1999, A1.
36. Roshan, "'Oh, Barbara! Your Dignity!'" 16.
37. "Want Lips like Monica Lewinsky?" NewsNet 5, March 5, 1999.
38. Charles Spencer, "Monica in Britain: Pure Televisual Viagra As 'Hot Lips' Melts Snow," *Daily Telegraph* (London), electronic version, March 5, 1999, 5.
39. Eddie Cantor, quoted in Lewis A. Erenberg, *Steppin' Out* (Westport, Conn: Greenwood Press, 1981), 196.
40. Sarah Blacher Cohen, "The Unkosher Comediennes," in *Jewish Wry*, ed. Sarah Blacher Cohen (Bloomington: Indiana University Press, 1987), 112.
41. Ibid., 114.
42. Barbara W. Grossman, *Funny Woman: The Life and Times of Fanny Brice* (Bloomington: Indiana University Press, 1991), 56.
43. *New York Times*, August 2, 1923, 10. Grossman, *Funny Woman*, 146.
44. Brendan Gill, introduction to *The Portable Dorothy Parker* (New York: Penguin Books, 1976), xxiii.
45. Grossman, *Funny Woman*, 149.
46. *Variety*, December 26, 1928, 11. Grossman, *Funny Woman*, 178.
47. Cohen, "Unkosher Comediennes," 115.
48. Joan Rivers, *The Life and Times of Heidi Abromowitz* (New York: Delacorte Press, 1984), table of contents; quoted in Cohen, "Unkosher Comediennes," 121.
49. Rivers, *Heidi Abromowitz*, 10.
50. Bill Bell, "Nothing to Hide: In Her New On-Woman Show, Sandra Bernhard Reveals (Almost) Everything," *New York Daily News*, November 1, 1998, "Sunday Extra" section, 18.
51. Bill Locey, "Queen of Outrageous Comedy Is Heading to Ventura," *Los Angeles Times* May 4, 1995, J6.

52. Betty Beard, "Twin Impersonators Bette You'll Get the Joke," *Arizona Republic*, February 2, 1996, D2.

53. Monique Polak, "A Star Is Revealed" (review of Ann Edwards, *Streisand; A Biography*), *Gazette* (Montreal), May 10, 1997, J1.

54. Bart Mills, "Model Teen; Alicia Silverstone Is More Clued In Than Roles She Plays on Screen," *Boston Herald*, July 21, 1995, S3.

55. Emma Forrest, "Alicia in Wonderland," *Guardian* (London), November 14, 1997, Features section, 2.

56. Arthur Gold and Robert Fizdale, *The Divine Sarah* (New York: Vintage, 1992), 13.

57. Ibid. 275. The quotation is from Bernhardt's former friend Marie Colombier's thinly veiled novel, *The Memoirs of Sarah Barnum*.

58. Heinrich Heiner, quoted in S. S. Prawer, *Heine's Jewish Comedy* (New York: Clarendon Press, 1983), 755. Rachel M. Brownstein, *Tragic Muse: Rachel of the Comédie-Francaise* (New York: Knopf, 1993), 87.

59. Brownstein, *Tragic Muse*, 82.

60. Christopher Marlowe, *The Jew of Malta*. New Mermaid edition, ed. T. W. Craik (New York: W. W. Norton, 1966), 1.2.376; 381–82; 289; 400.

61. Honoré de Balzac, *Le Cousin Pons* (Harmondsworth, England: Penguin, 1968), 143.

62. Eve Kosofsky Sedgwick, *Epistemology of the Closet* (Berkeley and Los Angeles: University of California Press, 1990), 82.

63. David Horovitz, "Latter-Day Esther a Boon to Jewish Right," *Irish Times*, January 26, 1998, 15.

64. Jonathan Rosenblum, "Joseph Lieberman, a Jewish Hero," *Jerusalem Post*, September 18, 1998, 9.

65. Frank Rich, "The 'New News,'" *New York Times,* October 28, 1998, A29.

66. "Is Lewinsky with the KGB?" *Guandong Writer;* cited in John Hiscock, "Scandal in the White House: Monica's Rabbi Tells President to Cleanse His Soul." *Daily Telegraph* (London) September 17, 1998, 20.

67. Hiscock, "Scandal in the White House, 20.

68. Cited in Horovitz, "Latter-Day Esther a Boon to Jewish Right," 15.

69. Amelia Richards and Jennifer Baumgardner, ""Why Young Feminists Should Support Monica," *The Nation*, December 20, 1998, A13.

70. Ari Hier, "Why David Was Not Impeached," *Denver Post*, January 29, 1999, F5.

71. Yossi Ben-Aharon, "Lewinsky, for Example," *Jerusalem Post*, October 8, 1998, 10.

72. Julian Borger, "At Last, Israelis Can Enjoy Their Own Lewinsky," *Guardian* (London), July 18, 1998, 16.

73. Tessa L. Auman, "Denigrating Description," *Jerusalem Post*, February 6, 1998, 8. Greer Fay Cashman, "Forced Insomnia," *Jerusalem Post,* February 3, 1998, 12.

74. Morton, *Monica's Story*, 225–26.

75. Associated Press report, "Lewinsky's Rabbi Blasted Clinton for His Behavior," *Star Tribune* (Minneapolis), September 16, 1998, 10A.

76. Wendy and Alec Roth, "Inappropriate Rabbinical Behavior," *Jerusalem Post*, September 20, 1998, 8.

77. Sam Abrams, "People in Glass Houses," *Jerusalem Post*, September 18, 1998, 8.

78. "Congressman Objects to Clinton Tapes on Rosh Hashana," *Jerusalem Post*, September 22, 1998, 1; David L. Greene, "Democrats Question Release of Tape on Rosh Hashana," *Baltimore Sun*, September 19, 1998, 6A; Tara George, "Jews Rip Rosh Hashanah Tape Release," *New York Daily News*, September 19, 1998, 4.

79. "A Theatrical Repentance" (editorial), *Denver Rocky Mountain News*, September 13, 1998, 2B.

80. Allan Hall, "Cosmetic Surgeon and Rich Admirer Give Paula Jones a New-Look Nose for Scandal," *The Scotsman*, July 20, 1998, 7.

81. Gilman, *The Jew's Body*, 185.
82. Paul Natvig, *Jacques Joseph: Surgical Sculptor* (Philadelphia: W. B. Saunders, 1982), 95; cited in Gilman, *The Jew's Body*, 187.
83. Corky Siemaszko, "TV Questioning Turns Paula Off," *New York Daily News*, November 18, 1998, 18.
84. Howard Rosenberg, "A Nose for News, from Tabs to TV," *Los Angeles Times*, August 17, 1998, F1.
85. Calev Ben-David, "My Evening with Monica," *Jerusalem Post*, March 5, 1999, 1. Jon Snow, interview with Lewinsky, Channel 4 (Britain), March 4, 1999.
86. Carole Corbeil, "Monica's Story: Sacrificed on Misogyny's Altar," *Gazette* (Montreal), March 13, 1999, J1.
87. Robert Winder, "Rubber-Necking at the Monica Freak Show." *Independent* (London), March 14, 1999, p. 12.
88. Christopher Reed, "However She Handles Herself, Lewinsky's Fame Is Guranteed," *Irish Times*, September 12, 1998, 14.
89. Burt A. Folkart, "Irving Wallace: Prolific Writer Reached Billion Readers," *Los Angeles Times*, June 30, 1990, A38.
90. Gabler, 372, from House Un-American Activities Committee transcripts.
91. Morton, *Monica's Story*, 66.
92. Ibid., 22.
93. Ibid., 24.
94. Ibid., 25.
95. Anne Beatts, "A Proposition for the Sake of Science," *Los Angeles Times*, February 15, 1998, E10.
96. Jack London, "His 'monica' was Skysail Jack," *The Road* (New York: Macmillan, 1907), 169:

Chapter 9

1. Samuel Johnson, "Preface to Shakespeare" (1765), in *Johnson on Shakespeare*, ed. Arthur Sherbo (New Haven, Conn.: Yale University Press, 1968), 94–95.
2. Johnson, "Preface," 105, 108, 109.
3. C. M. Ingleby, *The Still Lion: An Essay towards the Restoration of Shakespeare's Text* (London: Trübner, 1874), ix.
4. Fredson Bowers, *Textual and Literary Criticism* (Cambridge: Cambridge University Press, 1959), 120.
5. Fredson Bowers, *On Editing Shakespeare* (Charlottesville: University of Virginia Press, 1966), 116.
6. Ibid., 104-105.
7. Ibid., 177.
8. Donald Spoto, *The Dark Side of Genius: The Life of Alfred Hitchcock* (New York: Da Capo Press, 1999), 278.
9. Ibid., 145.
10. Mel Gussow, "With Math, a Playwright Explores a Family in Stress," (review of David Auburn, *Proof*), *New York Times*, May 29, 2000, B1.
11. Spoto, *The Dark Side*, 145.
12. Ibid.
13. "Master of Suspense: Being a Self-Analysis by Alfred Hitchcock," *New York Times*, June 4, 1950, sec. 2, p. 4. Reprinted in *Hitchcock on Hitchcock*, ed. Sidney Gottlieb (Berkeley and Los Angeles: University of California Press, 1995), 124.

14. Jacques Lacan, "Seminar on 'The Purloined Letter,'" in *The Purloined Poe: Lacan, Derrida, and Psychoanalytic Reading*, ed. John P. Muller and William J. Richardson (Baltimore: Johns Hopkins University Press, 1988), 46.
15. Slavoj Žižek, introduction to *Everything You Always Wanted to Know about Lacan (but Were Afraid to Ask Hitchcock)*, ed. Slavoj Žižek (London: Verso, 1992), 6, 8.
16. François Truffaut, *Hitchcock* (New York: Simon and Schuster, 1985), 268–69.
17. Spoto, *The Dark Side*, 286.
18. H. J. Oliver, *Timon of Athens*, Arden ed. (London: Methuen, 1959), 5.
19. Ingleby, *The Still Lion*, 111–12.
20. Harold Jenkins, ed., *Hamlet* (London: Routledge, 1982), 510.
21. Ingleby, *The Still Lion*, 120.
22. Jenkins, ed., *Hamlet*, 426.
23. Ibid., 357.
24. "If . . . we had but the First Folio, we should be called upon to explain or amend the following passage in Hamlet:

> To his good Friends, thus wide Ile ope my Armes:
> And like the kinde Life-rend'ring Politician,
> Repast them with my blood.

Such a crux as 'Life-rend'ring Politician' would have been . . . appetising and entertaining [to the critical taste] . . . and the game would naturally have been quickend by the fact, that when Hamlet was first indited Politician, occuring once, however, in this play ('the Pate of a Politician,' iv.1 [sic] 1]) was an insolens verbum, which we now believe to have been first used by George Puttenham in 1589 [in *The Arte of English Poesie*]. The misprint in an unusual expansion of the original word. It is most unlikely that Pelican (the word of the quarto editions) was (as some have asserted) a difficulty with the old compositor: on the contrary, we may be pretty sure that he set up Polician, and that a pedantic 'read' of the house improved upon this, converting it into Politician." Ingleby, *Still Lion*, 113.
25. Jenkins, ed., *Hamlet,* 481.
26. Harold Bloom, *Shakespeare: The Invention of the Human* (New York: Riverhead, 1998), 424.
27. A. C. Bradley, *Shakespearean Tragedy* (1904; reprint, London: Penguin, 1991), 99, 131.
28. John Dover Wilson, *What Happens in Hamlet?* (1935; reprint, Cambridge: Cambridge University Press, 1970), 162 .
29. Charles and Mary Cowden Clarke, *Cassell's Illustrated Shakespeare* (London: Cassell, 1864–1868), vol. 3,. 415; emphasis added.
30. W. T. Malleson and J. R. Seeley, *Which Are Hamlet's "Dozen or Sixteen Lines"?* (London: New Shakespere Society, 1874), 481.
31. Ibid., 471.
32. Ibid., 482.
33. Ibid., 490–91.
34. F. J. Furnivall, in Malleson and Seeley, *Which Are?* 494-495.
35. Richard Simpson, in Malleson and Seeley, *Which Are?* 496.
36. Charles Bathurst, *Remarks on the Differences in Shakespeare's Versification in Different Periods of His Life* (London: John W. Parker and Son, 1857), 70.
37. Horace H. Furness, ed., *New Variorum Hamlet* (1877; reprint, New York: Dover, 1963) vol. 1, 250–51. Summary of a paper by C. M. Ingleby, to be read at the New Shakspere Society, February 9, 1877.
38. Martin Dodsworth, *Hamlet Closely Observed* (London: Athlone Press, 1985), 153–54.
39. R. A. Foakes, *Hamlet versus Lear* (Cambridge: Cambridge University Press, 1993), 86–87.

40. Samuel Weller Singer, *The Text of Shakespeare Vindicated from the Interpolations and Corruptions Advocated by John Payne Collier in His Notes and Emendations* (London: William Pickering, 1853), x.

41. Ibid., x.

42. Affidavit of John Payne Collier, concerning his book *Notes and Emendations to the Text of Shakespeare's Plays, from Early Manuscript Corrections in a Copy of the Folio, 1632, in the Possession of J. Payne Collier* (1832), sworn to in the Court of Queen's Bench, 1856. Quoted in N. E. S. A. Hamilton, *Strictures on Mr. N. E. S. A. Hamilton's Inquiry into the Genuineness of the Manuscript Corrections in Mr. J. Payne Collier's Annotated Shakspere, Folio, 1632* (London: Richard Bentley, 1860), 16–17.

43. Sir Frederick Madden, Keeper of Manuscripts at the British Museum, private *Journal*, quoted in Samuel Schoenbaum, *Shakespeare's Lives* (New York: Oxford University Press, 1970), 355.

44. Ingleby's own autobiographical writings suggest that he saw himself in the same critical spirit as the Hamlet of act 3 ("I am very proud, revengeful, ambitious, with more offenses at my beck than I have thoughts to put them in...." [3.1.124–26]: "I am morally weak in many respects. In some matters I have been systematically deceptive, & occasionally cowardly & treacherous. I am passionately fond of personal beauty; but, on the whole, I dislike my kind, & my natural affections are weak.") Manuscript in Folger Shakespeare Library, quoted in Schoenbaum, *Shakespeare's Lives*, 357.

45. C. M. Ingleby, *A Complete View of the Shakespere Controversy, Concerning the Authenticity and Genuineness of the Manuscript Matter Affecting the Works and Biography of Shakspere, Published by Mr. J. Payne Collier As the Fruits of His Researches* (London: Nattali and Bond, 1861; reprint, New York: AMS Press, 1973), 14, 19, 21.

46. Ibid., 323.

47. Ibid., 324–25.

48. John Collier, *Reply to Mr. N. E. S. A. Hamilton's "Inquiry" into the Imputed Shakespeare Forgeries* (1860), 47–50.

49. Ingleby, *Complete View*, 323–24.

50. Samuel Butler, *Hudibras*, The Third and Last Part, canto 3, ll. 759–64.

51. Dewey Ganzel, *Fortune and Men's Eyes: The Career of John Payne Collier* (Oxford: Oxford University Press, 1982).

52. John Payne Collier, *Autobiography*, Folger Shakespeare Library MS. M.a.230, pp. 146–47; quoted in Schoenbaum, *Shakespeare's Lives*, 360.

53. Collier, *Autobiography*, 148; the comment is Schoenbaum's.

54. Marjorie Garber, *Shakespeare's Ghost Writers: Literature as Uncanny Causality* (New York: Methuen, 1987). Marjorie Garber, "As They Like It," *Harper's*, April 1999, 44–46.

Chapter 10

1. Claire McEachern, introduction to *Religion and Culture in Renaissance England*, ed. Claire McEachern and Debora Shuger (Cambridge: Cambridge University Press, 1997), 2.

2. Ibid.

3. Richard Bernstein, "We Happy Many, Playing Fast and Loose with History," *New York Times*, January 18, 2000, B1–B2.

4. Nabokov offers this piece of mindless and fictive "Ekwilist doctrine": "It is better for a man to have belonged to a politically incorrect organization than not to have belonged to any organization at all." Vladimir Nabokov, *Bend Sinister* (1947; reprint, New York: Vintage Books, 1990), 158.

5. Maurice Isserman recalls that among young people on the so-called New Left, the term was "always used in a tone mocking the pieties of our own insular political counterculture." Maurice Isserman, "Travels with Dinesh," *Tikkun* 6, no. 5 (1991): 82.

6. Ed Siegel, "Hazy Shade of 'Winter' at ART," *Boston Globe*, May 19, 2000, D1.

7. Clifford Longley, "Sacred and Profane: Labour and the Fall of Political Correctness," *Daily Telegraph*, November 26, 1999, 31. A recent publication by the British Institute of Economic Affairs, titled "Political Correctness and Social Work," insisted that "anti-oppressive practice" was itself "oppressive as well as practically ineffectual." See Social Workers Reject Political Correctness," *Times Home News*, November 22, 1999, n.p. Sue Clough, "Judge Attacks Irvine's Politically Correct Rules on Race," *Daily Telegraph*, October 1, 1999, 1.

8. Walter Benjamin, "Literary History and the Study of Literature," in *Selected Writings*, vol. 2 (1927–1934) (Cambridge, Mass.: Harvard University Press, 1999), 464.

9. See Samuel Kliger, *The Goths in England* (Cambridge, Mass.: Harvard University Press, 1952), cited in Jonathan Bate, ed. *Titus Andronicus*, Arden Shakespeare ed. (Walton-on-Thames, Surrey: Thomas Nelson, 1997), 19–20.

10. Alan F. Segal, "The Ten Commandments"; Michael Grant, "Julius Caesar"; Carolly Erickson, "The Scarlet Empress," all in *Past Imperfect: History according to the Movies*, ed. Mark C. Carnes (New York: Henry Holt, 1995), 38, 44, 88.

11. Peter Desmond, "The Roman Theater of Cruelty," *Harvard Magazine*, September/October 2000, 22.

12. Michel de Montaigne, "Of Thumbs," in *The Complete Essays of Montaigne*, trans. Donald M. Frame (Stanford, Calif.: Stanford University Press, 1958), 523:

> It was a sign of favor in Rome to close in and hold down the thumbs—
>
> > Your partisan with both his thumbs will praise your game
> > > Horace
>
> —and of disfavor to raise them and turn them outward:
>
> > When the people's thumb turns up.
> > They kill their man to please them.
> > > Juvenal

13. Philip Howard, "Blood and Circuses," *Times* (London), May 17, 2000, sec. 2, 3–4.

14. Steve Allen, *Meeting of Minds* (Buffalo, N.Y.: Prometheus Books, 1989), 161, 82.

15. Don Freeman, "Scripts Made a Meeting of the Minds," *San Diego Union-Tribune*, December 24, 1989, entertainment section, 6.

16. Sarah Boxer, "Snubbing Chronology as a Guiding Force in Art," *New York Times*, September 2, 2000, A19–A21. Boxer cites British art critic David Sylvester in the *London Review of Books* and Jed Perl in the *New Republic*.

17. Iwana Blazwick, quoted in Boxer, "Snubbing Chronology," A21.

18. Elmer Edgar Stoll, "Anachronism in Shakespeare Criticism," *Modern Philology* 7 (1910): 1, 5, 7, 12, 8, 1, 19.

19. Anne Bradstreet, "The Author to Her Book," in *The Works of Anne Bradstreet*, ed. Jeannine Hensley (Cambridge: Belknap Press of Harvard University Press, 1967), 221.

20. The editor of Bradstreet's works makes a similar claim: "In 'The Author to Her Book,' the metaphor of the book as a child expresses how the poet felt when she saw her work in print. It was her own child, even if she was ashamed of its errors...." Jeannine Hensley, introduction to Hensley, ed. *The Works of Anne Bradstreet*, xxxi. The "new historicist" twist not present in this 1960s reading is the presentation of period images from authors like Ambroise Paré.

21. Adrienne Rich, "Anne Bradstreet and Her Poetry," in Hensley, ed., *The Works of Anne Bradstreet*, x.

22. John Heminge and Henry Condell, "To the Great Variety of Readers," prefatory letter to the First Folio of Shakespeare; *The Norton Facsimile, The First Folio of Shakespeare*, prepared by Charlton Hinman (New York: W. W. Norton, 1968), 7.

23. August Wilhelm Schlegel, "The Art of Shakespeare's Romantic Drama," from *Lectures on Dramatic Art and Literature* (1808), trans. John Black (London: George Bell and Sons, 1909), 356.

24. David Daniell, introduction, *Julius Caesar*, Arden Shakespeare ed., 3d ser. (Walton-on-Thames, Surrey: Thomas Nelson, 1998), 17–22.

25. There is also in Julius Caesar the matter of "sleeves." "As they pass by, pluck Caska by the sleeve," Cassius instructs Brutus (1.2.178). "Togas had no sleeves," corrects John Dover Wilson in his Cambridge edition of the play. Once again, the redoubtable Daniell comes to the rescue, suggesting that nearby references to cloak (214) and doublet (264) are clues that "Shakespeare also had London in mind," and reading the combination of pluck plus sleeve as, again, "almost furtive." These anachronistic references to clothing are, in other words, both functional and double coded: their out-of-place-ness is a theatrical and interpretative marker, reminding the audience that the play is about *now* as well as *then* (Shakespeare's London as well as Caesar's Rome), while also drawing attention to a particular kind of affect (here "furtiveness").

26. David Patrick Stearns, "Akalaitis' Henry IV Conforms," *Gannett News Service*, March 19, 1991, n.p.

27. Charles Spencer, "The Arts: Shakespeare Meets Le Carre," *Daily Telegraph*, November 9, 1998, 19.

28. Herbert Mitgang, "Books of the Times," *New York Times*, April 18, 1986, C31.

29. Jacques Lacan, "Seminar on 'The Purloined Letter,'" trans. Jeffrey Mahlman, in *The Purloined Poe*, ed. John P. Muller and William J. Richardson (Baltimore: Johns Hopkins University Press, 1988), 39–40.

30. Ralph Waldo Emerson, "Shakspeare; Or, the Poet" in *Representative Men: Essays and Lectures* (New York: Library of America, 1983), 716–21.

31. Lisa Jardine has argued that the task of literary studies is "to bring historical studies and text studies into constructive tension with one another," suggesting that "what we should be looking at is the converging practices of social historians, intellectual and cultural historians, text critics and social anthropologists, as they move together towards a more sensitive integration of past and present cultural products." She closes her book in the same bitemporal spirit: "To read Shakespeare historically is to undertake a dialogue with these culturally freighted residues of our own past in order more clearly to illuminate the culture we currently inhabit." What is stressed here, crucially, is dialogue, and, by implication, dialectic. Reading historically means reading the present as well as the past, reading the past as that which produces the present but also the present as that which produces the past (by reading, by analysis, by the very protocols of scholarship). Lisa Jardine, *Reading Shakespeare Historically* (London: Routledge, 1996), 35–36; 148.

32. Theodor Adorno, "Gaps," in *Minima Moralia*, trans. E. F. N. Jephcott (London: Verso, 1978), 80.

33. William Shakespeare, *As You Like It*, 2.7.144–46.

Chapter 11

1. Carol McDaid, "There's No Escaping Mr. Darcy," *Independent* (London), June 9, 2000, Features section, 11.

2. Jane Austen, *Pride and Prejudice* (1813; reprint, New York: Penguin Books, 1985), 286.

3. Ibid., 302

4. Ibid., 228.

5. Ibid., 209.

6. Marjorie Garber, *Symptoms of Culture* (New York: Routledge, 1998), 4.

7. Ibid., 2.

8. Sheen's brother, Joe Estevez, is a handgun advocate who has appeared in films like *Bimbo Movie Bash* and *Slaves of the Vampire Werewolf*, and is currently making voice-over commercials in support of "America's firearms." Grace Bradberry, "Brothers in Small-Screen Gun Battle," *Times* (London), August 26, 2000, n.p.

9. "In Search of Jane Austen," *Fodor's 2000 Great Britain* (New York: Fodor's Travel Publications, 2000), 170.

10. *Frommer's 2000 England* (New York: Macmillan, 2000), 3.

11. Ibid., 320.

12. Sherry Thomas, "Love on the Open Page," *Houston Chronicle*, April 2, 2000, Texas Magazine section, 8.

13. Gary Taylor, *Reinventing Shakespeare* (New York: Weidenfeld and Nicolson, 1989), 119.

14. Brochure for the Jane Austen Centre at Bath.

15. Dorothy Sayers, *Five Red Herrings,* vol. 8 in the *Collected Edition of Detective Stories* (London: Gollence Ltd., 1931, reprint 1974), 254.

16. Olivia Lichtenstein, "Guess What Mummy Did Today?" *Times* (London), July 15, 2000, n.p.

17. David Benedict, "More Than Just a Pretty Voice," *Independent* (London), June 7, 2000, Features section, 10.

18. "Vicar: Assert Thyself," *Daily Telegraph,* May 1, 2000, 23.

19. Deborah Hargreaves, "World News: Europe" *Financial Times*, April 13, 2000, 3.

20. Liza Mundy, "Women and Investing," *Washington Post Magazine*, September 10, 2000, Magazine, W15.

21. Roger Henderson, "Grape Divide." *Sunday Times* (London), Features section, n.p.

22. Gillian Glover, "Madam, May I Be the Angel at Your Table?" *The Scotsman*, October 1, 1999, 19.

23. Steve Johnson, "Reality Shows Are Biting Back, but the Grim Reality Is That Worse Are Coming," *Chicago Tribune*, February 25, 2000, sec. 5, 3.

24. Deborah Mitchell, "Bloomberg: Terminally Single?" *Daily News* (New York), April 9, 2000, 22.

25. Linda Barrett Osborne, "Follies on the Strand," *Washington Post*, July 16, 2000, X7.

26. Jeremy Samuel, "It'll Take Some Persuasion," *Straits Times* (Singapore), March 4, 2000, Life! section, 22.

27. Sarah Hemming, "Too Fast a Gallop through Austen," *Financial Times*, April 19, 2000, Arts section, 18.

28. *Fordyce's Sermons to Young Women* were apparently a popular butt of jokes in the period. This very comic episode is clearly indebted to Richard Brinsley Sheridan's play *The Rivals*, in which a character called Lydia Languish, who is dreaming of an elopement rather than a too-respectable marriage, hides her novels when her aunt and her proper suitor arrive:

> *Lydia.* Here, my dear Lucy, hide these books—Quick, quick!—Fling *Peregrine Pickle* under the toilet—throw *Roderick Random* into the closet—put *The Innocent Adultery* into *The Whole Duty of Man*—thrust *Lord Aimsworth* under the sopha—cram Ovid behind the bolster—there—put *The Man of Feeling* into your pocket—so, so—now lay *Mrs. Chapone* in sight, and leave *Fordyce's Sermons* open on the table.
>
> *Lucy.* O burn it, Ma'am! The hair-dresser has torn away as far as *Proper Pride.*
>
> *Lydia.* Never mind—open at Sobriety.

Richard Brinsley Sheridan, *The Rivals* (1775; reprint, Boston: Houghton Mifflin, 1910), 1.2.186–96.

29. Sue Birtwhistle and Susie Conklin, *The Making of Pride and Prejudice* (London: Penguin, 1995), vi.

30. *Oxford English Dictionary*, "pride," 3b.

31. Jack Todd, "Pride and Prejudice: Aboriginal Runner Freeman's Triumph Stirs a Nation and a People," *The Gazette* (Montreal), September 26, 2000, D3.

32. Michael Ellison, "Pride and Prejudice: Anne Heche and Ellen DeGeneres, Hollywood's Only Publicly Acknowledged Lesbian Couple, Have Split Up. The Truth Is That It's Tough Being Gay in Hollywood," *Guardian* (London), August 22, 2000, 4.

33. Jay Rey and Lou Michel, "Pride or Prejudice? Schools Feeling Heat over Indian Nicknames," *Buffalo News*, April 15, 2000, 1A.

34. "Flagging South Carolina" (editorial), *San Francisco Chronicle*, April 14, 2000, A28.

35. Austen, *Pride and Prejudice*, 41.

36. Ibid., 142.

Chapter 12

1. Frank Kermode, introduction to *Antony and Cleopatra*, ed. G. Blakemore Evans. *Riverside Shakespeare*, 2d ed. (Boston: Houghton Mifflin, 1997), 1394.

2. John Dryden, "Rival Ladies," in *The Works of John Dryden*, ed. H. T. Swedenberg, vol. 8 (Berkeley and Lost Angeles: University of California Press, 1962), 95.

3. John Dryden, "An Essay of Dramatick Poesie and Shorter Works," in *The Works of John Dryden*, ed. H. T. Swedenberg, vol. 17 (Berkeley: University of California Press, 1971), 61.

4. Thomas Overbury, *The Miscellaneous Works in Prose and Verse*, ed. Edward F. Rimbault (London: John Russell Smith, 1856), 168.

5. Jean de La Bruyère, *Characters*, trans. Henri van Laun (London: Oxford University Press, 1963), 35, 37, 248–49, 254.

6. Charles Baudelaire, "The Painter of Modern Life," in *The Painter of Modern Life and Other Essays*, trans. Jonathan Mayne (London: Phaidon, 1964, 1995), 1–41.

7. C. G. Jung, *Psychological Types: or the Psychology of Individuation,* trans. H. Godwin Baynes (New York: Pantheon Books, 1923; reprint, 1953). Jung believed that individuals have four modes of apprehending the world: thinking/feeling and intuition/sensation. The first two are "rational" functions and the second two "irrational" functions. Each person is born with one of these modes "superior" or predominating, with two more "accessible," and with the fourth "inferior" and difficult to access. In addition, Jung posited two attitudes: extraversion and introversion (taking one's bearing from an object or person in the world; taking one's bearing from within oneself). This typological model of the psyche was central to his theories of personal development, and is not unlike a modern theory of humors.

8. J. Knight in *Atheneum*, March 16, 1878; *Stage*, November 9, 1883. Both cited in the *Oxford English Dictionary*, "character," 19.

9. Sigmund Freud, "General Theory of the Neuroses," in *The Standard Edition of the Complete Psychological Works of Sigmund Freud*, ed. James Strachey (London: Hogarth Press, 1963), 16:381.

10. Freud, "Those Wrecked by Success," (*Standard Edition* 14:324), quoted in Philip Rieff, *Freud: The Mind of the Moralist* (New York: Viking Press, 1959), 52.

11. Rieff, *Freud*, 130–131.

12. Samuel Johnson, notes to *Hamlet*, in *Johnson on Shakespeare*, ed. Arthur Sherbo. *The Yale Edition of the Works of Samuel Johnson* (New Haven, Conn.: Yale University Press, 1968), 8:971.

13. Again Johnson is a good barometer. "This speech, which the former edition give[s] to Miranda, is very judiciously bestowed by Mr. Theobald on Prospero." Notes to *The Tempest*, in Sherbo, ed., *Johnson on Shakespeare*, 7:124.

14. See, for a good example of this argument, Jacques Lacan: "The phenomenology that emerges from analytic experience is certainly of a kind to demonstrate in desire the paradoxical, deviant, erratic, eccentric, even scandalous character by which it is distinguished from need. This fact has been too often affirmed not to have been always obvious to moralists worthy of the name. . . . In any case, man cannot aim at being whole (the 'total personality' is another of the deviant premises of modern psychotherapy), while ever the play of displacement and condensation to which he is doomed in the exercise of his functions marks his relation as a subject to the signifier." Jacques Lacan, "The Signification of the Phallus," in *Écrits: A Selection*, trans. Alan Sheridan (New York: W. W. Norton, 1977), 286–87.

15. *Hamlet* 3.2.345–51.

16. *Antony and Cleopatra* 4.14.3–14 (Arden ed.).

17. Richard Brinsley Sheridan, *The Rivals* (1775; reprint, Boston: Houghton Mifflin, 1910), 3.4.230.

18. Lucy Hughes-Hallet, *Cleopatra: Histories, Dreams, Distortions* (New York: Harper and Row, 1990).

19. Edmund Spenser, *Fairie Queene*, 1.5.18–19, in *The Poetical Works of Edmund Spenser*, ed. J. C. Smith and E. De Selincourt (London: Oxford University Press, 1912), 18–19.

20. *2 Henry VI* 3.1.225–30. (Arden ed.).

21. *Antony and Cleopatra* 1.2.154–56 (Arden ed.).

22. Louisa May Alcott, *Little Women* (Oxford: Oxford University Press, 1994), 331.

23. Aristotle, *The Poetic,* trans. Stephen Halliwell (Chapel Hill: University of North Carolina Press, 1987), 38, 47.

> (a) first and foremost, that the characters be good. Characterisation will arise . . . where speech or action exhibits the nature of an ethical choice; and the character will be good when the choice is good. But this depends on each class of person: there can be a good woman and a good slave, even though perhaps the former is an inferior type, and the latter a wholly base one.
> (b) that the characters be appropriate. For it is possible to have a woman manly in character, but it is not appropriate for a woman to be so manly or clever.
> (c) Likeness of character—for this is independent of making character good and appropriate, as described.
> Consistency of character. For even where an inconsistent person is portrayed, and such a character is presupposed, there should still be consistency in the inconsistency.

24. Ibid., 139 and 139n. Halliwell cites Brian Vickers, "The Emergence of Character Criticism," in Stanley Wells, ed., *Shakespeare Survey* 34 (Cambridge: Cambridge University Press, 1981), 11:21.

25. Samuel Johnson, "Preface to Shakespeare," in Sherbo, ed., *Johnson on Shakespeare*, 7:62.

26. Samuel Johnson, in Sherbo, ed. *Johnson on Shakespeare*, 8: 873.

27. Hughes-Hallet, *Cleopatra*, 132–59.

28. John Dryden, preface to *All for Love, or the World Well Lost* (1678), in *Essays of John Dryden*, ed. W. P. Ker, vol. 1 (Oxford: Clarendon Press, 1900), 190–91.

29. T. R. Henn, *The Living Image* (London: Methuen, 1972), 117.

30. William Hazlitt, *Characters of Shakespeare's Plays* (London: J. S. Dent, 1906), 74, 75, 76.

31. A. C. Bradley, *Oxford Lectures on Poetry* (London: Macmillan, 1909), 300–303.

32. A. C. Swinburne, *Shakespeare* (London: H. Frowde, 1909) 76. A. C. Swinburne, *A Study of Shakespeare* (New York: R. Worthington, 1880), 191.

33. John Middleton Murry, *The Problem of Style* (1922; reprint, London: Oxford University Press, 1967), 32–36.

34. T. S. Eliot, "Hamlet" (1919), in *Selected Essays 1917–1932* (New York: Harcourt, Brace, and Company, 1932), 124–25.
35. Rosalie L. Colie, "Antony and Cleopatra: The Significance of Style," in *Shakespeare's Living Art* (Princeton, N.J.: Princeton University Press, 1974), 198, 202, 207.
36. A. C. Bradley, *Shakespearean Tragedy* (1904; reprint, London: Penguin, 1991), 35–36.
37. G. Wilson Knight, *The Imperial Theme* (1931; reprint, London: Methuen, 1965), 289–90.
38. Bradley, *Shakespearean Tragedy*, 44 and 44n. In his note Bradley says the following: "I have raised no objection to the idea of fate, because it occurs so often both in conversation and in books about Shakespeare's tragedies that I must suppose it to be natural to many readers. Yet I doubt whether it would be so if Greek tragedy had never been written; and I must in candour confess that to me it does not often occur when I am reading, or when I have just read, a tragedy of Shakespeare."
39. Johnson, "Preface to Shakespeare," 7:74.
40. William Shakespeare, "The Phoenix and Turtle," ll. 28–32, 38–40, *Riverside Shakespeare*, 2d ed., ed. G. Blakemore Evans (Boston: Houghton Mifflin, 1997), 1891.
41 George Puttenham, *The Arte of English Poesie* (1589; reprint, Kent, Ohio: Kent State University Press, 1970), 269.

Chapter 13

1. *PGA Tour Inc. v. Martin*, certoriari to the United States Court of Appeals for the Ninth Circuit. No. 00-24. Argued January 17, 2001. Decided May 29, 2001.
2. William Safire, "On Language: Compassion," *New York Times Magazine*, July 15, 2001, 22.
3. Justice Clarence Thomas, quoted in Linda Greenhouse, "Disabled Golfer May Use a Cart on the PGA Tour, Justices Affirm," *New York Times*, May 30, 2001, A1.
4. George F. Will, "'Compassionate' Courts," *Washington Post*, June 3, 2001, B7.
5. Joe Gordon, "FleetBoston Classic: Notebook," *Boston Herald*, June 24, 2001, B4.
6. Charles Chi Haleri, "Golf's Handicap" A Lack of Compassion, Logic" letter to the editor *Chicago Sun Times*, June 5, 2001, 30.
7. Steven D. Stark, "Practicing Inclusion, Consensus: Clinton's Feminization of Politics," *Los Angeles Times*, March 14, 1993, M2.
8. H. D. S. Greenway, "Compassion Overload," *Boston Globe*, May 17, 1991, 19.
9. Susan Moeller, *Compassion Fatigue: How the Media Sell Disease, Famine, War, and Death* (New York: Routledge, 1999), 321.
10. Herbert Kohl and Colin Green, eds., *A Call to Character: A Family Treasury* (New York: HarperCollins, 1996).
11. *Oxford English Dictionary*, "compassion," vol. 2, ed. Mozley (New York: Oxford University Press, 1989), 597.
12. Rev. James Gardner, *Faiths of the World, a dictionary of all religions and religious sects, their doctrines, rights, ceremonies, and customs*, Div. 3 (London: Fullarton, 1857), 570.
13. John Quincy Adams to A. Bronson, July 30, 1838, in *Bartletts Familiar Quotations*, 10th ed. (Boston: Little, Brown, and Company, 1919), 458.
14. In John 4:9 the woman of Samaria anticipates scorn from Jesus since "the Jews have no dealings with the Samarians."
15. Mickey Kaus, "Compassion, the Political Liability," *New York Times*, June 25, 1999, A23.
16. See, e.g. *Buddhist Acts of Compassion*; *Compassion: The Key to Great Awakening: Thought Training and the Bodhissattva Practices*; *Cultivating Compassion: A Buddhist Perspective*; *Meditation, Compassion and Loving Kindness: An Approach to Vipassana Practice*; *Science and Compassion: Dialogues between Biobehavioral Scientists and the Dalai Lama*.

17. Associated Press, "Dalai Lama Meets with Bush; China Lodges Formal Protest," *Newsday* (Long Island, N.Y.), May 24, 2001, A16.

Chapter 14

1. Madeleine Bunting, "The Morning After." *Guardian* (London), September 12, 2001, 14.
2. Joelle Sumner (John F. Kennedy High School, Bellmore, N.Y.), "Student Briefing Page on the News," *Newsday* (Long Island, N.Y.), October 4, 2001, A24.
3. Mimi Avins, Cara Mia DiMassa, "Amid Disaster, Heroes Ran toward Danger, Not from It," *Los Angeles Times*, September 21, 2001, sec. 5, 1.
4. Nicholas M. Christian, Glenn Collins, Jim Dwyer, Joseph P. Fried, Jan Hoffman, Mireya Navarro, Maria Newman, Mirta Ojito, Barbara Stewart, and Joyce Wadler, "A Nation Challenged: The Missing," *New York Times*, October 2, 2001, B9.
5. Madeleine Bunting, "The Launch of a TV Game That Trades on Our Dark Side," *Guardian* (London), May 21, 2001, 20.
6. Joyce Purnick, "Intern's Role Appears to Be Same Sad Tale," *New York Times*, July 12, 2001, B1.
7. Francine Prose, "The Big Surprise? Our Surprise," *Washington Post*, February 18, 2001, B1.
8. James Carville, quoted in Ellen Gamerman, "Hillary Clinton, Fund-Raiser," *Baltimore Sun*, April 25, 2001, 1A.
9. George F. Will, "A Principled Solution to Stem Cell Dilemma," *Baltimore Sun*, April 16, 2001, 19A.
10. Karl Marx, "Introduction to a Critique of Political Economy," in Karl Marx and Friedrich Engels, *The German Ideology*, ed. C. J. Arthur (New York: International Publishers, 1974), 124.
11. Anna Quindlen, *A Short Guide to a Happy Life* (New York: Random House, 2000), 1.
12. Ken Karnofsky, "Genome Project Can't Explain Human Nature" (letter to the editor), *Boston Globe*, February 16, 2001, A18.
13. "Mysteries of the Genes" (editorial), *New York Times*, February 17, 2001, A30.
14. Francis Fukuyama, *Our Posthuman Future* (New York: Farrar, Straus and Giroux, 2002), 83.
15. Clifford Geertz, *The Interpretation of Cultures*, (New York: Basic Books, 1973), 67.
16. Karl Marx, "Introduction to a Critique of Political Economy," 124.
17. For example, from *Human Nature and the Social Order* (1902) to *Human Nature and Railroads* (1915); to *Human Nature and Management* (1929) to *Human Nature and Christian Marriage* (1958); from *Human Nature in Its Fourfold State, Of Primitive Interiority, Entire Deprivation, Begun Recovery and Consummate Happiness or Misery in The Parents of Mankind in Paradise, The Unregenerate, The Regenerate, All Mankind in the Future State* (1729) to *Human Nature in Business: How to Capitalize Your Everyday Habits and Characteristics* (New York: G. P. Putnam's Sons 1920); *The Human Nature of Birds* (1993); *The Human Nature of Christ* (1965); *The Human Nature of a University* (1969).
18. J. Stanley Grimes, *The Mysteries of Human Nature Explained by a New System of Nervous Physiology, To Which Is Added, a Review of the Errors of Spiritualism, and Instructions for Developing or Refining the Influence by Which Subjects and Mediums Are Made* (Buffalo: R. M. Wanzer, 1857); Louis Berman, *The Glands Regulating Personality: A Study of the Glands of Internal Secretion in Relation to the Types of Human Nature* (New York: Macmillan, 1921), viii.
19. Berman, *The Glands Regulating Personality*, 21, 23, 26, 329.
20. John Dewey, *Human Nature and Conduct* (Madison, Wisc.: Henry Holt, 1944), 113–14.
21. Virginia Woolf, *The Common Reader* (1925; reprint, New York: Harcourt Brace and Company, 1984), 63, 93, 137, 167; emphasis added.

22. T. S. Eliot, *Selected Essays 1917–1932* (New York: Harcourt, Brace and Company, 1932), 111, 158, 279.
23. A few critical works using the phrase have continued to appear from time to time, though they are in a great minority: e.g., Ruth Caplan, *Human Nature in Richardson's Clarissa* (Ph.D diss. 1974) and David Green, *Human Nature in the Drawing Room: The Aristocratic World of George Meredith* (Ph.D diss. 1944).
24. Harold Bloom, *Shakespeare: The Invention of the Human* (New York: Riverhead Books, 1998), 1, 17.
25. Hannah Arendt, *The Human Condition*, 2d ed. (Chicago: University of Chicago Press, 1998), 11.
26. Jean-François Lyotard, *The Inhuman: Reflections on Time*, trans. Geoffrey Bennington and Rachel Bowlby (Cambridge: Polity Press, 1991), 2.
27. Robert Pepperell, *The Post-Human Condition* (Oxford: Intellect, 1995), i.
28. E. O. Wilson, *On Human Nature* (Cambridge, Mass.: Harvard University Press, 1978), 2.
29. Ibid., 167.
30. Ibid., 281.
31. Ibid., 196; 197.
32. E. O. Wilson, *Sociobiology* (Cambridge, Mass.: Belknap Press of Harvard University Press, 1980), 58.
33. Wilson, *On Human Nature*, 200.
34. Ibid., 203.
35. William Whewell, *Philosophical Inductions of Science* (1840, part 2, vol. 6, ed. G. Buchdahl and L. L. Sauden (London: Frank Cass and Co., Ltd. 1967) 65.): "[T]he cases in which inductions from classes of facts altogether or different have thus *jumped together*, belong only to the best established theories which the history of science contains. . . . [I] will term it the *Consilience of Inductions.*
36. Kenan Malik, *Man, Beast and Zombie: What Science Can and Cannot Tell Us about Human Nature* (New York: Weidenfeld, 2000).
37. Paul Ehrlich, *Human Natures* (Washington, D.C.: Island Press, 2000), ix.
38. Ibid., x. Even these footnotes are of the most perfunctory and summary kind (a "romantic response" to Enlightenment science, representing "a preference for feeling, intuition, imagination, and self-expression over rational analysis and intellect," is said to be "associated with such writers and thinkers as German philosopher Friedrich von Schelling and Johann von Goethe, John von Schiller, Samuel Taylor Coleridge, and Percy Bysshe Shelley." This is the sort of thing one finds in readers' encyclopedias and school texts; a generalization this unnuanced from a literary critic speaking about science would surely evoke protests from scientific theorists and practitioners.
39. Ibid., 426, n. 73.
40. Terry Burnham and Jay Phelan, *Mean Genes* (Cambridge, Mass.: Perseus, 2000), 8.
41. William R. Clark and Michael Grunstein, *Are We Hardwired?* (New York: Oxford University Press, 2000).
42. Jean-Paul Sartre, *Les Mots (The Words)*, trans. Bernard Frechtman (New York: G. Braziller, 1964), 254.
43. Lyotard, *The Inhuman*, 3.
44. Rowan Taylor of the Great Ape Project, quoted in Seth Mydans, "He's Not Hairy, He's My Brother," *New York Times,* August 12, 2001, sec. 4, 5.
45. Miguel de Unamuno, *Tragic Sense of Life*, trans. J. E. Crawford Fitch (New York: Dover, 1954), 90, 93.
46. Ian Hacking, *The Social Construction of What?* (Cambridge, Mass.: Harvard University Press, 1999), 4.
47. Francis Fukuyama, *Our Posthuman Future* (New York: Farrar, Straus & Giroux, 2002), 7.

Index